standard catalog of®

VOLKSWAGEN
1946-2004

John Gunnell

©2004 KP Books

Published by

 **kp books**
An imprint of F+W Publications, Inc.

700 East State Street • Iola, WI 54990-0001
715-445-2214 • 888-457-2873

Our toll-free number to place an order or obtain
a free catalog is (800) 258-0929.

Library of Congress Catalog Number: 2004093889

ISBN: 0-87349-761-9

Designed by Brian Brogaard

Edited by Tom Collins

Printed in the United States of America

ACKNOWLEDGMENTS

The author, editor and design team for
Standard Catalog of Volkswagen—1946-2004
would like to thank the following people
for their contributions to this book.

Der Kafer Fahrer, the national
organization of Volkswagen owners.

Richard (Dick) Dance and **Phil Hall** for their
automotive literature collections.

Dr. Mac Jones for allowing access
to his collection of rare Volkswagens.

Everett Barnes at the *Samba.com* and
Roy Short at *aircooledads.com* for their assistance.

Rob and **Sharon** at *McLellan's Automotive History*
for their generous contributions.

Volkswagen owners **Brian** and **Connie Holcomb** and
Duane Miller for their background information.

Professional photographers who
contributed to this book including:

Robert Best and **Kris Kandler** of KP Publishing

Tom Glatch

David Lyon

Paul Smith

Perrin Todd

And a special thanks to all the generous car owners
who submitted photos of their cars, whether used and credited
in this book or that were considered for these pages. We appreciate
your dedication to the Beetle and other Volkswagen cars.

standard catalog of®

VOLKSWAGEN

CONTENTS

1946–1949 VOLKSWAGEN

1950–1959 VOLKSWAGEN

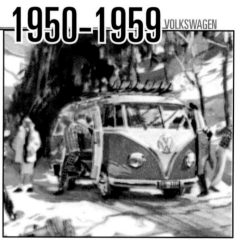

1960–1969 VOLKSWAGEN

1970–1979 VOLKSWAGEN

1980–1989 VOLKSWAGEN

5 Rabbit

1990–1999 VOLKSWAGEN

2000–2004 VOLKSWAGEN

INTRODUCTION

VOLKSWAGEN 1934-1945

Volkswagen history began, late in 1930, with the formation of a new company: Dr.-Ing. h.c. Ferdinand Porsche GmbH. As early as 1927, Dr. Ferdinand Porsche had the idea of building a German "people's car." Porsche's start-up staff included body designer Erwin Komenda and air-cooled engine expert Joseph Kales, as well as his son Ferry. Porsche saw the creation of small cars as a challenge. Over the prior decade, he'd worked on such early attempts as the Sascha (for Austro-Daimler).

Early in the new engineering firm's history came Project 12, which evolved into the Beetle. Most of the car's basic elements were selected early. Designers chose a rear-mounted engine, partly because it eliminated the need for a long driveshaft. To go the rear-engine route without impairing safe weight distribution, however, such an engine would have to be light in weight. Thus, aluminum and magnesium castings found their way into the concept. Air cooling meant no radiator would be needed, and owners would not have to worry about coolant freeze-ups. Finally, the horizontally-opposed cylinder configuration allowed a short crankshaft and would mate neatly with the proposed rear transaxle. Instead of a separate body and frame, the car would have a platform-type chassis with a central backbone and integral floor pan. Torsion bars were the choice for a front suspension, and swing axles for the rear.

Rather than pursuing this small-car project further at the time, Porsche took on other work for such companies as Wanderer and Zundapp, including development of prototypes for a Zundapp Volksauto (which also translates to "people's car"), powered by a five-cylinder radial engine. After Zundapp nixed that project in 1932, Porsche established a connection with NSU to develop yet another set of prototypes, which evolved from the Project 12 design with a flat-four engine.

By 1933, Adolf Hitler had risen to power and made the first announcement of his desire to create not only the Autobahnen (high-speed highway network), but also a "people's car" for the ordinary workingman's family. As outlined by automotive historian Dan R. Post, Hitler wanted a car that could travel at 100-kph (62-mph) speeds, deliver fuel mileage of 33 mpg, demand minimal repair and maintenance, contain space for four or five occupants and have an air-cooled engine (since so few people in Germany had garages).

Hitler publicly endorsed Porsche's idea at the 1934 Berlin Auto Show. Porsche continued work on the Zundapp/NSU concept, to create what would be called the "Volkswagen Series 3." Late in 1936, the final prototypes were ready with a body

Above: **An early Porsche-built "V" series prototype appeared in 1935.** *(Old Cars Weekly Archives)*

design generally credited to Erwin Komenda. The German automaker's association undertook extensive testing of the car.

By 1937, it was determined that a separate government company would be needed to complete development of the car and bring it to production. Later that year, 30 prototypes were prepared with the assistance of Daimler-Benz. This version was known as the Series 30 and was road tested by Nazi storm troopers. Dr. Porsche twice visited the United States and met with auto-industry leaders, including Henry Ford. He also sought engineers of German ancestry to come back and help set up the factory. Work began on the plant at Wolfsburg, then called KDF-Stadt, in mid-1938. The first cars scheduled to emerged late the following year.

Meanwhile, Porsche people kept refining the car's design until it finally emerged as the ready-for-production Series 38. This same basic car was destined to become an automotive icon. It was initially sold as the KdF-Wagen. "Kraft durch Freude" means "Strength through Joy" in German. That was the slogan of the Nazi ministry in charge of workers, the German Labor Front. The car quickly adopted the Volkswagen nickname that had been hung on it for several years. The factory was called the Volkswagenwerk consistently. The letters "VW" were used in wheel covers and in logos inside the car. Both 704- and 984-cc air-cooled engines were installed in early versions.

The earliest KDF-Wagens were to be sold by a stamp-purchase plan. When workers filled five red or blue books of stamps, each worth about $240, they could take delivery of the car. World War II intervened with that notion, as civilian production was hampered. Diligent workers continued to save for the cars. Years later, quite a few Germans presented their collections of saved-up KdF-Wagen-Sparkarte stamp books and, in 1961, Volkswagen allowed those people a 600 Deutsch marks credit toward a new car or 100 Deutsch marks in cash.

During World War II, Volkswagens with larger (1131-cc) engines were manufactured for military use. The Jeep-like "Kubelwagen" was also produced, an all-purpose military vehicle especially praised by Field Marshall Rommel in North Africa. Kubel bodies were reportedly supplied by Berlin-based Ambi-Budd. KdF-Wagens also were modified in four-wheel-drive "Kommandeur" configurations. The "Schwimmwagen" was another vehicle built for the military with KdF-Wagen components and was at home on land or in the water. Some sources report their effective use in the snows of the Russian Front as well. Actual passenger-car production of the KdF-Wagen began after the war.

In early April 1945, the American army entered KdF-Stadt, the factory town that Hitler had set up to build the promised cars for workers. Some 18,000 people were living there, many in emergency accommodations. Late that May, the first town council meeting was held and hosted representatives appointed by the British military government. They choose to call the town Wolfsburg, in honor of a local castle, and the auto factory was temporarily renamed Wolfsburg Motor Works. (The Nazis had called it Volkswagenwerk G. m.b.h. and the British toyed with

eliminating the Volkswagen reference the same way KdF-Wagen had been erased. The British thought of calling the cars the Type 1. Yet, the Volkswagen name remained though it all.)

Technically, the military government seized the company's assets. Press tools and parts were still on hand despite heavy Allied bombing in the area during the war. A small work force remained. The work of building cars desperately needed in the British Zone started on a limited basis. Some 1,785 cars were built between May and the end of 1945. These were made mostly for use by members of the occupying forces, but some were used for other purposes, such as German postal vans. Repair work on British military vehicles was also carried out at the factory during this period. The French forces noticed the car's potential and requested some as well. During 1946, production of the cars rose in to the 10,000 car range. For a time, the future of the Wolfsburg plant was uncertain as some countries and even automotive industry leaders in America saw its dismantling in terms of war reparations. Firm British leadership dissuaded that direction.

Heinrich "Heinz" Nordhoff took over as general manager of the Volkswagen' factory on January 1, 1948. Formerly with Opel, Nordhoff directed the company in a brilliant fashion, steering it towards international distribution that began in 1949 with the exportation of Volkswagens. Referred to as limousines in France, Belgium and Germany or saloons for British audiences, these first sedans were called "5 persoons-wagen" in Dutch language literature when they were sent to The Netherlands. Nordhoff presided over the car's development into a 1950s phenomenon. By May of 1949, the 50,000th Volkswagen made since the end of the war was built. On June 30, 1949 the Volkswagen Finance Company was formed. On July 1, 1949 a new export model (11A) was introduced at a price of 5450 DM and a Karmann-bodied convertible was released.

The convertible had been conceived and some promos were built during the Nazi period but the drop-top was not released officially in Kdf-Wagen form. In postwar production, both the Karmann and Hebmueller versions were built. The Hebmueller used a closed-coupe look to its roofline, plus a neater top fold. Its design did cut rear seat room to make the flush top fold down happen.) On September 6, 1949, the British departed from the operation, returning the company to German control via military government directive No. 202.

Just as American owners of British-built sports cars in the 1950s shared a camaraderie, so too did early Volkswagen owners feel a kinship, often expressed by waves and horn toots. A succession of improvements—some significant, others not—arrived through the 1950s and '60s, often promoted in advertisements. For that reason, tracing the evolution of the Beetle is far easier than comparable changes for other imported makes. A synchronized gearbox (except for first gear) arrived on 1952 models. The original split rear window was replaced by a single oval pane the next year. A bigger (1192-cc) engine replaced the original 1131-cc unit for 1954, boosting horsepower to 36. Horsepower wasn't increased again until 1961 and again in 1966, when the engine grew to 1285-cc (nomimally 1300) displacement. A year later, another enlargement sent it to 1493-cc (1500). Then, in 1970, came a final increase to 1585-cc size (1600).

Early in 1972, the Volkswagen Beetle set a production record for a single model, topping even the long-lived Model T Ford. Volkswagen even displayed a Model T next to a row of brand-new Beetles at the 1972 Geneva Auto Show. It was, perhaps, ironic that this display of the model's longevity came hot on the heels of Volkswagen's losing its leading rank in Switzerland's car market to fall to third, behind Opel and Fiat. *Motor Trend* (June 1972) noted: "It was also symbolic that VW had no new product to offer, while most of its rivals came to the show loaded down."

Beetle sedans were exported to the United States until 1977, while the convertible lasted two years longer. Even though manufacture came to a halt in Germany, Beetles remained in production elsewhere in the world into the 1980s. They were especially popular in Mexico where the Beetle was called the "Fusca."

Volkswagen expanded its model lineup on a regular basis. As early as 1949, the boxy Transporter became available, using regular Beetle mechanical components. In addition to what German VW literature called the "Achtsitzer" and what enthusiasts still love to call the "barn door" versions, the Transporters came sans back windows in the "Kastenwagen" delivery van version and the versatile "Pritschenwagen" pickup. The VW Transporter station wagons soon were adapted as campers in the aftermarket, then officially by Volkswagen into the fully outfitted Camper buses. In the 1960s, Volkswagen buses would become a "trademark" of the burgeoning counterculture. The buses and camper versions were popular among "hippies" for their combination of economy and practicality—and the ease with which their slab sides could be adorned with decals and decorations.

For a brief time in the 1950s, the Rometsch coachbuilding company sold Volkswagen-based cars designed by Johannes Beeskow and Bert Lawrence. These sporty versions paved the way for Volkswagen's own "sports bug," built by Karmann of Osnabruk, Germany, and designed by Ghia of Italy. The Karmann-Ghia was a stylish 2 + 2 coupe based upon the Beetle chassis, first offered in 1956. A cabriolet (convertible) joined the line two years later. A much different form of sedan, the Type 3 (1500), debuted in Europe in 1961, rear-engined like its mates but with a squarish body and larger (1493-cc) power plant. (It was popularly called the Notchback.) Two years later, the Volkswagen 1500S came along. It had even more power. Next came the 1600TL, with a 1.6-liter engine. Both fastback sedan and squareback wagon versions were produced.

By 1968, both the Beetle and the 1600 got an early form of automatic shift. The Type 411 came next, making it to the market in 1969. It featured unibody construction and MacPherson struts up front. Fuel injection became available on some models in 1970. Also new was the open-air Jeep-like Type 181, which

became known as "The Thing" when it debuted on the American market for 1973.

Volkswagen began turning away from rear-mounted, air-cooled engines as early as 1971, offering a variant of the Audi/NSU model with an inline four-cylinder engine. That happened because Volkswagen had taken over NSU in 1969, just as it had obtained Audi earlier. The front-engined Dasher arrived in America in1974. The first Rabbit came a year later, along with the sporty Scirocco coupe (styled by the well-known Italian designer Giugiaro). By 1978, Rabbits were being manufactured in the United States (at New Stanton, Pennsylvania), though that venture wouldn't last through the 1980s. The Rabbit led to Golf and Jetta models of the 1980s, marketed along with a Rabbit-based Cabriolet (one of the few convertibles to survive in the United States marketplace at that time). Diesel engines also were part of the picture. Later in the 1980s, the Brazilian-built Fox debuted.

For 1990, the Volkswagen lineup included a Corrado sports car and a new Passat sedan and station wagon. Evolutions of the long-lived Transporter still remained available, too, after a succession of changes. Long before that time, though, the original Beetle and its variants were largely forgotten, though many mourned their passing. In the Beetle's heyday, some people cherished it, while others hated it. Most owners seemed to experience a unique love/hate relationship unlike that connected to most other automobiles.

Volkswagen sales in the United States, which had been at around 130,000 when the 1980s ended, declined to 96,700 in 1991 when the Corrado sports car and a "designer" edition of the Cabrio were making news. Fox, Golf, Golf-GTI, Jetta, Passat, Cabrio and Corrado series offered a total of 15 models priced from about $7,200 to as high as $18,700. Only four-cylinder engines were used, but they included the ECO diesel and the hot 16-valve power plant that was standard in the GTI and Passat and could be had in Jettas.

Little of substance changed in 1992. The two door Jetta sedan was dropped and the Passat line gained a fancier GLS sedan and wagon. This raised the overall model count to 16. The sporty Corrado got a new narrow-angle six, also available in Passats, that substantially raised its horsepower and its price (which was up to $21,840). That would be the start of a trend for the 1990s at Volkswagen. Stateside sales declined to just below 76,000 units.

The year 1993 was truly a bad one for Volkswagen in the United States, with sales slipping to below 50,000 units. Enthusiasts, however, got a restyled GTI with a more powerful 8-valve overhead-cam four. The offerings remained fairly stable, with most activity taking place in the Passat line where the GLS wagon disappeared and even fancier GLX sedans and wagons were added. The 2.8-liter six gave the Passat sedan a top speed of 130 mph, making it VW's hottest offering. The Jetta also got a GLX sedan, but not the VR6 power plant. A collector's editon of the drop-top Cabrio was offered.

In 1994, the Jetta was totally redstyled and did get the V-6. These changes made a big difference in performance, as well as American sales. Jetta deliveries in the U.S. jumped from 15,000 the previous year to nearly 56,000. Also leaving the launch pad was a Gen III Golf. Total model count dropped way back to 10 and the price range crept up again. The lowest-cost VW was the $12,325 Golf GL two-door hatchback and the top-of-the line Corrado went out the door for $25,150. Total United States sales nearly doub led to 97,000 cars.

In 1995 you could get a V-6 in the Golf. The golf-based Cabrio was given the updated Gen III look. The Jetta got some small refinements, while the Passat got a major overhaul. No longer on the market was the slow-selling Corrado. Golf fans got a new Sport model and one more Jetta was added, too. Sales in the United States were up to 115,000 and going in the right direction for Volkswagen.

For its 50th year in the country, Volkswagen advertised the new 1996 Passat with the 1.9-liter four as "the lowest-priced European mid-size model sold in the United States. American sales rose again, to 135,807 cars. Engine choises included just one four-cylinder and one V-6. Model offerings were consolidated to 10.

Starting in 1997, Volkswagen began to "grow" its model list again. There were still four series—Golf, Cabrio, Jetta and Passat — but new engines and trim levels were provided in cars like the Passat TDI sedan, which were then merchandised as separate models. TDI stood for "Turbo Diesel Injection." That was a turbochared overhead-cam four-cylinder diesel that generated 116 hp combined with fuel economy improvements. The Cabrio was treated to a new "High Line" model. All in all, there were 12 models priced between $13,500 and $22,300 and U.S. sales rose again to nearly 138,000.

A new car that looked old-fashioned and modern at the same time was the star of Volkswagen's 1998 hit parade. This New Beetle resembeled the classic "Bug," but had a tranverse-mounted water-cooled engine up front and a hatchback body configuration and incorporated moden technology. It was offered in two New Beetle models. The base $15,200 version used a four-cylinder gas engine, but a TDI model was about $1,500 more. Also new for 1998 was the Passat. There were now five series offering a total of 16 models priced from $15,200 to $26,250. Sales here hopped again to 219,679. That included 55,842 New Beetles.

For the last year of the century, Volkswagen continued with the same five series, but the list of individual models was almost twice as long as just two years earlier. New GLS and GLX versions of the retro Beetle included a 1.8T turbocharged four that produced 150 zoomy horsepower. The TDI engine was back too. It was available in Golf and Jetta models. The news of the year was a Gen IV Golf that was bigger, stronger and speedier. The Passat got a new 2.8-liter V-6 previously used in Audis.

For a New Millennium, the New Beetle got a few new upgrades. There were now five models, two with GLS trim, one with GLX trim and two with 1.8-liter turbos. Six Golfs were available including two each of GLS and TDI models and a GLX. The fanciest GTI got standard traction control. The Cabrio came in GL and GLS models. The Jetta models aped the Golf models, although they were sedans instead of hatchbacks and there was no Jetta GTI. The Passat got two GL, two GLS and two GLX models. There were 25 Volkswagens in all and they cost between $15,900 and $28,455. United States sales were 355,479 units.

Upgraded audio systems, added safety and new wheels were common alterations to 2001 Volkswagens. The Passat sedan and wagon were available with a 4Motion all-wheel-drive system in GLS and GLX trim. This was considered a model, rather than an option. There were now 33 models in the same five series and pricing stayed relatively stable. Sales by United States dealers rose aggain to 241,639 units.

At its Annual Press Conference held at the Transparent Factory in Dresden, Germany, in March 2003, the Volkswagen Group presented the second best results in corporate history. It had delivered 4.984 million vehicles to customers worldwide during 2002, achieving a 12.1 percent share of the world passenger car market. Nearly one of every five cars bought in Europe was a Volkswagen.

"I would like to say a special thank you to all our employees in the Group whose personal commitment has helped us to achieve such an excellent performance even in the midst of economic recession," Dr. Bernd Pischetsrieder, Chairman of the Board of Management, told some 300 journalists. "Our financial statements are characterized by healthy incomes and sound capital structures", said Dr. Bruno Adelt, a member of the Board of Management of Volkswagen AG responsible for controlling and accounting. "Our production costs have developed favorably. We have achieved one of the primary objectives of our cost cutting measures."The Volkswagen Group invested heavily in the expansion of the product range and the updating of manufacturing facilities. 2002 saw the start of production of the Volkswagen Phaeton, the Touareg off-road vehicle and the Touran minivan. Other investments were made in the successor models to the Audi A8, the Audi A3, the SEAT Cordoba, the Golf and the New Beetle Cabriolet.

In Western Europe the Volkswagen Group delivered 2,827,472 vehicles. Germany saw a total of 940,129 vehicles delivered, making it the Group's largest market once again. Deliveries in North America were slightly down at 663,278 units, but The Group's share of the region's passenger car market rose slightly to 6.7 percent. In the South American/South African Region the Volkswagen Group sold 477,473 units. Volkswagen's largest increase in sales was achieved in the Asia-Pacific Region, where it delivered 620,624 vehicles. China was the largest single market in Asia and over half a million vehicles were sold there for the first time. Deliveries to customers increased to 512,548. The Group's market share in China was a strong 38.5 percent. In Japan, Volkswagen increased deliveries by 3.5 percent to 70,931 units.

Volkswagen introduced a convertible version of the New Beetle in 2003, but did not have its best year in terms of sales and profits. The company had a negative cash flow of 2.5 billion euros in its automotive division. That was in contrast to a loss of 993 million euros the previous year. Its two biggest markets were in Germany, where 943,000 vehicles were sold, and in China, where 697,000 new vehicles found customers. In July 2003, Standard & Poor's cut the firm's long-term credit rating because of concerns over future profitability. Volkswagen remained China's largest automaker in 2003, but its market share in that country was also falling. It had dropped by half between 1999 and 2003, as General Motors and Honda expanded their Chinese operations.

In April 2004, Volkswagen advised that its first-quarter profit had fallen 87 percent to 26 million euros ($31 million). This was the lowest in a decade. The company cited higher costs to introduce new models, sales incentives for the new Golf car and currency shifts as reasons for the decline. The German car market segment, which was still Volkswagen's largest, had declined by 2.5 percent, including a 7.3 percent fall in the fall of 2003, according to the European Automobile Manufacturers Association. Volkswagen's May 2004 sales, in the 18 countries of Western Europe, fell 2.1 percent to 224,315 cars.

In June 2004, Volkswagen again had its long-term credit rating cut one level by Standard & Poor's due to concerns over ``weakening profitability.'' investment guru Henning Gebhardt said, ``Their domestic market isn't very well, the dollar isn't helping and China is a much more challenging market than before. That's quite a lot of problems to deal with at once.''

Volkswagen was faced with intensifying competition in Europe's car industry. In addition, the euro's strength against the dollar made Volkswagen models more expensive in the U.S., while reducing earnings returned to Germany. Still, Volkswagen announced plans to open three more factories in China as part of a plan to double production in that country by 2008. And the company also predicted that its full-year 2004 operating profit would exceed 2003's 2.5 billion euros. The company planned 4 billion euros in cost cuts and the elimination of 5,000 jobs by 2005 to help boost its 2004 profit.

DATA NOTES: This catalog is designed to guide the efforts of Volkswagen collectors. We have attempted to use a variety of reputable sources to accumulate a massive database that will be useful to Volkswagen collectors. The basic data in this book was originally compiled by James M. Flammang for the *Standard Catalog of Imported Cars*. It was later updated by Mike Covello in the *Standard Catalog of Imported Cars 1946-2002*. We have greatly enhanced the database for this book, added color images and updated the collector price estimates to current market conditions. Determining prices and weights, especially for early Volkswagen models, is *not* an exact science. Source material contemporary to the cars, as well as later historical references, often give conflicting information. Also, prices and specifications often change from the beginning to the end of a model year. Differences in calendar-year and model-year dating can affect factors such as production totals. Even when using factory-supplied statistics, body-style production numbers may not add up to the same total as reported numbers for annual production which may include chassis without bodies. We have attempted to give the model numbers for U.S. market cars with left-hand drive. Right-hand drive units may have had different model numbers. The tables printed below will help sort out early Volkswagen model numbers. We are always open to constructive criticism that will improve future editions of this work.

BEETLE MODEL NUMBERS

1945-1954

11A-Standard sedan left-hand drive
11B-Standard sedan right-hand drive
11C-Deluxe/Export sedan left-hand drive
11D-Deluxe/Export sedan right-hand drive
11E-Standard Sunroof sedan left-hand drive
11F-Standard Sunroof sedan right-hand drive
11G-Deluxe/Export Sunroof sedan left-hand drive
11H-Deluxe/Export Sunroof sedan right-hand drive
14A-Hebmuller Cabriolet (convertible) left-hand drive
15A-Karmann Cabriolet (convertible) left-hand drive
15B-Karmann Cabriolet (convertible) right-hand drive

1954-1967

1/11-Standard Sedan left-hand drive
1/12-Standard Sedan right-hand drive
1/13-Deluxe Sedan left-hand drive
1/14-Deluxe Sedan right-hand drive
1/15-Standard Sunroof Sedan left-hand drive
1/16-Standard Sunroof Sedan right-hand drive
1/17-Deluxe Sunroof Sedan left-hand drive
1/18-Deluxe Sunroof Sedan right-hand drive
1/51-Karmann Convertible left-hand drive
1/52-Karmann Convertible right-hand drive

1967-1977

1111-Standard Sedan left-hand drive
1121-Standard Sedan right-hand drive
1131-Deluxe Sedan left-hand drive
1141-Deluxe Sedan right-hand drive
1151-Standard Sunroof Sedan left-hand drive
1161-Standard Sunroof Sedan right-hand drive
1171-Deluxe Sunroof Sedan left-hand drive
1181-Deluxe Sunroof Sedan right-hand drive
1511-Convertible left-hand drive
1512-Convertible left-hand drive

Note 1: Tables in this catalog focus on the most popular American-market Volkswagen models.

1940-1945 VOLKSWAGEN ENGINE/CHASSIS NUMBERS

Year	Chassis Numbers	Engine Numbers
1940	1-00001 to 1-01000	1-00001 to 1-01000
1941	1-01001 to 1-05656	1-01001 to 1-06251
1942	1-05657 to 1-014383	1-06252 to 1-017113
1943	1-014384 to 1-0032302	1-017114 to 1-045707

1946

TYPE 11 (BEETLE)--FOUR Few people who were alive at the time of the Beetle's rise to prominence need to be reminded of its appearance. Many described the two-door sedan, with its rounded profile, as an "ugly duckling." Volkswagen would later capitalize upon the image, rather than attempt to dispute it. As everyone would eventually realize, the shape of the Beetle would change little over the next three decades. Volkswagen still promoted a continuous sequence of mechanical and detail improvements. For 1946, the engine size was increased from 985 cc to 1131 cc. This 1.1-liter power plant was used from 1945 through 1950. The sealing tubes for the engine push rods had new corrugated tube ends. Early engines were rated 24.5 hp and often referred top as "25-hp" models. The 25-hp Standard version was actually introduced during 1945 and 1,785 cars were made in that calendar year. An unsynchronized four-speed gear box meant plenty of double clutching was required to change gears, especially when downshifting. Next to the gearshift lever was the manual choke button. Early Volkswagen models had a split-oval rear window with a rather thick pillar between the tiny panes. American cars had abandoned running boards before World War II, but Volkswagen kept them—though they weren't the kind that anyone could stand on. A notch below the rear bumper permitted insertion of a hand crank. Characteristics of early cars included a rear axle with single-acting shocks (1945 to 1951), a T-shaped luggage compartrment handle (1945 to 1949), pull-out door handles (1945 through1959) and a license plate pressing on the rear engine cover (until 1949). Early examples wore nipple-shaped chrome hubcaps. The gas tank, which was mounted higher than on earlier models, sat under the hood. The hood had to be raised with each fill up. Lighted turn-signal semaphores were activated by a switch on the dashboard. Also on the dashboard sat a pair of glove boxes, neither of which contained a door. There was no gas gauge, but when the driver noticed evidence that fuel might be running out, he could reach down to the firewall and turn a tap to open the reserve tank, which held an extra gallon or so. Lack of body insulation contributed to a noisy-running car. This trait actually helped endear early Volkswagens to their owners. These cars had the front lubrication fittings on the inner track rod joints and they no longer sat at right angles to the track rod. The brake cable had a new lubrication nipple. The early 4.50 x 16 tires were replaced with size 5.00 x 16 rubber. Some efforts were made to reduce engine noise, such as the use of cardboard insulation in the engine compartment.

Above: **The 1946 Volkswagen split window sedan differs little from the KDF-Wagen.**

(Owner: Dr. Mac Jones / Photographer: Perrin Todd)

Model Code	Body Type & Seating	POE Price	Weight (lbs.)	ProductionTotal
11	2d Sedan-4P	NA	1600	10,020

I.D. DATA: Serial number is on a plate on the front hood center and at back of spare tire and stamped on chassis backbone under rear seat. Engine number is stamped on the generator support and on the crankcase. Chassis numbers: 1-053815 to 1-063796. Engine numbers: 1-079094 to 1-090732.

ENGINE

BASE FOUR: Horizontally opposed, overhead-valve four-cylinder (air cooled). Light alloy block with cast-iron cylinders. Displacement: 69.0 cid (1131 cc). Bore & Stroke: 2.95 x 2.52 in. (75 x 64 mm). Compression Ratio: 5.8:1. Brake Horsepower: 24.5 at 3000 rpm. Torque: 51 ft.-lbs. at 2000 rpm. Solid valve lifters. Downdraft carburetor. 6-volt electrical system.

CHASSIS

Wheelbase: 94.5 in. Overall Length: 160 in. Height: 61.0 in. Width: 60.5 in. Front Tread: 51.0 in. Rear Tread: 49.2 in. Standard Tires: 5.00 x 16. Turn circle: 37 ft. Turns lock-to-lock: 2.4.

TECHNICAL

Layout: rear-engine, rear-drive. Transmission: four-speed manual (unsynchronized). Gear ratios: (1st) 3.60:1, (2nd) 2.07:1, (3rd) 1.25:1, (4th) 0.80:1, (reverse) 6.60:1. Standard Final Drive Ratio: 4.43:1. Steering: worm and cap nut. Suspension (front): king pins with transverse torsion bars and upper/lower trailing arms. Suspension (rear): swing axles with trailing arms and torsion bars. Brakes: mechanical, front/rear drum. Body Construction: steel unibody on stamped steel floor pan. Fuel Tank: 8.8 gallons.

HISTORICAL FOOTNOTES: Allied forces entered the area of the Volkswagen factory on April 10, 1945. A total of 17,109 people lived in the town, then called KdF-Stadt, and nearly half of them were auto workers. Around 336,000 workers (called "Volkswagen Savers") had put 267 million German Reichsmarks into a special account to earn a car. The account was adminstered by the German Labor Front. Volkswagens rise from the ashes was not a smooth or easy journey. As *Motor Trend* noted in its *1954 Worldwide Automotive Yearbook* "Nine years ago (1944) British auto manufacturers refused to give consideration to the

Right: **Many 1946 Volkswagens were used as British and French military staff cars.**

(Owner: Dr. Mac Jones / Photographer: Perrin Todd)

possibility of getting the British Zone Wolfsburg plant for the 'people's car' back into production. Located less than 15 miles from the Russian-occupied East German sector, 60 percent of the plant had been destroyed by Allied aircraft bombings. Rain and pilfering had added to the loss, so that in late 1945, the possibility of converting the bomb-pocked rubble into a successful business seemed extremely remote."

At its first meeting in late May, the town council voted to name the town, then under British military governance, Wolfsburg. For a time, the assets of the auto company were seized and it was renamed Wolfsburg Motor Works. Near the end of spring 1945, car building began on a limited basis and 1,785 vehicles were manufactured, primarily for use by the occupying British and French forces. Some government vehicles, such as postal vans, were also constructed. In addition, repairs were made to British military vehicles. On October 14, 1946, the 10,000th Beetle produced since the end of World war II rolled down the assembly line. The early Beetle required a full 39 seconds to move from 0 to 60 mph. Its top speed was a reported 65 mph. It delivered 35 mpg fuel economy.

The distinctive split window can be seen from this rear view of the 1946 Volkswagen.

(Owner: Dr. Mac Jones / Photographer: Perrin Todd)

1947

TYPE 11 (BEETLE)—FOUR The 1947, Volkswagen remained largely the same as in 1946, although running changes were made from time to time. Effective with chassis number 071 377 the fastenings for the spare wheel were changed and there was a new bracket for the chain and lock. A new "choke" type cooling-air throttle valve with a swing handle replaced the old slide-valve style effective with chassis number 071 616 (assembly number 099610). The 1947 models retained all the early-car characteristics, including a rear axle with single-acting shocks (1945-1951), a T-shaped luggage compartrment handle (1945-

1949), pull-out door handles (1945-1959) and a license plate pressing on the rear engine cover (which was used until 1949).

I.D. DATA: Serial number is on a plate on the front hood center and at back of spare tire and stamped on chassis backbone under rear seat. Engine number is stamped on the generator support and on the crankcase. Chassis numbers 1-063797 to 1-072743. Engine numbers 1-090733 to 1-0100788.

Above: **The early postwar Beetles like this 1947 car varied little from KdF-Wagens.**
(Dick Dance Collection)

The 1947 VW horn was mounted externally and bumper guards were curved forward.

Dick Dance Collection

The 1947 Beetle was much like the KdF-Wagen predecessor inside.

Dick Dance Collection

Model Code	Body Type & Seating	POE Price	Weight (lbs.)	Production Total
11	2d Sedan-4P	NA	1600	8,987

Note 1: Model-year production for 1947 ended on December 31, 1947 with chassis number 072 743 and engine number 100788.

By 1947, Volkswagens were exported to France and Holland.

Old Car Weekly Archives

ENGINE

BASE FOUR: Horizontally opposed, overhead-valve four-cylinder (air cooled). Light alloy block with cast-iron cylinders. Displacement: 69.0 cid (1131 cc). Bore & Stroke: 2.95 x 2.52 in. (75 x 64 mm). Compression Ratio: 5.8:1. Brake Horsepower: 24.5 at 3000 rpm. Torque: 51 ft.-lbs. at 2000 rpm. Solid valve lifters. Downdraft carburetor. 6-volt electrical system.

CHASSIS

Wheelbase: 94.5 in. Overall Length: 160 in. Height: 61.0 in. Width: 60.5 in. Front Tread: 51.0 in. Rear Tread: 49.2 in. Standard Tires: 5.00 x 16. Turn circle: 37 ft. Turns lock-to-lock: 2.4.

TECHNICAL

Layout: rear-engine, rear-drive. Transmission: four-speed manual (unsynchronized). Gear ratios: (1st) 3.60:1, (2nd) 2.07:1, (3rd) 1.25:1, (4th) 0.80:1, (reverse) 6.60:1. Standard Final Drive Ratio: 4.43:1. Steering: worm and cap nut. Suspension (front): king pins with transverse torsion bars and upper/lower trailing arms. Suspension (rear): swing axles with trailing arms and torsion bars. Brakes: mechanical, front/rear drum. Body Construction: steel unibody on stamped steel floor pan. Fuel Tank: 8.8 gallon.

HISTORICAL FOOTNOTES: Operated as Volkswagenwerk GmbH, Wolfsburg, West Germany. Production for 1947 was 8,987 cars. A total of 56 Volkswagen Saloons were exported to the Netherlands during 1947. The Pon brothers were the exporters in Holland.

1948

TYPE 11 (BEETLE)—FOUR By 1948 the Volkswagen chassis number was being stenciled on the chassis tunnel, between the gear shifter and the handbrake. The Volkswagen Sedan (affectionately known to most enthusiasts as the "Beetle") remained largely the same as in 1947, with running changes made from time to time. During the year a crankshaft with a 48.5-mm diameter for the flywheel was adopted. The flywheel had a 48.5-mm bore. The use of an "unsprung" choke cable was also adopted in 1948. This was the last full year for a T-shaped handle to be seen on the luggage compartment in the front of the car. The 1948 models otherwise retained early-car characteristics including a rear axle with single-acting shocks, a T-shaped luggage compartment handle, pull-out door handles and a license plate pressing on the rear engine cover.

I.D. DATA: Serial number is on a plate on the front hood center and at back of spare tire and stamped on chassis backbone under rear seat. Engine number is stamped on the generator support and on the crankcase. The model year ended on December 31, 1948 with chassis number 091 921 and engine number 122649.

ENGINE

BASE FOUR: Horizontally opposed, overhead-valve four-cylinder (air cooled). Light alloy block with cast-iron cylinders. Displacement: 69.0 cid (1131 cc). Bore & Stroke: 2.95 x 2.52 in. (75 x 64 mm). Compression Ratio: 5.8:1. Brake Horsepower: 24.5 at 3000 rpm. Torque: 51 ft.-lbs. at 2000 rpm. Solid valve lifters. Downdraft carburetor. 6-volt electrical system.

CHASSIS

Wheelbase: 94.5 in. Overall Length: 160 in. Height: 61.0 in. Width: 60.5 in. Front Tread: 51.0 in. Rear Tread: 49.2 in. Standard Tires: 5.00 x 16. Turning circle: 37 ft. Turns lock-to-lock: 2.4.

TECHNICAL

Layout: rear-engine, rear-drive. Transmission: four-speed manual (unsynchronized). Gear ratios: (1st) 3.60:1, (2nd) 2.07:1, (3rd) 1.25:1, (4th) 0.80:1, (reverse) 6.60:1. Standard Final Drive Ratio: 4.43:1. Steering: worm and cap nut. Suspension (front): king pins with transverse torsion bars and upper/lower trailing arms. Suspension (rear): swing axles with trailing arms and torsion bars. Brakes: mechanical, front/rear drum. Body Construction: steel unibody on stamped steel floor pan. Fuel Tank: 8.8 gallon.

MANUFACTURER: Made by Volkswagenwerk GmbH, Wolfsburg, West Germany. On January 1, 1948 Heinz Nordoff became General Manager of the Wolfsburg factory. Production for 1948 was 19,244 cars. In May the 25,000th Volkswagen was made. Corporate headquarters relocated to Wolfsburg, from Berlin, on July 29, 1948. In October the Association of Former Volkswagen Savers was founded and some members complained of not getting the car they had saved for under the savings scheme started 10 years earlier.

1948 VOLKSWAGEN PRODUCTION CHART

Model Code	Body Type & Seating	POE Price	Weight (lbs.)	Production Total
11	2d Sedan-4P	Note 1	1600	19,244

Note 1: In June 1948 the price changed to 5300 RM/DM. RM refers to the German currency Reichsmark used by the Nazi regime, before the Deutschemark of Germany's new government following the war.

1949

1100 (BEETLE) — FOUR — Over 51 changes were made in 1949 Volkswagens, but they did not all happen at once. Early in the year, an under-dash pull cable replaced the former locking-handle hood release. This meant that the engine cover in the rear of the car was no longer lockable. Another early-year change was the addition of a block-out plate on the right-hand side of the standard dashboard. This was added so that the sheet metal did not have to be cut out to install a radio. In addition, the front and rear bumpers were redesigned to have wider sections and the manufacture of convex-curved bumper guards stopped. Smaller, more rounded bumper guards were used on export models. Also, a double heating conduit was adopted and a double heater cable was added. A "mushroom" air filter was substituted for the the former pan-shaped type. The lower portion of the warm air conduit got a modified heat flap without a hinge and the cork seal on the gasoline petcock was replaced with a Thiokol seal. A front seat with a straight backrest replaced the previous slanted-backrest style and a new throttle cable with an elbow at

the front was adopted. In February, the intake pipe bracket was modified and two lengthwise metal rails were added in the luggage compartment. In March, a new Electron gear box was used on some models, the use of a cooling fan control was discontinued and the torsion bars got five upper leaves and four lower ones. (This was an experient and 1,000 cars were built before the new configuration was adopted for production). In April, Volkswagen started using a new fuel pump with blue Solex diaphragms fitted

Above and Right: **The first 1949 Volkswagens imported to the U.S. looked like these.** *(Old Car Weekly Archives)*

with four gaskets. Also, exhaust valves with case-hardened stems were adopted and the Electron gear box was made standard equipment. Around the same time, an additional lubrication nipple was added for the pedal bearings. In May, the dashboared was completely changed in Export models and a new two-spoke steering wheel appeared in them. The heater cables got rubber stoppers at their ends and the fuse box was moved to the left front side of the instrument panel. A strap was added to secure the fiber material in the glove box. Many changes were made during June; the engine got a new breather pipe and a cylinder head ventilation holes filter. Production of the Export Saloon model began on June 2 and production of Export Cabriolets began a day later. The same day, Volkswagen began using high-gloss synthetic body paint, instead of cellulose type. Late in June, Volkswagen began printing the chassis number lengthwise, on the smooth surface of the frame tunnel, using a die. The rear window glass design was modified and a new rear view mirror was securec more firmly to reduce vibrations. In July, a felt cone air filter was adoptedfor export models and the engine lid inset for the license plate was discontinued. Changes made by Volkswagen late in the year, after the annual company holidays, are generally associated with the subsqent "model year," so modification made in the latter part of 1949 are listed in our 1950 section.

SEDAN COLORS: (January 1949-July 1949) L11=Pastel Green, L13=Medium Green, L14=Reseda Green, L21=Pearl Gray, L23=Silver Gray, L32=Dark Blue, L41=Black, L51=Bordeaux Red. (uly 1949-December 1949) L11=Pastel Green, L13=Medium Green, L14=Reseda Green, L21=Pearl Gray, L23=Silver Gray, L32=Dark Blue, L41=Black, L50=Coral Red, L51=Bordeaux Red and L70=Medium Brown. All models used a Beige interior throughout the year. Headliner color was Beige or Gray depending on body color. Carpets were Gray, Beige or Honey Brown depending on body color. Until July all cars had Black rubber mats. After July standard models came with Black mats and Deluxe models Black and Beige.

I.D. DATA: Serial number is on a plate on the front hood center and at back of spare tire and stamped on chassis tunnel (backbone) under the rear seat. Engine number is stamped on the generator support and on the crankcase. Serial number range: 91922-138554. The model year ended on December 31, 1949 with chassis number 138 554 and engine number 169 913.

ENGINE

BASE FOUR: Horizontally opposed, overhead-valve four-cylinder (air cooled). Light alloy block. Light alloy heads. Finned cylinders with cast-iron cylinder liners. Displacement: 69.0 cid (1131 cc). Bore & Stroke: 2.95 x 2.52 in. (75 x 64 mm). Compression Ratio: 5.8:1. Torque: 51 ft.-lbs. at 2000 rpm. Brake Horsepower: 24.5 at 3300 rpm. Solid valve lifters. Solex carburetor. 6-volt electrical system.

CHASSIS

Wheelbase: 94.5 in. Overall Length: (sedan) 160 in. Height: (sedan) 61.0 in. Width: (sedan) 60.5 in. Front Tread: (sedan) 51.0 in. Rear Tread: (sedan) 49.2 in. Standard Tires: (sedan) 5.00 x 16. Turn circle: 37 ft. Turns lock-to-lock: 2.4.

1949 VOLKWAGEN PRODUCTION CHART

Model Code	Body Type & Seating	POE Price	Weight (lbs.)	Production Total
1100 STANDARD				
11A	2d Sedan-4P	1280	1600	Note 1
1100 DELUXE				
11C	2d Sedan-4P	1480	1600	Note 1
11G	2d Sunroof Sedan-4P	1550	1600	Note 1
1400/1500 CONVERTIBLE				
15A	2d Convertible-4P	1997	1600	Note 1

Note 1: 46,146 Volkswagen passenger cars were produced in 1949; 45,782 Sedans and 346 Cabriolets were produced in 1949.

1950

1100 (BEETLE)—FOUR Initiated in August 1949 were many changes associated with "1950 models" including a new fuel tank design, the use of a fuel filler cap with a VW emblem and a beefed-up front axle. On some cars, the old single-acting lever-type shock absorbers were replaced with a new double-acting type. The left-hand door lost its armrest and running-in stickers were no longer placed on the windshield. On August 28, a new seven-digit chassis numbering system was adopted. September brought changes to the clutch disc and piston clearance specs. In the suspension, a track rod with left- and right-hand threading was made standard. In October, Volkswagen stopped providing an engine crank-starting handle. A beefier clutch lever was put into production. Inside, the use of a brown molded-type rubber front floor mat and rubber footwell trim began. Rubber rear floor mats were no longer used. An accelerator pedal with a larger roller was adopted in October and the runner for the driver's seat was raised a bit. In December 1949, the push rod tubes were changed to have corrugated ends only. In 1950, Volkswagen marketed the Standard Sedan and the Deluxe Export Sedan, also called the Saloon and Limousine depending on the market. A rare Cabriolet (Convertible) also was marketed. About two months into the year, buyers could request a sunroof for their Sedan at additional cost. "Export" models were designed for the taste of overseas (mainly American) buyers and came with equipment that was more deluxe than that used on the Standard

Above: **The distinctive Volkswagen Cabriolet styling is modeled by this 1950 version.**

Owner: Dr. Mac Jones / Photographer: Perrin Todd

model in Germany. The Export Sedan was identifiable by its chrome bumpers, bright hub caps, chrome headlight rims and shiny door handles. Interior appointments were also of a better quality. The new Cabriolet was based on the two-door sedan. It had a convertible top that was unusually bulky when folded. *Motor Trend* observed that a Volkswagen was capable of 34-mpg fuel economy. The car could easily hit 60 mph. Four-wheel independent suspension was featured. The Standard model could be identified by looking for the horn attached to the outside of the front bumper bracket, which eliminated the use of a protective grille. On the Export Sedan the horn was attached under the left fender, behind a small grille. Running changes were made to the Volkswagen sedan throughout 1950. In January, the crankcase was modified to alter the oil level and to allow complete draining of the oil. The use of an oil splash guard was discontinued and the number 4 main bearing was grooved. Another change was the gasket between the cylinder and cylinder head. Up front, the upper torsion bar now had the same five leafs as the lower one (instead of four). A larger knob was used on the lock cable for the up-front trunk. The main beam and turn signal indicator lights were on the left side of the dashboard, with the generator and oil warning lights on the right. The oil dipstick was given a black phosphate coating. A sealing ring was used between the headlights and front fenders. In February, Volkswagen began using a 19-mm hexagonal oil drain plug on some cars. The accelerator cable elbow was replaced by a pin and clip arrangement. The cord carpets previously used in the rear were replaced with Honey Brown molded rubber mats. Starting in March, some Export Sedans and Karmann-

Below: The 1950 Volkswagen sunroof sedan had a canvas roof that could be folded back.

Dick Dance Collection

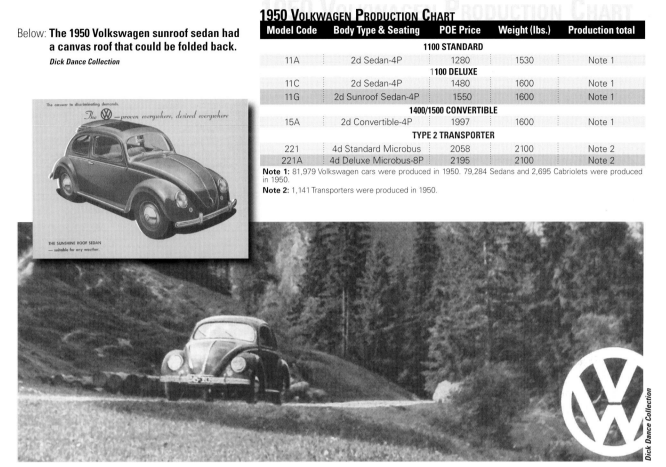

1950 VOLKSWAGEN PRODUCTION CHART

Model Code	Body Type & Seating	POE Price	Weight (lbs.)	Production total
	1100 STANDARD			
11A	2d Sedan-4P	1280	1530	Note 1
	1100 DELUXE			
11C	2d Sedan-4P	1480	1600	Note 1
11G	2d Sunroof Sedan-4P	1550	1600	Note 1
	1400/1500 CONVERTIBLE			
15A	2d Convertible-4P	1997	1600	Note 1
	TYPE 2 TRANSPORTER			
221	4d Standard Microbus	2058	2100	Note 2
221A	4d Deluxe Microbus-8P	2195	2100	Note 2

Note 1: 81,979 Volkswagen cars were produced in 1950. 79,284 Sedans and 2,695 Cabriolets were produced in 1950.

Note 2: 1,141 Transporters were produced in 1950.

One of the earliest VW brochures shows a 1950 Beetle on a mountain road.

Dick Dance Collection

bodied Cabriolets got hydraulic brakes (which were made standard on all Type11A and Type 15 cars a month later). Volkswagen began stamping its chassis number on the vertical side panel of the left-hand rear crossmember, instead of on the smooth surface of the chassis tunnel. The exhaust pipe diameter was enlarged. In April, the door windows got a curved cutout at the front upper "corner" for improved draft-free fresh-air ventilation and a locking right-hand door handle went into production. On April 28, Volkswagen put the Sunroof Sedan into production. The next day, a new turn handle was used with the heater flap cable. In May, a heating pipe with noise suppressors was adopted. Volkswagen changed to automatic cooling-air regulation, which eliminated use of the swivel-handled control valve. Now the air-control valve was regulated by a thermostat that reacted to engine temperature. A connecting pipe was added to the exhaust box to help preheat the gas/fuel mixture. Mahle Autothermic pistons went into some engines and a brake fluid reservoir with a float replaced the old filter type. The diameters of the master cylinder and rear wheel cylinders were reduced. In June, ashtrays were added to the dashboard and the rear

right interior side panel. A single-spring clutch became standard equipment.

SEDAN COLORS: L11=Pastel Green, L13=Medium Green, L14=Reseda Green, L21=Pearl Gray, L23=Silver Gray, L32=Dark Blue, L41=Black, L50=Coral Red, L51=Bordeaux Red, L70=Medium Brown, L71=Beige, L76=Brown Beige, L87=Pearl White. All models had a standard Beige cloth interior. Beige and Red Beige leatherette interiors were available depending on body color. Headliner color was Beige or Gray depending on body color. Carpets were Gray Beige or Honey Brown depending on body color. Standard Sedans came only with Black rubber mats. Deluxe Export models came with Black or Beige mats depending on choice and body color.

TYPE 2 TRANSPORTER—FOUR Ben Pon, one of the Dutch brothers reponsible for getting the first Volkswagen Beetles to New York, drew up plans for the boxy Type 2 Transporter as early as 1947, convinced that such a vehicle would sell in his native Holland. The engineers went to work and eight Transporters were displayed late in 1949. Production of the pioneering minivan began early in 1950. Early Volkswagen literature referred to the vehicles as a "Micro Bus," but the single word "Microbus" was more commonly used. Standard and Deluxe models were offered. The latter carried eight passengers and cost a bit more. Transports were not officially exported to the United States until 1952, when 10 were sold here.

I.D DATA: Serial number is on a plate on the front hood center and at back of spare tire and stamped on chassis tunnel (backbone) under the rear seat. Engine number is stamped on the generator support and on the crankcase. Serial number range: 138555-220471. The model year ended on December 31, 1950 with chassis number 220 133 and engine number 265 999. On Transporters the serial number is on a plate mounted on the firewall in the engine compartment.

ENGINE

BASE FOUR (All): Horizontally opposed, overhead-valve four-cylinder (air cooled). Light alloy block. Light alloy heads. Finned cylinders with cast-iron cylinder liners. Displacement: 69.0 cid (1131 cc). Bore & Stroke: 2.95 x 2.52 in. (75 x 64 mm). Compression Ratio: 5.8:1. Brake Horsepower: 24.5 at 3300 rpm. Torque: 51 ft.-lbs. at 2000 rpm. Solid valve lifters. Solex carburetor. 6-volt electrical system.

CHASSIS

(BEETLE) SEDAN: Wheelbase: 94.5 in. Overall Length: 160.2 in. Height: 61.0 in. Width: 60.5 in. Front Tread: 51.0 in. Rear Tread: 49.2 in. Standard Tires: 5.00 x 16. Turning circle: 37 ft. Turns lock-to-lock: 2.4.

TRANSPORTER: Wheelbase: 94.5 in. Overall Length: (Transporter) 155 in., (Deluxe Transporter) 166.1 inches. Height: 74.5 in. Width: 67 in. Front Tread: 53.4 in. Rear Tread: 53.5 in. Standard Tires: 5.50 x 16.

TECHNICAL

(BEETLE SEDAN): Layout: rear-engine, rear-drive. Transmission: four-speed manual. Standard Final Drive Ratio: (sedan) 4.43:1. Steering: worm and cap nut. Suspension (front): king pins with transverse torsion bars and upper/lower trailing arms. Suspension (rear): swing axles with trailing arms and torsion bars. Brakes: (early) mechanical, (March-April on) hydraulic, front/rear drum. Body Construction: steel unibody on stamped steel floor pan. Fuel Tank: 8.8 gallon.

(TRANSPORTER): Layout: rear-engine, rear-drive. Transmission: four-speed manual. Standard Final Drive Ratio: 6.2:1. Steering: manual. Suspension (front): Independent: two square section torsion bars. Suspension (rear): Independent: circular torsion bars each side. Brakes: hydraulic, front/rear drum. Body Construction: steel unibody on stamped steel floor pan. Fuel Tank: 10.5 gallon.

PERFORMANCE: Top speed (Beetle): 60+ mph. Fuel mileage (Beetle): about 34 mpg.

HISTORICAL FOOTNOTES: Manufacturer: Volkswagenwerk GmbH, Wolfsburg, West Germany. Distributor: Hoffman Motor Car Co., New York City. Production for 1950 was 81,979 cars. The 100,000th Volkswagen was put together on March 4. A total of 270 Volkswagens were sold in the United States during 1950. According to *Ward's 1952 Automotive Yearbook*, 157 Volkswagens were registered in the United States in calendar-year 1950. The trade magazine, which rarely makes mistakes, misspelled the company name as "Volkswagon." *Motor Trend* tested a Volkswagen Beetle in late 1950. "Roadability is said to be phenomenal for a light sedan," advised the magazine. The German car was said to be rapidly becoming an "outstanding success." *Motor Trend* said that "several hundred" had been sold in the New York area. The January 1950 issue of *Motor Trend* carried a reader's letter from Hans B. Kirchner of Long Beach, California, an early Volkswagen "Bug" fan. It was entitled "60,000 miles in a Volkswagen." Kirchner told of how he had purchased a Volkswagen in 1947 and used it to travel the Southern Alps to Italy. He had crossed the Gross Glockner Strasse (highest highway in Austria) and Germany in his car, then brought it to the United States. He drove it from coast to coast, including Southern and Northern California and brought it to Long Beach in 1949. It must of been one of very fw VWs in the country then. In the "Transatlantic Newsletter" section of the July 1950 *Motor Trend* a photo of a Volkswagen and a Porsche appeared. The caption read, "The cars in this pleasant Alpine setting are both engineered by Dr. Ferdinand Porsche." In the September "Transatlantic Newsletter" the columnist noted, "Volkswagen's latest models have been reduced in price and improved in quality. Lockheed hydraulic brakes are now standard. Cooling air to the engine is at last thermostatically regulated." Despite such press exposure for Volkswagen products, *Motor Trend* seemed to be more interested in the German DKW in 1950, than it was in the Volkswagen.

1951

It is easy to spot a 1951 Volkswagen built after January 6, 1951 — just look for the ventilation flaps on the body panel between the front fender and the door. This was one of at least 25 significant running changes. Also in January, the generator pulley was redesigned, a sleeve for guiding the accelerator cable return spring was added and the original magnesium-aluminum alloy crankcase was replaced by the Electron type experimented with earlier. In February 5, Volkswagen decided to "bench test" the Standard sedan, rather than run it in on a test track. In March, a synthetic cam gear was put into production and the exhaust silencer pipe was modified. "Windows" appeared in both halves of the crankcase starting in April. A Wolfsburg crest was added to the front hood of Export models. Also, the front heater flaps were moved inside the heat exchangers and telescopic shocks relaced the lever-action style on Export models and Cabriolets. Bright metal trim was added to the windshield of Export models, the front side panels got pull-out flaps and a locking glove compartment was added to the Cabriolet (which also got concealed door hinges, a single interior door pocket on each side and an additional interior-light switch. Also in April, the generator was uprated and in July a rubber boot was added to cover the hand-brake lever. In August, the ventilation flaps were improved through the use of a new mesh screen and an operating lever.

SEDAN COLORS: L11=Pastel Green, L13=Medium Green, L14=Reseda Green, L21=Pearl Gray, L23=Silver Gray, L31=Dove Blue, L32=Dark Blue, L36=Azure Blue, L37=Medium Blue, L41=Black, L55=Maroon Red, L70=Medium Brown, L73=Chestnut Brown, L87=Pearl

The top folded flush on the 1951 Hebmueller but it sacrificed rear seating space.

Paul Smith

Above: **A 1951 VW Hebmueller shows off its special craftsmanship.**

Paul Smith

Below: **Early Transporter fans call them "barn doors" because of the rear door's shape.**
Dick Dance Collection

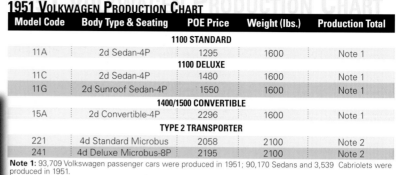

Model Code	Body Type & Seating	POE Price	Weight (lbs.)	Production Total
1100 STANDARD				
11A	2d Sedan-4P	1295	1600	Note 1
1100 DELUXE				
11C	2d Sedan-4P	1480	1600	Note 1
11G	2d Sunroof Sedan-4P	1550	1600	Note 1
1400/1500 CONVERTIBLE				
15A	2d Convertible-4P	2296	1600	Note 1
TYPE 2 TRANSPORTER				
221	4d Standard Microbus	2058	2100	Note 2
241	4d Deluxe Microbus-8P	2195	2100	Note 2

Note 1: 93,709 Volkswagen passenger cars were produced in 1951; 90,170 Sedans and 3,539 Cabriolets were produced in 1951.

Note 2: 3,074 Transporters were produced in 1951.

The 1951 VW Transporter series bus was ahead of its time in terms of practicality.

White, L90=Sand Beige. All models had a standard Beige cloth interior. Beige and Red Beige leatherette interiors were available depending on body color. Headliner color was Beige or Gray depending on body color. Carpets were Gray Beige or Honey Brown depending on body color. Standard Sedans came only with Black rubber mats. Deluxe Export models came with Black or Beige mats depending on choice and body color.

TYPE 2 TRANSPORTER—FOUR Production of the boxy Microbus station wagon continued with little change. It used the same drivetrain layout as the sedan. Standard and Deluxe models were offered. The latter carried eight passengers and cost a bit more.

I.D. DATA: Serial number is on a plate on the front hood center and at back of spare tire and stamped on chassis tunnel (backbone) under the rear seat. Engine number is stamped on the generator support and on the crankcase. Serial number range: 220472-313829. The model year ended on December 31, 1951 with chassis number 313 829 and engine number 379 470. On Transporters the serial number is on a plate mounted on the firewall in the engine compartment.

ENGINE

BASE FOUR: Horizontally opposed, overhead-valve four-cylinder (air cooled). Light alloy block and heads and finned cylinders with cast-iron cylinder liners. Displacement: 69.0 cid (1131 cc). Bore & Stroke: 2.95 x 2.52 in. (75 x 64 mm). Compression Ratio: 5.8:1. Brake Horsepower: 24.5 at 3300 rpm. Torque: 51 ft.-lbs. at 2000 rpm. Solid valve lifters. Solex carburetor. 6-volt electrical system.

CHASSIS

(BEETLE) SEDAN: Wheelbase: 94.5 in. Overall Length: 159.3 in. Height: 59.1 in. Width: 60.6 in. Front Tread: 50.8 in. Rear Tread: 49.2 in. Standard Tires: 5.00 x 16. Turning circle: 37 ft. Turns lock-to-lock: 2.4.

TRANSPORTER: Wheelbase: 94.5 in. Overall Length: 159.3 in. Height: 74.8 in. Width: 66.9 in. Front Tread: 53.4 in. Rear Tread: 53.5 in. Standard Tires: 5.50 x 16.

TECHNICAL

(BEETLE) SEDAN: Layout: rear-engine, rear-drive. Transmission: four-speed manual. Final Drive type: Spiral bevel. tandard Final Drive Ratio: 4.43:1. Steering: worm and cap nut. Suspension (front): king pins with transverse torsion bars and upper/lower trailing arms. Suspension (rear): swing axles with trailing arms and torsion bars. Brakes: hydraulic, front/rear drum. Body Construction: steel body welded to floor pan with tubular center section. Fuel Tank: 8.8 gallon.

(TRANSPORTER): Layout: rear-engine, rear-drive. Transmission: four-speed manual. Final drive type: Spiral bevel, double reduction. Standard Final Drive Ratio: 6.2:1. Steering: manual. Suspension (front): Independent: two square section torsion bars. Suspension (rear): Independent: circular torsion bars each side. Brakes: hydraulic, front/rear drum. Body Construction: steel unibody on stamped steel floor pan. Fuel Tank: 10.5 gallon.

PERFORMANCE: Top speed (Beetle): 60 mph. Fuel mileage (Beetle): up to 34 mpg.

HISTORICAL FOOTNOTES: Manufacturer: Volkswagenwerk GmbH, Wolfsburg, West Germany. Distributor: Hoffman Motor Car Co., New York City. Production for 1951 was 93,709 vehicles. A total of 550 Volkswagens were sold in the United States during 1950. According to *Ward's 1952 Automotive Yearbook*, 390 Volkswagens were registered in the United States in calendar-year 1951. On January 30, 1951, Dr. Ferdinand Porsche, the father of Volkswagen, passed away at age 75. With international communications being much slower in 1951, it wasn't until June that *Motor Trend* noted his passing. "He was best known for his revolutionary Volkswagen and recent Porsche automobile and for his famous rear-engined racing machines, which were operated by Auto Union between '34 and '37," said the magazine. Also in June 1951, *Motor Trend* printed Volkswagen specifications which varied from those in other references used to research this book. They put the price of the Beetle sedan at $1,380 and the weight at 1,533 lbs. The same issue also noted, "Newest model in the Volkswagen line is this convertible with typically German padded top. It's costliest VW, sells for $1,655." (Note that the price in the photo caption was significantly lower than the convertible price given in many other sources.) On October 5, 1951 the 250,000th Volkswagen made since the end of the war was built.

Owner: Dr. Mac Jones/ Photographer: Perrin Todd

A new 1951 Volkswagen Beetle would have been a rare sight on a country road.

1952

1100 (BEETLE)—FOUR Late-1951 changes used on 1952 models included strengthened jacking point on the Beetle and the deletion of wheel bolts from the tool kit. In November, the rear seat bolsters that had been used in the Export Sedan since 1949 were discontinued and the exhaust valves were improved. Starting in Decermber, new 6-volt 0.6-watt dashboard indicator lamps were used. The Volkswagen underwent numerous changes during the 1952 calendar year, but not all at once. For instance, the use of vent windows, associated with the 1952 Beetle, didn't go into effect until October 1, 1952. In January a hollow bolt with a felt ring was adopted to prevent grease leaks and the handbrake lever boot on the chassis tunnel of Export models was modified. Starting in February, the hydraulic brake reservoir no longer had a float and Volkswagen made some electrical changes involving parking lights, which were in the headlight and attached to a different system terminal. In March, a Klettermaxe jack was added to the tool kit. In March, the use of a connecting pipe between the tailpipe and the exhaust silencer was dropped. In May, the use of double valve springs stopped and a single spring was used. In June, the diameter of the clutch cable adjusting nut was reduced. A new clutch cable operating lever with a conical "eye" was adopted.

SEDAN COLORS: L11=Pastel Green, L13=Medium Green, L14=Reseda Green, L21=Pearl Gray, L23=Silver Gray, L31=Dove Blue, L32=Dark Blue, L36=Azure Blue, L37=Medium Blue, L41=Black, L55=Maroon Red, L70=Medium Brown, L73=Chestnut Brown, L87=Pearl White, L90=Sand Beige. All models had a standard Beige cloth interior. Beige and Red Beige leatherette interiors were available depending on body color. Headliner color was Beige or Gray depending on body color. Carpets were Gray Beige or Honey Brown depending on body color. Standard Sedans came only with Black rubber mats. Deluxe Export models came with Black or Beige mats depending on choice and body color.

TYPE 2 TRANSPORTER FOUR Production of the boxy rear-engined Transporter "station wagon" continued with little change. Standard and Deluxe models were offered. The latter carried eight passengers and cost a bit more. Transporters were officially exported to the United States this year and 10 were sold here.

TRANSPORTER COLORS: L11=Pastel Green, L14=Mignonette, L73=Chestnut Brown.

Model Code	Body Type & Seating	POE Price	Weight (lbs.)	Production Total
1100 STANDARD				
11A	2d Sedan-4P	1395	1600	Note 1
1100 DELUXE				
11C	2d Sedan-4P	1595	1600	Note 1
11G	2d Sunroof Sedan-4P	1667	1600	Note 1
1400/1500 CONVERTIBLE				
15A	2d Convertible-4P	2395	1700	Note 1
TYPE 2 TRANSPORTER				
221	4d Standard Microbus	1995	2200	Note 2
222	4d Deluxe Microbus-8P	2169	2240	Note 2

Note 1: 114,348 Volkswagen cars were produced in 1952; 110,095 Sedans and 4,253 Cabriolets were produced in 1952.

Note 2: 5,194 Transporters were produced in 1952.

Left: **By 1952, producing VWs had become efficient and quality was high.**

Above and Left: **This 1952 Volkswagen sunroof sedan is a well-preserved Beetle.**

Tom Glatch

I.D. DATA: Serial number is on a plate on the front hood center and at back of spare tire and stamped on chassis tunnel (backbone) under the rear seat. Engine number is stamped on the generator support and on the crankcase. Serial number range: 313830-428156. The model year ended on December 31, 1952 with chassis number 397 023 and engine number 481 713. On Transporters the serial number is on a plate mounted on the firewall in the engine compartment.

ENGINE

BASE FOUR: Horizontally opposed, overhead-valve four-cylinder (air cooled). Light alloy block and heads and finned cylinders with cast-iron cylinder liners. Displacement: 69.0 cid (1131 cc). Bore & Stroke: 2.90 x 2.52 in. (75 x 64 mm). Compression Ratio: 5.8:1. Brake Horsepower: 24.5 at 3300 rpm. Four main bearings. Solid valve lifters. Solex carburetor. 6-volt electrical system.

CHASSIS

(BEETLE) SEDAN: Wheelbase: 94.5 in. Overall Length: 159.4 in. Height: 59.1 in. Width: 60.6 in. Front Tread: 50.8 in. Rear Tread: 49.2 in. Standard Tires: 5.00 x 16. Turningcircle: 37 ft.

TRANSPORTER: Wheelbase: 94.5 in. Overall Length: (Transporter) 161.5 in. Height: 74.8 in. Width: 66.9 in. Front Tread: 53.4 in. Rear Tread: 53.5 in. Standard Tires: 5.50 x 16.

TECHNICAL

(BEETLE) SEDAN: Layout: rear-engine, rear-drive. Transmission: four-speed manual. Final Drive Type: Spiral bevel. Standard Final Drive Ratio: 4.43:1. Steering: worm and cap nut. Suspension (front): king pins with transverse torsion bars and upper/lower trailing arms. Suspension (rear): swing axles with trailing arms and torsion bars. Brakes: hydraulic, front/rear drum. Body Construction: steel body welded to floor pan with tubular center section. Fuel Tank: 8.8 gallon.

TRANSPORTER: Layout: rear-engine, rear-drive. Transmission: four-speed manual. Final Drive Type: Spiral bevel double reduction. Standard Final Drive Ratio: 6.2:1. Steering: manual. Suspension (front): Independent: two square section torsion bars. Suspension (rear): Independent: circular torsion bars each side. Brakes: hydraulic, front/rear drum. Body Construction: steel unibody on stamped steel floor pan. Fuel Tank: 10.5 gallon.

PERFORMANCE: Top speed (Beetle): 65 mph. Fuel mileage: (Beetle) 34 mpg.

HISTORICAL FOOTNOTES: Manufacturer: Volkswagenwerk GmbH, Wolfsburg, West Germany. Distributor: Hoffman Motor Car Co., New York City. Production for 1952 was 114,348 vehicles. According to *Ward's 1953 Automotive Yearbook*, 601 Volkswagens were registered in the United States in calendar-year 1952. The trade magazine, which rarely makes mistakes, again misspelled the company name as "Volkswagon." Volkswagen of Canada was formed on September 11, 1952 to sell Volkswagens in Canada. For the year, 41.4 percent of all Volkswagens made were exported. During the fourth quarter of the year Volkswagen workers were building 734 cars per day.

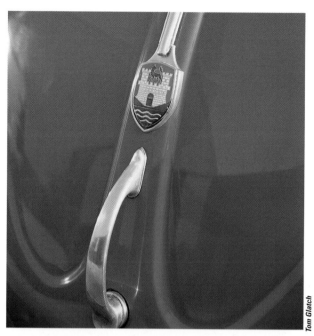

Volkswagen added a hood ornament to the 1952 Beetle.

Tools could be found in the center of the spare tire in the 1952 Volkswagen.

1953

1100 (BEETLE)—FOUR Late-1952 changes used on 1953 Volkswagens included a new rotary knob for heating adjustments. The front torsion bars got a sixth leaf and the shock absorber travel was increased. A new 28 PCI carburetor was used. The transmission used in the Export sedan got synchronizers on all gears but first. New rubber-and-steel gearbox mountings were used. Rear torsion bar diameters were reduced a bit. A change was made to smaller but wider 5.60-15 wheels and increased-diameter rear wheel brake cylinders were introduced. As mentioned earlier, use of the vent windows also kicked-in on October 1. Other improvement were made to the heating system demisters and noise suppression. Opening the windows now took just over three turns of the crank handle, rather than 10-1/2 turns. The engine lid got a T-handle instead of a vertical one. The bumpers had a broader section (profile) and beefier guards. Polished annodized metal moldings replaced the old aluminum body trim. For better security the glove compartment got a lid and a push-button latching mechanism. The dashboard was completely redesigned and

rubber floor mats with press studs were also new. There was a new ash tray on the passenger side of the dash and different cloth upholstery. The rear light lenses had heart-shaped brake lamp lenses on top of each taillight The fuse box for the brake/taillights was on the reverse side of the dashboard. Wider-sweeping windshields wipers were fitted. New battery hold-down springs were fitted. Single-pull switches were used for the lights and the wipers. The starter button was now on the left side of the steering wheel. The turn signal indicator switch was to the left of the column. A new larger-diameter speedometer was fitted. The horn was now concealed behind a decorative oval grille. The horn button on the center of the steering wheel had a Wolfsburg crest. Volkswagen continued making running changes to its "People's Car" in 1953, but there were fewer modifications than in the past few years. An oil-bath air cleaner with a clamping strap was introduced. The carburetor air-correction jet was revised and bronze check valves replaced the steel ones. Engine valve clearances were reduced. New adjustable door striker plates appeared on production cars beginning on Valentine's Day. In March, the electric fuses were changed to a brass-wire type, the fuel tank filler neck doubled in size to 80 mm and new reflecting trim moldings were

Above: **The 1953 Volkswagen Beetle is carefully preserved.**
Tom Glatch

Model Code	Body Type & Seating	POE Price	Weight (lbs.)	Production Total
1100 STANDARD				
11A	2d Sedan-4P	Note 1	1520	Note 2
1100 DELUXE				
11C	2d Sedan-4P	Note 3	1540	Note 2
11G	2d Sunroof Sedan-4P	1675	1554	Note 2
1400/1500 CONVERTIBLE				
15A	2d Convertible-4P	2350	1790	Note 2
TRANSPORTER				
221	4d Standard Microbus	NA	2200	Note 4
241	4d Deluxe Microbus -8P	NA	2200	Note 4

Note 1: *Official Automobile Guide* (1958) says $1,455. In April 1953 *Motor Trend* noted "The German automotive industry has been quiet since Volkswagen reduced the price on its standard model to $1,056."
Note 2: 151,323 Volkswagen cars were produced in 1953; 147,153 Sedans and 4,170 Cabriolets were produced in 1953.
Note 3: *Official Automobile Guide* (1958) says $1,655. In January 1953 *Motor Trend* foreign car specifications chart the price of the Volkswagen sedan was given as $1,790.
Note 4: 5,375 Transporters were produced in 1953.

Below: **VW buyers could purchase a spotlight and roof rack for their 1953 Beetle.**

Tom Glatch

adopted, along with a new, 23-percent larger, curved safety glass rear window with no division bar. The lid for the ashtray in the dashboard got a new, short and horizontal handle. A new interior light came with an on-off switch and a 10-watt bulb instead of a 5-watt bulb. A wider new "combined" indicator arrow appeared in the speedometer. In July, a new rearview mirror that was integral with the sun visor was introduced and the quarter windows got new locking catches.

SEDAN COLORS: (October-March) L11=Pastel Green, L21=Pearl Gray, L36=Azure Blue, L37=Medium Blue, L41=Black, L55=Maroon Red, L70=Medium Brown, L73=Chestnut Brown, L90=Sand Beige. All models had a standard Gray Beige cloth interior. Beige and Red Beige leatherette interiors were available depending on body color. Headliner color was Beige or Gray depending on body color. Carpets were Gray Beige or Honey Brown depending on body color. Black rubber mats were provided. (March-December) L11=Pastel Green, L19=Atlantic Green, L35=Metallic Blue, L37=Medium Blue, L41=Black, L73=Chestnut Brown, L225=Jupiter Gray, L271=Texas Brown, L272=Sahara Tan. All models had a standard Gray Beige cloth interior. Beige, Black and Red Beige leatherette interiors were available depending on body color. Headliner color was Beige or Gray depending on body color. Carpets were Gray Beige or Honey Brown depending on body color. Black rubber mats were provided.

TRANSPORTER—FOUR Production of the boxy rear-engined Transporter (Transporter) station wagon continued with little change.

Dick Dance Collection

The art used in the 1953 VW brochure was memorable.

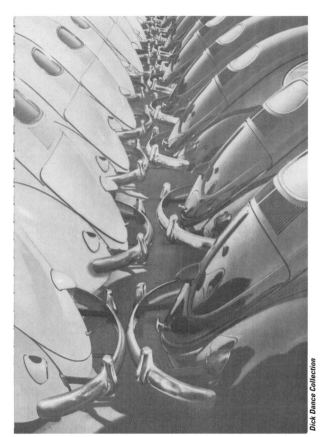

Dick Dance Collection

There is no question where the power comes from in these posed VWs.

TRANSPORTER COLORS: L11=Pastel Green, L14=Mignonette, L73=Chestnut Brown.

I.D. DATA: Serial number is on a plate on the front hood center and at back of spare tire and stamped on chassis tunnel (backbone) and under the rear seat. Engine number is stamped on the generator support and on the crankcase. Serial number range: (Sedan) 428157 to 575414. On Transporters the serial number is on a plate mounted on the firewall in the engine compartment.

ENGINE

BASE FOUR: Horizontally opposed, overhead-valve four-cylinder (air cooled). Light alloy block and heads and finned cylinder with cast-iron cylinder liners. Displacement: 69.0 cid (1131 cc). Bore & Stroke: 2.95 x 2.52 in. (75 x 64 mm). Compression Ratio: 5.8:1. Brake Horsepower: 24.5 at 3300 rpm. Torque: 51 ft.-lbs. at 2000 rpm. Four main bearings. Solid valve lifters. Solex carburetor. 6-volt electrical system.

CHASSIS

(BEETLE) SEDAN: Wheelbase: 94.5 in. Overall Length: 160.2 in. Height: 59.1 in. Width: 60.6 in. Front Tread: 50.6 in. Rear Tread: 49.08 in. Standard Tires: 5.60 x 15. Turning Diameter: 36 ft. Turns lock-to-lock: 2.4.

Note: The tread widths given above are from *Motor Trend* (January 1953). Other reference sources show the same tread widths as for previous cars with 5.00 x 16 tires, but it is logical that the wider 5.60 x 15 tires of 1953 narrowed tread width very slightly.

TRANSPORTER: Wheelbase: 94.5 in. Overall Length: 161.5 in. Height: 74.8 in. Width: 66.9 in. Front Tread: 53.4 in. Rear Tread: 53.5 in. Standard Tires: 5.50 x 16. Turning diameter: 37 ft.

TECHNICAL

(BEETLE) SEDAN: Layout: rear-engine, rear-drive. Transmission: four-speed manual. Final Drive Type: Spiral bevel. Standard Final Drive Ratio: 4.40:1. Steering: worm and cap nut. Suspension (front): king pins with transverse torsion bars and upper/lower trailing arms. Suspension (rear): swing axles with trailing arms and torsion bars. Brakes: hydraulic, front/rear drum. Body Construction: steel body welded to floor pan with tubular center section. Fuel Tank: 8.8 gallon.

TRANSPORTER: Layout: rear-engine, rear-drive. Transmission: four-speed manual. Final Drive Type: Spiral bevel double reduction. Standard Final Drive

Ratio: 6.20:1. Steering: manual. Suspension (front): Independent: two square section torsion bars. Suspension (rear): Independent: circular torsion bars each side. Brakes: hydraulic, front/rear drum. Body Construction: steel unibody on stamped steel floor pan. Fuel Tank: 10.5 gallon.

PERFORMANCE: Top Speed (Beetle): 66 mph. 0-60 mph acceleration (Beetle): 42.1 sec. Fuel Mileage (Beetle): 22-28 mpg average.

HISTORICAL FOOTNOTES: Manufacturer: Volkswagenwerk GmbH, Wolfsburg, West Germany. Distributor: Hoffman Motor Car Co., New York City. Production for 1953 was 151,323 vehicles. According to *Ward's 1955 Automotive Yearbook*, 1,237 new Volkswagens were registered in the United States in calendar-year 1953. The trade magazine, which did not report U.S. registrations of foreign cars in its 1954 yearbook, corrected the spelling of "Volkswagen" in its 1955 edition, a clear sign that people in America were becoming more aware of the German import. "Handling qualities are exceptional," declared *Motor Trend* of the Beetle in 1953. "You can break the rear end loose, but only if you work at it" said the magazine, which also noted that the "interior trim is as good as in some cars costing an additional $1,000." One of the reasons that the Volkswagen was more in the spotlight in America in 1953 was because the first dealerships opened this year. According to an article in the February 1959 issue of *Motor Trend*, Volkswagen sent the first mechanics and their families over from Germany. Each dealer was assigned one or more factory mechanics to assure that parts and service departments would meet stringent qualifications requirements. *Motor Trend* gave "ink" to the Volkswagen at least three times during 1953. In the September issue, Dr. Ferdinand Porsche was mentioned as the creator of the Volkswagen and Porsche automobiles. In October an article entitled "Seven Economy Cars" covered the Volkswagen sedan in minute detail. "The whole car is crammed with features as unusual as the engine," the magazine said. "Do you want a car that breaks sharply with tradition and does so with undeniable competence? If so, the Volkswagen deserves your attention," said the magazine. An article entitled "German Auto Industry" appeared in the December issue. "Best known German export car is the Volkswagen, rear-powered by an air-

This 1953 accessory was an air vent called the "beecatcher."

cooled flat four and finished like an expensive car," said the caption under the picture of a Beetle sedan. The article also stated, "For 1953, the Volkswagen plant alone expects a production of 160,000 passenger cars." It was hard to determine who actually owned Volkswagen in 1953. Each year since 1945 a certain amount of the company's profits had been put into escrow, awaiting a decision by the West German courts and there was $50 million in the kitty. More than 200,000 VWs had been exported from Germany to 83 countries by that point. *All The Worlds' 1954 Cars* said, "To date, over 2000 Americans and 500,000 Europeans have bought these durable, economical, well-finished and sprightly Volkswagens." The *Motor Trend Worldwide Yearbook 1954* noted, "The Deluxe Export Sedan and Cabriolet offer between 30 and 32 miles to the U.S. gallon. The 24.5-hp engine does not sound overly exciting, however the Volkswagen combines simplicity, ease of repair and cheapness of replacement parts which led to the Model T's fabulous popularity. Although the normal maximum speed does not exceed 65 mph, that speed is accomplished at just over 3,000 rpm, a noteworthy factor in reducing

engine wear. Its pound-per-horsepower ratio is a relatively unimpressive 63.43, but despite this, the Volkswagen can hold its own under normal traffic conditions. The ride offered by this surprisingly roomy car is fairly comfortable. Its handling qualities are superior, aside from a tendency toward overly quick steering in the turns."

Old Cars Weekly Archive

By 1953, Volkswagen had refined the car's interior in many ways.

Volkswagen quickly earned a repuatation as economical, yet well-built cars.

1954

1200 (BEETLE)—FOUR Late 1953 changes used on 1954 Volkswagen models included eight-leaf torsion bars and greaseless front wheel bearing caps. In October, a juicier generator was used on some cars. In November, VW went to a heater control knob with no inscription. A new steering wheel with two downward-pointing spokes that provided a clearer view of the speedometer was used. In December, a new 1192-cc 30-hp engine with a 6.1:1 compression ratio was used for the first time. Volkswagens got an oil-bath air cleaner and larger heating outlets up front (instead of at the rear) with a protective grille. A new 160-watt generator replaced the previous 130-watt model and adjustable automatic instrument illumination was provided. The windshield wipers were improved and finished with metallic paint (instead of chrome plating). Tool kit ingredients were shuffled again and the use of a push-button starter was dropped. The engine distributor was built with a new type of vacuum control (cars only) and a new over-center battery clamp was used. By late December, the door and ignition locks were identical. In January 1954 Volkswagen adopted a dip

stick with an integral loop handle and cap. In February, Volkswagen began marking the month and year of production on the underside of the oil cooler. In March,

This image of a Volkswagen was two panels wide in the 1954 brochure.

Dick Dance Collection

A Volkswagen Cabriolet is shown with its top up in this 1954 brochure.

Dick Dance Collection

Above: **The popular 1954 VW Cabriolet featured four-place seating and a unique folded top.**

Dick Dance Collection

1954 VOLKSWAGEN PRODUCTION CHART

Model Code	Body Type & Seating	POE Price	Weight (lbs.)	Production Total
1200 STANDARD				
111	2d Sedan-4P	1395	1565	Note 1
1200 DELUXE				
113	2d Sedan-4P	1495	1600	Note 1
116	2d Sunroof Sedan-4P	1575	1609	Note 1
151	2d Convertible-4P	1995	1700	Note 1
TRANSPORTER				
231-M13	4d Kombi-8P	NA	2260	Note 2
221	4d Microbus-8P	NA	2403	Note 2
241	4d Deluxe Microbus -8P	NA	NA	Note 2

Note 1: 202,174 Volkswagen cars were produced in 1954; 197,620 Sedans and 4,554 Cabriolets were produced in 1954.

Note 2: 7,630 Transporters were produced in 1954.

Owner: Dr. Mac Jones/ Photographer: Perrin Todd

By 1954, the VW Kombi was earning a reputation as a versatile vehicle.

a new style starting crank was supplied. It was made of 3-mm gauge seamless tubing. In April, the distributor was upgraded with improved springs for the bob weights. In May, the carburetor was improved with a nylon float and the body finish on the Cabriolet was changed from cellulose to synthetic resin. Volkswagen added a driving mirror with two sun visors, a passenger grab handle, a tailpipe extension and several interior changes. In July, the filter mesh was removed from the oil filter cap.

SEDAN COLORS: L41=Black, L213=Iceland Green, L225=Jupiter Gray (Standard Sedan only), L227=Strato

Silver, L271=Texas Brown, L275=Light Beige, L276=Ultramaroon. Cloth interiors were Beige, Green, Gray or Slate Blue depending on body color. Headliner color was Beige or Gray depending on body color. Carpets were Gray Beige, Gray Blue or Honey Brown depending on body color. Black rubber mats were provided.

TRANSPORTER—FOUR Production of the rear-engined Transporter Microbus station wagon continued with little change, except for the adoption of the larger engine. A Deluxe version was available with "skylight" style mini windows and a sunroof. American used-car guides such as

Red Book National Market Reports Official Used Car Evaluations often listed the Transporter series as simply the "Station Wagon" Series. The 1954 Transporter sales brochure listed six models, of which three (Eight-passenger Microbus, Deluxe Microbus and Kombi) were passenger vehicles and three were commercial vehicles (Delivery Van, Pickup Truck and Ambulance). The Kombi van was offered with or without occasional passenger seating. The seats were removable, but a Kombi could carry 8 to 9 passengers with all seats in place. The rear windows pivoted outward for extra ventilation. Since the center and rear seats were removable, the Kombi could be a passenger car or a cargo van. The cargo area lacked a headliner and interior panels. The Eight-Passenger Microbus was available with a Golde brand sunroof at extra cost. The Deluxe Microbus included the Golde sunroof, windows all around the body and side observation panels in the roof. Enthusiasts of today identify different models by counting the number of windows.

TRANSPORTER COLORS: L11=Pastel Green, L14=Mignonette, L73=Chestnut Brown, L271=Texas Brown.

I.D. DATA: Serial number is on a plate on the front hood center and at back of spare tire and stamped on chassis tunnel (backbone) and under the rear seat. Engine number is stamped on the generator support and on the crankcase. Serial number range: (sedan) 575415 to 722934. On Transporters the serial number is on a plate mounted on the firewall in the engine compartment.

ENGINE

BASE FOUR: Horizontally opposed, overhead-valve four-cylinder (air cooled). Light alloy block and heads and finned cylinder with cast-iron cylinder liners. Displacement: 72.7 cid (1192 cc). Bore & Stroke: 3.03 x 2.52 in. (77 x 64 mm). Compression Ratio: 6.6:1. Brake Horsepower: 30 at 3400 rpm. Four main bearings. Solid valve lifters. Solex down-draft carburetor. 6-volt electrical system.

CHASSIS

(BEETLE) SEDAN: Wheelbase: 94.5 in. Overall Length: 160.2 in. Height: 59.1 in. Width: 60.6 in. Front Tread: 50.8 in. Rear Tread: 49.2 in. Standard Tires: 5.60 x 15. Turning circle: 36 ft.

Dick Dance Collection

Volkswagen used art that stylized the car in its 1950s advertising literature.

TRANSPORTER: Wheelbase: 94.5 in. Overall Length: (Standard)161.5, (Deluxe) 168.1 in. Height: 74.8 in. Width: 66.9 in. Front Tread: 53.4 in. Rear Tread: 53.5 in. Standard Tires: 5.50 x 16. Turning circle: 37 ft.

TECHNICAL

(BEETLE) SEDAN: Layout: rear-engine, rear-drive. Transmission: four-speed manual. Final Drive Type: Spiral bevel. Standard Final Drive Ratio: 4.40:1. Steering: worm and cap nut. Suspension (front): king pins with transverse torsion bars and upper/lower trailing arms. Suspension (rear): swing axles with trailing arms and torsion bars. Brakes: hydraulic, front/rear drum. Body Construction: steel body welded to floor pan with tubular center section. Fuel Tank: 8.8 gallon.

TRANSPORTER: Layout: rear-engine, rear-drive. Transmission: four-speed manual. Final Drive Type: Spiral bevel double reduction. Standard Final Drive Ratio: 6.20:1. Steering: manual. Suspension (front): Independent: two square section torsion bars. Suspension (rear): Independent: circular torsion bars each side. Brakes: hydraulic, front/rear drum. Body Construction:

steel unibody on stamped steel floor pan. Fuel Tank: 10.5 gallon.

PERFORMANCE: Top Speed (Beetle): 66 mph. 0-60 mph acceleration (Beetle): 42.1 sec. Fuel Mileage (Beetle): 22-28 mpg average. Top Speed (Transporter): 50 mph. 0-60 mph acceleration (Transporter): NA. Fuel Mileage (Transporter): 25 mpg average.

HISTORICAL FOOTNOTES: Manufacturer: Volkswagenwerk GmbH, Wolfsburg, West Germany. Distributor: Hoffman Motor Car Co., New York City. A total of 202,174 Volkswagens were built in 1954. According to *Ward's 1955 Automotive Yearbook*, 6,344 new Volkswagens were registered in the United States in calendar-year 1954. On September 10, 1954 the 100,000th Volkswagen leaves the Wolfsburg factory. For the first time Volkswagen generated one billion DM for the year. The company started an annual "success" bonus for its workforce. A used 1948 Volkswagen was advertised in the August 1954 issue of *Motor Trend*. The car was said to be in nice condition with a radio and paint (new paint?). Mr. B. Dierke of Chicago was asking $25 but offered to "trade up on an MG."

Old Car Weekly Archives

Bugs, bugs everywhere! It's the VW Beetle assembly plant, circa 1954.

1955

1200 (BEETLE)—FOUR In 1955, Volkswagen switched to making changes on a model-year basis with the model year running from August to August. On August 31, 1954, some engine improvements went into effect and the distributor rotor arm was redesigned to stay dust free. Other changes made included the spare V-belt once again being dropped from the tool kit contents. In October, the "window" lens on the brake light housing was discontinued and new double-filament bulbs were used in cars destined for the United States and Canada. Volkswagen also began using shatterproof windshield glass and, later, a taillight housing with a drain hole in it went into production. In December, the door hinge was modified to use an oil slot instead of a hole for hinge pin lubrication. A key-type starter replaced the earlier push-button starter and a three-way dome light was installed. Volkswagen engines no longer required a break-in period. Calendar year 1955 was one of very minimal change. Starting on April 1, cars sold in the United States, Canada and Guam had fender-mounted turn-signal flashers instead of semaphores.

SEDAN COLORS: L41=Black, L225=Jupiter Gray (Standard Sedan only), L227=Strato Silver, L313=Reed Green, L315=Jungle Green, L324=Polar Silver, L370=Nile Beige. Cloth interiors were Beige, Green, Gray, Blue or Rusty Red depending on body color. Headliner color was Beige, Gray or Brown Beige depending on body color. Black rubber mats were provided. About the Volkswagen interior, *Motor Trend* (June 1955), said, "Interiors are odd-smelling, durable plastic with most screws concealed, workmanship expected of much more expensive car."

TRANSPORTER—FOUR The 1955 Transporter series included the same three passenger-carrying models. The Kombi van was offered with or without occasional passenger seating. The seats were removable, but a Kombi could carry 8 to 9 passengers with all seats in place. The rear windows pivoted outward for extra ventilation. Since the center and rear seats were removable, the Kombi could be used as a passenger car or a cargo van. The cargo area lacked a headliner and interior panels. The eight-passenger Microbus was available with or without the optional Golde sunroof. The Deluxe Microbus included the Golde sunroof, windows all around the body and side observation panels in the roof. The June 1955 issue of *Motor Trend* stated, "Heavier Microbus uses the same engine (as Beetle), has high, wide compartment for nine people or much cargo. Deluxe version has roll-back roof. For use as a station wagon where little power needed."

TRANSPORTER COLORS: L11=Pastel Green, L14=Mignonette, L53=Sealing Wax Red, L73=Chestnut Brown, L271=Texas Brown, L315=Jungle Green Metallic.

I.D. DATA: Serial number is on a plate on the front hood center and at back of spare tire and stamped on chassis tunnel (backbone) and under the rear seat. Engine number is stamped on the generator support and on the crankcase. Chassis number range: 722935-929745. On Transporters the serial number is on a plate mounted on the firewall in the engine compartment.

Left: The 1955 Volkswagen cabriolet was an alternative choice for convertible buyers.

Robert and Ellen Flood

1955 Volkswagen Production Chart

Model Code	Body Type & Seating	POE Price	Weight (lbs.)	Production Total
	1200 DELUXE			
113	2d Sedan-4P	1595	1609	Note 1
117	2d Sunroof Sedan-4P	1675	1690	Note 1
151	2d Convertible-4P	2195	1764	Note 1
	TRANSPORTER			
231-M13	4d Kombi-8P	NA	2127	Note 2
221	4d Microbus-8P	NA	NA	Note 2
241	4d Deluxe Microbus-8P	NA	NA	Note 2

Note 1: 279,986 Volkswagens were produced in 1955.
Note 2: 10,152 Transporters were produced in 1955.

The 1955 Volkswagen Beetle sunroof sedan was listed at $1,575 when it was new.

Tom Glatch

Engine

BASE FOUR: Horizontally opposed, overhead-valve four-cylinder (air cooled). Light alloy block and heads and finned cylinders with cast-iron cylinder liners. Displacement: 72.7 cid (1192 cc). Bore & Stroke: 3.03 x 2.52 in. (77 x 64 mm). Compression Ratio: 6.6:1. Brake Horsepower: 30 at 3400 rpm. Four main bearings. Solid valve lifters. Solex downdraft carburetor. 6-volt electrical system.

CHASSIS

(BEETLE) SEDAN: Wheelbase: 94.5 in. Overall Length: 160.2 in. Height: 59.1 in. Width: 60.6 in. Front Tread: 50.8 in. Rear Tread: 49.2 in. Standard Tires: 5.60 x 15. Turning circle: 36 ft. Ground clearance: 6.8 in.

TRANSPORTER: Wheelbase: 94.5 in. Overall Length: (Standard)165, (Deluxe) 168.1 in. Height: 74.8 in. Width: 68.0 in. Front Tread: 53.4 in. Rear Tread: 53.5 in. Standard Tires: 5.50 x 16. Turning circle: 37 ft. Ground clearance: 11.2 in.

TECHNICAL

(BEETLE) SEDAN: Layout: rear-engine, rear-drive. Transmission: four-speed manual. Final Drive Type: Spiral bevel. Standard Final Drive Ratio: 4.40:1. Steering: worm and cap nut. Suspension (front): king pins with transverse torsion bars and upper/lower trailing arms. Suspension (rear): swing axles with trailing arms and torsion bars. Brakes: hydraulic, front/rear drum. Body Construction: steel body welded to floor pan with tubular center section. Fuel Tank: 8.8 gallon.

TRANSPORTER: Layout: rear-engine, rear-drive. Transmission: four-speed manual. Final Drive Type: Spiral bevel double reduction. Standard Final Drive Ratio: 6.20:1. Steering: manual. Suspension (front): Independent: two square section torsion bars. Suspension (rear): Independent: circular torsion bars each side. Brakes: hydraulic, front/rear drum. Body Construction: steel unibody on stamped steel floor pan. Fuel Tank: 10.5 gallon.

PERFORMANCE: Top Speed (Beetle): 68 mph. Fuel Mileage (Beetle): 28 mpg average. Top Speed (Transporter): 50 mph. Fuel Mileage (Transporter): 25 mpg average.

HISTORICAL FOOTNOTES: Manufacturer: Volkswagenwerk GmbH, Wolfsburg, West Germany. Distributor: Hoffman Motor Car Co., New York City. Volkswagen made a total of 279,986 cars in 1955. According to *Ward's 1956 Automotive Yearbook*, 28,907 new Volkswagens were registered in the United States in calendar-year 1955. This made the Volkswagen the largest selling imported car behind Jaguar and MG, in order. The previous year the 1-2-3 order had been Volkswagen, MG, Jaguar. In 1955, *Motor Trend* said, "Having shot in a short time to the top of imported car sales lists, the familiar VW is worth a close look" . . "For a lot of people, gives near-sports feel, comfort, high quality, economy, practical innovations." On August 5, 1955 the one millionth Volkswagen came off the Wolfsburg assembly line. Volkswagen of America was founded on October 27, 1955 in Englewood Cliffs, N.J. This trading company was responsible for United States sales of Volkswagen products. In Germany, the production of the Volkswagen passed the 1,000 units per day mark.

Old Car Weekly Archives

The Volkswagenwerk photo shows the company was an automotive giant by 1955.

1956

1956

1200 (BEETLE)—FOUR Most of Volkswagen's "1956" changes went into effect on August 4, 1953, when the taillights were redesigned and mounted higher on the fenders. Twin tailpipes jutted out the rear of the car (bright tailpipes on Export models). A new easy-grip steering wheel had deeper-set spokes and a smaller hub. Door panels on Export models got leatherette trim. The interior door handles now moved towards the rear of the car. The jack attached with a snap-on clip and was nearer the spare tire than before. The front seats were made wider. Seats in the Export Sedan were on a higher-at-the-front rail and adjusted three ways. The gear shift lever was now bent backwards. A sports car based on the Beetle was announced on July 14, 1955. This sporty coupe had a Ghia-styled body and was constructed by the German coachbuilder Karmann. It would enter regular production as a 1956 model. In February, 1956, VWs got a distributor with a new power curve. Beginning in March, the Export Sedan had less ground clearance. April brought 15-mm longer front seats with rubber-based hair padding. In June, the engine vacuum pipe was moved from above the choke cable to under the accelerator cable and tubeless tires were

Above: **The 1956 Rometsch-Beeskow was a limited production car based on the Volkswagen.**

Owner: Dr. Mac Jones / Photographer: Perrin Todd

tested on 800 cars (they were later installed on all VWs). Other new-for-1956 features included self-cancelling directional lights and adjustable seat backs.

SEDAN COLORS (EARLY 1956): L41=Black, L225=Jupiter Gray (Standard Sedan only), L227=Strato Silver, L313=Reed Green, L315=Jungle Green, L324=Polar Silver, L370=Nile Beige. Cloth interiors were Green, Gray, Blue or Rusty Red depending on body color. Headliner color was Beige, Gray or Brown Beige depending on body color. Black rubber mats were provided. These colors were used from August 1955 to March 1956. **(LATE 1956):** L41=Black, L225=Jupiter Gray (Standard Sedan only), L240=Agave Green, L324=Polar Silver, L331=Horizon Blue, L351=Coral Red, L378=Prairie Beige and L412=Diamond Green. Black rubber mats were provided. These colors were used from April to July 1956 and for 1957.

KARMANN-GHIA—FOUR This was the first year for the stylish Karmann-Ghia coupe, which blended the mechanical components and structure of the Beetle with a handsome Italian-designed 2 + 2 coupe body. Body manufacture was performed by Karmann, the firm that also turned out Volkswagen convertibles. The driving position

Most of Volkswagen's "1956" changes went into effect on August 4, 1953, when the taillights were redesigned and mounted higher on the fenders.

1956 VOLKSWAGEN PRODUCTION CHART

1956 VOLKSWAGEN PRODUCTION CHART

Model Code	Body Type & Seating	POE Price	Weight (lbs.)	ProductionTotal
1200 DELUXE				
113	2d Sedan-4P	1495	1609	Note 1
117	2d Sedan-4P	1575	1690	Note 1
151	2d Convertible-4P	1995	1764	Note 1
KARMANN-GHIA				
143	2d Coupe-2 + 2P	2395	1720	Note 1
TRANSPORTER				
231-M13	4d Kombi-8P	1995	2100	Note 2
221	4d Microbus-8P	2095	2400	Note 2
241	4d Deluxe Microbus-8P	2545	2450	Note 2

Note 1: 333,190 Volkswagen cars were produced in 1956.
Note 2: 11,798 Transporters were produced in 1956.
Note 3: According to *Motor Trend* (May 1956) the sedan was $100 more on the West Coast.

Paul Smith

This 1956 VW Cabriolet is still a beautiful car nearly 40 years later.

was lower than in a sedan, described by *Motor Trend* as "more like Porsche." The shapely body had a sculpted line leading from the lower door, upward and along the rear quarter panel. There was more of a "hood" up front than in the Beetle. The roof line was low; it looked great, but would touch a tall person's head. Rear quarter windows were installed, along with curved door windows. *Motor Trend* said, Interor finish is flawless and chastely classic. There were bucket seats in front and a bench in the rear, Either cloth or leatherette upholstery was available. Controls were similar to those of the sedan, but not identical. The small grilles on each side of the nose admitted floor-level fresh air. The rear end was less skitterish than that of the Beetle thanks to the Karmann-Ghia's front-end roll bar and wider frame rails. It had better low-end acceleration than other VWs. "On a lonely stretch," declared *Motor Trend* of their test coupe, the "Ghia's high-speed behavior proved impeccable." According to the magazine, this was a result of the car's weight and streamlining.

KARMANN-GHIA COLORS (JANUARY 1956-JULY 1957): L41=Black, L317=Lizard Green, L375 Antelope Brown, L259=Pelican Red, L330=Trout Blue, L376-=Gazelle Beige.

TRANSPORTER–FOUR The 1956 Transporter included three models. The Kombi came with or without occassional seating. The seats were removable, but a Kombi could carry 8 to 9 passengers with all seats in place. The rear windows pivoted outward. The Eight-Passenger Microbus was available with a Golde brand sunroof. The Deluxe Microbus included the Golde sunroof, windows all around the body and side observation panels in the roof. What *Motor Trend* (October 1956) described as "the ingenious German-made Kamper Kit" was also available for the 1956 Microbus. It included a folding table, a little folding bench, a plaid-covered full-length bench, a cupboard, a camp ice box, a camp stove, a fold-out bed, storage cabinets, a roof transom, an awning, lockers and curtains.

TRANSPORTER COLORS: L11=Pastel Green, L14=Mignonette, L53=Sealing Wax Red, L73=Chestnut Brown, L271=Texas Brown, L315=Jungle Green Metallic.

I.D. DATA: Serial number is on a plate on the front hood center and at back of spare tire and stamped on chassis tunnel (backbone) and under the rear seat. Engine number is stamped on the generator support and on the crankcase. Chassis number range: 929746-1246618. On Transporters the serial number is on a plate mounted on the firewall in the engine compartment.

ENGINE

BASE FOUR: Horizontally opposed, overhead-valve four-cylinder (air cooled). Light alloy block, heads and finned cylinder with cast-iron cylinder liners. Displacement: 72.7 cid (1192 cc). Bore & Stroke: 3.03 x 2.52 in. (77 x 64 mm). Compression Ratio: 6.6:1. Brake Horsepower: 36 at 3700 rpm. Four main bearings. Solid valve lifters. Solex 28 PCI downdraft carburetor. 6-volt electrical system.

CHASSIS

(BEETLE) SEDAN: Wheelbase: 94.5 in. Overall Length: 160.2 in. Height: 59.1 in. Width: 60.6 in. Front Tread:

Paul Smith

By 1956, Beetles were a popular choice among North American drivers.

Dick Dance Collection

The Karmann-built, Ghia-designed sports car Volkswagen appeared in 1956.

50.8 in. Rear Tread: 49.2 in. Standard Tires: 5.60 x 15. Turning circle: 36 ft. Ground clearance: 6.8 in.

KARMANN-GHIA: Wheelbase: 94.5 in. Overall Length: 163 in. Height: 52.2. Width: 64.2 in. Front Tread: 50.8 in. Rear Tread: 49.2 in. Standard Tires: 5.60 x 15.

TRANSPORTER: Wheelbase: 94.5 in. Overall Length: (Standard)165, (Deluxe) 166.1 in. Height: 76.5 in. Width: 68.0 in. Front Tread: 53.9 in. Rear Tread: 53.5 in. Standard Tires: 6.40 x 16. Turning circle: 37 ft. Ground clearance: 11.2 in.

TECHNICAL

(BEETLE) SEDAN: Layout: rear-engine, rear-drive. Transmission: four-speed manual. Gear ratios: (1st) 3.60:1, (2nd) 1.88:1, (3rd) 1.23:1, (4th) 0.82:1, (reverse) 4.63:1. Final Drive Type: Spiral bevel. Standard Final Drive Ratio: 4.40:1. Steering: worm and cap nut. Suspension (front): king pins with transverse torsion bars and upper/lower trailing arms. Suspension (rear): swing axles with trailing arms and torsion bars. Brakes: hydraulic, front/rear drum. Body Construction: steel body welded to floor pan with tubular center section. Fuel Tank: 8.8 gallon.

KARMANN-GHIA: Layout: rear-engine, rear-drive. Transmission: four-speed manual. Final Drive Type: Spiral bevel. Standard Final Drive Ratio: 4.40:1. Steering: worm and cap nut. Suspension (front): Independent: upper and lower trailing arms with square torsion bars. Suspension (rear): Independent: swinging half axle shafts with torsion bars. Brakes: hydraulic, front/rear drum. Body Construction: Tubular center section, forked at rear, with welded on platform. Fuel Tank: 10.6 gallon.

TRANSPORTER: Layout: rear-engine, rear-drive. Transmission: four-speed manual. Final Drive Type: Spiral bevel double reduction. Standard Final Drive Ratio: 6.20:1. Steering: manual. Suspension (front): Independent: two square section torsion bars. Suspension (rear): Independent: circular torsion bars each side. Brakes: hydraulic, front/rear drum. Body Construction: steel unibody on stamped steel floor pan. Fuel Tank: 10.5 gallon.

OPTIONS: (Sedan) Sliding canvas roof $80. Plastic upholstery ($25). (Karmann-Ghia) Fitted luggage.

PERFORMANCE: Top Speed: (Beetle) 68 mph claimed. Top Speed: (Karmann-Ghia) "over 70" mph claimed. Top Speed: (Transporter) 50 mph. Fuel Mileage (Beetle): 32 mpg claimed. Fuel mileage (Karmann-Ghia): NA. Fuel mileage (Transporter): 25 mpg.

HISTORICAL FOOTNOTES: Manufacturer: Volkswagenwerk GmbH, Wolfsburg, West Germany. Importer: Volkswagen of America, Englewood Cliffs, N.J. Volkswagen made a total of 333,190 cars in 1956. According to *Ward's 1958 Automotive Yearbook*, 50,011 new Volkswagens were registered in the United States in calendar-year 1956. Volkswagen had 50.9 percent of the imported car market in 1956, Metropolitan was second and Jaguar was third. "Analyzing the growing Volkswagen Family" said the tag line on the cover of the May 1956 issue of *Motor Trend*. The cover photo showed the new Karmann-Ghis coupe, a Volkswagen microbus and 13 Beetle sedans. Inside was a comparison road test of the '56 Volkswagen and Renault. Subjectively, the magazine tester, Pete Molson, liked the renault best. He admitted, however, "But there is a combination of civilized U.S.-type comfort and fun in the VW that the Renault does not approach." Aftermarket accessories available for the Volkswagen in 1956 included a '40-Ford-like front end called the "Classic Kit" that Kit enterprises of San Bernardino, California sold for $135. Garden Supply Co., of Grass Valley, California, advertised a Volkswagen luggage rack for $20. "Haul lumber, ladders, luggage" said their advertisement. Judson Research and Mfg. Co. of Conshohocken, Pennsylvania offered a supercharger with six pounds of boost for $144. It gave a 45 percent boost in rear-wheel horsepower and cut 0-to-60 mph times to 15.5 seconds. Carrosseire Zund of Switzerland made a large, wraparound rear window treatment. In Germany, a Volkswagen-based car called the Rometsch Sportswagen was available on a built-to-order basis. One brought into the United States by Beverly Hills, California, dealer Jack Berman was showcased in the September 1956 edition of *Motor Trend*. It was the first (and possibly only) such car to reach America. Available as a package priced at $2,995 for a coupe and $3,195 for a convertible, it included a completely custom body with a full wraparound rear window that had a touch of Studebaker Starlight Coupe to it.

1956 VW drivers seeking more room could add an optional, spacious roof rack.

1957

1200 (BEETLE)—FOUR Volkswagen's "1957" changes started appearing on cars leaving the factory in August 1956. They included an adjustable door lock plate and new ignition coil specs. A light alloy cam timing gear was adopted. Starting in September, the VW emblems on the hubcaps was finished in black. A new Cabriolet top was fastened with brass pins and studs instead of steel ones. Starting in October, a new starter with four commutator brushes was used. All home-market cars got an outside rearview mirror. The door hinges no longer had lubrication nipples. December brought new Pearl Blue and Bambo colors for the Cabriolet, but Iris Blue and Sepia Silver were dropped. There was slightly more room throughout the Beetle, including in the up-front luggage compartment. Numerous changes were made to Volkswagens throughout calendar-year 1957. In January, the front heater outlets were moved rearward, to within a foot of the doors, in order to improve heat distribution. This required some modifications to the body side panels. In February, Volkswagen adopted the use of a new windshield wiper motor and made improvements to the

license plate lighting. Starting at the end of the first week in June, a steering wheel with twice as many (48) splines was put into use.

SEDAN COLORS (1957-1958): L41=Black, L225=Jupiter Gray (Standard Sedan only), L240=Agave Green, L324=Polar Silver, L331=Horizon Blue, L351=Coral Red, L378=Prairie Beige and L412=Diamond Green. Black rubber mats were provided. These colors were used from April to July 1956 and for 1957. **(August 1, 1957 and 1958 model year):** L41=Black, L225=Jupiter Gray (Standard Sedan only), L243=Diamond Gray, L245=Light Bronze,

Above: **By 1957, the distinctive Volkswagen profile was immediately recognizable.**

By 1957, the Volkswagen Beetle had new turn signals and bumper overriders.

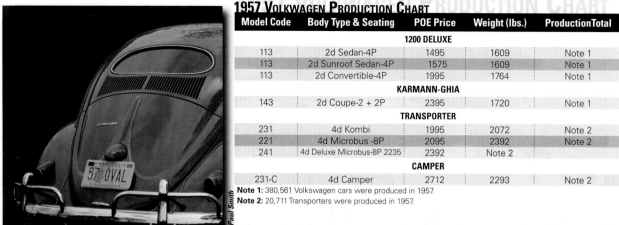

Model Code	Body Type & Seating	POE Price	Weight (lbs.)	ProductionTotal
	1200 DELUXE			
113	2d Sedan-4P	1495	1609	Note 1
113	2d Sunroof Sedan-4P	1575	1609	Note 1
113	2d Convertible-4P	1995	1764	Note 1
	KARMANN-GHIA			
143	2d Coupe-2 + 2P	2395	1720	Note 1
	TRANSPORTER			
231	4d Kombi	1995	2072	Note 2
221	4d Microbus -8P	2095	2392	Note 2
241	4d Deluxe Microbus-8P	2235	2392	Note 2
	CAMPER			
231-C	4d Camper	2712	2293	Note 2

Note 1: 380,561 Volkswagen cars were produced in 1957.
Note 2: 20,711 Transporters were produced in 1957.

Paul Smith

Alex and Angela Vena

From the front or back, there was nothing like a Volkswagen Beetle.

L334=Glacier Blue, L335=Capri Blue and L351=Coral Red. Black rubber mats were provided were provided in Jupiter Gray cars; Gray mats in other cars. These colors were used from April to July 1956 and for 1957.

CABRIOLET COLORS (1957-1958): L41=Black, L241=Bamboo Green, L258=Inca Red, L316=Almond Green, L320=Light Dolphin Gray, L329=Shetland Gray, L331=Horizon Blue, L336-Deep Blue, L351=Coral Red . **(August 1, 1957 and 1958 model year):** L41=Black,

L241=Bamboo Green, L243=Diamond Gray, L244=Moss Green, L258=Inca Red, L329=Shetland Gray, L338=Atlas Blue and L473=Alabaster Gray. Gray mats in all cars.

KARMANN-GHIA—FOUR Production of the 2 + 2 Sport Coupe continued with minor changes. In midyear, at the Frankfurt International Automobile Show, Volkswagen introduced a Karmann-Ghia Cabriolet. The open model went into production on August 1, 1957. This car was the highlight attraction at the Karmann assembly plant

The 1957 Beetle convertible could get a healthy 32 miles per gallon.

in Osnabruck, where it was showcased on September 19. The new ragtop's introductory price was 8250 DM.

KARMANN-GHIA COLORS (JANUARY 1956-JULY 1957): L41=Black, L317=Lizard Green, L375 Antelope Brown, L259=Pelican Red, L330=Trout Blue, L376=Gazelle Beige.

TRANSPORTER—FOUR The 1957 Transporter series again included three regular passenger models. The Kombi van was offered with or without occassional passenger seating. The seats were removable, but a Kombi could carry 8 to 9 passengers with all seats in place. The rear windows pivoted outward for extra ventilation. Since the center and rear seats were removable, the Kombi could be a passenger car or a cargo van. The cargo area lacked a headliner and interior panels. The Eight-Passenger Microbus was available with a Golde brand sunroof at extra cost. The Deluxe Microbus included the Golde sunroof, windows all around the body and side observation panels in the roof. Enthusiasts of today identify different models by counting the number of windows. A Camper bus was also available starting this year. It was fitted with such extras as a folding table and fold-out beds.

TRANSPORTER COLORS: L11=Pastel Green, L14=Mignonette, L31=Dove Blue, L53=Sealing Wax Red, L73=Chestnut Brown, L271=Texas Brown, L315=Jungle Green Metallic.

I.D. DATA: Serial number is on a plate on the front hood center and at back of spare tire and stamped on chassis

The most obvious change to the 1957 Volkswagen interior was the steering wheel.

tunnel (backbone) and under the rear seat. Engine number is stamped on the generator support and on the crankcase. On Transporters the serial number is on a plate mounted on the firewall in the engine compartment. Serial number range: (Beetle sedan and Karmann-Ghia) 1246619-1600439, (Transporter) 191842 up.

ENGINE

BASE FOUR: Horizontally opposed, overhead-valve four-cylinder (air cooled). Light alloy block, heads and finned cylinder with cast-iron cylinder liners. Displacement: 72.7 cid (1192 cc). Bore & Stroke: 3.03 x 2.52 in. (77 x 64 mm). Compression Ratio: 6.6:1. Brake Horsepower: 36 at 3700 rpm. Four main bearings. Solid valve lifters. Solex 28 PCI downdraft carburetor. 6-volt electrical system.

CHASSIS

(BEETLE) SEDAN: Wheelbase: 94.5 in. Overall Length: 160.2 in. Height: 59.1 in. Width: 60.6 in. Front Tread: 50.8 in. Rear Tread: 49.2 in. Standard Tires: 5.60 x 15. Turning circle: 36 ft. Ground clearance: 6.8 in.

KARMANN-GHIA: Wheelbase: 94.5 in. Overall Length: 163 in. Height: 52.2. Width: 64.2 in. Front Tread: 50.8 in. Rear Tread: 49.2 in. Standard Tires: 5.60 x 15.

TRANSPORTER: Wheelbase: 94.5 in. Overall Length: (Standard)165, (Deluxe) 166.1 in. Height: 76.5 in. Width: 68.0 in. Front Tread: 53.9 in. Rear Tread: 53.5 in. Standard Tires: 6.40 x 15. Turning circle: 37 ft. Ground clearance: 11.2 in.

TECHNICAL

(BEETLE) SEDAN: Layout: rear-engine, rear-drive. Transmission: four-speed manual. Gear ratios: (1st) 3.60:1, (2nd) 1.88:1, (3rd) 1.23:1, (4th) 0.82:1, (reverse) 4.63:1. Final Drive Type: Spiral bevel. Standard Final Drive Ratio: 4.40:1. Steering: worm and cap nut. Suspension (front): king pins with transverse torsion bars and upper/lower trailing arms. Suspension (rear): swing axles with trailing arms and torsion bars. Brakes: hydraulic, front/rear drum. Body Construction: steel body welded to floor pan with tubular center section. Fuel Tank: 8.8 gallon.

KARMANN-GHIA: Layout: rear-engine, rear-drive. Transmission: four-speed manual. Final Drive Type: Spiral bevel. Standard Final Drive Ratio: 4.40:1. Steering: worm and cap nut. Suspension (front): Independent: upper and lower trailing arms with square torsion bars. Suspension (rear): Independent: swinging half axle shafts with torsion bars. Brakes: hydraulic, front/rear drum. Body Construction: Tubular center section, forked at rear, with welded on platform. Fuel Tank: 10.6 gallon.

Late in 1957, Volkswagen introduced the convertible Karmann-Ghia to North America.

TRANSPORTER: Layout: rear-engine, rear-drive. Transmission: four-speed manual. Final Drive Type: Spiral bevel double reduction. Standard Final Drive Ratio: 6.20:1. Steering: manual. Suspension (front): Independent: two square section torsion bars. Suspension (rear): Independent: circular torsion bars each side. Brakes: hydraulic, front/rear drum. Body Construction: steel unibody on stamped steel floor pan. Fuel Tank: 10.5 gallon.

PERFORMANCE: Top Speed: (Beetle) 68 mph claimed. Top Speed: (Karmann-Ghia) "over 70" mph claimed. Top Speed: (Transporter) 50 mph. Fuel Mileage (Beetle): 32 mpg claimed. Fuel mileage (Karmann-Ghia): NA. Fuel mileage (Transporter): 25 mpg.

HISTORICAL FOOTNOTES: Manufacturer: Volkswagenwerk GmbH, Wolfsburg, West Germany. Importer: Volkswagen of America, Englewood Cliffs, N.J. Volkswagen continued its upward march and manufactured 380,561 cars in 1957. According to *Ward's 1958 Automotive Yearbook*, 64,242 new Volkswagens were registered in the United States in calendar-year 1957. Volkswagen had 50.9 percent of the imported car market in 1956, Metropolitan was second and Jaguar was third. The "As We Go To Press" column in the October 1957 issue of *Motor Trend* highlighted VW's larger windshield, new dashboard and new pedal design, giving a good idea of when the "1958" features were gaining awareness in the United States. Early automotive publisher Flord Clymer, of Los Angeles, was selling a *Volkswagen Owners Handbook* for $2 in 1957. The 100,000th Volkswagen to be exported to Sweden was shipped on New Year's Day 1957. Also, the 300,000th VW transporter was made on November 15. On December 28, the two millionth Volkswagen was made. VW took over the Henschel factory in Germany and also started a subsidiary in Australia this year. Despite the increase in new-car registrations this year, VW's share of the import car market fell from almost 51 percent to 31.1 percent. The "Big 3" in this market segment were Volkswagen first, Renault second and British Ford third.

*Volkswagen Station Wagon
and De Luxe Station Wagon*

1958

1200 (BEETLE)—FOUR As usual, Volkswagen's main "1958" product changes came after the company holidays, late in the summer of 1957. A number of changes took place August 1. There was a completely new dashboard with the radio loudspeaker to the left of the steering wheel, all-new control knobs and a glovebox lid that dropped automatically when a button was pushed. Export and Cabriolet models had a bright metal molding running across the center of the dash from side to side. The old-fashioned roller–type pedal was replaced with a pad type. A higher, but smaller, air cleaner was fitted. Fuel economy was improved. The windshield wipers moved closer together to give a wider sweep. Several modifications were made to bodies. The cool-air inlets were redesigned to improve drainage. The engine cover seal was imporved. A larger windshield and back window were fitted. The new windshield narrowed the front corner posts (this was promoted as a safety feature). There were new exterior colors for Beetle Sedans and Cabriolets. A second roup of changes came on September 16, 1957. At that time the steering column was shortened, a new steering wheel was used, more new colors were introduced and Volkswagen improved the seats, the soundproofing and added outlets with short vertical louvers below the rear window of Sedans. Instead of using this arrangement, Beetle Cabriolets had a stack of short horizontal lovers on each side of the engine cover. In October, VW started using a different type of bulb in the license plate lamp and brake indicator lamp.

On December 20, VW offered maintenance-free tie rods as an option in 20,000 cars. A small number of additional changes were made during calendar-year 1958. In January, many Cabriolets (depending on body color) got Pearl White wheels and the factory began using magnetic oil drain plugs on Export Sedans. A control flap was added to the rear window demister system. In February, coat hooks were added to the interior. In March, the spark plug wrench that came with the car was changed to a rubber-sleeve type instead of the retaining-spring type. In April, Volkswagen began using 13-mm bolts to attach mud guards, running boards and horns. On April 29, Wolfsburg initiated use of a rolled bronze swivel-pin bushing, with a lengthwise slit, in the steering system. A plastic carburetor venturi tube replaced the aluminum type in June. Starting in July, the distributor rotor and spark plug caps were of a different design. In April 1958, *Motor Trend* selected the Volkswagen Beetle as The Best Foreign Car Buy in the $1,500-$2,000 range. "You have to go a long way to beat the Volkswagen as the best dollar-for-dollar buy in the economy class" said the write up. The magazine found the paint, trim and upholstery of incredibly high quality and credited its full-torsion-bar suspension for "top-of-the-list" ride quality. Real-life top speed was said to be in the 70-72-mph bracket, although the speedometer read 80 mph. "The air-

Above: **This inviting cover promoted the VW station wagons in 1958.**

Dick Dance Collection

Model Code	Body Type & Seating	POE Price	Weight (lbs.)	Production Total
1200 DELUXE				
113	2d Sedan-4P	1545	1609	Note 1
117	2d Sunroof Sedan-4P	1625	1609	Note 1
151	2d Convertible-4P	2045	1764	Note 1
1200 KARMANN-GHIA				
143	2d Sport Coupe 2 + 2P	2445	1720	Note 1
141	2d Cabriolet 2 + 2P	2725	1786	Note 1
TRANSPORTER				
231	4d Kombi	2020	2127	Note 2
221	4d Microbus	2120	2447	Note 2
241	4d Deluxe Microbus	2576	2447	Note 2
CAMPER				
231C	4d Camper	2886	2293	Note 2

Note 1: 451,526 Volkswagen cars were produced in 1958.
Note 2: 23,841 Transporters were produced in 1958.

Bottom: **Whether its top was open or closed, the Karmann-Ghia was a handsome car.**

Dick Dance Collection

Dick Dance Collection

The Karmann-Ghia coupe was displayed artistically in this 1958 Volkswagen brochure.

cooled, flat-opposed, four-cylinder engine, nestling aft, never overworks itself," said *Motor Trend*. "Piston speed at full throttle is ridiculously low." The article noted that the seats did not offer much support and mentioned the fact that there were no instruments except a speedometer and monitor lights for the oil and generator, but visibilitry was praised highly. The magazine warned "don't overfill the front-mounted gas tank or you'll ride with fumes." On the plus side, it pointed out that Volkswagen's service and parts situation was "likely the best in America."

SEDAN COLORS (1958): L41=Black, L225=Jupiter Gray, L240=Agave Green, L243=Diamond Gray, L245=Light Bronze, L334=Glacier Blue, L335=Capri Blue and L351=Coral Red. Black mats were provided in Jupiter Gray cars; Gray mats in other cars.

CABRIOLET COLORS (1958): L41=Black, L241=Bamboo Green, L243=Diamond Gray, L244=Moss Green, L258=Inca Red, L329=Shetland Gray, L338=Atlas Blue and L473=Alabaster Gray. Gray mats in all cars.

KARMANN-GHIA—FOUR The Karmann-Ghia line continued to offer the Coupe introduced in 1956 and the Cabriolet introduced in mid-1957. Starting January 3, 1958, Karmann-Ghia produced for the American marketplce got reinforced front and rear bumpers. Starting January 7, Karmann-Ghia Pearl White wheel finish was used on Karmann-Ghia Coupes and Cabriolets in 10 colors.

TRANSPORTER—FOUR The Transporter series again included three regular passenger models. The Kombi van was offered with or without occassional passenger seating.

The seats were removable, but a Kombi could carry 8 to 9 passengers with all seats in place. The rear windows pivoted outward for extra ventilation. Since the center and rear seats were removable, the Kombi could be a passenger car or a cargo van. The cargo area lacked a headliner and interior panels. The Eight-Passenger Microbus was available with a Golde brand sunroof at extra cost. The Deluxe Microbus included the Golde sunroof, windows all around the body and side observation panels in the roof. Enthusiasts of today identify different models by counting the number of windows. A Camper bus was also available and included such extras as a folding table and fold-out beds.

TRANSPORTER COLORS: L14=Mignonette, L31=Dove Blue, L53=Sealing Wax Red, L73=Chestnut Brown, L82=Silver White, L87=Pearl White, L345=Pale Gray, L346=Mango Green, L472=Beige Gray.

I.D. DATA: Serial number is on a plate on the front hood center and at back of spare tire and stamped on chassis tunnel (backbone) and under the rear seat. Engine number is stamped on the generator support and on the crankcase. Chassis number range: 1600440-2007615. On Transporters the serial number is on a plate mounted on the firewall in the engine compartment.

ENGINE

BASE FOUR: Horizontally opposed, overhead-valve four-cylinder (air cooled). Light alloy block, heads and finned cylinder with cast-iron cylinder liners. Displacement: 72.7 cid (1192 cc). Bore & Stroke: 3.03 x 2.52 in. (77 x 64 mm). Compression Ratio: 6.6:1. Brake Horsepower: 36 at 3700 rpm. Torque: 56 lbs.-ft. at 2000 rpm. Four main bearings. Solid valve lifters. Solex downdraft carburetor. 6-volt electrical system.

CHASSIS

(BEETLE) SEDAN: Wheelbase: 94.5 in. Overall Length: 160.2 in. Height: 59.1 in. Width: 60.6 in. Front Tread: 51.4 in. Rear Tread: 49.2 in. Standard Tires: 5.60 x 15.

KARMANN-GHIA: Wheelbase: 94.5 in. Overall Length: 163 in. Height: 52.2. Width: 64.2 in. Front Tread: 51.4 in. Rear Tread: 49.2 in. Standard Tires: 5.60 x 15.

TRANSPORTER: Wheelbase: 94.5 in. Overall Length: (Standard)165, (Deluxe) 166.1 in. Height: 76.5 in. Width: 68.0 in. Front Tread: 53.9 in. Rear Tread: 53.5 in. Standard Tires: 6.40 x 15.

TECHNICAL

(BEETLE) SEDAN: Layout: rear-engine, rear-drive. Transmission: four-speed manual. Gear ratios: (1st) 3.60:1,

Volkswagens were placed in fashionable locations in this 1958 brochure.

By 1958, buyers knew the Volkswagen Kombi was a reliable vehicle.

The 1958 VW Deluxe bus could carry many people economically.

In the U.S.A., the Station Wagon is a familiar friendly sight everywhere.

Clubs find their own Station Wagon popular with members.

Sightseeing in Paris — an elegant bus in the city of elegance.

Volkswagen Transporters were shown in artistic settings in the late 1950s.

(2nd) 1.88:1, (3rd) 1.23:1, (4th) 0.82:1, (reverse) 4.63:1. Final Drive Type: Spiral bevel. Standard Final Drive Ratio: 4.40:1. Steering: worm and cap nut. Suspension (front): king pins with transverse torsion bars and upper/lower trailing arms. Suspension (rear): swing axles with trailing arms and torsion bars. Brakes: hydraulic, front/rear drum. Body Construction: steel body welded to floor pan with tubular center section. Fuel Tank: 8.8 gallon.

KARMANN-GHIA: Layout: rear-engine, rear-drive. Transmission: four-speed manual. Final Drive Type: Spiral bevel. Standard Final Drive Ratio: 4.40:1. Steering: worm and cap nut. Suspension (front): Independent: upper and lower trailing arms with square torsion bars. Suspension (rear): Independent: swinging half axle shafts with torsion bars. Brakes: hydraulic, front/rear drum. Body Construction: Tubular center section, forked at rear, with welded on platform. Fuel Tank: 10.6 gallon.

TRANSPORTER: Layout: rear-engine, rear-drive. Transmission: four-speed manual. Final Drive Type:

Spiral bevel double reduction. Standard Final Drive Ratio: 6.20:1. Steering: manual. Suspension (front): Independent: two square section torsion bars. Suspension (rear): Independent: circular torsion bars each side. Brakes: hydraulic, front/rear drum. Body Construction: steel unibody on stamped steel floor pan. Fuel Tank: 10.5 gallon.

PERFORMANCE: Top Speed (Beetle): 70-72 mph (75 mph in table) noted in *Motor Trend* April 1958. Top Speed: (Karmann-Ghia) "over 70" mph claimed. Top Speed: (Transporter) 50 mph. Fuel Mileage (Beetle): Fuel Mileage (Beetle): 35-40 mpg noted in *Motor Trend* April 1958. Fuel mileage (Karmann-Ghia): NA. Fuel mileage (Transporter): 25 mpg.

HISTORICAL FOOTNOTES: Manufacturer: Volkswagenwerk GmbH, Wolfsburg, West Germany. Importer: Volkswagen of America, Englewood Cliffs, N.J. Volkswagen manufactured 451,526 cars in 1958. According to *Ward's 1959 Automotive Yearbook*, 78,261 new Volkswagens were registered in the United States in

A memorable vision of the Volkswagen is captured on the cover of the 1958 brochure.
Dick Dance Collection

calendar-year 1958. This year Volkswagen's share of the imported car market in the United States was 20.7 percent. Renault was second with 12.7 percent and Englisdh Ford was third with 8.9 percent. The 400,000th Volkswagen Transporter was manufactured on October 16, 1958. In its April issue, *Motor Trend* published a story about visiting the German auto industry in 1958. "When you stand at one end of a corridor on the 'office' side of the factory, you cannot see the other end," wrote Walt Woron. "Where you see cars rolling off the ends of four assembly lines at the rate of one every 30 seconds. Then, and only then, do you get the true impression of Volkswagenwerk GMBH, located in the small town of Wolfsburg, near Hanover, in Western Germany, just seven short miles from the Iron Curtain." Woron noted that 818,000 Volkswagens were registered in Germany alone. He also pictured a "Porsche Jeep" that was virtually the same vehicle as The Thing that arrived in the United States, as a Volkswagen product, in the 1970s. In 1958, Volkswagen engine production was transferred from the Wolfsburg factory to a new addition in the Hanover plant. The August 1958 issue of *Motor Trend* carried a classified ad from Charles Pasco, of

Seattle, offering to trade his '55 Morgan Drophead Coupe for a Volkswagen Beetle or Karmann-Ghia. Possibly he contacted D.E. Salmeier, of Clovis, New Mexico, who had an ad on the same page offering a 1958 Karmann-Ghia with 3,000 miles for $2,625. Mr. Salmeier even noted that he was willing to trade for an older model car. During 1958, W. Robert Nitske authored a book called *The Amazing Porsche and Volkswagen Story* that was published by Comet Press and sold for $5. The September 1958 issue of *Motor Trend* noted the availability of a replacement body for the VW chassis from Alken Corporation of Venice, California. The Alken D-2 was a fiberglass convertible sports car that was 300 pounds lighter than a bug when completed. The body sold for $1,295 and supposedly took "a few hours" to fit to a VW chassis. A prototype of the Alken D-2 was raced at Riverside Raceway in June 1958 as part of a product testing program. A full story on this interesting VW variant appeared in the October issue of *Motor Trend*. Also in the October issue was an interesting article entitled "Wortld's Coldest Highway" in which James Joseph drove a modified Beetle across the Alaska Highway. The car was equipped with oversize tires, a gas heater and two types of crankcase immersion heaters.

There were plenty of great views everywhere from inside a 1958 VW Deluxe bus.

Dick Dance Collection

1959

1200 (BEETLE)—FOUR On September 19, 1958, the handle that operated the "trunk" lid was relocated to a spot nearer the steering column. A larger outside rearview mirror was used on German Volkswagens. Quite a few additional technical changes put into effect during calendar-year 1959, though the overall appearance of the cars changed very little. Starting in January, the tool kit included a hub cap removing hook. A new padded inside sun visor replaced the old see-through plastic type. Volkswagen began using a covered and padded dashboard for improved safety in Beetle Cabriolets. The tie rod lengths were modified (shorter on left, longer on right). Another safety feature, a front passenger grab handle, was added at the same time. The fuel tank ventilation system was modified and a new 80-mm cap was used. Starting in February 23, some 5,000 cars got carburetor modifications including a double vacuum unit and a vacuum-advance-only type distributor. New no.175 spark plugs were used in the VW engine starting in April. In May, the heating exchangers and associated parts were redesigned. A new cork seal was used on the fuel tap. Silencer-to-tailpipe joints were improved and the silencer stub pipes were shortened. In July, a heat-resistant V-belt was used and fewer pulley spacers were required.

Above: **A natural setting brings out the best features of this 1959 Karmann-Ghia coupe.**

Owner: Dr. Mac Jones / Photographer: Perrin Todd

SEDAN COLORS (1959): L14=Mignonette Green, L41=Black, L225=Jupiter Gray, L243=Diamond Gray, L335=Capri Blue, L343=Kalahari Beige, L344=Rush Green, L358=Garnet Red and L434=Fjord Blue. Black mats were provided in Jupiter Gray cars; Gray mats in other cars.

CABRIOLET COLORS (1959): L41=Black, L241=Bamboo Green, L258=Inca Red, L329=Shetland Gray, L333=Pearl Blue and L473=Alabaster Gray. Gray mats in all cars.

KARMANN-GHIA—FOUR The 1959 Karmann-Ghia also had a number of running changes. The Karmann-Ghia Coupe got the new padded design sun visor on January 20. It replaced the old transparent plastic type. On January 26, the Karmann-Ghia convertible got this change. Also on January 26, the studded trim on the front of the Cabriolet's folding top was eliminated. At the same time the top covering and the method of weather sealing were improved and the passenger grab handle was redesigned. On July 6, the dashboard cover was modified to include new shutters for the heating outlets and a lower retaining strip. On August 6, new colors were introduced for both Karmann-Ghia body styles. The side windows were modified to pivot at the rear. Also, the armrest on the right got a recess for better gripping. A new two-spoke steering wheel with a deep-set hub and a bright horn ring was used and the steering column design was changed. The majority of mechanical changes listed above for the Beetle were also done to the Karmann-Ghias.

1959 VOLKSWAGEN PRODUCTION CHART

Model Code	Body Type & Seating	POE Price	Weight (lbs.)	ProductionTotal
1200 DELUXE				
113	2d Sedan-4P	1545	1609	Note 1
117	2d Sunroof Sedan-4P	1625	1609	Note 1
151	2d Convertible-4P	2045	1764	Note 1
1200 KARMANN-GHIA				
143	2d Sport Coupe 2 + 2P	2445	1720	Note 1
141	2d Cabriolet 2 + 2P	2725	1786	Note 1
TRANSPORTER DELUXE				
231	4d Kombi	2045	2127	Note 2
221	4d Microbus	2120	2447	Note 2
241	4d Deluxe Microbus	2576	2447	Note 2
DELUXE CAMPER				
231C	4d Camper	2886	2293	Note 2

Note 1: 575,407 Volkswagen cars were produced in 1959.
Note 2: 29,184 Transporters were produced in 1959.

Paul Smith

A two-tone color scheme and roof rack make this 1959 Beetle stand out.

KARMANN-GHIA COLORS (AUGUST 1959-JULY 1960):
L41=Black, L346=Mango Green, L362=Midnight Nlue, L364=Strato Blue, L444=Malachite Green, L452=Paprika Red.

TRANSPORTER—FOUR The Transporter series again included three regular passenger models. The Kombi van was offered with or without occassional passenger seating. The seats were removable, but a Kombi could carry 8 to 9 passengers with all seats in place. The rear windows pivoted outward for extra ventilation. Since the center and rear seats were removable, the Kombi could be a passenger car or a cargo van. The cargo area lacked a headliner and interior panels. The Eight-Passenger Microbus was available with a Golde brand sunroof at extra cost. The Deluxe Microbus included the Golde sunroof, windows all around the body and side observation panels in the roof. Enthusiasts of today identify different models by counting the number of windows. A Camper bus was also available and included such extras as a folding table and fold-out beds. The engine used in Transporters was the same used in other models and had the same mechanical improvements.

TRANSPORTER COLORS: L14=Mignonette, L31=Dove Blue, L53=Sealing Wax Red, L54=Poppy Red, L59=Cherry Red, L73=Chestnut Brown, L82=Silver White, L87=Pearl White, L345=Pale Gray, L346=Mango Green, L351=Coral, L472=Beige Gray, L1009=Yukon Yellow.

I.D. DATA: Serial number is on a plate on the front hood center and at back of spare tire and stamped on chassis tunnel (backbone) and under the rear seat. Engine number is stamped on the generator support and on the crankcase. Chassis number range: 2007616-2528667. On Transporters the serial number is on a plate mounted on the firewall in the engine compartment.

ENGINE

BASE FOUR: Horizontally opposed, overhead-valve four-cylinder (air cooled). Light alloy block, heads and finned cylinder with cast-iron cylinder liners. Displacement: 72.7 cid (1192 cc). Bore & Stroke: 3.03 x 2.52 in. (77 x 64 mm). Compression Ratio: 6.6:1. Brake Horsepower: 36 at 3700 rpm. Torque: 56 lbs.-ft. at 2000 rpm. Four main bearings. Solid valve lifters. Solex downdraft carburetor. 6-volt electrical system.

CHASSIS

(BEETLE) SEDAN: Wheelbase: 94.5 in. Overall Length: 160.6 in. Height: 59.1 in. Width: 60.6 in. Front Tread: 51.4 in. Rear Tread: 49.2 in. Standard Tires: 5.60 x 15.

KARMANN-GHIA: Wheelbase: 94.5 in. Overall Length: 163 in. Height: 52.2. Width: 64.3 in. Front Tread: 51.4 in. Rear Tread: 49.2 in. Standard Tires: 5.60 x 15.

TRANSPORTER: Wheelbase: 94.5 in. Overall Length: 166.1 in. Height: 76.5 in. Width: 68.9 in. Front Tread: 53.9 in. Rear Tread: 53.5 in. Standard Tires: 6.40 x 15.

TECHNICAL

(BEETLE) SEDAN: Layout: rear-engine, rear-drive. Transmission: four-speed manual. Final Drive Type: Spiral bevel. Standard Final Drive Ratio: 4.40:1. Steering: worm and cap nut. Suspension (front): king pins with transverse torsion bars and upper/lower trailing arms. Suspension (rear): swing axles with trailing arms and torsion bars. Brakes: hydraulic, front/rear drum. Body Construction: steel body welded to floor pan with tubular center section. Fuel Tank: 8.8 gallon.

KARMANN-GHIA: Layout: rear-engine, rear-drive. Transmission: four-speed manual. Final Drive Type: Spiral bevel. Standard Final Drive Ratio: 4.40:1. Steering: worm and cap nut. Suspension (front): Independent: upper and lower trailing arms with square torsion bars. Suspension (rear): Independent: swinging half axle shafts with torsion bars. Brakes: hydraulic, front/rear drum. Body Construction: Tubular center section, forked at rear, with welded on platform. Fuel Tank: 10.6 gallon.

TRANSPORTER: Layout: rear-engine, rear-drive. Transmission: four-speed manual. Final Drive Type: Spiral bevel. Standard Final Drive Ratio: 6.20:1. Steering: manual. Suspension (front): Independent: two square section torsion bars. Suspension (rear): Independent: circular torsion bars each side. Brakes: hydraulic, front/rear drum. Body Construction: steel unibody on stamped steel floor pan. Fuel Tank: 10.6 gallon.

OPTIONS: Front and rear chrome stone shields ($4.50 per pair). Chrome headlamp sun visors ($1.95 each). Chrome wheel trim rings (four types available from $18.95 per set up).

PERFORMANCE: Top Speed (Beetle): 70-72 mph (75 mph in table) noted in *Motor Trend* April 1958. Top Speed: (Karmann-Ghia) "over 70" mph claimed. Top Speed: (Transporter; level) 60 mph. Fuel Mileage (Beetle): Fuel Mileage (Beetle): 35-40 mpg noted in *Motor Trend* April 1958. Fuel mileage (Karmann-Ghia): NA. Fuel mileage (Transporter): 20.3-22.3 mpg. The January issue of *Motor Trend* featured a two-page article entitled "The Mighty Micro" that reported on the 1959 Microbus. The idea was to take the Transaporter over the hardest, roughest road to test its reliability and durability. The Micro came through with flying colors. According to an article in the July 1959 *Motor Trend*, the stock Volkswagen Beetle did 0-to-60 mph in 31.4 seconds. And it covered the quarter-mile in 24.9 seconds. At 51 mph. with a Weber stroker kit, performance was 12.7 seconds and 0-to-60 was 20.6 seconds.

HISTORICAL FOOTNOTES: Manufacturer: Volkswagenwerk GmbH, Wolfsburg, West Germany. Importer: Volkswagen of America, Englewood Cliffs, N.J. Volkswagen manufactured 575,407 cars in 1959. According to *Ward's 1960 Automotive Yearbook*, 119,899 new Volkswagens were registered in the United States in calendar-year 1959. In November 1958, *Motor Trend* mentioned that Volkswagen "swings into its 20th year of production" in 1959. At this point the company claimed to have built nearly 2.5 million cars. The company was the largest seller of imported cars in the United States and the fourth-largest automaker in the world. A new book called *All About the Volkswagen*, by Henry Elfrink, was aimed at Volkswagen owners, mechanics and tuners. The 192-page book had over 200 photos and sold for $3.50.

1960

1200 (BEETLE)—FOUR August 1959 brought the initial "1960" product changes. The dipstick markings were changed and the oil drain plug was moved from the crankcase to the sump plate. The carburetor modification tested on 5,000 cars starting in late February 1959 was extended to all models. A new two-spoke steering wheel with a deep-set hub and a bright horn ring was used and the steering column design was changed. A number of new colors also arrived. New push-button door handles were introduced. The right-hand armrest was redesigned with an open grip and the door striker plates were improved. Many interior upgrades were made including curved seat backrests, rear seat heel boards, a front passenger foot rest, five-section rubber mats, two-piece floor coverings and better soundproofing. Padded sun visors were installed in place of the previous transparent plastic type. A plastic headlining replaced the earlier "mouse hair" fabric version. A number of electrical upgrades were made. The front turn-signal indicator lamps were now mounted on the tops of the front fenders in chrome housings. The rear blinkers were integrated into the taillights. In its October 1959 "Overseas News Reports" column, *Motor Trend* noted "For roadability, transmission is mounted differently and front has stabilizer bar. Also, defroster pipes are bigger, steering hub is recessed." In January 1960, the valve-clearance adjusting nut was slightly enlarged and resistor-type ignition leads were adopted. In March several modifications were made to the front trailing arm and the steering damper. Plastic warm air ducts, designed to reduce noise, went into production in May.

Dick Dance Collection

Above: **This red Beetle fits in well with the red barn.**
Paul Smith

Here is a Karmann-Ghia image from the 1960 VW brochure.

Model Code	Body Type & Seating	POE Price	Weight (lbs.)	Production Total
1200 DELUXE				
113	2d Sedan-4P	1565	1631	Note 1
117	2d Sunroof Sedan-4P	1665	1631	Note 1
151	2d Convertible-4P	2055	1764	Note 1
1200 KARMANN-GHIA				
143	2d SportCoupe-2P	2430	1720	Note 1
141	2d Convertible-2P	2695	1786	Note 1
TRANSPORTER				
231	4d Kombi–8P	2095	2127	Note 2
221	4d Microbus-8P	2245	2447	Note 2
241	4d Microbus Deluxe-8P	2620	2447	Note 2
CAMPER				
231C	4d Camper	2886	2293	Note 2

Note 1: 725,939 Volkswagens were produced in 1960.
Note 2: 30,350 Transporters were produced in 1960.

Dick Dance Collection

Here is a Karmann-Ghia image from the 1960 VW brochure.

KARMANN-GHIA—FOUR Production of the sporty Karmann-Ghia coupe and convertible continued, with some of the changes noted above. In January 1960, a resistor type ignition system was introduced. In March, the plastic frame was removed from the Karmann-Ghia outside rearview mirror. Door window sealing and convertible top sealing were also improved. In October, *Motor Trend* said, "On Ghia models, windshield washers are standard, directionals are self cancelling, there is more soundproofing."

KARMANN-GHIA COLORS (AUGUST 1959-JULY 1960): L41=Black, L346=Mango Green, L362=Midnight Nlue, L364=Strato Blue, L444=Malachite Green, L452=Paprika Red.

STATION WAGON—FOUR The Transporter series again included three regular passenger models. The Kombi van was offered with or without occassional passenger seating. The seats were removable, but a Kombi could carry 8 to 9 passengers with all seats in place. The rear windows pivoted outward for extra ventilation. Since the center and rear seats were removable, the Kombi could be a passenger car or a cargo van. The cargo area lacked a headliner and interior panels. The Eight-Passenger Microbus was available with a Golde brand sunroof at extra cost. The Deluxe Microbus included the Golde sunroof, windows all around the body and side observation panels in the roof. Enthusiasts of today identify different models by counting the number of windows. A Camper bus was also available and included such extras as a folding table and fold-out beds. Commercial variations of the Transporter were also available as well as optional double-door treatments.

TRANSPORTER COLORS: L31=Dove Blue, L53=Sealing Wax Red, L54=Poppy Red, L82=Silver White, L87=Pearl White, L289=Pale Blue, L345=Pale Gray, L346=Mango Green, L360=Sea Blue, L380=Turquoise Green, L390=Gulf Blue, L398=Pacific Blue, L456=Ruby Red, L472=Beige Gray, L478=Beryl Green, L1009=Yukon Yellow.

I.D. DATA: Serial number is on a plate on the front hood center and at back of spare tire and stamped on chassis tunnel (backbone) and under the rear seat. Engine number is stamped on the generator support and on the crankcase. On Transporters the serial number is on a plate mounted on the firewall in the engine compartment. Serial number range: (sedan/Karmann-Ghia) 2528668-3192506, (Transporter) 491002.

ENGINE

BASE FOUR: Horizontally opposed, overhead-valve four-cylinder (air cooled). Light alloy block, heads and finned cylinder with cast-iron cylinder liners. Displacement: 72.7 cid (1192 cc). Bore & Stroke: 3.03 x 2.52 in. (77 x 64 mm). Compression Ratio: 6.6:1. Brake Horsepower: 36 at 3700 rpm. Torque: 56 lbs.-ft. at 2000 rpm. Four main bearings. Solid valve lifters. Solex downdraft carburetor. 6-volt electrical system.

CHASSIS

(BEETLE) SEDAN: Wheelbase: 94.5 in. Overall Length: 160.6 in. Height: 59.1 in. Width: 60.6 in. Front Tread: 51.4 in. Rear Tread: 50.7 in. Standard Tires: 5.60 x 15. Steering: 2.4 turns lock-to-lock. Turning circle: 36 ft. curb-to-curb. Ground clearance. 7.2 in. Front seat headroom: 36 in. Interior width: 48 in. Legroom: 43 in. Trunk capacity: 9 cu. ft.

KARMANN-GHIA: Wheelbase: 94.5 in. Overall Length: 163 in. Height: 52.4. Width: 64.3 in. Front Tread: 51.4 in. Rear Tread: 50.7 in. Standard Tires: 5.60 x 15.

TRANSPORTER: Wheelbase: 94.5 in. Overall Length: 168.9 in. Height: 76.5 in. Width: 68.9 in. Front Tread: 53.9 in. Rear Tread: 53.5 in. Standard Tires: 6.40 x 15.

TECHNICAL

(BEETLE) SEDAN: Layout: rear-engine, rear-drive. Transmission: four-speed manual. Final Drive Type: Spiral bevel. Standard Final Drive Ratio: 4.375:1. Steering: worm and cap nut. Suspension (front): king pins with transverse torsion bars and upper/lower trailing arms. Suspension (rear): swing axles with trailing arms and torsion bars.

Brakes: hydraulic, front/rear drum. Body Construction: steel body welded to floor pan with tubular center section. Fuel Tank: 10.6 gallon.

KARMANN-GHIA: Layout: rear-engine, rear-drive. Transmission: four-speed manual. Final Drive Type: Spiral bevel. Standard Final Drive Ratio: 3.60:1. Steering: worm and cap nut. Suspension (front): Independent: upper and lower trailing arms with square torsion bars. Suspension (rear): Independent: swinging half axle shafts with torsion bars. Brakes: hydraulic, front/rear drum. Body Construction: Tubular center section, forked at rear, with welded on platform. Fuel Tank: 10.6 gallon.

TRANSPORTER: Layout: rear-engine, rear-drive. Transmission: four-speed manual. Final Drive Type: Spiral bevel. Standard Final Drive Ratio: 6.20:1. Steering: manual. Suspension (front): Independent: two square section torsion bars. Suspension (rear): Independent: circular torsion bars each side. Brakes: hydraulic, front/rear drum. Body Construction: steel unibody on stamped steel floor pan. Fuel Tank: 10.6 gallon.

PERFORMANCE: Top Speed (Beetle): 70-72 mph (75 mph in table) noted in *Motor Trend* April 1958. Top Speed: (Karmann-Ghia) "over 70" mph claimed. Top Speed: (Transporter; level) 60 mph. Fuel Mileage (Beetle): Fuel Mileage (Beetle): 28-36 mpg noted in *Motor Trend* May 1960. Fuel mileage (Karmann-Ghia): NA. Fuel mileage (Transporter): 20.3-22.3 mpg. In March 1960, *Motor Trend* did a comparison test of a stock Volkswagen Beetle sedan against two similar cars with aftermarket performance kits installed. The first kit was manufactured by Harry Weber of Los Angeles. It featured a 1/2-in. stroker crankshaft, domed pistons, a wild cam, a special exhaust system and twin Solex carbs. The second car was a 1954 Volkswagen with a well-known kit made by European Motor Products, Inc. (EMPI) of Riverside, California. It had special Okrasa manifolding and heads, large EMPI valves, stiffer valve springs, a 6-mm stroker crank, twin Solex carburetors and Porsche brakes. The stock VW did 0-60 mph in 32 seconds and the quarter mile in 23.9 seconds at 52 mph. It had a 68-mph top speed. The Weber VW did 0-60 mph in 17 seconds and the quarter mile in 20.9 seconds at 66 mph. It had a 91-mph top speed. The EMPI VW did 0-60 mph in 18.8 seconds and the quarter mile in 21.4 seconds at 63 mph. It also had a 91-mph top speed.

HISTORICAL FOOTNOTES: Manufacturer: Volkswagenwerk GmbH, Wolfsburg, West Germany. Importer: Volkswagen of America, Englewood Cliffs, N.J. Volkswagen manufactured 739,443 cars in 1960. According to *Ward's 1961 Automotive Yearbook*, 159,995 new Volkswagens were registered in the United States in calendar-year 1960. Sales of imported cars in the United States fell in 1960, when several American automakers brought out compact-sized economy cars. However, Germany's share of imported car registrations climbed to 44.4 percent, up from 33.7 percent in 1959. As Ward's put it, "Close to half of the 498,785 new foreign cars sold in the U.S. during 1960 had been shipped in from West Germany, a phenomenon attributable to Volkswagen, the mainstay of the import market. Among the 15 German makes imported, Volkswagen accounted for 72.2 percent of the cars of German origin registered in the U.S." Volkswagen, by itself, built 32.1 percent of all imports sold here in 1960. Ward's said that this was "reminisecent of earlier years." On April 27, 1960, the 600,000th Volkswagen Transporter was put together. On June 15, the 500,000th Volkswagen was exported to the United States and the one millionth person to tour the Volkswagen factory since 1949 was mentioned in corporate press releases. In November, the Volkswagen Foundation was organized to support science and technology. A French marketing branch was also set up this year. During 1960, the German auto industry employed 50,000 people to make 3,000 vehicles per day—one every 19 seconds. Everyth third one of these cars was a Volkswagen. During 1959, a proving grounds was constructed next to the Wolfsburg factory. It included an endurance test course, a banked high-speed test track, washboard roads, dirt roads and other durability courses. In Germany, it was possible to buy a Volkswagen Standard Sedan with no options for as little as $911 (the Export Sedan went for $1,109). During the 1960 Australian National Speedboat Championships in Sydney's Kogarah Bay, the local VW distributor stole the show with a publicity stunt that turned the car into a boat. This was done by installing plugs in the drain holes beneath the car, sealing the control cables, plastic sealing on the ignition system components, sealing the engine, adding "snorkel" exhausts and hooking up a 3-bladed 10-in. prop so that it would drive off the generator drive wheel at the end of the crankshaft. After thrilling crowds at the boating event, the car went on a promotional tour to help pull buyers into Volkswagen show rooms. In June 1960, *Motor Trend* spotlighted a customized Volkswagen built by William Neumann of Spremberg Lausitz, Germany. The car had a interesting fender and body side treatment that lengthened its overall appearance. Trim parts from a German Wartburg were used to brighten it up. A Volkswagen came in first in Class C (1100-1599-cc) in the 1960 Mobil Mileage Rally and got 34.77 miles per gallon.

By 1960, Volkswagen made 3,000 vehicles per day or one per every 19 seconds.

Below: **The Beetle, like the Model T, was a popular source of humor around the world.**

1961

1200 (BEETLE)—FOUR "The 1961 Volkswagen sedan provides the kind of happy surprise that comes when an excellent motor car is made even better," said *Motor Trend*. "And inclusion of the rugged, higher-horsepower transporter engine in this new Volkswagen provides a real surprise, even to long time owners of previous models of this marque. Four more horsepower at first seem like just too little to talk about, but the boost from 36 hp at 3700 rpm to today's output of 40 hp at 3900 revs makes a world of difference in this 1631-pound (dry weight) automobile." In addition, the '61 Volkswagen got a full-synchronized four-speed manual transmission. *Motor Trend* suggested that people who drove 1955 and earlier Volkswagens would have "difficulty realizing this is the same automobile," although that seems to be a bit of an exaggeration. The factory promoted 27 changes in the new model, though some were quite minor. The more important alterations included an automatic choke, an anti-icing carburetor heater, a redesigned ful tank that increased luggage space, an external gas tank vent (to keep fuel odors out of the car), a concave washer on the third gear drive pinion (to reduce transmission noise), softer transmission mountings, a transparent brake fluid reservoir, a front passenger grab handle, standard windshield washers and a new ignition switch that prevented jamming the starter into action when the engine was running. All electrical connections were now push-on or plug-in types. The fuse box was relocated below the instrument panel, to the right of the steering column. A passenger inside sun visor was now provided. Other improvements included a quieter air intake pipe, new paint colors, color-keyed running boards, new leatherette upholstery, color-coordinated fender beading, a colored steering wheel and a 90-mph speedometer. Side marker lights and a non-repeating starter switch were also new. Key slots in the doors were now horizontal instead of vertical. Mechanical parts receiving minor revisions included the air cleaner (with a new heating duct), the automatic-choke carburetor and the fuel pump. The spark generated by the distributor was now controlled only by vacuum advance. Also new was a detachable generator support that eliminated the threat of casting fractures.

SEDAN COLORS (1961): L41=Black, L391=Pastel Blue, L456=Ruby Red, L478=Beryl Green, L380=Turquoise, L87=Pearl White, L390=Gulf Blue.

ADDITIONAL CABRIOLET COLORS (1961): L54=Poppy Red, L398=Pacific Blue, L10009=Yukon Yellow, L10018=Brunswick Blue.

Above: **Even in basic black, the 1961 Beetle has a very memorable image.**
Paul Smith

Model Code	Body Type & Seating	POE Price	Weight (lbs.)	Production Total
1200 DELUXE				
113	2d Sedan-4P	1565	1631	Note 1
117	2d Sunroof Sedan-4P	1655	1631	Note 1
151	2d Convertible-4P	2055	1764	Note 1
1200 KARMANN-GHIA				
143	2d Coupe-2 + 2P	2430	1786	Note 1
141	2d Convertible 2 + 2P	2695	1786	Note 1
TRANSPORTER				
231	4d Kombi	1995	2161	Note 2
221	4d Station Wagon	2245	2315	Note 2
241/M130	4d Deluxe Wagon	2620	2315	Note 2
CAMPER				
231-C	4d Camper	2973	NA	Note 2

Note 1: 807,488 Volkswagen passenger cars were produced in 1961.
Note 2: 33,506 Transporters were produced in 1961.

"The 1961 Volkswagen sedan provides the kind of happy surprise that comes when an excellent motor car is made even better."

– Motor Trend

Juanita Pritchard

This 1961 Beetle is pretty in white and a veteran survivor.

KARMANN-GHIA—FOUR Although the smartly-styled Karmann-Ghia was a Volkswagen under its outer skin, its completely different coachwork gave it a new function and put it in its own class. One slight variation was a slightly wider platform than that used for the Beetle. Due to its improved streamlining, the Karmann-Ghia was about three miles per hour faster than the Beetle sedan. Handling, braking and ride quality were about the same for both models and highly rated. The Karmann-Ghia was almost seven inches lower and three inches longer than the Beetle and held two people in semi-bucket seats. There was a padded platform in the rear where children could sit or luggage could be stored. The seat backs folded to increase luggage space. On the convertible model, the outside of the top was padded to hide the top bows. The inside was also padded, giving the open car a hardtop look when the roof was raised.

KARMANN-GHIA COLORS (1961): L41=Black, L87=Pearl White, L360=Sea Blue, L384=Pampas Green, L397=Lavender, L398=Pacific Blue, L452=Paprika Red, L456=Ruby Red, L469=Anthracite, L490=Sierra Beige.

TRANSPORTER—FOUR The "split windshield" Volkswagen Transporter continued to be offered in the 1960s. The Microbuses got a horsepower boost like the Beetle sedan. The series still offered three different passenger transporters. The Kombi had 8 to 9 passenger seating with all of the removable seats in place. The rear windows pivoted outward for extra ventilation. The cargo area was untrimmed. The Eight-Passenger Station Wagon (the term Microbus seems to have been dropped) was fully trimmed inside and a Golde sunroof cost extra. The Deluxe Station Wagon included the sunroof, windows all around and side observation windows. A Camper was also available and included such extras as a sink, ice box, folding table and fold-out beds. Volkswagen also marketed panel and pickup truck versions of the Transporter in the United States

TRANSPORTER COLORS (1961): L31=Dove Blue, L53=Sealing Wax Red, L54=Poppy Red, L82=Silver White, L87=Pearl White, L289=Pale Blue, L345=Pale Gray, L346=Mango Green, L360=Sea Blue, L380=Turquoise Green, L390=Gulf Blue, L398=Pacific Blue, L456=Ruby Red, L472=Beige Gray, L478=Beryl Green, L1009=Yukon Yellow.

I.D. DATA: Serial number is on a plate behind the spare tire, and on the frame tunnel, under the back seat. Engine number is stamped on the generator support and on the crankcase. Serial number range: (sedan/Karmann-Ghia) 3192507-4010994, (Transporter) 623734-802426.

ENGINE

BASE FOUR: Horizontally opposed, overhead-valve four-cylinder (air cooled). Light alloy block, heads and finned cylinder with cast-iron cylinder liners. Displacement: 72.7 cid (1192 cc). Bore & Stroke: 3.03 x 2.52 in. (77 x 64 mm). Compression Ratio: 7.0:1. Brake Horsepower: 40 at 3900 rpm. Torque: 64.4 lbs.-ft. at 2400 rpm. Four main bearings. Solid valve lifters. Solex single-barrel carburetor. 6-volt electrical system.

CHASSIS

(BEETLE) SEDAN: Wheelbase: 94.5 in. Overall Length: 160.6 in. Height: 59.1 in. Width: 60.6 in. Front Tread: 51.4 in. Rear Tread: 50.7 in. Standard Tires: 5.60 x 15. Steering ratio: 14.2:1. Turns lock-to-lock: 2.4. Turning circle: 36 ft. curb-to-curb. Ground clearance. 7.2 in. Front seat headroom: 36 in. Interior width: 48 in. Legroom: 43 in. Trunk capacity: 9 cu. ft.

KARMANN-GHIA: Wheelbase: 94.5 in. Overall Length: 163 in. Height: 52.4. Width: 64.3 in. Front Tread: 51.4 in. Rear Tread: 50.7 in. Standard Tires: 5.60 x 15.

TRANSPORTER: Wheelbase: 94.5 in. Overall Length: 168.9 in. Height: 76.5 in. Width: 68.9 in. Front Tread: 53.9 in. Rear Tread: 53.5 in. Standard Tires: 6.40 x 15.

TECHNICAL

(BEETLE) SEDAN: Layout: rear-engine, rear-drive. Transmission: four-speed manual. Final Drive Type: Spiral bevel. Standard Final Drive Ratio: 4.375:1. Steering: worm and cap nut. Suspension (front): king pins with transverse torsion bars and upper/lower trailing arms. Suspension (rear): swing axles with trailing arms and torsion bars. Brakes: hydraulic, front/rear drum. Body Construction: steel body welded to floor pan with tubular center section. Fuel Tank: 10.6 gallon.

KARMANN-GHIA: Layout: rear-engine, rear-drive. Transmission: four-speed manual. Final Drive Type: Spiral bevel. Standard Final Drive Ratio: 3.60:1. Steering: worm and cap nut. Suspension (front): Independent: upper and lower trailing arms with square torsion bars. Suspension (rear): Independent: swinging half axle shafts with torsion bars. Brakes: hydraulic, front/rear drum. Body Construction: Tubular center section, forked at rear, with welded on platform. Fuel Tank: 10.6 gallon.

TRANSPORTER: Layout: rear-engine, rear-drive. Transmission: four-speed manual. Final Drive Type: Spiral bevel. Standard Final Drive Ratio: 6.20:1. Steering: manual. Suspension (front): Independent: two square section torsion bars. Suspension (rear): Independent: circular torsion bars each side. Brakes: hydraulic, front/rear drum. Body Construction: steel unibody on stamped steel floor pan. Fuel Tank: 10.6 gallon.

The unique Volkswagen could easily poke fun at conventional auto styles.
Old Cars Weekly Archive

PERFORMANCE: Fuel Mileage (Beetle): 28-32 mpg noted in *Motor Trend* January 1961. Fuel mileage (Karmann-Ghia): NA. Fuel mileage (Transporter): NA. The stock 1961 VW Beetle did 0-30 mph in 6.5 sec., 0-45 mph in 12.5 sec. and 0-60 mph in 32 seconds. The weight-power ratio was 40.8 lbs. Per horsepower. Horsepower per cubic inch was 550.

HISTORICAL FOOTNOTES: Manufacturer: Volkswagenwerk GmbH, Wolfsburg, West Germany. Importer: Volkswagen of America, Englewood Cliffs, N.J. Dr. C. H. Hahn was in charge of the U.S. operations. There were 15 Volkswagen distributors in the U.S.: Hansen-MacPhee Engineering of Bedford, Massachusetts, World-Wide Automobiles Corporation of Long Island City, N.Y., Auto Associates, Incorporated of King of Prussia, Pennsylvania, Capitol Car Distributors, Ltd., of Takoma Park, Maryland, Brundage Motors, Inc., of Jacksonville, Florida, International Sales and Service, Inc., of New Orleans, Louisianna, Midwestern VW Corp., of Columbus, Ohio, Import Motors, Ltd., of Grand Rapids, Michigan, Import Motors of Chicago, Inc., of Northbrook, Illinois, Mid-America Cars, Inc., of St. Louis, Missouri, Inter-Continental Motors Corporation of San Antonio, Texas, Competition Motors Distributors, Inc., of Hollywood, California, Reynold C. Johnson Co., of Burlingame, California, Riviera Motors, Inc., of Portland, Oregon, and Volkswagen Hawaii, inc., of Honolulu, Hawaii. Volkswagen manufactured 827,850 cars in 1961. According to *Ward's 1962 Automotive Yearbook*, 177,308 new Volkswagens were registered in the United States in calendar-year 1961. That total represented 46.8 percent of the imported car market in the United states, Volkswagen's highest market share since 1956 when it had 50.9 percent. Sales rose 10.8 percent from 1960. Production of the new Type 3 (also called 1500) began during 1961, but that car would not become readily available in the United States market until the 1966 model year. Through the 1960s, Type 3 Karmann-Ghias were produced, which differed in appearance from the familiar coupes and convertibles, but they were not sold in America. Some Volkswagens were already getting collectible by 1961. In the May issue of *Motor Trend* that year, D.E. Richards of Hopkins, Minnesota, advertised a "rare" early Volkswagen convertible (no year was mentioned) for $1,395. Despite the fact that Volkswagen registrations in the United States moved steadily upwards (1955=28,907; 1956=50,011; 1957=64,242; 1958=78,588; 1959=120,442; 1960=159,995 and 1961=177,308) there were early signs of trouble brewing. In his "Memo From the Editor" in the October 1961 *Motor Trend*, Don Werner noted, "Five years ago, out of every ten imported cars sold, six were Volkswagens. Latest figures show the ratio is now down to abouit four VWs out of every ten. If the current VW starts to slip the new 1500, soon to be introduced, probably will be imported to justify the more than 600 VW dealers and the $100 million investment in facilities." Werner went on to say that the 1500 had not impressed industry executives "on both sides of the Atlantic."

It seemed Volkswagen buses had openings everywhere in 1961.

1962

1200 (BEETLE)—FOUR Most "1962" Volkswagen changes went into production at the Wolfsburg factory on July 31, 1961. A conventional fuel gauge was installed, replacing the original tap lever for a reserve tank. A worm-and-roller steering system, introduced a month earlier for Karmann-Ghias and Cabriolets, replaced the former spindle arrangement. Larger new two-section taillights were used. The hood was now supported by a pair of spring-loaded rods. Three-point seat belt mountings were provided on both sides up front. The front heater outlets now had sliding covers. There were new air outlets in the heel boards. New door retainers replaced the old stay rods and the door hinges were improved. Longer rails were used for the front seats, which also had new backrests with an improved adjustment system. Also new was a compressed-air windshield washer. Adjustable, permanently lubricated tie rods were used at both sides. New paint and interior trim choices were seen. A steering/starter lock was a new option.

SEDAN COLORS (1962): L41=Black, L456=Ruby Red, L478=Beryl Green, L380=Turquoise, L87=Pearl White, L390=Gulf Blue, L469=Anthracite.

Above: **In 1962, the sunroof option continued to be popular choice for Volkswagen buyers.**
Paul Smith

ADDITIONAL CABRIOLET COLORS (1962): L54=Poppy Red, L398=Pacific Blue, L10009=Yukon Yellow, L10018=Brunswick Blue.

1500 TYPE 3—FOUR Anyone who guessed that Volkswagen would not introduce another model must have been stunned when the 1962 Type 3 (1500) Squareback sedan arrived at the Frankfurt Auto Show, in Germany, in the fall of 1961. Some called the 1500 a "Beetle in disguise," although it had a completely different appearance and a slightly larger engine. The first 1500 was a conventional notchback sedan with squarish lines. A wagon was added during calendar-year 1962. A convertible was planned and a prototype was made, but it was not put into production. However photos of the pilot model exist, even in some Volkswagen product literature of that time. The 1500 engine was mounted under the floor of a trunk at the rear, providing luggage compartments at both ends of the car.

Dick Dance Collection

The 1962 catalog showed a VW 1500 convertible but production of it was cancelled.

Model Code	Body Type & Seating	POE Price	Weight (lbs.)	Production Total
1200 DELUXE				
113	2d Sedan-4P	1595	1565	Note 1
117	2d Sunroof Sedan-4P	1685	1565	Note 1
151	2d Convertible-4P	2095	1698	Note 1
1500 TYPE 3 SQUAREBACK (EUROPE)				
1500-31	2d Notchback	1895	1829	Note 1
1500-31	2d Station Wagon	1995	1918	Note 1
1500 TYPE 34 KARMANN-GHIA (EUROPE)				
1500-34	Karmann-Ghia coupe	NA	NA	Note 1
1200 KARMANN-GHIA				
143	2d Coupe-2 + 2P	2295	1742	Note 1
141	2d Convertible 2 + 2P	2495	1742	Note 1
TRANSPORTER				
231	4d Kombi	1995	2095	Note 2
221	4d Station Wagon	2275	2414	Note 2
241/M130	4d Deluxe Station Wagon	2655	2414	Note 2
231-C	4d Camper	2982	2547	Note 2

Note 1: 876,255 Volkswagen passenger cars were produced in 1962.
Note 2: 41,179 Transporters were produced in 1962.

Dick Dance Collection

The Volkswagen 1500 series was sold everywhere but the United States in 1962.

The Type 3 Volkswagen was sold mainly in the European market at this point, but occasionally made its way into the United States and some did appear on the highways here.

1500 TYPE 34 (T2) KARMANN-GHIA—FOUR Also available outside the U.S. was a new Karmann-Ghia that shared the 1500 engine. It looked something like a cross between a Karmann-Ghia and a Corvair. It was introduced in Germany as the Type 34, bowing at the Frankfurt Auto Show, and became known as "der Grosse Karmann-Ghia." Britons called in the "Razor Edge"

Karmann-Ghia and Americans knew it as the Type 3. The completely fresh body design was styled by the Italian design firm Carrozzeria Ghia and bore no resemblance to its successful older brother. It shared the chassis and drive train with the Volkswagen 1500 notchback and fastback models. Production began late in 1961 as a 1962 model. Karmann planned a 1500 convertible that was scheduled for production. VW even printed literature and did a show launch, but technical problems with body flexing kept the ragtop from reaching the assembly line. At least three were made: one was displayed by Karmann, another is in the hands of the Karmann family and a

third was retained by Volkswagen. The 1962 coupe had a rectangular front emblem and small Karmann nameplates on the lower front section of each rear quarter panel. Like the 1500 Squareback, it featured front and rear luggage compartments.

KARMANN-GHIA—FOUR Production of Volkswagen's Sport Coupe and convertible continued without major change. Several modifications for "1962" models went into effect with chassis nuumber 3933247 built on June 30, 1961. At that point a worm-and-roller steering system was adopted and a combination ignition/starter switch was used in home market cars. A non-repeat starter was optional on these units.

KARMANN-GHIA COLORS (1962): L41=Black, L87=Pearl White, L360=Sea Blue, L384=Pampas Green, L397=Lavender, L398=Pacific Blue, L452=Paprika Red, L456=Ruby Red, L469=Anthracite, L490=Sierra Beige.

TRANSPORTER—FOUR Microbuses and related station wagons remained available with the same powertrain as other Volkswagens. The series still offered three different passenger transporters. The Kombi had 8 to 9 passenger seating with all of the removable seats in place. The rear windows pivoted outward for extra ventilation. The cargo area was untrimmed. The Eight-Passenger Station Wagon was fully trimmed inside and a Golde sunroof cost extra. The Deluxe Station Wagon included the sunroof, windows all around and side observation windows. A Camper was also available and included such extras as a sink, ice box, folding table and fold-out beds.

TRANSPORTER COLORS (1962): L31=Dove Blue, L53=Sealing Wax Red, L54=Poppy Red, L82=Silver White, L87=Pearl White, L289=Pale Blue, L345=Pale Gray, L360=Sea Blue, L380=Turquoise Green, L390=Gulf Blue, L398=Pacific Blue, L456=Ruby Red, L469=Anthracite, L472=Beige Gray, L478=Beryl Green, L532=Polar Blue, L560=Manilla Yellow, L1009=Yukon Yellow.

I.D. DATA: The serial number is on a plate behind the spare tire and on the frame tunnel under the back seat. Engine number is stamped on the generator support and on the crankcase. Serial number range: (sedan/Karmann-Ghia) 4010995-4846835, (Transporter) 802427-971550, (1500) Not reported in U.S.

ENGINE

BASE FOUR (1200): Horizontally opposed, overhead-valve four-cylinder (air cooled). Light alloy block, heads and finned cylinder with cast-iron cylinder liners. Displacement: 72.7 cid. Bore & Stroke: 3.03 x 2.52 in. Compression Ratio: 7.0:1. Brake Horsepower: 40 at 3900 rpm. Torque: 64.4 lbs.-ft. at 2400 rpm. Four main bearings. Solid valve lifters. Solex single-barrel downdraft carburetor. 6-volt electrical system.

BASE FOUR (1500): Horizontally opposed, overhead-valve four-cylinder (air cooled). Light alloy block, heads and finned cylinder with cast-iron cylinder liners. Displacement: 91.1 cid. Bore & Stroke: 3.27 x 2.72 in. Compression Ratio: 7.2:1. Brake Horsepower: 53 at 4000 rpm. Torque: 82.5 lbs.-ft. at 2400 rpm. Four main bearings. Solid valve lifters. Single-barrel sidedraft carburetor. 6-volt electrical system.

CHASSIS

(BEETLE) SEDAN: Wheelbase: 94.5 in. Overall Length: 160.6 in. Height: 59.1 in. Width: 60.6 in. Front Tread: 51.4 in. Rear Tread: 50.7 in. Standard Tires: 5.60 x 15.

(SQUAREBACK) 1500 TYPE 3: Wheelbase: 94.5 in. Overall Length: (Style 31) 166.3 in., (Style 34 Karmann-Ghia Type 3) 168.5 in. Height: (Style 31) 58.1 in., (Style 34 Karmann-Ghia Type 3) 52.6 in. Width: 63.2 in. Front Tread: 51.6 in. Rear Tread: 53.0 in. Standard Tires: 6.00 x 15.

KARMANN-GHIA: Wheelbase: 94.5 in. Overall Length: 163 in. Height: 52.4. Width: 64.3 in. Front Tread: 51.4 in. Rear Tread: 50.7 in. Standard Tires: 5.60 x 15.

TRANSPORTER: Wheelbase: 94.5 in. Overall Length: 166.1 in. Height: 76.4 in. Width: 68.9 in. Front Tread: 53.9 in. Rear Tread: 53.5 in. Standard Tires: 6.40 x 15.

TECHNICAL

(BEETLE) SEDAN: Layout: rear-engine, rear-drive. Transmission: four-speed manual. Final Drive Type: Spiral bevel. Steering: worm and cap nut. Suspension (front): king pins with transverse torsion bars and upper/lower trailing arms. Suspension (rear): swing axles with trailing arms and torsion bars. Brakes: hydraulic, front/rear drum. Body Construction: steel body welded to floor pan with tubular center section. Fuel Tank: 10.6 gallon.

1500 TYPE 3: Layout: rear-engine, rear-drive. Transmission: four-speed manual. Final Drive Type: Spiral bevel. Steering: worm and cap nut. Suspension (front): king pins with transverse torsion bars and upper/lower trailing arms. Suspension (rear): swing axles with trailing arms and torsion bars. Brakes: hydraulic, front/rear drum. Body Construction: steel body welded to floor pan with tubular center section. Fuel Tank: 10.6 gallon.

KARMANN-GHIA: Layout: rear-engine, rear-drive. Transmission: four-speed manual. Final Drive Type: Spiral bevel. Steering: worm and cap nut. Suspension (front): Independent: upper and lower trailing arms with square torsion bars. Suspension (rear): Independent: swinging half axle shafts with torsion bars. Brakes: hydraulic, front/rear drum. Body Construction: Tubular center section, forked at rear, with welded on platform. Fuel Tank: 10.6 gallon.

TRANSPORTER: Layout: rear-engine, rear-drive. Transmission: four-speed manual. Final Drive Type: Spiral bevel. Steering: manual. Suspension (front): Independent: two square section torsion bars. Suspension (rear): Independent: circular torsion bars each side.

Brakes: hydraulic, front/rear drum. Body Construction: steel unibody on stamped steel floor pan. Fuel Tank: 10.6 gallon.

PERFORMANCE: Top Speed: (Beetle 1200) 74 mph cruising speed, (Karmann-Ghia) 75 mph. 0-60 mph acceleration: (Beetle) 32 sec., (1500) 30 sec. Standing start quarter mile (Beetle): 23.9 sec. at 56 mph. Fuel Mileage: (Beetle) 28-32 mpg.

HISTORICAL FOOTNOTES: Manufacturer: Volkswagenwerk GmbH, Wolfsburg, West Germany. Importer: Volkswagen of America, Englewood Cliffs, N.J. Dr. C. H. Hahn was in charge of the U.S. operations. There were again 15 Volkswagen distributors in the U.S.: Hansen-MacPhee Engineering of Bedford, Massachusetts, World-Wide Automobiles Corporation of Long Island City, N.Y., Auto Associates, Incorporated of King of Prussia, Pennsylvania, Capitol Car Distributors, Ltd., of Takoma Park, Maryland, Brundage Motors, Inc., of Jacksonville, Florida, International Auto Sales and Service, Inc., of New Orleans, Louisianna, Midwestern VW Corp., of Columbus, Ohio, Import Motors, Ltd., of Grand Rapids, Michigan, Import Motors of Chicago, Inc., of Northbrook, Illinois, Mid-America Cars, Inc., of St. Louis, Missouri, Inter-Continental Motors Corporation of San Antonio, Texas, Competition Motors Distributors, Inc., of Hollywood, California, Reynold C. Johnson Co., of Burlingame, California, Riviera Motors, Inc., of Portland, Oregon, and Volkswagen Hawaii, Inc., of Honolulu, Hawaii. Volkswagen manufactured 876,255 cars in 1962. According to *Ward's 1963 Automotive Yearbook*, 192,570 new Volkswagens were registered in the United States in calendar-year 1962. That represented 56.8 percent of the imported cars sold here, up from 46.8 percent in 1961. The introduction of new Volkswagen models (the 1500s) was big news and made good copy in the car buff magazines. In May 1961, *Motor Trend* ran a two-page article entitled "The New VW" that covered the notchback and station wagon models in some detail. This article noted that the 1500 would be "exported from Germany to every country in the world except the United States" and explained that this was the case because sales of the Beetle were still increasing at the time. A month later the same magazine printed what it said was "The first complete picture report on the new Volkswagen." The Karmann-Ghia version of the 1500 was mentioned near the end of this article. In the October 1961 issue, *Motor Trend* ran a third story called "Official Debut of the VW-1500." It estimated that the cost of a 1500 with required U.S. market equipment would be "in excess of $2,000." The Karman-Ghia 1500 Type 2 was depicted in the "European Report" in the December 1961 issue of *Motor Trend*.

1963

1200 (BEETLE)—FOUR Volkswagen's "1963" changes began to appear at the factory level on July 30, 1962. The oil filter was modified with an air filter. Some manifolding was slightly enlarged and the cooling fan housing was redesigned. Larger-diameter cylinder head induction ports were used. Cars with sunroofs got a flatter inside crank handle that was hinged to fold flush into the headliner. The headliner and window guides were now made of plastic. The Wolfsburg crest that had decorated Volkswagen hoods since 1951 was replaced by "Volkswagen" lettering and the VW emblem in the hubcaps was no longer trimmed with black paint. Foam insulation was added to the floorboards. Fresh-air heating also was new. Shortly after the 1963 calendar-year started, the crankcase vent was modified to incorporate a new sludge-draining pipe with a rubber vent. In April, a new plastic (instead of rubber) seal was used around the bumper bracket and the front seat backrest adjustment was changed.

SEDAN COLORS (1963): L41=Black, L456=Ruby Red, L478=Beryl Green, L380=Turquoise, L87=Pearl White, L390=Gulf Blue, L469=Anthracite.

Above: **Beetle popularity continued in 1963 in both the sedan and convertible versions.**
Paul Smith

ADDITIONAL CABRIOLET COLORS (1963): L54=Poppy Red, L398=Pacific Blue, L10009=Yukon Yellow, L10018=Brunswick Blue.

1500 TYPE 3 SQUAREBACK—FOUR The Type 3 was not well received in Europe, where reviewers found it disappointing, unreliable and downright undesirable. Volkswagen even sued *Deutsche Mark* magazine (Germany's answer to *Consumer Reports*) for a story reporting that its test car had to go to the repair shop eight times. Nevertheless, sedan and wagon models continued to be marketed overseas. These cars were not officially sold in the U.S., but some made their way here through Canada, Mexico or the "black market." In April 1963, *Motor Trend* printed a comparison test of the Volkswagen 1200 and the Volkswagen 1500. "It's rare that we devote a road test to a European car not currently being imported to the U.S., but in the case of the VW 1500, there seems good reason to make an exception," wrote Wayne Thoms. "The fact is that the car's now available in Canada and Mexico and significant numbers have been brought in from Europe by servicemen and tourists, so you're likely you see the 1500 with fair regularity in larger cities." The magazine found both models to be "top-quality" small automobiles, but picked the 1500 as the most desirable because it was bigger, faster and more deluxe. It had a fully-padded dashboard

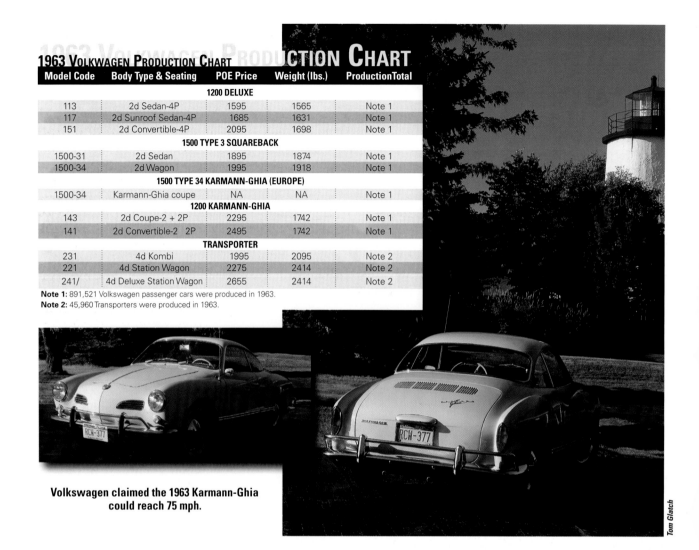

Model Code	Body Type & Seating	POE Price	Weight (lbs.)	Production Total
1200 DELUXE				
113	2d Sedan-4P	1595	1565	Note 1
117	2d Sunroof Sedan-4P	1685	1631	Note 1
151	2d Convertible-4P	2095	1698	Note 1
1500 TYPE 3 SQUAREBACK				
1500-31	2d Sedan	1895	1874	Note 1
1500-34	2d Wagon	1995	1918	Note 1
1500 TYPE 34 KARMANN-GHIA (EUROPE)				
1500-34	Karmann-Ghia coupe	NA	NA	Note 1
1200 KARMANN-GHIA				
143	2d Coupe-2 + 2P	2295	1742	Note 1
141	2d Convertible-2 2P	2495	1742	Note 1
TRANSPORTER				
231	4d Kombi	1995	2095	Note 2
221	4d Station Wagon	2275	2414	Note 2
241/	4d Deluxe Station Wagon	2655	2414	Note 2

Note 1: 891,521 Volkswagen passenger cars were produced in 1963.
Note 2: 45,960 Transporters were produced in 1963.

**Volkswagen claimed the 1963 Karmann-Ghia
could reach 75 mph.**

Tom Glatch

that hooded three circular instruments. The steering wheel was of the locking type and a button on back of the turn signal stalk operated the headlight dimmer. The 1500 was about 12 mph faster than the 1200. A seven-position front seat was standard equipment. Recessed interior door handles were featured. The engine was similar in design to the flat four used in the Beetle, but it included a cooling fan driven off the front of the crankshaft. The engine was quieter and flatter than the 1200 version. There was a front luggage compartment, plus a second one in the rear, above the engine. An external dipstick was provided in the rear of the car to allow checking the oil level without opening the engine cover.

1500 TYPE 34 (T2) KARMANN-GHIA—FOUR Also available again, outside the U.S., was the Karmann-Ghia Type 34 (a.k.a. Type 3) that shared the 1500 engine. As in 1962, it had a rectangular front emblem and small Karmann nameplates on the lower front section of each rear quarter panel.

1200 KARMANN-GHIA—FOUR Production of Volkswagen's Karmann-Ghia Sport Coupe and convertible continued without major change, except for most of the same modifications noted above for Beetles.

KARMANN-GHIA COLORS (1963): L41=Black, L60Z=Emerald Green, L87=Pearl White, L360=Sea Blue, L398=Pacific Blue, L456=Ruby Red, L469=Anthracite, L532=Polar Blue, L560=Manilla Yellow, N/A=Terra Brown.

TRANSPORTER—FOUR Beginning in 1963, larger round front turn-signal indicators were installed on Microbuses. A fresh-air heating system also became available. The series again offered three different passenger transporters. The Kombi had 8 to 9 passenger seating with all of the removable seats in place. The rear windows pivoted outward for extra ventilation. The cargo area was untrimmed. The Eight-Passenger Station Wagon was fully trimmed inside and a Golde sunroof cost extra. The Deluxe Station Wagon included the sunroof, windows all around and side observation windows. Transporter-based commercial models included the Model 211 Panel Delivery, the Model 261 Pickup and the Model 265 Deluxe Cab Pickup. Late in 1962, Volkswagen announced that 10 camper "kits" would be available for Transporters at various prices, so it was no longer necessary to buy the expensive Westfalia Camper. However, eight of the kits were still made by that German company. A camper model was no longer listed separately.

TRANSPORTER COLORS (1963): L31=Dove Blue, L53=Sealing Wax Red, L54=Poppy Red, L82=Silver White, L87=Pearl White, L289=Pale Blue, L345=Pale Gray, L360=Sea Blue, L380=Turquoise Green, L390=Gulf Blue, L398=Pacific Blue, L456=Ruby Red, L469=Anthracite, L472=Beige Gray, L478=Beryl Green, L532=Polar Blue, L560=Manilla Yellow, L1009=Yukon Yellow.

I.D. DATA: Serial number is on a plate behind the spare tire and on the frame tunnel under the back seat. Engine number is stamped on the generator support and on the crankcase. Serial number range: (Beetle sedan) 4846836- 5677118, (Beetle convertible) 4765156 up, (Karmann-Ghia coupe) 4763000 up, (Karmann-Ghia convertible) 4763007 up, (Transporter) 971551 up, (Type 3) not reported in U.S.

ENGINE

BASE FOUR (1200): Horizontally opposed, overhead-valve four-cylinder (air cooled). Light alloy block, heads and finned cylinder with cast-iron cylinder liners. Displacement: 72.7 cid (1192 cc). Bore & Stroke: 3.03 x 2.52 in. (77 x 64 mm). Compression Ratio: 7.0:1. Brake Horsepower: 40 at 3900 rpm. Torque: 64.4 lbs.-ft. at 2400 rpm. Four main bearings. Solid valve lifters. Solex single-barrel downdraft carburetor. 6-volt electrical system.

BASE FOUR (1500): Horizontally opposed, overhead-valve four-cylinder (air cooled). Light alloy block, heads and finned cylinder with cast-iron cylinder liners. Displacement: 91.1 cid. Bore & Stroke: 3.27 x 2.72 in. Compression Ratio: 7.8:1. Brake Horsepower: 53 at 4000 rpm. Torque: 82.5 lbs.-ft. at 2000 rpm. Four main bearings. Solid valve lifters. Single-barrel sidedraft carburetor. 6-volt electrical system.

Dick Dance Collection

Fresh air heating was available beginning with the 1963 Volkswagen buses.

The "21 window" Volkswagen Microbus offered passengers space and great sight lines.

CHASSIS

(BEETLE) SEDAN: Wheelbase: 94.5 in. Overall Length: 156 in. Height: 59.1 in. Width: 60.6 in. Front Tread: 51.4 in. Rear Tread: 50.7 in. Standard Tires: 5.60 x 15.

(SQUAREBACK) 1500 TYPE 3: Wheelbase: 94.5 in. Overall Length: (Style 31) 166.3 in., (Style 34 Karmann-Ghia Type 3) 168.5 in. Height: (Style 31) 58.1 in., (Style 34 Karmann-Ghia Type 3) 52.6 in. Width: 63.8 in. Front Tread: 51.6 in. Rear Tread: 53.0 in. Standard Tires: 6.00 x 15.

KARMANN-GHIA: Wheelbase: 94.5 in. Overall Length: 163 in. Height: 52.4. Width: 64.3 in. Front Tread: 51.4 in. Rear Tread: 50.7 in. Standard Tires: 5.60 x 15.

TRANSPORTER: Wheelbase: 94.5 in. Overall Length: 166.1-168.9 in. Height: 76.4 in. Width: 68.9 in. Front Tread: 53.9 in. Rear Tread: 53.5 in. Standard Tires: 6.40 x 15.

TECHNICAL

(BEETLE) SEDAN: Layout: rear-engine, rear-drive. Transmission: four-speed manual. Final Drive Type: Spiral bevel. Steering: worm and cap nut. Suspension (front): king pins with transverse torsion bars and upper/lower trailing arms. Suspension (rear): swing axles with trailing arms and torsion bars. Brakes: hydraulic, front/rear drum. Body Construction: steel body welded to floor pan with tubular center section. Fuel Tank: 10.6 gallon.

(SQUAREBACK) 1500 TYPE 3: Layout: rear-engine, rear-drive. Transmission: four-speed manual. Final Drive Type: Spiral bevel. Steering: worm and cap nut. Suspension (front): king pins with transverse torsion bars and upper/lower trailing arms. Suspension (rear): swing axles with trailing arms and torsion bars. Brakes: hydraulic, front/rear drum. Body Construction: steel body welded to floor pan with tubular center section. Fuel Tank: 10.6 gallon.

KARMANN-GHIA: Layout: rear-engine, rear-drive. Transmission: four-speed manual. Final Drive Type: Spiral bevel. Steering: worm and cap nut. Suspension (front): Independent: upper and lower trailing arms with square torsion bars. Suspension (rear): Independent: swinging half axle shafts with torsion bars. Brakes: hydraulic, front/rear drum. Body Construction: Tubular center section, forked at rear, with welded on platform. Fuel Tank: 10.6 gallon.

TRANSPORTER: Layout: rear-engine, rear-drive. Transmission: four-speed manual. Final Drive Type:

Spiral bevel. Steering: manual. Suspension (front): Independent: two square section torsion bars. Suspension (rear): Independent: circular torsion bars each side. Brakes: hydraulic, front/rear drum. Body Construction: steel unibody on stamped steel floor pan. Fuel Tank: 10.6 gallon.

PERFORMANCE: Top Speed: (Beetle sedan) 72 mph cruising, (1500) 82 mph, (Karmann-Ghia) 75 mph. 0-60 mph acceleration (Beetle sedan) 32 seconds, (1500) 20.8 seconds. 1/4-Mile: ((Beetle) 23.9 sec. At 56 mph, (1500) 21.9 sec. At 61 mph. Fuel Mileage: (Beetle sedan) 28-35 mpg, (1500) 25-35 mpg.

HISTORICAL FOOTNOTES: Manufacturer: Volkswagenwerk GmbH, Wolfsburg, West Germany. Importer: Volkswagen of America, Englewood Cliffs, N.J. J. Stuart Perkins was general manager. There were again 15 Volkswagen distributors in the U.S.: Hansen-MacPhee Engineering of Bedford, Massachusetts, World-Wide Automobiles Corporation of Long Island City, N.Y., Auto Associates, Incorporated of King of Prussia, Pennsylvania, Capitol Car Distributors, Ltd., of Takoma Park, Maryland, Brundage Motors, Inc., of Jacksonville, Florida,

International Auto Sales and Service, Inc., of New Orleans, Louisianna, Midwestern VW Corp., of Columbus, Ohio, Import Motors, Ltd., of Grand Rapids, Michigan, Import Motors Ltd., of Deerfield, Illinois, Mid-America Cars, Inc., of Overland, Missouri, Inter-Continental Motors Corporation of San Antonio, Texas, Competition Motors Distributors, Inc., of Hollywood, California, Reynold C. Johnson Co., of Burlingame, California, Riviera Motors, Inc., of Portland, Oregon and Volkswagen Hawaii, Inc., of Honolulu, Hawaii. Volkswagen held a 62.3 percent share of the U.S. imported car market in 1963. The company registered 240,143 new cars in the U.S., about twice the 1959 total. It was also a gain of 24.7 percent from 1962. This represented a strong 3.2 percent of all new cars sold in the country. Volkswagen beat both foreign competitors and the new U.S.-built compact cars. Building on its image in America, Volkswagen ran advertisements poking fun at itself and its hardly-ever-changed Beetle sedan. Due to factory limitations, Volkswagen postponed the U.S. introduction of the 1500 model until 1965. During the year, Volkswagen increased its dealer count from 687 stores to 744. The company reported that it employed 20,000 Americans and had made a total investment of some $200,000,000 in the U.S. economy.

This convertible is one of more than 240,000 1963 Volkswagens sold in the U.S.

1964

1200 (BEETLE)—FOUR The date for the 1964 model changeover at Volkswagen was August 5, 1963. Perforated vinyl upholstery replaced the former non-porous leatherette material and a sliding steel sun roof (with a crank) replaced the familiar fold-back fabric unit. The rear license-plate light grew larger and dual thumb buttons on the steering wheel replaced the horn half-ring. A new Silver Beige color was used on the control knobs and steering wheel, which were previously black. The Volkswagen emblem on the hubcaps was no longer colored. Rear tire pressure specifications were modified. A new synthetic seat covering material was used and foam door seals were adopted. There were minor alterations to the curved part of the engine cover and the license plate fastening holes. Effective February 5, the old aluminum running board moldings were replaced with chrome-steel moldings. Starting in March, the oil filter cover plate was sealed with cap nuts and copper washers and new gasket material was used.

SEDAN COLORS (1964): L41=Black, L456=Ruby Red, L360=Sea Blue, L87=Pearl White, L469=Anthracite, L518=Java Green, L519=Bahama Blue, L572=Panama Beige, L1009=Yukon Yellow.

ADDITIONAL CABRIOLET COLORS (1964): L54=Poppy Red, L398=Pacific Blue, L10018=Brunswick Blue.

1500S TYPE 3 SQUAREBACK—FOUR Since the Type 3 had not been well received in Europe, Volkswagen launched the 1500S two years later. In addition to more chrome trim, it had a 66-hp engine with twin carburetors. This was another model that was not officially sold in the United States. The few that made it to this country had to be snuck in.

1500 TYPE 34 (T2) KARMANN-GHIA—FOUR The rare Karmann-Ghia 1500S was also sold outside the U.S. again this year. Though styled by Ghia, it had only a vague family resemblance to the Karmann-Ghia introduced in the '50s.

1200 KARMANN-GHIA—FOUR Production of Volkswagen's Karmann-Ghia Sport Coupe and convertible continued. After the start of the model year, the license plate grew larger.

KARMANN-GHIA COLORS (1964): (Body color/Roof or Convertible Top Color) Terra Brown/Pearl White, Manilla Yellow/Black, Sea Blue/Blue White, Pacfic Blue/Blue White, Pearl White/Black, Emerald Green/Blue White, Ruby Red/Black, Black/Pearl White, Polar Blue/Blue White and Anthracite/Pearl White..

TRANSPORTER—FOUR Microbus production continued without major change and with the option of a new larger 50-hp engine. The series again offered three different

Left: **Beetle popularity continued in 1963 in both the sedan and convertible versions.**

Paul Smith

Above: **This Wisconsin-based 1964 Volkswagen Beetle brightens its natural settings.**

Kris Kandler

Model Code	Body Type & Seating	POE Price	Weight (lbs.)	ProductionTotal
1200 DELUXE				
113	2d Sedan-4P	1595	1609	Note 1
117	2d Sunroof Sedan-4P	1685	1609	Note 1
151	2d Convertible-4P	2095	1720	Note 1
1500S TYPE 3 SQUAREBACK				
1500-31	2d Sedan	NA	1874	Note 1
1500-31N	2d Wagon	NA	1918	Note 1
1500 TYPE 34 KARMANN-GHIA (EUROPE)				
1500-34	Karmann-Ghia Coupe	NA	1918	Note 1
1200 KARMANN-GHIA				
143	2d Coupe-2 + 2P	2295	1742	Note 1
141	2d Convertible-2 + 2P	2495	1742	Note 1
TRANSPORTER				
2313	4d Kombi	2140	2282	Note 2
2213	4d Station Wagon	2385	2469	Note 2
2413/M130	4d Deluxe Wagon	2605	2469	Note 2

Note 1: 1,034,797 Volkswagen passenger cars were produced in 1964.
Note 2: 54,146 Transporters were produced in 1964.

passenger transporters. The Kombi had 8 to 9 passenger seating with all of the removable seats in place. Its rear windows pivoted outward for extra ventilation. The cargo area was untrimmed. The Eight-Passenger Station Wagon was fully trimmed inside and a Golde sunroof was optional. The Deluxe Station Wagon included the Golde sunroof, windows all around and side observation windows. A number of camper kits were offered at a range of prices. Also available were the same three commercial models offered in 1963, although the "Deluxe Cab" pickup was now listed as the "Double Cab" pickup.

TRANSPORTER COLORS (1964): L31=Dove Blue, L53=Sealing Wax Red, L54=Poppy Red, L82=Silver White, L87=Pearl White, L289=Pale Blue, L345=Pale Gray, L360=Sea Blue, L380=Turquoise Green, L390=Gulf Blue, L398=Pacific Blue, L456=Ruby Red, L469=Anthracite, L472=Beige Gray, L478=Beryl Green, L479=Tan Beige, L513=Sea Green, L518=Java Green, L519=Bahama Blue, L532=Polar Blue, L539=Baltic Blue, L560=Manilla Yellow, L563=Safari Beige, L572=Panama Beige, L573=Nutria, L1009=Yukon Yellow.

I.D. DATA: Serial number is on a plate behind the spare tire and on the frame tunnel and under the back seat. Engine number is stamped on the generator support and on the crankcase. Serial number range: (Beetle) 5677119-6502399, (Transporter) 1144303 up, (Karmann-Ghia] NA, {1500S) NA.

ENGINE

BASE FOUR (1200): Horizontally opposed, overhead-valve four-cylinder (air cooled). Light alloy block and heads and finned cylinder with cast-iron cylinder liners. Displacement: 72.7 cid (1192 cc). Bore & Stroke: 3.03 x 2.52 in. (77 x 64 mm). Compression Ratio: 7.0:1. Brake Horsepower: 40 at 3900 rpm. Torque: 64.4 lbs.-ft. at 2400 rpm. Four main bearings. Solid valve lifters. Solex single-barrel downdraft carburetor. 6-volt electrical system.

BASE FOUR (1500S): Horizontally opposed, overhead-valve four-cylinder (air cooled). Light alloy block, heads and finned cylinder with cast-iron cylinder liners. Displacement: 91.1 cid. Bore & Stroke: 3.27 x 2.72 in. Compression Ratio: 8.5:1. Brake Horsepower: 66 at 4800 rpm. Torque: NA. Four main bearings. Solid valve lifters. Twin sidedraft carburetors. 6-volt electrical system.

OPTIONAL FOUR (TRANSPORTER): Horizontally opposed, overhead-valve four-cylinder (air cooled). Light alloy block, heads and finned cylinder with cast-iron cylinder liners. Displacement: 91.1 cid (1493 cc). Bore & Stroke: 3.27 x 2.72 in. (83 x 69 mm). Compression Ratio: 7.8:1. Brake Horsepower: 50 at 3900 rpm. Four main bearings. Solid valve lifters. Solex single-barrel downdraft carburetor. 6-volt electrical system.

CHASSIS

(BEETLE) SEDAN: Wheelbase: 94.5 in. Overall Length: 160.6 in. Height: 59.1 in. Width: 60.6 in. Front Tread: 51.4 in. Rear Tread: 50.7 in. Standard Tires: 5.60 x 15.

(SQUAREBACK) 1500 TYPE 3: Wheelbase: 94.5 in. Overall Length: (Style 31) 166.3 in., (Style 34 Karmann-Ghia Type 3) 168.5 in. Height: (Style 31) 58.1 in., (Style 34 Karmann-Ghia) 52.6 in. Width: 63.2 in. Front Tread: 51.6 in. Rear Tread: 53.0 in. Standard Tires: 6.00 x 15.

KARMANN-GHIA (1200): Wheelbase: 94.5 in. Overall Length: 163 in. Height: 52.4. Width: 64.3 in. Front Tread: 51.4 in. Rear Tread: 50.7 in. Standard Tires: 5.60 x 15.

TRANSPORTER: Wheelbase: 94.5 in. Overall Length: 166.1-168.9 in. Height: 76.4 in. Width: 68.9 in. Front Tread: 54.1 in. Rear Tread: 53.5 in. Standard Tires: 7.00 x 14.

TECHNICAL

(BEETLE) SEDAN: Layout: rear-engine, rear-drive. Transmission: four-speed manual. Final Drive Type: Spiral bevel. Steering: worm and cap nut. Suspension (front): king pins with transverse torsion bars and upper/lower trailing arms. Suspension (rear): swing axles with trailing arms and torsion bars. Brakes: hydraulic, front/rear drum. Body Construction: steel body welded to floor pan with tubular center section. Fuel Tank: 10.6 gallon.

(SQUAREBACK) 1500S TYPE 3: Layout: rear-engine, rear-drive. Transmission: four-speed manual. Final Drive Type: Spiral bevel. Steering: worm and cap nut. Suspension (front): king pins with transverse torsion bars and upper/lower trailing arms. Suspension (rear): swing axles with trailing arms and torsion bars. Brakes: hydraulic, front/rear drum. Body Construction: steel body welded to floor pan with tubular center section. Fuel Tank: 10.6 gallon.

KARMANN-GHIA: Layout: rear-engine, rear-drive. Transmission: four-speed manual. Final Drive Type: Spiral bevel. Steering: worm and cap nut. Suspension (front): Independent: upper and lower trailing arms with square torsion bars. Suspension (rear): Independent: swinging half axle shafts with torsion bars. Brakes: hydraulic, front/rear drum. Body Construction: Tubular center section, forked at rear, with welded on platform. Fuel Tank: 10.6 gallon.

TRANSPORTER: Layout: rear-engine, rear-drive. Transmission: four-speed manual. Final Drive Type: Spiral bevel. Steering: manual. Suspension (front): Independent: two square section torsion bars. Suspension (rear): Independent: circular torsion bars each side. Brakes: hydraulic, front/rear drum. Body Construction: steel unibody on stamped steel floor pan. Fuel Tank: 10.6 gallon.

PERFORMANCE: Top Speed: (Beetle sedan) 72 mph cruising, (1500) 82 mph, (Karmann-Ghia) 75 mph. 0-60 mph acceleration (Beetle sedan) 32 seconds, (1500) 20.8 seconds. 1/4-Mile: ((Beetle) 23.9 sec. At 56 mph, (1500) 21.9 sec. At 61 mph. Fuel Mileage: (Beetle sedan) 28-35 mpg, (1500) 25-35 mpg.

HISTORICAL FOOTNOTES: Manufacturer: Volkswagenwerk GmbH, Wolfsburg, West Germany. Importer: Volkswagen of America, Englewood Cliffs, N.J. J. Stuart Perkins was general manager. There were again 15 Volkswagen distributors in the U.S.: Hansen-MacPhee Engineering of Waltham, Massachusetts, World-Wide Automobiles Corporation of Long Island City, N.Y., Auto Associates Incorporated of King of Prussia, Pennsylvania, Capitol Car Distributors, Ltd., of Takoma Park, Maryland, Brundage Motors, Inc., of Jacksonville, Florida, International Auto Sales and Service, Inc., of New Orleans, Louisiana, Midwestern VW Corp., of Columbus, Ohio, Import Motors, Ltd., of Grand Rapids, Michigan, Import Motors of Chicago, Inc., of Deerfield, Illinois, Mid-America Cars, Inc., of Overland, Missouri, Inter-Continental Motors Corporation of San Antonio, Texas, Competition Motors Distributors, Inc., of Culver City, California, Reynold C. Johnson Co., of Burlingame, California, Riviera Motors, Inc., of Beaverton, Oregon and Volkswagen Hawaii, Inc., of Honolulu, Hawaii. Volkswagen continued to hold the lion's share of the market for imported cars in the United States. For 1964, six out of every 10 imported cars sold in this nation were Volkswagen Beetles. The company's growth was leveling off a bit and amounted to just 1.1 percent for 1964. The company continued to run humorous ads highlighting the bug-like shape of its most popular model, as well as its design simplicity and ease of repair. During the year the number of dealers grew from 750 to 845. The company estimated that approximately 1,600,000 Volkswagens were on American highways. Volkswagen's 307,173 unit sales in the United States amounted to 63.4 percent of the market.

This convertible is one of more than 240,000 1963 Volkswagens sold in the U.S.

1965

1200 (BEETLE)—FOUR Let there be light! The Volkswagen's windshield and windows grew larger for 1965. This gave the Beetle a total of 15 percent more glass area. A push-button mechanism replaced the former T-type handle on the engine lid. The front seat backs were now slightly thinner and more contoured, while the rear seat folded almost flat. Twin levers operated the heater, which delivered greater heating volume due to the use of four thermostically-controlled flaps at the fan housing instead of the former throttle ring. This redesign allowed heated air to flow immediately after the engine was started. Pivoting sun visors were also installed. The windshield wiper blades were longer and they were now operated by a more powerful motor. The blades now "parked" on the left side instead of the right side. The braking system was also improved.

1500S TYPE 3 SQUAREBACK—FOUR Little changed in 1965, although a new version of the Type 3 Volkswagen was coming soon.

1200 KARMANN-GHIA—FOUR Production of Volkswagen's Sport Coupe and convertible continued without major change. Katmann-Ghias got most of the same refinements given Beetles.

Above: **In 1965, VW owners continued to add the optional roof rack for more load space.**

Paul Smith

TRANSPORTER—FOUR Microbus production continued without major change, except that the formerly-optional "1500" engine was now standard equipment in this model. Wider 14-in. tires were used. The series again offered three passenger transporters. The Kombi had 8 to 9 passenger seating with all removable seats in place. Its rear windows pivoted outward for extra ventilation. The cargo area was untrimmed. The Eight-Passenger Station Wagon was fully trimmed inside. The Deluxe Station Wagon included a sunroof, windows all around and side observation windows. Camper kits were offered at a range of prices. Also available were the same three commercial models offered in 1964.

John Gunnell

By 1965, owners were enjoying cranked steel sun roofs on their Beetles.

Model Code	Body Type & Seating	POE Price	Weight (lbs.)	ProductionTotal
1200 (BEETLE)				
113	2d Sedan-4P	1563	1609	Note 1
117	2d Sunroof Sedan-4P	1653	1609	Note 1
151	2d Convertible-4P	2053	1720	Note 1
1500S TYPE 3 SQUAREBACK				
1500-31	2d Sedan	NA	1940	Note 1
1500-34	2d Wagon	NA	1940	Note 1
1500	Karmann-Ghia	NA	1940	Note 1
1200 KARMANN-GHIA				
143	2d Coupe-2 + 2P	2250	1742	Note 1
141	2d Convertible-2 + 2P	2445	1742	Note 1
TRANSPORTER				
23121	4d Kombi	2195	2282	Note 2
2212/2812	4d Station Wagon	2385	2436	Note 2
2412/2512	4d Deluxe Station Wagon	2765	2469	Note 2

Note 1: 1,174,687 Volkswagen passenger cars were produced in 1965.
Note 2: 50,400 Transporters were produced in 1965.

Dick Dance Collection

Dick Dance Collection

Popular in North America in 1965 was the VW 1500 Fastback.

I.D. DATA: Serial number is on a plate behind the spare tire and on the frame tunnel under the back seat. A new nine-digit numbering system was used starting in 1965. The first two digits indicate the model, the next digit identifies the model year and the final six digits formed the sequential production number. Engine number is stamped on the generator support and on the crankcase. Serial number range: (Beetle sedan) 11-5000001-11-5979202, (Karmann-Ghia) 14-5000001 up, (Transporter) 2()-5000001 up, (Others) NA.

ENGINE

BASE FOUR (EXCEPT TRANSPORTER): Horizontally opposed, overhead-valve four-cylinder (air cooled). Light alloy block and heads and finned cylinder with cast-iron cylinder liners. Displacement: 72.7 cid (1192 cc). Bore & Stroke: 3.03 x 2.52 in. (77 x 64 mm). Compression Ratio: 7.0:1. Brake Horsepower: 40 at 3900 rpm. Torque: 64.4 lbs.-ft. at 2400 rpm. Four main bearings. Solid valve lifters. Solex single-barrel downdraft carburetor. 6-volt electrical system.

BASE FOUR (1500S): Horizontally opposed, overhead-valve four-cylinder (air cooled). Light alloy block, heads and finned cylinder with cast-iron cylinder liners. Displacement: 91.1 cid. Bore & Stroke: 3.27 x 2.72 in. Compression Ratio: 8.5:1. Brake Horsepower: 66 at 4800 rpm. Torque: NA. Four main bearings. Solid valve lifters. Twin sidedraft carburetors. 6-volt electrical system.

BASE FOUR (TRANSPORTER): Horizontally opposed, overhead-valve four-cylinder (air cooled). Light alloy block, heads and finned cylinder with cast-iron cylinder liners. Displacement: 91.1 cid (1493 cc). Bore & Stroke: 3.27 x 2.72 in. (83 x 69 mm).Compression Ratio: 7.8:1. Brake Horsepower: 50 at 3900 rpm. Four main bearings. Solid valve lifters. Solex single-barrel downdraft carburetor. 6-volt electrical system.

CHASSIS

(BEETLE) SEDAN: Wheelbase: 94.5 in. Overall Length: 160.6 in. Height: 59.1 in. Width: 60.6 in. Front Tread: 51.4 in. Rear Tread: 50.7 in. Standard Tires: 5.60 x 15.

(SQUAREBACK) 1500 TYPE 3: Wheelbase: 94.5 in. Overall Length: (31) 166.3 in., (34 Karmann-Ghia) 168.5 in. Height: (31) 58.1 in., (34 Karmann-Ghia) 52.6 in. Width: 63.8 in. Front Tread: 51.6 in. Rear Tread: 53.0 in. Standard Tires: 6.00 x 15.

KARMANN-GHIA (1200): Wheelbase: 94.5 in. Overall Length: 163 in. Height: 52.4 in. Width: 64.3 in. Front Tread: 51.4 in. Rear Tread: 50.7 in. Standard Tires: 5.60 x 15.

TRANSPORTER: Wheelbase: 94.5 in. Overall Length: 166.1-168.9 in. Height: 76.4 in. Width: 68.9 in. Front

Above Right: **A very practical world was portrayed in this 1965 VW bus ad.**

If the world looked like this,
and you wanted to buy a car that sticks out a little,
you probably wouldn't buy a Volkswagen Station Wagon.
But in case you haven't noticed, the world doesn't look like this.
So if you've wanted to buy a car that sticks out a little,
you know just what to do.

Old Cars Weekly Archive

David Lyon

The 1965 Beetles had 15 percent more glass area—and plenty of room with a roof rack.

Tread: 54.1 in. Rear Tread: 53.5 in. Standard Tires: 7.00 x 14.

TECHNICAL

(BEETLE) SEDAN: Layout: rear-engine, rear-drive. Transmission: four-speed manual. Final Drive Type: Spiral bevel. Steering: worm and cap nut. Suspension (front):

The first car at the bottom of the world.

It comes in its own box.

king pins with transverse torsion bars and upper/lower trailing arms. Suspension (rear): swing axles with trailing arms and torsion bars. Brakes: hydraulic, front/rear drum. Body Construction: steel body welded to floor pan with tubular center section. Fuel Tank: 10.6 gallon.

(SQUAREBACK) 1500S TYPE 3: Layout: rear-engine, rear-drive. Transmission: four-speed manual. Final Drive Type: Spiral bevel. Steering: worm and cap nut. Suspension (front): king pins with transverse torsion bars and upper/lower trailing arms. Suspension (rear): swing axles with trailing arms and torsion bars. Brakes: hydraulic, front/rear drum. Body Construction: steel body welded to floor pan with tubular center section. Fuel Tank: 10.6 gallon.

KARMANN-GHIA: Layout: rear-engine, rear-drive. Transmission: four-speed manual. Final Drive Type: Spiral bevel. Steering: worm and cap nut. Suspension (front): Independent: upper and lower trailing arms with square torsion bars. Suspension (rear): Independent: swinging half axle shafts with torsion bars. Brakes: hydraulic, front/rear drum. Body Construction: Tubular center section, forked at rear, with welded on platform. Fuel Tank: 10.6 gallon.

TRANSPORTER: Layout: rear-engine, rear-drive. Transmission: four-speed manual. Final Drive Type: Spiral bevel. Steering: manual. Suspension (front): Independent: two square section torsion bars. Suspension (rear): Independent: circular torsion bars each side. Brakes: hydraulic, front/rear drum. Body Construction: steel unibody on stamped steel floor pan. Fuel Tank: 10.6 gallon.

PERFORMANCE: Top Cruising Speed: (sedan) 72 mph, (Karmann-Ghia) 75 mph. Acceleration (0-60 mph): (sedan) 22 seconds. Fuel Mileage: (sedan) 28-32 mpg.

PRODUCTION/SALES: 371,222 Volkswagens were sold in the United States during 1965 (including tourist deliveries).

MANUFACTURER: Volkswagenwerk AG, Wolfsburg, West Germany.

DISTRIBUTOR: Volkswagen of America Inc., Englewood Cliffs, New Jersey.

Above Left: **An air-cooled Beetle drove in the icy Antarctic and was promoted in this 1965 ad.** *(Old Cars Weekly Archive)*

Below Left: **All wrapped for Christmas in this ad was the 1965 VW bus.** *(Old Cars Weekly Archive)*

1966

1300 (BEETLE)—FOUR A boost from 40 to 50 hp was Volkswagen's major change for 1966. Engine displacement grew to 1285cc. That change put a "1300" emblem on the engine lid. The wheels now contained vent slots and flat hubcaps. Inside, the car, the half horn-ring that had been deleted two years earlier was reinstated. Safety latches were added to the front seat back rests. The headlight dimmer now was mounted on the steering column and the dashboard held a central defroster outlet.

1300 KARMANN-GHIA—FOUR Production of Volkswagen's Karmann-Ghia Sport Coupe and convertible continued. Both body styles now utilized the larger engine described above.

TRANSPORTER—FOUR Microbus production continued with a boost to 53 hp. The series again offered three passenger transporters. The Kombi had 8 to 9 passenger seating with all removable seats in place. Its rear windows pivoted outward for extra ventilation. The cargo area was untrimmed. The Eight-Passenger Station Wagon was fully trimmed inside. The Deluxe Station Wagon included a sunroof, windows all around and side observation windows. Camper kits were offered at a range of prices. Also available were the same three commercial models offered in 1965.

1600—FOUR The 1600 model was an all-new Volkswagen. This car evolved from the European Type 3 and came

Above and Below: **In 1966, the Beetle engine earned a boost from 45 to 50 hp.**

Paul Smith

in two-door fastback or "squareback" (Station Wagon) form. It used a 1585-cc horizontally-opposed engine that developed 65 hp. The 1600's appearance was completely different from that of the Beetle or Karmann-Ghia, but it was similar to the "1500" that had been marketed elsewhere in the world (and occasionally brought into the United States). The fastback's body had long rear quarter windows, a sharply-slanted back window and vertical taillights at the rear fender tips. The squareback's rear window was almost vertical, similar to that of a station wagon.

1966 VOLKSWAGEN PRODUCTION CHART

Model Code	Body Type & Seating	POE Price	Weight (lbs.)	ProductionTotal
1300 (BEETLE)				
113	2d Sedan-4P	1585	1653	Note 1
117	2d Sunroof Sedan-4P	1675	1653	Note 1
151	2d Convertible-4P	2075	1742	Note 1
1300 KARMANN-GHIA				
143	2d Coupe-2 + 2P	2250	1764	Note 1
141	2d Convertible-2 + 2P	2445	1764	Note 1
1600 FASTBACK				
311	2d Sedan-4P	2140	1962	Note 1
1600 SQUAREBACK				
361	2d Sedan-4P	2295	2029	Note 1
TRANSPORTER				
23121	4d Kombi	2150	2283	Note 2
2212/2812	4d Station Wagon	2337	2436	Note 2
2412/2512	4d Deluxe Station Wagon	2595	2469	Note 2

Note 1: 1,168,146 Volkswagen passenger cars were produced in 1966.
Note 2: 49,557 Transporters were produced in 1966.

A poster-perfect Volkswagen is this 1966 Beetle in blue.

I.D. DATA: Serial number is on a plate behind the spare tire and on the frame tunnel under the back seat. The first two digits indicate the model, the next digit identifies the model year and the final digits form the sequential production number. Engine number is stamped on the generator support and on the crankcase. Serial number range: (sedan/convertible) 116-000001-116-1021298, (Karmann-Ghia) 146-000001 up, (1600 fastback) 316-000001, (1600 squareback) 366-000001, (Transporter) 2()6-000001 up.

ENGINE

BASE FOUR (1300): Horizontally opposed, overhead-valve four-cylinder (air cooled). Light alloy block and heads and finned cylinders with cast-iron cylinder liners. Displacement: 78.4 cid (1285 cc). Bore & Stroke: 3.03 x 2.72 in. (77 x 69 mm). Compression Ratio: 7.3:1. Brake Horsepower: 50 at 4600 rpm. Torque: 69 lbs.-ft. at 2600 rpm. Four main bearings. Solid valve lifters. Solex single-barrel sidedraft carburetor. 6-volt electrical system.

Above and Right: **In addition to the Beetle, the 1966 Squareback was a memorable VW shape.**

BASE FOUR (TRANSPORTER): Horizontally opposed, overhead-valve four-cylinder (air cooled). Light alloy block and heads and finned cylinders with cast-iron cylinder liners. Displacement: 91.1 cid (1493 cc). Bore & Stroke: 3.27 x 2.72 in. (83 x 69 mm). Compression Ratio: 7.8:1. Brake Horsepower: 53 at 4200 rpm. Four main bearings. Solid valve lifters. Solex single-barrel sidedraft carburetor. 6-volt electrical system.

BASE FOUR (1600): Horizontally opposed, overhead-valve four-cylinder (air cooled). Light alloy block and heads and finned cylinders with cast-iron cylinder liners. Displacement: 96.7 cid (1585 cc). Bore & Stroke: 3.36 x 2.72 in. (85 x 69 mm). Compression Ratio: 7.7:1. Brake Horsepower: 65 at 4600 rpm. Torque: 87 lbs.-ft. at 2800 rpm. Four main bearings. Solid valve lifters. Twin Solex single-barrel sidedraft carburetors. 6-volt electrical system.

CHASSIS

(BEETLE) SEDAN: Wheelbase: 94.5 in. Overall Length: 160.6 in. Height: 59.1 in. Width: 60.6 in. Front Tread: 51.4 in. Rear Tread: 51.2 in. Standard Tires: 5.60 x 15.

1600: Wheelbase: 94.5 in. Overall Length: (31) 166.3 in., (34 Karmann-Ghia) 168.5 in. Height: (31) 58.1 in., (34 Karmann-Ghia) 52.5 in. Width: 63.8 in. Front Tread: 51.6 in. Rear Tread: 53.0 in. Standard Tires: 6.00 x 15.

KARMANN-GHIA (1300): Wheelbase: 94.5 in. Overall Length: 163 in. Height: 52.4. Width: 64.3 in. Front Tread: 51.4 in. Rear Tread: 51.2 in. Standard Tires: 5.60 x 15.

TRANSPORTER: Wheelbase: 94.5 in. Overall Length: 166.1-168.9 in. Height: 76.4 in. Width: 68.9 in. Front Tread: 54.1 in. Rear Tread: 53.5 in. Standard Tires: 7.00 x 14.

TECHNICAL

(BEETLE) SEDAN: Layout: rear-engine, rear-drive. Transmission: four-speed manual. Final Drive Type: Spiral bevel. Steering: worm and sector. Suspension (front): king pins with transverse torsion bars and upper/lower trailing arms. Suspension (rear): swing axles with trailing arms and torsion bars. Brakes: hydraulic, front/rear drum. Body Construction: steel body welded to floor pan with tubular center section. Fuel Tank: 10.6 gallon.

1600: Layout: rear-engine, rear-drive. Transmission: four-speed manual. Final Drive Type: Spiral bevel. Steering: worm and sector. Suspension (front): king pins with transverse torsion bars and upper/lower trailing arms.

Suspension (rear): swing axles with trailing arms and torsion bars. Brakes: hydraulic, front disc/rear drum. Body Construction: steel body welded to floor pan with tubular center section. Fuel Tank: 10.6 gallon.

KARMANN-GHIA: Layout: rear-engine, rear-drive. Transmission: four-speed manual. Final Drive Type: Spiral bevel. Steering: worm and sector. Suspension (front): Independent: upper and lower trailing arms with square torsion bars. Suspension (rear): Independent: swinging half axle shafts with torsion bars. Brakes: hydraulic, front/rear drum. Body Construction: Tubular center section, forked at rear, with welded on platform. Fuel Tank: 10.6 gallon.

TRANSPORTER: Layout: rear-engine, rear-drive. Transmission: four-speed manual. Final Drive Type: Spiral bevel. Steering: worm and sector. Suspension (front): Independent: two square section torsion bars. Suspension (rear): Independent: circular torsion bars each side. Brakes: hydraulic, front/rear drum. Body Construction: steel unibody on stamped steel floor pan. Fuel Tank: 10.6 gallon.

PERFORMANCE: Top Speed (Beetle 1300): 82 mph. Top Speed (Transporter): 72 mph. Fuel Mileage (Beetle 1300): about 25 mpg. Fuel mileage (Transporter): about 23 mpg.

PRODUCTION/SALES: 427,694 Volkswagens were sold in the United States during 1966 (including tourist deliveries).

MANUFACTURER: Volkswagenwerk AG, Wolfsburg, West Germany.

DISTRIBUTOR: Volkswagen of America Inc., Englewood Cliffs, New Jersey.

Top: **Volkswagen's 1966 camper brought the comforts of home to any outdoor setting.**

Bottom: **Drivers of the 1966 Karmann-Ghia convertible also enjoyed the new 50-hp engine.**
Floyd Stough

1967

1500 (BEETLE)—FOUR Still another engine enlargement sent horsepower from 50 to 53. Glass headlight covers were no longer were and the parking lamps became part of the turn signals. Back-up lights were added for 1967 and a 'Volkswagen' script went on the rear engine cover, which now held the license plate vertically. Locking door buttons were installed, as was a dual brake system. The electrical system was now 12-volt, after two decades of 6-volt operation. Two-speed windshield wipers were installed.

1500 KARMANN-GHIA—FOUR Production of Volkswagen's Sport Coupe and convertible continued, with the larger "1500" engine described above. The seat backrests now locked in position when the door was closed.

1600—FOUR Production of the fastback and squareback sedans, introduced to the United States in 1966, continued without major change. These two models used a different form of horizontally-opposed engine than the Beetle. This power plant was sometimes referred to as a "suitcase" engine because of its overall shape. Both body types were available with or without a sunroof.

TRANSPORTER—FOUR In the last year of the "split-windshield" design, Microbus production continued with minimal change. Microbus production continued with a

Above: **Volkswagen added 12 volt electrical systems for 1967.**
Paul Smith

boost to 53 hp. The series again offered three passenger Transporters. The Kombi had 8 to 9 passenger seating with all removable seats in place. Its rear windows pivoted outward for extra ventilation. The cargo area was untrimmed. The Eight-Passenger Station Wagon was fully trimmed inside. The Deluxe Station Wagon included a sunroof, windows all around and side observation windows. A Campmobile was available. It had wood paneling, cabinets, an icebox, a sink, folding beds, a folding table, louvered glass windows and curtains.

I.D. DATA: Serial number is on a plate behind the spare tire, and on the frame tunnel, under the back seat. 1600 serial number is on a plate in front luggage compartment, ahead of the spare tire. Transporter serial number is on right side of engine-compartment floor. The first two digits indicate the model, the next digit identifies the model year, and the final digits form the sequential production number. Engine number is stamped on the generator support and on the crankcase. Starting serial number: (1500 sedan/convertible 117-000001, (1600) 317-000001, (Transporter) 217-000001 up.

ENGINE

BASE FOUR (1500, Transporter): Horizontally opposed, overhead-valve four-cylinder (air cooled). Light alloy block and heads and finned cylinder with cast-iron cylinder liners. Displacement: 91.1 cid (1493 cc). Bore & Stroke: 3.27 x 2.72 in. (83 x 69 mm). Compression Ratio: 7.5:1. Brake Horsepower: 53 at 4200 rpm. Torque: 78 lbs.-ft. at 2600 rpm. Four main bearings. Solid valve lifters. Single-barrel carburetor. 12-volt electrical system.

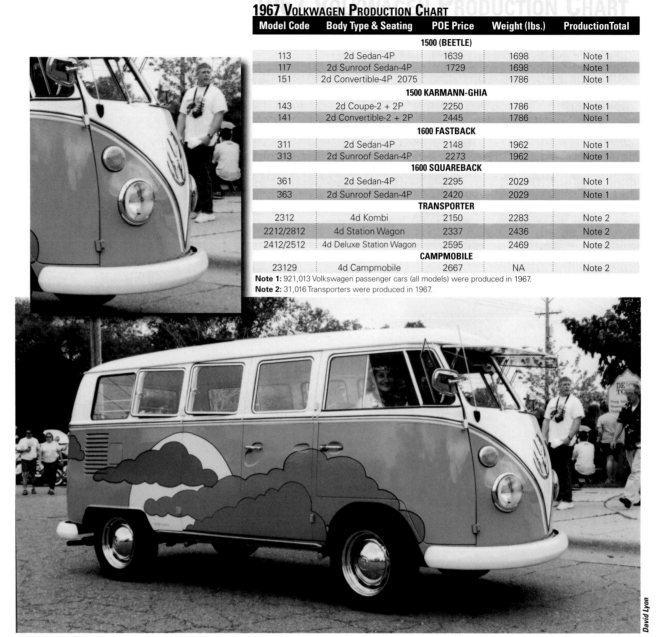

Model Code	Body Type & Seating	POE Price	Weight (lbs.)	Production Total
1500 (BEETLE)				
113	2d Sedan-4P	1639	1698	Note 1
117	2d Sunroof Sedan-4P	1729	1698	Note 1
151	2d Convertible-4P	2075	1786	Note 1
1500 KARMANN-GHIA				
143	2d Coupe-2 + 2P	2250	1786	Note 1
141	2d Convertible-2 + 2P	2445	1786	Note 1
1600 FASTBACK				
311	2d Sedan-4P	2148	1962	Note 1
313	2d Sunroof Sedan-4P	2273	1962	Note 1
1600 SQUAREBACK				
361	2d Sedan-4P	2295	2029	Note 1
363	2d Sunroof Sedan-4P	2420	2029	Note 1
TRANSPORTER				
2312	4d Kombi	2150	2283	Note 2
2212/2812	4d Station Wagon	2337	2436	Note 2
2412/2512	4d Deluxe Station Wagon	2595	2469	Note 2
CAMPMOBILE				
23129	4d Campmobile	2667	NA	Note 2

Note 1: 921,013 Volkswagen passenger cars (all models) were produced in 1967.
Note 2: 31,016 Transporters were produced in 1967.

David Lyon

A 1960s icon was the painted VW bus, like this 1967 model with smiling passenger.

BASE FOUR (1600): Horizontally opposed, overhead-valve four-cylinder (air cooled). Light alloy block and heads and finned cylinder with cast-iron cylinder liners. Displacement: 96.7 cid (1585 cc). Bore & Stroke: 3.36 x 2.72 in. (85 x 69 mm). Compression Ratio: 7.7:1. Brake Horsepower: 65 at 4600 rpm. Torque: 87 lbs.-ft. at 2800 rpm. Four main bearings. Solid valve lifters. Two single-barrel carburetors. 12-volt electrical system.

CHASSIS

(BEETLE) 1500 SEDAN: Wheelbase: 94.5 in. Overall Length: 160.6 in. Height: 59.1 in. Width: 60.6 in. Front Tread: 51.4 in. Rear Tread: 51.2 in. Standard Tires: 5.60 x 15.

1600: Wheelbase: 94.5 in. Overall Length: (31) 166.3 in., (34 Karmann-Ghia) 168.5 in. Height: (31) 58.1 in., (34 Karmann-Ghia) 52.5 in. Width: 63.8 in. Front Tread: 51.6 in. Rear Tread: 53.0 in. Standard Tires: 6.00 x 15.

Looking at home next to a pond is this 1967 VW camper, a home away from home.

Perrin Todd

KARMANN-GHIA (1500): Wheelbase: 94.5 in. Overall Length: 163 in. Height: 52.4. Width: 64.3 in. Front Tread: 51.4 in. Rear Tread: 51.2 in. Standard Tires: 5.60 x 15.

TRANSPORTER: Wheelbase: 94.5 in. Overall Length: 168.9-169.3 in. Height: 76.4 in. Width: 68.9 in. Front Tread: 54.1 in. Rear Tread: 53.5 in. Standard Tires: 7.00 x 14.

TECHNICAL

(BEETLE) SEDAN: Layout: rear-engine, rear-drive. Transmission: four-speed manual. Final Drive Type: Spiral bevel. Steering: worm and sector. Suspension (front): king pins with transverse torsion bars and upper/lower trailing arms. Suspension (rear): swing axles with trailing arms and torsion bars. Brakes: hydraulic, front/rear drum. Body Construction: steel body welded to floor pan with tubular center section. Fuel Tank: 10.6 gallon.

1600: Layout: rear-engine, rear-drive. Transmission: four-speed manual. Final Drive Type: Spiral bevel. Steering: worm and sector. Suspension (front): king pins with transverse torsion bars and upper/lower trailing arms. Suspension (rear): swing axles with trailing arms and torsion bars. Brakes: hydraulic, front disc/rear drum. Body Construction: steel body welded to floor pan with tubular center section. Fuel Tank: 10.6 gallon.

KARMANN-GHIA: Layout: rear-engine, rear-drive. Transmission: four-speed manual. Final Drive Type: Spiral bevel. Steering: worm and sector. Suspension (front): Independent: upper and lower trailing arms with square torsion bars. Suspension (rear): Independent: swinging half axle shafts with torsion bars. Brakes: hydraulic, front/rear drum. Body Construction: Tubular center section, forked at rear, with welded on platform. Fuel Tank: 10.6 gallon.

TRANSPORTER: Layout: rear-engine, rear-drive. Transmission: four-speed manual. Final Drive Type: Spiral bevel. Steering: worm and sector. Suspension (front): Independent: two square section torsion bars. Suspension (rear): Independent: circular torsion bars each side. Brakes: hydraulic, front/rear drum. Body Construction: steel unibody on stamped steel floor pan. Fuel Tank: 10.6 gallon.

PERFORMANCE: Top Speed (1500 Beetle): 82 mph. Top Speed (Transporter): 72 mph. Fuel Mileage (1500 Beetle): 25 mpg. Fuel mileage (Transporter): 23 mpg.

PRODUCTION/SALES: 454,801 Volkswagens were sold in the United States during 1967 (including tourist deliveries).

MANUFACTURER: Volkswagenwerk AG, Wolfsburg, West Germany.

DISTRIBUTOR: Volkswagen of America Inc., Englewood Cliffs, New Jersey.

1968

1500 (BEETLE)—FOUR Changes for 1968 included a switch to one-piece single-bar bumpers without overriders. This decreased the Beetle's overall length. Other revisions included larger taillights with integrated back-up lights, an external gas filler with spring-loaded door and flatter door handles with trigger-type releases. The rear engine cover was bulged slightly. The car now had a cowl air inlet and the hood release was moved to the outside. A collapsible steering column became standard equipment, while a "Stick Shift" automatic transmission became optional. The semi-automatic unit could be shifted from low to driving range simply by moving the gearshift lever and without using the clutch. "Sarcophagus" seat backs were now used, with integrated head restraints. A certification sticker on the door post advised that the car met United States' federal safety standards.

Above: **More than one-half million Volkswagens were sold to buyers in 1968.**

Dick Dance Collection

1500 KARMANN-GHIA—FOUR Production of Volkswagen's Sport Coupe and convertible continued with some of the same changes noted above. Front disc brakes were new.

1600—FOUR Production of the fastback and squareback sedans continued in much the same format, except that the fuel filler door went on the right front fender and the engine gained electronic fuel injection during the year (though many specifications sheets show the twin carburetors used on early 1968 models). An automatic transmission also became available during the model year.

TRANSPORTER (CLIPPER)—FOUR Microbuses and Campmobiles were restyled for 1968, taking on an appearance closer to American vans, with a sliding-type side door. Some reference sources of the time called these "Clipper" models for 1968. Later they were simply identified as the Type 22 and the Type 24. The "24" was an "L" trim version with bumper guards and equipment

Model Code	Body Type & Seating	POE Price	Weight (lbs.)	ProductionTotal
1500 (BEETLE)				
1131	2d Deluxe Sedan-4P	1699	1742	Note 1
1171	2d Sunroof Sedan-4P 1789	1742	Note 1	
1511	2d Convertible-4P	2099	1852	Note 1
1500 KARMANN-GHIA				
1431	2d Coupe-2 + 2P	2254	1852	Note 1
1411	2d Convertible-2 + 2P	2449	1852	Note 1
1600 FASTBACK				
3111	2d Sedan-4P	2179	2050	Note 1
3131	2d Sunroof Sedan-4P	2299	2050	Note 1
1600 SQUAREBACK				
3611	2d Sedan-4P	2349	2050	Note 1
3631	2d Sunroof Sedan-4P	2469	2050	Note 1
TRANSPORTER (CLIPPER)				
23101	3d Kombi	2269	2535	Note 2
2211	3d Station Wagon	2499	2634	Note 2
23129	3d Campmobile	2110	NA	Note 2

Note 1: 1,191,854 Volkswagen passenger cars (all models) were produced in 1968.
Note 2: 64,411 Transporters were produced in 1968.

A "Stick Shift" automatic transmission was made optional on 1968 Volkswagens.

Below: **A 1968 VW ad showed actor Paul Newman as a car owner/ driver.**

Dick Dance Collection

that made it a little longer and wider. It also came with radial tires. Both trim levels gained a larger "1600" engine. These vehicles had the same wheelbase as the older Microbus style, but they were 5-1/2 inches longer. They were also about one inch wider and higher. A one-piece wraparound windshield with rounded corners was used. The side windows were longer, larger and vented. A sliding door replaced the double swing-out doors on the curbside. This reduced the number of doors from four to three. A sunroof was still optional, but it was now made

of metal and was smaller than before. New safety features included a deep-dish steering wheel, a padded dashboard and sun visors, impact-absorbing outside mirrors and rubber-covered interior knobs. The driver got a new vinyl-trimmed seat. A new fresh air vent system ducted into the front and rear compartment. A new double-jointed rear suspension was used. Cargo volume, without center or rear seats, rose to 177 cubic feet. Station Wagons got a 28-

Dick Dance Collection

More than one-half million Volkswagens were sold to buyers in 1968.

cubic-foot luggage compartment that was accessible via a two-hinged rear door. Passenger models included a Kombi, a Station Wagon and a Campmobile. The redesigned Type 2 also included a full line of commercial models.

I.D. DATA: Serial number is on a plate behind the spare tire and on the frame tunnel under the back seat. 1600 serial number is in the front luggage compartment beside the hood lock. Transporter serial number is on right side of engine compartment floor. The first two digits indicate the model, the next digit identifies the model year and the final digits form the sequential production number. Engine number is stamped on the generator support and on the crankcase. Serial number range: (1500 sedan/convertible) 118-000001-119-1016098, (Karmann-Ghia) 148-000001 up, (1600 Fastback) 318-000001 up, (1600 Squareback) 368-000001 up, (Station Wagon) 218-000001 up, (Kombi) 238-000001 up.

ENGINE

BASE FOUR (1500 BEETLE, 1500 KARMANN-GHIA): Horizontally opposed, overhead-valve four-cylinder (air cooled). Light alloy block, heads and finned cylinder with cast-iron cylinder liners. Displacement: 91.1 cid (1493 cc). Bore & Stroke: 3.27 x 2.72 in. (83 x 69 mm). Compression Ratio: 7.5:1. Brake Horsepower: 53 at 4200 rpm. Torque: 78 lbs.-ft. at 2600 rpm. Four main bearings. Solid valve lifters. Single-barrel carburetor. 12-volt electrical system.

BASE FOUR (TRANSPORTER): Horizontally opposed, overhead-valve four-cylinder (air cooled). Light alloy block, heads and finned cylinder with cast-iron cylinder liners. Displacement: 96.7 cid (1585 cc). Bore & Stroke: 3.36 x 2.72 in. (85 x 69 mm). Compression Ratio: 7.5:1. Brake Horsepower: 57 at 4400 rpm. Torque: 81.7 lbs.-ft. at 3000 rpm. Four main bearings. Solid valve lifters. Single-barrel carburetor. 12-volt electrical system.

BASE FOUR (1600): Horizontally opposed, overhead-valve four-cylinder (air cooled). Light alloy block and heads and finned cylinder with cast-iron cylinder liners. Displacement: 96.7 cid (1585 cc). Bore & Stroke: 3.36 x 2.72 in. (85 x 69 mm). Compression Ratio: 7.7:1. Brake Horsepower: 65 at 4600 rpm. Torque: 87 lbs.-ft. at 2800 rpm. Four main bearings. Solid valve lifters. (Early 1968) Two single-barrel carburetors. (Late 1968) Electronic fuel injection. 12-volt electrical system.

CHASSIS

(BEETLE) 1500 SEDAN: Wheelbase: 94.5 in. Overall Length: 158.6 in. Height: 59.1 in. Width: 61.0 in. Front Tread: 51.4 in. Rear Tread: 53.1 in. Standard Tires: 5.60 x 15.

1600: Wheelbase: 94.5 in. Overall Length: (31) 166.3 in., (34 Karmann-Ghia) 168.5 in. Height: (31) 57.9 in., (34 Karmann-Ghia) 52.4 in. Width: (31) 64.6 in., (34 Karmann-Ghia) 63.8 in. Front Tread: 51.6 in. Rear Tread: 53.0 in. Standard Tires: 6.00 x 15.

KARMANN-GHIA (1500): Wheelbase: 94.5 in. Overall Length: 163 in. Height: 52.4. Width: 64.3 in. Front Tread: 51.4 in. Rear Tread: 53.1 in. Standard Tires: 5.60 x 15.

TRANSPORTER (CLIPPER): Wheelbase: 94.5 in. Overall Length: (22) 174 in., ("L" 24) 175 in. Height: 76.4 in. Width: (22) 69.5 in., ["L" 24) 71.5 in. Front Tread: 54.5 in. Rear Tread: 56.1. Standard Tires: (22) 7.00 x 14, ("L" 24) P185-14 radials.

TECHNICAL

(BEETLE) SEDAN: Layout: rear-engine, rear-drive. Transmission: four-speed manual. Final Drive Type: Spiral bevel. Steering: worm and sector. Suspension (front): transverse torsion bars with upper/lower trailing arms. Suspension (rear): swing axles with trailing arms and torsion bars.. Brakes: hydraulic, front/rear drum. Body Construction: steel body welded to floor pan with tubular center section. Fuel Tank: 10.6 gallon.

1600: Layout: rear-engine, rear-drive. Transmission: four-speed manual. Final Drive Type: Spiral bevel. Steering: worm and sector. Suspension (front): king pins with transverse torsion bars and upper/lower trailing arms. Suspension (front): transverse torsion bars with upper/lower trailing arms. Suspension (rear): swing axles with trailing arms and torsion bars. Brakes: hydraulic, front disc/rear drum. Body Construction: steel body welded to floor pan with tubular center section. Fuel Tank: 10.6 gallon.

KARMANN-GHIA: Layout: rear-engine, rear-drive. Transmission: four-speed manual. Final Drive Type: Spiral bevel. Steering: worm and sector. Suspension (front): transverse torsion bars with upper/lower trailing arms. Suspension (rear): swing axles with trailing arms and torsion bars. Brakes: hydraulic, front disc/rear drum. Body Construction: Tubular center section, forked at rear, with welded on platform. Fuel Tank: 10.6 gallon.

TRANSPORTER: Layout: rear-engine, rear-drive. Transmission: four-speed manual. Final Drive Type: Spiral bevel. Steering: worm and sector. Suspension (front): transverse torsion bars with upper/lower trailing arms. Suspension (rear): swing axles with trailing arms and torsion bars. Brakes: hydraulic, front/rear drum. Body Construction: steel unibody on stamped steel floor pan. Fuel Tank: 10.6 gallon.

PERFORMANCE: Top Speed (1500): 82 mph. Top Speed (Transporter): 72 mph. Fuel Mileage: (1500) 25 mpg. Fuel Mileage: (Transporter): 23 mpg.

PRODUCTION/SALES: 582,009 Volkswagens were sold in the United States during 1968 (including tourist deliveries).

MANUFACTURER: Volkswagenwerk AG, Wolfsburg, West Germany.

DISTRIBUTOR: Volkswagen of America Inc., Englewood Cliffs, New Jersey.

The Karmann-Ghia styling had changed little by the 1968 model year.

1969

1500 (BEETLE)—FOUR For the first time, the Beetle had truly independent rear suspension with a double-jointed rear axle and semi-trailing arms, instead of the customary swing axles. After being moved to the outside a year earlier, the hood release was moved inside the glovebox. Warm air outlets at the bases of the doors moved to the rear of the interior. An electric rear-window defogger/defroster was installed, as was an inside fuel-door release, a steering wheel and a day/night mirror. Later in the year, the odometer added readings in tenths of a mile.

KARMANN-GHIA—FOUR Production of Volkswagen's Sport Coupe and convertible continued with most of the same changes noted above.

1600 — FOUR — Production of the fastback and squareback sedans continued without major change, with either manual shift or an automatic transmission available. The 1.6- liter horizontally-opposed engine used fuel injection.

TRANSPORTER—FOUR Restyled for 1968, Volkswagen's Microbuses and Campmobiles continued without major

Above: **The 1969 Volkswagens enjoyed improved suspension systems.**
Old Cars Weekly Archive

change this year. Passenger models included a Kombi, a Station Wagon and a Campmobile.

I.D. DATA: Serial number is on the upper left of the dashboard, near the windshield. 1600 serial number is in front luggage compartment, beside the hood lock. Transporter serial number is on right side of engine-compartment floor. The first two digits indicate the model, the next digit identifies the model year, and the final digits form the sequential production number. Engine number is stamped on the generator support and on the crankcase. Serial number range: (1500 sedan/convertible) 119-000001-119-1093704, (Karmann-Ghia) 149-000001 up, (1600 Fastback) 319-000001 up, (1600 Squareback) 369-000001 up, (Kombi) 239-000001 up, (Transporter) 229-000001 up.

ENGINE

BASE FOUR (BEETLE, KARMANN-GHIA): Horizontally opposed, overhead-valve four-cylinder (air cooled). Light alloy block, heads and finned cylinder with cast-iron cylinder liners. Displacement: 91.1 cid (1493 cc). Bore & Stroke: 3.27 x 2.72 in. (83 x 69 mm). Compression Ratio: 7.5:1. Brake Horsepower: 53 at 4200 rpm. Torque: 78 lbs.-ft. at 2600 rpm. Four main bearings. Solid valve lifters. Single-barrel carburetor. 12-volt electrical system.

The VW Beetle received truly independent suspension for the first time in 1969.

1969 Volkswagen Production Chart

Model Code	Body Type & Seating	POE Price	Weight (lbs.)	ProductionTotal
1500 (BEETLE)				
1131	2d Sedan-4P	1799	1742	Note 1
1171	2d Sunroof Sedan-4P	1889	1742	Note 1
1511	2d Convertible-4P	2209	1852	Note 1
1500 KARMANN-GHIA				
1431	2d Coupe-2 + 2P	2365	1852	Note 1
1411	2d Convertible-2 + 2P	2575	1852	Note 1
1600 FASTBACK				
3111	2d Sedan-4P	2295	2050	Note 1
3131	2d Sunroof Sedan-4P	2415	2050	Note 1
1600 SQUAREBACK				
3611	2d Sedan-4P	2470	2050	Note 1
3631	2d Sunroof Sedan-4P	2590	2050	Note 1
TRANSPORTER				
23101	3d Kombi	2414	2469	Note 2
2211	3d Station Wagon -7P	2650	2634	Note 2
2215	3d Station Wagon -9P	2672	2634	Note 2
23109	3d Campmobile	2850	NA	Note 2

Note 1: 1,241,580 Volkswagen passenger cars (all models) were produced in 1969.
Note 2: 64,411 Transporters were produced in 1969.

The 1969 Volkswagens enjoyed improved suspension systems.

Old Cars Weekly Archive

BASE FOUR (TRANSPORTER): Horizontally opposed, overhead-valve four-cylinder (air cooled). Light alloy block, heads and finned cylinder with cast-iron cylinder liners. Displacement: 96.7 cid (1585 cc). Bore & Stroke: 3.36 x 2.72 in. (85 x 69 mm). Compression Ratio: 7.5:1. Brake Horsepower: 57 at 4400 rpm. Torque: 81.7 lbs.-ft. at 3000 rpm. Four main bearings. Solid valve lifters. Single-barrel carburetor. 12-volt electrical system.

BASE FOUR (1600): Horizontally opposed, overhead-valve four-cylinder (air cooled). Light alloy block and heads and finned cylinder with cast-iron cylinder liners.

Displacement: 96.7 cid (1585 cc). Bore & Stroke: 3.36 x 2.72 in. (85 x 69 mm). Compression Ratio: 7.7:1. Brake Horsepower: 65 at 4600 rpm. Torque: 87 lbs.-ft. at 2800 rpm. Four main bearings. Solid valve lifters. Electronic fuel injection. 12-volt electrical system.

CHASSIS: Wheelbase: 94.5 in. Overall Length: (1500 sedan) 158.7 in., (Karmann-Ghia) 163 in., (1600) 166.3 in., (Transporter) 174.0 in. Height: (1500 sedan) 59.1 in., (Karmann-Ghia) 52.4 in., (1600) 57.9 in. Width: (1500 sedan) 61.0 in., (Karmann-Ghia) 64.3 in., (1600) 63.2 in., (Transporter) 69.5 in. Front Tread: (1500 sedan)

51.6 in., (Karmann-Ghia) 51.8 in., (1600) 51.6 in. Rear Tread: (1500 sedan/Karmann-Ghia) 53.3 in., (1600) 53 in. Standard Tires: (1500 sedan/Karmann-Ghia) 5.60 x 15, (1600) 6.00 x 15, (Transporter) 7.00 x 14.

CHASSIS

(BEETLE) 1500 SEDAN: Wheelbase: 94.5 in. Overall Length: 158.6 in. Height: 59.1 in. Width: 61.0 in. Front Tread: 51.4 in. Rear Tread: 53.1 in. Standard Tires: 5.60 x 15.

1600: Wheelbase: 94.5 in. Overall Length: (31) 166.3 in., (34 Karmann-Ghia) 168.5 in. Height: (31) 57.9 in., (34 Karmann-Ghia) 52.4 in. Width: (31) 64.6 in., (34 Karmann-Ghia) 63.8 in. Front Tread: 51.6 in. Rear Tread: 53.0 in. Standard Tires: 6.00 x 15.

KARMANN-GHIA (1500): Wheelbase: 94.5 in. Overall Length: 163 in. Height: 52.4. Width: 64.3 in. Front Tread: 51.4 in. Rear Tread: 53.1 in. Standard Tires: 5.60 x 15.

TRANSPORTER (22/24): Wheelbase: 94.5 in. Overall Length: (22) 174 in., ("L" 24) 175 in. Height: 76.4 in. Width: (22) 69.5 in., ["L" 24) 71.5 in. Front Tread: 54.5 in. Rear Tread: 56.1. Standard Tires: (22) 7.00 x 14, ("L" 24) P185-14 radials.

TECHNICAL

(BEETLE) SEDAN: Layout: rear-engine, rear-drive. Transmission: four-speed manual. Final Drive Type: Spiral bevel. Steering: worm and sector. Suspension (front): transverse torsion bars with upper/lower trailing arms. Suspension (rear): swing axles with trailing arms and torsion bars.. Brakes: hydraulic, front/rear drum. Body Construction: steel body welded to floor pan with tubular center section. Fuel Tank: 10.6 gallon.

1600: Layout: rear-engine, rear-drive. Transmission: four-speed manual. Final Drive Type: Spiral bevel. Steering: worm and sector. Suspension (front): king pins with transverse torsion bars and upper/lower trailing arms. Suspension (front): transverse torsion bars with upper/lower trailing arms. Suspension (rear): swing axles with trailing arms and torsion bars. Brakes: hydraulic, front disc/rear drum. Body Construction: steel body welded to floor pan with tubular center section. Fuel Tank: 10.6 gallon.

KARMANN-GHIA: Layout: rear-engine, rear-drive. Transmission: four-speed manual. Final Drive Type: Spiral bevel. Steering: worm and sector. Suspension (front): transverse torsion bars with upper/lower trailing arms. Suspension (rear): swing axles with trailing arms

Old Cars Weekly Archive

It can manage the whole team.

A Volkswagen Station Wagon will take half a ball game to a ball game. It will hold nine players, fifteen pieces of luggage, balls, bats, bases and a goodly supply of crying towels. It will do all that while averaging a good 23 miles to a gallon of gasoline. (A feat comparable to hitting .400 or winning 30 games.) It will do all that on 5 pints of oil instead of 5 quarts. (Like going 5 for 5 instead of 5 for 20.) It will do all that without a radiator. (No radiator, no water to boil over, no errors.) And finally it will do all that for as little as $2,672.* Now. Let's play ball.

Even the local baseball team could fit into the VW station wagon in 1969.

and torsion bars. Brakes: hydraulic, front disc/rear drum. Body Construction: Tubular center section, forked at rear, with welded on platform. Fuel Tank: 10.6 gallon.

TRANSPORTER: Layout: rear-engine, rear-drive. Transmission: four-speed manual. Final Drive Type: Spiral bevel. Steering: worm and sector. Suspension (front): transverse torsion bars with upper/lower trailing arms. Suspension (rear): swing axles with trailing arms and torsion bars. Brakes: hydraulic, front/rear drum. Body Construction: steel unibody on stamped steel floor pan. Fuel Tank: 10.6 gallon.

PERFORMANCE: Top Speed (1500): 82 mph. Top Speed (Transporter) 72 mph. Fuel Mileage (1500): 25 mpg. Fuel Mileage (Transporter): 23 mpg.

PRODUCTION/SALES: 566,356 Volkswagens were sold in the United States during 1969 (including tourist deliveries).

MANUFACTURER: Volkswagenwerk AG, Wolfsburg, West Germany.

DISTRIBUTOR: Volkswagen of America Inc., Englewood Cliffs, New Jersey.

1970

1500 (BEETLE)—FOUR Displacement grew to 1585 cc for 1970, with a horsepower boost from 53 to 57. Despite the increase to 1.6 liters, the Beetle was still commonly referred to as a "1500" sedan. Front turn signals grew larger and were combined with the side marker lights. The engine lid added air-intake slots (introduced earlier on the convertible), and reflectors went on the rear bumper and tail lamp housings. Head restraints were smaller this year, and the glove box added a lock. Remote-control knobs for the warm air outlets were dropped. A buzzer now went off when the door was opened, if the key was in the ignition. Volkswagen's diagnosis and maintenance program was introduced this year.

KARMANN-GHIA—FOUR Production of Volkswagen's Sport Coupe and convertible continued with changes noted above.

1600—FOUR Production of the fastback and squareback sedans continued without major change. A three-speed automatic transmission was available.

TRANSPORTER—FOUR Restyled for 1968, Volkswagen's Microbuses and Campmobiles continued without major change.

Above: **The 1970 Beetles convertible claimed a top speed of 82 mph with their 57-hp engines.**
Paul Smith

I.D. DATA: Serial number is on the upper left of the dashboard, near the windshield. Fastback/squareback serial number is in front luggage compartment, beside the hood lock. Transporter serial number is on right side of engine-compartment floor. A 10-symbol identification number was now used. The first two digits indicate the model, the next digit identifies the model year, and the final seven digits form the sequential production number. Engine number is stamped on the generator support and on the crankcase. Starting serial number: (Beetle) 1102000001, (Karmann-Ghia) 1402000001, (1600 Fastback) 3102000001, (1600 Squareback) 3602000001, (Kombi) 2302000001, (Transporter) 2202000001.

ENGINE

BASE FOUR (Except 1600): Horizontally opposed, overhead-valve four-cylinder (air cooled). Light alloy block, heads and finned cylinder with cast-iron cylinder liners. Displacement: 96.7 cid (1585 cc). Bore & Stroke: 3.36 x 2.72 in. (85 x 69 mm). Compression Ratio: 7.5:1. Brake Horsepower: 57 at 4400 rpm. Torque: 81.7 lbs.-ft. at 3000 rpm. Four main bearings. Solid valve lifters. Single-barrel carburetor. 12-volt electrical system.

BASE FOUR (1600): Horizontally opposed, overhead-valve four-cylinder (air cooled). Light alloy block and heads and finned cylinder with cast-iron cylinder liners. Displacement: 96.7 cid (1585 cc). Bore & Stroke: 3.36 x

Model Code	Body Type & Seating	POE Price	Weight (lbs.)	ProductionTotal
1500 (BEETLE)				
113	2d Sedan-4P	1839	1807	Note 1
117	2d Sunroof Sedan-4P	1929	1807	Note 1
151	2d Convertible-4P	2249	NA	
KARMANN-GHIA				
143	2d Coupe-2 + 2P	2399	1978	Note 1
141	2d Convertible-2 + 2P	2609	1918	Note 1
1600 FASTBACK				
311	2d Sedan-4P	2339	2226	Note 1
313	2d Sunroof Sedan-4P	2459	2226	Note 1
1600 SQUAREBACK				
361	2d Sedan-4P	2499	2282	Note 1
363	2d Sunroof Sedan-4P	2619	2282	Note 1
TRANSPORTER				
23101	3d Kombi	2495	2665	Note 2
2211	3d Station Wagon -7P	2750	2743	Note 2
2215	3d Station Wagon -9P	2772	NA	Note 2
23109	3d Campmobile	3077	2921	Note 2

Note 1: 1,193,853 Volkswagen passenger cars (all models) were produced in 1970.
Note 2: 71,729 Transporters were produced in 1970.

Bottom: The 1970 Beetle was listed at $1,839, a great value in almost any decade.

Paul Smith

Deep-dish steering wheel.
Steering wheel lock. That locks the front wheels in position when you remove the key. And a buzzer to remind you to remove the key.
Collapsible steering column.

Emergency flasher button. Synchronizes flashing of front and rear lights.

Rear luggage compartment is 5 cu. ft. Can easily hold 2 good-size suitcases. Plus a few small bags.

A fresh-air ventilation system built into the top of the dash. Has separate controls for each person.
Two-speed windshield wipers. Plus windshield washers.

Electric rear-window defogger. Cleans up ice and fog at the flip of a switch.

Hand-assembled aluminum-magnesium engine sits above the drive wheels for extra traction. It's air-cooled, so there's no radiator. And no need for anti-freeze. And no radiator problems.

Front luggage compartment under the front hood is 5 cu. ft. Holds 2 suitcases easily. Plus a few small bags. And a spare tire.

Dual hydraulic brake system operating on front and rear paired wheels.

Sealed bottom keeps out rust and corrosion. And protects vital parts of the car.

Lockable backrest with locks on front and back seats.

Shoulder safety belts that snap easily into place.

Built-in front-seat headrests.

Back-up lights have rugged plastic shields.

Dick Dance Collection

Volkswagen used diagrams to show the inner workings of its cars, like this 1970 version.

2.72 in. (85 x 69 mm). Compression Ratio: 7.7:1. Brake Horsepower: 65 at 4600 rpm. Torque: 87 lbs.-ft. at 2800 rpm. Four main bearings. Solid valve lifters. Electronic fuel injection. 12-volt electrical system.

CHASSIS

(BEETLE) 1500 SEDAN: Wheelbase: 94.5 in. Overall Length: 158.6 in. Height: 59.1 in. Width: 64.0 in. Front Tread: 51.6 in. Rear Tread: 53.1 in. Standard Tires: 5.60 x 15.

1600: Wheelbase: 94.5 in. Overall Length: (31) 166.3 in. Height: 57.9 in. Width: 64.6 in. Front Tread: 51.6 in. Rear Tread: 53.0 in. Standard Tires: 6.00 x 15.

KARMANN-GHIA (1500): Wheelbase: 94.5 in. Overall Length: 163 in. Height: 52.0. Width: 64.3 in. Front Tread: 54.3 in. Rear Tread: 52.7 in. Standard Tires: 5.60 x 15.

TRANSPORTER (22/24): Wheelbase: 94.5 in. Overall Length: 175 in. Height: 76.4 in. Width: 71.5 in. Front Tread: 54.5 in. Rear Tread: 56.1. Standard Tires: 185R14 radials.

TECHNICAL

(BEETLE) SEDAN: Layout: rear-engine, rear-drive. Transmission: four-speed manual. Final Drive Type: Spiral bevel. Steering: worm and sector. Suspension (front): transverse torsion bars with upper/lower trailing arms. Suspension (rear): swing axles with trailing arms and torsion bars.. Brakes: hydraulic, front/rear drum. Body Construction: steel body welded to floor pan with tubular center section. Fuel Tank: 10.6 gallon.

1600: Layout: rear-engine, rear-drive. Transmission: four-speed manual. Final Drive Type: Spiral bevel. Steering: worm and sector. Suspension (front): king pins with transverse torsion bars and upper/lower trailing arms. Suspension (front): transverse torsion bars with upper/lower trailing arms. Suspension (rear): swing axles with trailing arms and torsion bars. Brakes: hydraulic, front disc/rear drum. Body Construction: steel body welded to floor pan with tubular center section. Fuel Tank: 10.6 gallon.

KARMANN-GHIA: Layout: rear-engine, rear-drive. Transmission: four-speed manual. Final Drive Type: Spiral bevel. Steering: worm and sector. Suspension (front): transverse torsion bars with upper/lower trailing arms. Suspension (rear): swing axles with trailing arms and torsion bars. Brakes: hydraulic, front disc/rear drum. Body Construction: Tubular center section, forked at rear, with welded on platform. Fuel Tank: 10.6 gallon.

TRANSPORTER: Layout: rear-engine, rear-drive. Transmission: four-speed manual. Final Drive Type: Spiral bevel. Steering: worm and sector. Suspension (front): transverse torsion bars with upper/lower trailing arms. Suspension (rear): swing axles with trailing arms and torsion bars. Brakes: hydraulic, front/rear drum. Body Construction: steel unibody on stamped steel floor pan. Fuel Tank: 10.6 gallon.

PERFORMANCE: Top Speed (Beetle sedans): 82 mph. Top Speed (Transporter): 72 mph. Fuel Mileage (Beetle Sedan): 25-26 mpg.

PRODUCTION/SALES: 582,573 Volkswagens were sold in the United States during 1970 (including tourist deliveries).

MANUFACTURER: Volkswagenwerk AG, Wolfsburg, West Germany.

DISTRIBUTOR: Volkswagen of America Inc., Englewood Cliffs, New Jersey.

Dick Dance Collection

The 1970 Karmann-Ghia continued to be a popular, sporty car.

Presenting the car of the future.

Dick Dance Collection

Larger turn signals and side marker lights were some of the 1970 Volkswagen changes.

1971

1500 (BEETLE)—FOUR The regular Beetle continued much the same as in 1970. Computer-analysis plugs were installed in models built during the second half of the 1971 model year.

BEETLE/SUPER BEETLE—FOUR A Super Beetle debuted for 1971 with a coil-spring front suspension and a bigger trunk. Volkswagen promoted the fact that the car had 89 improvements, including a boost to 60 hp. New flow-through vent ports went behind the side windows. The Super Beetle had chrome trim around its side windows and a modified front-lid shape. The front tread dimension grew wider and the turning radius was smaller. These cars also got computer-analysis plugs.

KARMANN-GHIA–FOUR Production of Volkswagen's Sport Coupe and convertible continued with changes noted above.

1600—FOUR Production of the squareback sedan and the fastback sedan (the latter now named the Type 3) continued without major change.

411—TYPE 4—FOUR Marketed elsewhere in the world since the 1969 model year, the Volkswagen Type 4 now was available in the United States. Two body styles were offered: a three-door hatchback and four-door sedan. The rear-mounted 1679-cc horizontally-opposed engine developed 85 hp.

TRANSPORTER—FOUR Volkswagen's Microbuses and Campmobiles continued without major change, except that the amber side safety light was now oblong in shape and was positioned farther forward.

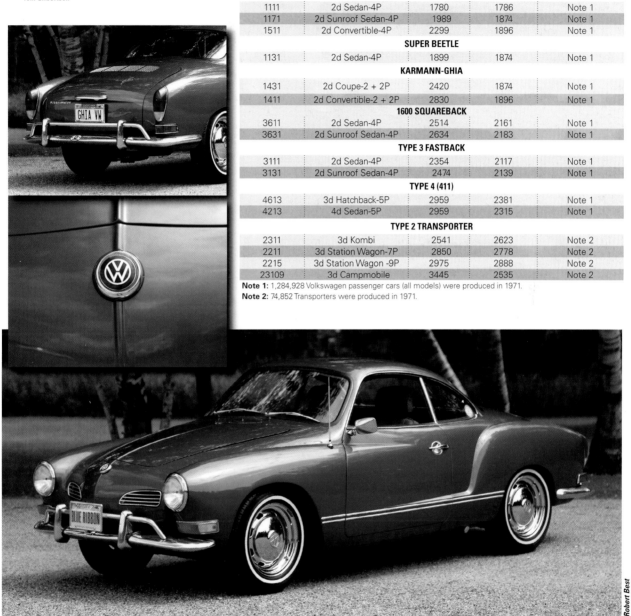

Left: **The Beetle was joined by a dressed-up Super Beetle edition in 1971.**

Tom Gilbertson

1971 VOLKSWAGEN PRODUCTION CHART

Model Code	Body Type & Seating	POE Price	Weight (lbs.)	Production Total
BEETLE				
1111	2d Sedan-4P	1780	1786	Note 1
1171	2d Sunroof Sedan-4P	1989	1874	Note 1
1511	2d Convertible-4P	2299	1896	Note 1
SUPER BEETLE				
1131	2d Sedan-4P	1899	1874	Note 1
KARMANN-GHIA				
1431	2d Coupe-2 + 2P	2420	1874	Note 1
1411	2d Convertible-2 + 2P	2830	1896	Note 1
1600 SQUAREBACK				
3611	2d Sedan-4P	2514	2161	Note 1
3631	2d Sunroof Sedan-4P	2634	2183	Note 1
TYPE 3 FASTBACK				
3111	2d Sedan-4P	2354	2117	Note 1
3131	2d Sunroof Sedan-4P	2474	2139	Note 1
TYPE 4 (411)				
4613	3d Hatchback-5P	2959	2381	Note 1
4213	4d Sedan-5P	2959	2315	Note 1
TYPE 2 TRANSPORTER				
2311	3d Kombi	2541	2623	Note 2
2211	3d Station Wagon-7P	2850	2778	Note 2
2215	3d Station Wagon -9P	2975	2888	Note 2
23109	3d Campmobile	3445	2535	Note 2

Note 1: 1,284,928 Volkswagen passenger cars (all models) were produced in 1971.
Note 2: 74,852 Transporters were produced in 1971.

Robert Best

The Karmann-Ghia coupe continued to be a popular choice for many Volkswagen buyers.

I.D. DATA: Serial number is on the upper left of the dashboard, visible through the windshield. Beetle/ Karmann-Ghia serial number may also be behind the spare tire. Fastback/ Type 3 serial number adjacent to the hood lock under the front hood. Transporter serial number stamped on right engine-cover plate. A 10-symbol vehicle identification number was used. The first two digits indicate the model, the next digit identifies the model year and the final seven digits form the sequential production number. Engine number is stamped on the generator support and on the crankcase. Starting serial number: (Beetle) 1112000001, (convertible) 1512000001, (Karmann-Ghia) 1412000001, (1600 Squareback) 3612000001, (Type 3 Fastback) 31120000001, (411 Squareback 3d) 4612000001, (411 four-door sedan) 42120000001, (Kombi/Campmobile) 2312000001, (Transporter) 2212000001.

Robert Best

The Karmann-Ghia with its top down always was an attractive car.

ENGINE

BASE FOUR (Beetle, Karmann-Ghia, Transporter): Horizontally opposed, overhead-valve four-cylinder (air cooled). Displacement: 96.7 cid (1585 cc). Bore & Stroke: 3.36 x 2.72 in. (85 x 69 mm). Compression Ratio: 7.5:1. Brake Horsepower: 60 at 4400 rpm. Torque: 81.7 lbs.-ft. at 3000 rpm. Four main bearings. Solid valve lifters. Single-barrel carburetor. 12-volt electrical system.

BASE FOUR (1600): Horizontally opposed, overhead-valve four-cylinder (air cooled). Light alloy block and heads and finned cylinder with cast-iron cylinder liners. Displacement: 96.7 cid (1585 cc). Bore & Stroke: 3.36 x 2.72 in. (85 x 69 mm). Compression Ratio: 7.7:1. Brake Horsepower: 65 at 4600 rpm. Torque: 87 lbs.-ft. at 2800 rpm. Four main bearings. Solid valve lifters. Electronic fuel injection. 12-volt electrical system.

BASE FOUR (411 Type 4): Horizontally opposed, overhead-valve four-cylinder (air cooled). Displacement: 102.5 cid (1679 cc). Bore & Stroke: 3.54 x 2.60 in. (90 x 66 mm). Compression Ratio: 8.2:1. Brake Horsepower: 85 at 5000 rpm. Torque: 99.4 lbs.-ft. at 3500 rpm. Four main bearings. Solid valve lifters. Bosch fuel injection.

CHASSIS

(BEETLE) 1500 SEDAN: Wheelbase: 94.5 in. Overall Length: 158.6 in. Height: 59.1 in. Width: 61.0 in. Front Tread: 51.6 in. Rear Tread: 53.1 in. Standard Tires: 5.60 x 15.

SUPER BEETLE: Wheelbase: 95.3 in. Overall Length: 161.8 in. Height: 59.1 in. Width: 62.3 in. Front Tread: 54.3 in. Rear Tread: 53.1 in. Standard Tires: 5.60 x 15.

TYPE 3 1600: Wheelbase: 94.5 in. Overall Length: 170.9 in. Height: 57.9 in. Width: 64.6 in. Front Tread: 51.6 in. Rear Tread: 53.0 in. Standard Tires: 6.00 x 15.

TYPE 4 411: Wheelbase: 98.4 in. Overall Length: 179.2 in. Height: 58.5 in. Width: 65.0 in. Front Tread: 54.2 in. Rear Tread: 53.1 in. Standard Tires: 155SR15.

KARMANN-GHIA (1500): Wheelbase: 94.5 in. Overall Length: 163 in. Height: 52.0 in. Width: 64.3 in. Front Tread: 54.3 in. Rear Tread: 52.7 in. Standard Tires: 5.60 x 15.

TRANSPORTER (22/24): Wheelbase: 94.5 in. Overall Length: 175 in. Height: 76.4 in. Width: 71.5 in. Front Tread: 54.5 in. Rear Tread: 56.1. Standard Tires: 185R14 radials.

TECHNICAL

(BEETLE) SEDAN: Layout: rear-engine, rear-drive. Transmission: four-speed manual. Final Drive Type: Spiral bevel. Steering: worm and sector. Suspension (front): transverse torsion bars with upper/lower trailing arms. Suspension (rear): swing axles with trailing arms and torsion bars.. Brakes: hydraulic, front/rear drum. Body

Construction: steel body welded to floor pan with tubular center section. Fuel Tank: 10.6 gallon.

SUPER BEETLE: Layout: rear-engine, rear-drive. Transmission: four-speed manual. Final Drive Type: Spiral bevel. Steering: worm and sector. Suspension (front): MacPherson struts with coil springs. Suspension (rear): swing axles with trailing arms and torsion bars..

Randy Ullenbrauck

New to the American market in 1971 was the 411 sedan by Volkswagen.

Dick Dance Collection

The 1971 Squareback continued to be a popular Volkswagen in its time.

Brakes: hydraulic, front/rear drum. Body Construction: steel body welded to floor pan with tubular center section. Fuel Tank: 10.6 gallon.

1600: Layout: rear-engine, rear-drive. Transmission: four-speed manual. Final Drive Type: Spiral bevel. Steering: worm and sector. Suspension (front): king pins with transverse torsion bars and upper/lower trailing arms. Suspension (front): transverse torsion bars with upper/lower trailing arms. Suspension (rear): swing axles with trailing arms and torsion bars. Brakes: hydraulic, front disc/rear drum. Body Construction: steel body welded to floor pan with tubular center section. Fuel Tank: 10.6 gallon.

411: Layout: rear-engine, rear-drive. Transmission: four-speed manual. Final Drive Type: Spiral bevel. Steering: recirculating ball. Suspension (front): king pins with transverse torsion bars and upper/lower trailing arms. Suspension (front): transverse torsion bars with upper/lower trailing arms. Suspension (rear): semi-trailing arms with coil springs. Brakes: hydraulic, front disc/rear drum. Body Construction: steel body welded to floor pan with tubular center section. Fuel Tank: 10.6 gallon.

KARMANN-GHIA: Layout: rear-engine, rear-drive. Transmission: four-speed manual. Final Drive Type: Spiral bevel. Steering: worm and sector. Suspension (front): transverse torsion bars with upper/lower trailing arms. Suspension (rear): swing axles with trailing arms and torsion bars. Brakes: hydraulic, front disc/rear drum. Body Construction: Tubular center section, forked at rear, with welded on platform. Fuel Tank: 10.6 gallon.

TRANSPORTER: Layout: rear-engine, rear-drive. Transmission: four-speed manual. Final Drive Type: Spiral bevel. Steering: worm and sector. Suspension (front): transverse torsion bars with upper/lower trailing arms. Suspension (rear): swing axles with trailing arms and torsion bars. Brakes: hydraulic, front/rear drum. Body Construction: steel unibody on stamped steel floor pan. Fuel Tank: 10.6 gallon.

PRODUCTION/SALES: 532,904 Volkswagens were sold in the United States during 1971 (including tourist deliveries).

MANUFACTURER: Volkswagenwerk AG, Wolfsburg, West Germany.

DISTRIBUTOR: Volkswagen of America Inc., Englewood Cliffs, New Jersey.

Volkswagen's Beetle still was a very popular car around the world in 1971.

The 1971 VW convertible and a body of water just seemed well matched.

1972

1500 (BEETLE)—FOUR Changes to the 1972 Beetle were modest, including installation of an energy-absorbing safety steering wheel and inertia-reel seat belts. The rear window grew larger and a hinged parcel shelf covered the luggage well.

BEETLE/SUPER BEETLE—FOUR A Super Beetle returned in 1972.

KARMANN-GHIA–FOUR Production of Volkswagen's Sport Coupe and convertible continued. The Karmann-Ghia models had changes similar to those made to the 1500 :Beetle."

SQUAREBACK/TYPE 3 (1600)—FOUR Production of the Squareback sedan and the Fastback sedan (or Type 3) continued without major change.

411—TYPE 4—FOUR The Type 4 three-door hatchback and four-door sedan returned. A three-door station wagon was added for 1972. The rear- mounted 1679-cc horizontally-opposed engine developed 85 hp.

Above: **The Volkswagen convertible continued to be a popular choice in 1972.**
Paul Smith

TRANSPORTER—FOUR Volkswagen's Microbuses and Campmobiles continued without major change.

I.D. DATA: Serial number is on the upper left of the dashboard, visible through the windshield. Beetle/ Karmann-Ghia serial number may also be behind the spare tire, fastback/ squareback, adjacent to the hood lock under the front hood, Transporters, stamped on right engine-cover plate. A 10-symbol identification number was used. The first two digits indicate the model, the next digit identifies the model year, and the final seven digits form the sequential production number. Engine number is stamped on the generator support and on the crankcase. Starting serial number (1971 models): (Beetle) 1112000001,(Beetle convertible) 1512000001,(Karmann-Ghia) 1412000001, (1600 Squareback) 3612000001, (Type 3 Fastback) 31120000001, (411 Squareback three-door sedan) 4612000001, (411 four-door sedan) 42120000001, (Kombi/Campmobile) 2312000001, (Transporter) 2212000001.

ENGINE

BASE FOUR (Beetle, Karmann-Ghia, Transporter): Horizontally opposed, overhead-valve four-cylinder (air cooled). Displacement: 96.7 cid (1585 cc). Bore & Stroke: 3.36 x 2.72 in. (85 x 69 mm). Compression Ratio: 7.3:1. Brake Horsepower: 60 at 4400 rpm. Torque: 81.7 lbs.-

ft. at 3000 rpm. Four main bearings. Solid valve lifters. Single-barrel carburetor. 12-volt electrical system.

BASE FOUR (1600): Horizontally opposed, overhead-valve four-cylinder (air cooled). Light alloy block and heads and finned cylinder with cast-iron cylinder liners. Displacement: 96.7 cid (1585 cc). Bore & Stroke: 3.36 x 2.72 in. (85 x 69 mm). Compression Ratio: 7.7:1. Brake Horsepower: 65 at 4600 rpm. Torque: 87 lbs.-ft. at 2800 rpm. Four main bearings. Solid valve lifters. Electronic fuel injection. 12-volt electrical system.

BASE FOUR (411 Type 4): Horizontally opposed, overhead-valve four-cylinder (air cooled). Displacement: 102.5 cid (1679 cc). Bore & Stroke: 3.54 x 2.60 in. (90 x 66 mm). Compression Ratio: 8.2:1. Brake Horsepower:

85 at 5000 rpm. Torque: 99.4 lbs.-ft. at 3500 rpm. Four main bearings. Solid valve lifters. Bosch fuel injection.

CHASSIS

(BEETLE) 1500 SEDAN: Wheelbase: 94.5 in. Overall Length: 158.6 in. Height: 59.1 in. Width: 61.0 in. Front Tread: 51.6 in. Rear Tread: 53.1 in. Standard Tires: 5.60 x 15.

SUPER BEETLE: Wheelbase: 95.3 in. Overall Length: 161.8 in. Height: 59.1 in. Width: 62.3 in. Front Tread: 54.3 in. Rear Tread: 53.1 in. Standard Tires: 5.60 x 15.

TYPE 3 1600: Wheelbase: 94.5 in. Overall Length: 170.9 in. Height: 57.9 in. Width: 64.6 in. Front Tread: 51.6 in. Rear Tread: 53.0 in. Standard Tires: 6.00 x 15.

Bottom: A special edition of Volkswagen that is memorable from 1972 is the Baja.

Old Cars Weekly Archive

1972 VOLKSWAGEN PRODUCTION CHART

Model Code	Body Type & Seating	POE Price	Weight (lbs.)	ProductionTotal
	BEETLE			
1111	2d Sedan-4P	1999	1786	Note 1
1171	2d Sunroof Sedan-4P	2249	1874	Note 1
1511	2d Convertible-4P	2599	1896	Note 1
	SUPER BEETLE			
1131	2d Sedan-4P	2159	1874	Note 1
	KARMANN-GHIA			
1431	2d Coupe-2 + 2P	2750	1874	Note 1
1411	2d Convertible-2 + 2P	3099	1896	Note 1
	1600 SQUAREBACK			
3611	2d Sedan-4P	2749	2161	Note 1
3631	2d Sunroof Sedan-4P	2875	NA	Note 1
	TYPE 3 FASTBACK			
3111	2d Sedan-4P	2549	2117	Note 1
3131	2d Sunroof Sedan-4P	2675	NA	Note 1
	TYPE 4 (411)			
4613	3d Hatchback-5P	2975	2300	Note 1
4213	4d Sedan-5P	3275	2315	Note 1
	TYPE 2 TRANSPORTER			
2311	3d Kombi	2989	2623	Note 2
2211	3d Station Wagon-7P	3299	2778	Note 2
2215	3d Station Wagon -9P	3329	NA	Note 2
23109	3d Campmobile	3848	2535	Note 2

Note 1: 1,082,098 Volkswagen passenger cars (all models) were produced in 1972.
Note 2: 66,400 Transporters were produced in 1972.

TYPE 4 411: Wheelbase: 98.4 in. Overall Length: 179.2 in. Height: 58.5 in. Width: 65.0 in. Front Tread: 54.2 in. Rear Tread: 53.1 in. Standard Tires: 155SR15.

KARMANN-GHIA (1500): Wheelbase: 94.5 in. Overall Length: 163 in. Height: 52.0. Width: 64.3 in. Front Tread: 54.3 in. Rear Tread: 52.7 in. Standard Tires: 5.60 x 15.

TRANSPORTER (22/24): Wheelbase: 94.5 in. Overall Length: 175 in. Height: 76.4 in. Width: 71.5 in. Front Tread: 54.5 in. Rear Tread: 56.1. Standard Tires: 185R14 radials.

TECHNICAL

(BEETLE) SEDAN: Layout: rear-engine, rear-drive. Transmission: four-speed manual. Final Drive Type: Spiral bevel. Steering: worm and sector. Suspension (front): transverse torsion bars with upper/lower trailing arms. Suspension (rear): swing axles with trailing arms and torsion bars.. Brakes: hydraulic, front/rear drum. Body Construction: steel body welded to floor pan with tubular center section. Fuel Tank: 10.6 gallon.

SUPER BEETLE: Layout: rear-engine, rear-drive. Transmission: four-speed manual. Final Drive Type: Spiral bevel. Steering: worm and sector. Suspension (front): MacPherson struts with coil springs. Suspension (rear): swing axles with trailing arms and torsion bars.. Brakes: hydraulic, front/rear drum. Body Construction: steel body welded to floor pan with tubular center section. Fuel Tank: 10.6 gallon.

1600: Layout: rear-engine, rear-drive. Transmission: four-speed manual. Final Drive Type: Spiral bevel. Steering: worm and sector. Suspension (front): king pins with transverse torsion bars and upper/lower trailing arms. Suspension (front): transverse torsion bars with upper/lower trailing arms. Suspension (rear): swing axles with trailing arms and torsion bars. Brakes: hydraulic, front disc/rear drum. Body Construction: steel body welded to floor pan with tubular center section. Fuel Tank: 10.6 gallon.

411: Layout: rear-engine, rear-drive. Transmission: four-speed manual. Final Drive Type: Spiral bevel. Steering: recirculating ball. Suspension (front): king pins with transverse torsion bars and upper/lower trailing arms. Suspension (front): transverse torsion bars with upper/lower trailing arms. Suspension (rear): semi-trailing arms with coil springs. Brakes: hydraulic, front disc/rear drum. Body Construction: steel body welded to floor pan with tubular center section. Fuel Tank: 10.6 gallon.

KARMANN-GHIA: Layout: rear-engine, rear-drive. Transmission: four-speed manual. Final Drive Type: Spiral bevel. Steering: worm and sector. Suspension (front): transverse torsion bars with upper/lower trailing arms. Suspension (rear): swing axles with trailing arms and torsion bars. Brakes: hydraulic, front disc/rear drum. Body Construction: Tubular center section, forked at rear, with welded on platform. Fuel Tank: 10.6 gallon.

TRANSPORTER: Layout: rear-engine, rear-drive. Transmission: four-speed manual. Final Drive Type: Spiral bevel. Steering: worm and sector. Suspension (front): transverse torsion bars with upper/lower trailing arms. Suspension (rear): swing axles with trailing arms and torsion bars. Brakes: hydraulic, front/rear drum. Body Construction: steel unibody on stamped steel floor pan. Fuel Tank: 10.6 gallon.

PRODUCTION/SALES: 491,742 Volkswagens were sold in the United States during 1972 (including tourist deliveries).

MANUFACTURER: Volkswagenwerk AG, Wolfsburg, West Germany.

DISTRIBUTOR: Volkswagen of America Inc., Englewood Cliffs, New Jersey.

Dick Dance Collection

While race cars careened past, these 1972 Karmann-Ghias were posed at trackside.

1973

BEETLE—FOUR Volkswagen's Beetle had only minor changes this year.

SUPER BEETLE—FOUR Volkswagen's Super Beetle had a bigger windshield and improved flow-through ventilation, while all Beetles had black windshield-wiper arms. Larger taillights were installed, along with 5-mph bumpers. They had new front seats that could be adjusted 77 ways! Improved intake-air preheating was intended to deliver quicker starts in cold weather.

KARMANN-GHIA—FOUR Production of Volkswagen's Sport Coupe and convertible continued with changes noted above.

SQUAREBACK/TYPE 3—FOUR This would be the final year for the rear-engined squareback sedan and Type 3 fastback sedan.

412—TYPE 4—FOUR The 412 model replaced the 411 this year in the Type 4 series. It was offered in two- and four-door sedan styles, as well as a station wagon. The horizontally-opposed engine was rated 76 hp (SAE net).

TRANSPORTER—FOUR An automatic transmission now was available in Volkswagen's Microbuses and Campmobiles. Front amber safety lights moved to a higher position. The new 102.5-cid engine developed 63 hp (SAE net).

THE THING—FOUR Introduced this year was "The Thing" (Type 81). This was an open Jeep-like vehicle with a folding top. Its basic design was derived from the Type 82 World War II Kubelwagen. Introduced elsewhere in the world during 1969, the "Thing" became available in the United States in 1973, after production moved to a Volkswagen factory in Mexico. Power came from the same rear-mounted 46-hp engine used in the Beetle. The car's spare tire was under the tall front hood. The doors were removable and the windshield folded flat. Three colors were offered: Pumpkin Orange, Sunshine Yellow and Blizzard White. All came with a Black convertible top and Black leatherette interior. Also available was the Acapulco Thing with a striped surrey top, striped seats and Blue and White body paint. Volkswagen claimed a 71-mph top speed.

I.D. DATA: Volkswagen's 10-symbol serial number is on the upper left of the dashboard, visible through the

Left Top: **In 1973, the Volkswagen Beetle produced 46 hp from its base 96.7-cid engine.**
Jim Hannum

Left Bottom: **This 1973 VW Beetle looks perfect in the spring setting.**
Jim Hannum

The Volkswagen Type 81, given the name "The Thing," was introduced in 1973.

Volkswagen claimed drivers could adjust its car seats in 77 ways for 1973.

Model Code	Body Type & Seating	POE Price	Weight (lbs.)	ProductionTotal
BEETLE				
1111	2d Sedan-4P	2299	1742	Note 1
1511	2d Convertible-4P	3050	1979	Note 1
SUPER BEETLE				
1131	2d Sedan-4P	2499	1911	Note 1
KARMANN-GHIA				
1431	2d Coupe-2 + 2P	3050	1853	Note 1
1411	2d Convertible-2 + 2P	3450	1853	Note 1
SQUAREBACK				
3611	2d Sedan-4P	2995	2217	Note 1
TYPE 3 (FASTBACK)				
3111	2d Sedan-4P	2795	2161	Note 1
3131	2d Sunroof Sedan-4P	2650	2161	Note 1
412 (TYPE 4)				
4111	2d Sedan-5P	3299	2300	Note 1
4213	4d Sedan-5P	3599	2345	Note 1
4613	2d Station Wagon-5P	3699	3549	Note 1
TRANSPORTER				
2301	3d Kombi	3500	2759	Note 2
2211	3d Station Wagon -7P	3799	2946	Note 2
2231	3d Station Wagon -9P	3850	3096	Note 2
2391	3d Campmobile	4449	3105	Note 2
THE THING				
1811	2d Roadster	2750	1984	Note 2

Note 1: 1,128,784 Volkswagen passenger cars (all models) were produced in 1973.
Note 2: 58,442 Transporters were produced in 1973.

windshield. The first two digits indicate the model, the next digit identifies the model year, and the final seven digits form the sequential production number. Starting serial number: (Beetle) 1132000001, (Super Beetle) 1332000001, (convertible) 1532000001, (Karmann-Ghia) 1432000001, (Squareback) 3632000001, (Type 3 Fastback) 31320000001, (412 coupe) 4132000001, (412 sedan) 42320000001, (Kombi/Campmobile) 2332000001, (Transporter) 2232000001.

ENGINE

BASE FOUR (Beetle, Super Beetle, Karmann-Ghia, The Thing): Horizontally opposed, overhead-valve four-cylinder (air cooled). Displacement: 96.7 cid (1585 cc). Bore & Stroke: 3.36 x 2.72 in. (85 x 69 mm). Compression Ratio: 7.3:1. Brake Horsepower: 46 (SAE net) at 4000 rpm. Torque: 72 lbs.-ft. at 2800 rpm. Four main bearings. Solid valve lifters. Single-barrel carburetor. 12-volt electrical system.

BASE FOUR (Squareback, Type 3 Fastback): Horizontally opposed, overhead-valve four-cylinder (air cooled). Displacement: 96.7 cid (1585 cc). Bore & Stroke: 3.36 x 2.72 in. (85 x 69 mm). Compression Ratio: 7.3:1. Brake Horsepower: 52 (SAE net) at 4000 rpm. Torque: 77 lbs.-ft. at 2200 rpm. Four main bearings. Solid valve lifters. . Fuel injection. 12-volt electrical system.

BASE FOUR (412 Type 4): Horizontally opposed, overhead-valve four-cylinder (air cooled). Displacement:

102.5 cid (1679 cc). Bore & Stroke: 3.54 x 2.60 in. (90 x 66 mm). Compression Ratio: 8.2:1. Brake Horsepower: 76 at 4900 rpm. Torque: 95 lbs.-ft. at 2700 rpm. Four main bearings. Solid valve lifters. Bosch fuel injection.

CHASSIS

(BEETLE) 1500 SEDAN: Wheelbase: 94.5 in. Overall Length: 159.8 in. Height: 59.1 in. Width: 61.0 in. Front Tread: 52.1 in. Rear Tread: 53.6 in. Standard Tires: 6.00 x 15L.

SUPER BEETLE: Wheelbase: 95.3 in. Overall Length: 163 in. Height: 59.1 in. Width: 62.3 in. Front Tread: 54.6 in. Rear Tread: 53.6 in. Standard Tires: 5.60 x 15.

TYPE 3 1600: Wheelbase: 94.5 in. Overall Length: 170.8 in. Height: 57.9 in. Width: 64.6 in. Front Tread: 53.1 in. Rear Tread: 53.1 in. Standard Tires: 6.00 x 15L.

TYPE 4 412: Wheelbase: 98.4 in. Overall Length: 180.4 in. Height: 58.1 in. Width: 65.0 in. Front Tread: 54.2 in. Rear Tread: 53.1 in. Standard Tires: 165SR15.

KARMANN-GHIA (1500): Wheelbase: 94.5 in. Overall Length: 165 in. Height: 52.0 in. Width: 64.3 in. Front Tread: 52.7 in. Rear Tread: 52.7 in. Standard Tires: 6.00 x 15L.

TRANSPORTER (22/24): Wheelbase: 94.5 in. Overall Length: 175 in. Height: 76.4 in. Width: 71.5 in. Front

Tread: 54.6 in. Rear Tread: 56.6. Standard Tires: 185R14 radials.

THE THING: Wheelbase: 94.5 in. Overall Length: 148.8 in. Height: NA. Width: 64.6 in. Front Tread: NA. Rear Tread: NA. Standard Tires: 165R14 radials.

TECHNICAL

(BEETLE) SEDAN: Layout: rear-engine, rear-drive. Transmission: four-speed manual. Final Drive Type: Spiral bevel. Steering: worm and sector. Suspension (front): transverse torsion bars with upper/lower trailing arms. Suspension (rear): swing axles with trailing arms and torsion bars.. Brakes: hydraulic, front/rear drum. Body Construction: steel body welded to floor pan with tubular center section. Fuel Tank: 10.6 gallon.

SUPER BEETLE: Layout: rear-engine, rear-drive. Transmission: four-speed manual. Final Drive Type: Spiral bevel. Steering: worm and sector. Suspension (front): MacPherson struts with coil springs. Suspension (rear): swing axles with trailing arms and torsion bars. Brakes: hydraulic, front/rear drum. Body Construction: steel body welded to floor pan with tubular center section. Fuel Tank: 10.6 gallon.

1600: Layout: rear-engine, rear-drive. Transmission: four-speed manual. Final Drive Type: Spiral bevel. Steering: worm and sector. Suspension (front): king pins with transverse torsion bars and upper/lower trailing arms. Suspension (front): transverse torsion bars with upper/lower trailing arms. Suspension (rear): swing axles with trailing arms and torsion bars. Brakes: hydraulic, front disc/rear drum. Body Construction: steel body welded to floor pan with tubular center section. Fuel Tank: 10.6 gallon.

411: Layout: rear-engine, rear-drive. Transmission: four-speed manual. Final Drive Type: Spiral bevel. Steering: recirculating ball. Suspension (front): king pins with transverse torsion bars and upper/lower trailing arms. Suspension (front): transverse torsion bars with upper/lower trailing arms. Suspension (rear): semi-trailing arms with coil springs. Brakes: hydraulic, front disc/rear drum. Body Construction: steel body welded to floor pan with tubular center section. Fuel Tank: 10.6 gallon.

KARMANN-GHIA: Layout: rear-engine, rear-drive. Transmission: four-speed manual. Final Drive Type: Spiral bevel. Steering: worm and sector. Suspension (front): transverse torsion bars with upper/lower trailing arms. Suspension (rear): swing axles with trailing arms and torsion bars. Brakes: hydraulic, front disc/rear drum.

A memorable color choice for 1973 Beetle buyers was Maya Gold.

Body Construction: Tubular center section, forked at rear, with welded on platform. Fuel Tank: 10.6 gallon.

THE THING: Layout: rear-engine, rear-drive. Transmission: four-speed manual. Final Drive Type: Spiral bevel. Steering: worm and sector. Suspension (front): transverse torsion bars with upper/lower trailing arms. Suspension (rear): swing axles with trailing arms and torsion bars. Brakes: hydraulic, front disc/rear drum. Fuel Tank: 11.1 gallon.

TRANSPORTER: Layout: rear-engine, rear-drive. Transmission: four-speed manual. Final Drive Type: Spiral bevel. Steering: worm and sector. Suspension (front): transverse torsion bars with upper/lower trailing arms. Suspension (rear): swing axles with trailing arms and torsion bars. Brakes: hydraulic, front/rear drum. Body Construction: steel unibody on stamped steel floor pan. Fuel Tank: 10.6 gallon.

PRODUCTION/SALES: 480,602 Volkswagens were sold in the United States during 1973 (including tourist deliveries).

MANUFACTURER: Volkswagenwerk AG, Wolfsburg, West Germany.

DISTRIBUTOR: Volkswagen of America Inc., Englewood Cliffs, New Jersey.

HISTORICAL FOOTNOTES: In 1973, Volkswagen's Beetle surpassed the production total set long before by the Model T Ford. Several "The Things" competed in the 1972 Baja 1000 race and one placed second in its class. Actor James Garner drove one to a second-in-class finish at the "Dam 500" off-road race. Some of these vehicles were used as police cars in Mexico.

1974

DASHER—FOUR The Dasher replaced the Fastback and the Squareback. It featured a front-mounted, water-cooled engine and front-wheel drive. *Road Test* magazine (May 1974) said, "It's a luxury, econo, sport sedan all rolled into one" The car had a full-width grille with single, round headlights at either side. There was a large, round VW emblem in the center. The front was slimlined, while the rear end had a wedge shape with an unusual rear quarter window on the sedan. The styling was done by Italian designer Giorgetto Giugiaro. The sedan model had a 17.3-cu.-ft. trunk. A three-speed automatic transmission was optional.

BEETLE—FOUR The 1974 Beetle got energy-absorbing bumpers, new wheels and a seatbelt-ignition interlock system. The front seat headrests were smaller.

SUPER BEETLE—FOUR The 1974 Super Beetle got the same changes as the Beetle. This was the final year for the "Super Beetle." *Road Test* magazine (April 1974) said that the last Super Beetle "had a heavy feeling, sits high and gives a cramped feeling to one used to more spacious cars. (The) chair-high seats might be right for

Above: One VW that stood out in the 1974 model year was the 412 series squareback.

Randy Ullenbrauck

some. Performance is not starling." The magazine noted that the only instrument was a large, center speedometer. The fuel gauge was inside the one circular dial. The seats were high and firm. There was little room for the driver's left foot and not much rear legroom. The test driver noted a blind spot to the left, but good vision to the rear. The steering was hard. The car was subject to crosswinds and gave a choppy, bouncy ride. *Road Test* said riders could feel the road surfaces. Seeming to contradict its first opinion, the magazine said the car had "a good performance feel"

This 1974 VW squareback is a well-preserved car that is carefully attended to by its owner.

Randy Ullenbrauck

Model Code	Body Type & Seating	POE Price	Weight (lbs.)	Production Total
DASHER				
3441	4d Hatchback-4/5P	4225	2050	Note 1
3241	2d Hatchback-4/5P	3975	1995	Note 1
3641	4d Station Wagon-4/5P	4295	2037	Note 1
BEETLE				
1111	2d Sedan-4P	2625	1831	Note 1
1511	2d Convertible-4P	3475	2043	Note 1
SUPER BEETLE				
1131	2d Sedan-4P	2849	1955	Note 1
KARMANN-GHIA				
1431	2d Coupe-2 + 2P	3475	1919	Note 1
1411	2d Convertible-2 + 2P	3935	1919	Note 1
412 (TYPE 4)				
4111	2d Sedan-5P	3775	2322	Note 1
4213	4d Sedan-5P	4100	2365	Note 1
4613	2d Station Wagon-5P	4200	2411	Note 1
TRANSPORTER				
2301	3d Kombi	4000	2946	Note 2
2211	3d Station Wagon-7P	4350	2946	Note 2
2231	3d Station Wagon-9P	4400	NA	Note 2
2391	3d Campmobile	5274	NA	Note 2

Note 1: 955,355 Volkswagen passenger cars (all models) were produced in 1974.
Note 2: 38,700 Transporters were produced in 1974.

The venerable Volkswagen Karmann-Ghia was discontinued after the 1974 model year.

Dick and Mary Lu Zellers

The venerable Karmann-Ghia continued its sporty look in 1974.

and advised that the brakes worked good. It had a high overall noise level, but only light wind noise was heard. The Super Beetle was 7th among nine imports tested for fuel economy.

KARMANN-GHIA—FOUR This was the final year for the stylish Karmann-Ghia Sport Coupe and convertible. *Road Test* (February 1974) noted the Karmann-Ghia had a few improvements for quieter running and greater durability. The sporty VW was now covered by a "Security Blanket" warrantee. It offered 14 cu. ft. of storage space behind its bucket seats. New for 1974 were "space-saving" front disc brakes with floating calipers and larger pads, self-restoring energy-absorbing bumpers that added 1/2-inch to vehicle length. A new alloy cylinder head was used in the Karmann-Ghia engine and a new muffler system reduced noise. The Karmann-Ghia also had wider front and rear track measurements and a computer-analysis function.

412—TYPE 4—FOUR This was the final season for the Type 4 series. A larger (109.5-cid) engine went into the four-door sedan and station wagon.

TRANSPORTER—FOUR A larger engine went into the Kombi and station wagons this year.

I.D. DATA: Volkswagen's 10-symbol serial number is on the upper left of the dashboard, visible through the windshield. The first two digits indicate the model, the next digit identifies the model year and the final seven digits form the sequential production number. Starting serial number: (Beetle) 1142000001, (Super Beetle) 1342000001, (convertible) 1542000001, (Karmann-Ghia) 1442000001, (412 two-door Sedan) 4142000001, (412 four-door Sedan) 42420000001, (412 Station Wagon) 46420000001, (Dasher sedan) 3242000001, (Dasher wagon) 33420000001, (Kombi) 2342000001, (Transporter) 2242000001.

ENGINE

BASE FOUR (Dasher): Inline. Single overhead cam. Overhead-valve. Four-cylinder (water cooled). Displacement: 89.7 cid (1471 cc). Bore & Stroke: 3.01 x 3.15 in. (76.5 x 80 mm). Compression Ratio: 8.5:1. Brake Horsepower: 75 at 5800 rpm. Torque: 81 lbs.-ft. at 4000 rpm. Solid valve lifters. Single two-barel carburetor.

BASE FOUR (Beetle, Super Beetle, Karmann-Ghia, The Thing): Horizontally opposed, overhead-valve four-cylinder (air cooled). Displacement: 96.7 cid (1585 cc). Bore & Stroke: 3.36 x 2.72 in. (85 x 69 mm). Compression Ratio: 7.3:1. Brake Horsepower: 46 at 4000 rpm. Torque: 72 lbs.-ft. at 2800 rpm. Four main bearings. Solid valve lifters. Single carburetor.

BASE FOUR (412): Horizontally opposed, overhead-valve four-cylinder (air cooled). Displacement: 102.5 cid (1679 cc). Bore & Stroke: 3.54 x 2.60 in. (90 x 66 mm). Compression Ratio: 8.2:1. Brake Horsepower: 76 at 4900 rpm. Torque: 95 lbs.-ft. at 2700 rpm. Four main bearings. Solid valve lifters. Bosch fuel injection.

BASE FOUR (TRANSPORTER): Horizontally opposed, overhead-valve four-cylinder (air cooled). Displacement: 109.5 cid (1795 cc). Bore & Stroke: 3.66 x 2.59 in. (93 x 66 mm). Compression Ratio: 7.3:1. Brake Horsepower: 65 at 4200 rpm. Torque: 91 lbs.-ft. at 3000 rpm. Four main bearings. Solid valve lifters.

CHASSIS

DASHER: Wheelbase: 97.2 in. Overall Length: 172.8 in. Height: 53.9. Width: 63 in. Front Tread: 52.7 in. Rear Tread: 52.6 in. Standard Tires: 155SR13.

BEETLE: Wheelbase: 94.5 in. Overall Length: 163.4 in. Height: 59.1 in. Width: 61.0 in. Front Tread: 51.5 in. Rear Tread: 53.1 in. Standard Tires: 6.00 x 15L.

SUPER: Wheelbase: 95.3 in. Overall Length: 164.8 in. Height: 59.1 in. Width: 62.4 in. Front Tread: 54.9 in. Rear Tread: 53.2 in. Standard Tires: (Beetle/Karmann-Ghia) 6.00 x 15L.

KARMANN-GHIA: Wheelbase: 94.5 in. Overall Length: 165.8 in. Height: 52 in. Width: 64.3 in. Front Tread: 51.7 in. Rear Tread: 53.1 in. Standard Tires: 6.00 x 15L.

412: Wheelbase: 98.4 in. Overall Length: 183.7 in. Height: NA. Width: NA. Front Tread: (54.6 in. Rear Tread: 53.2 in. Standard Tires: 155SR15.

TRANSPORTER: Wheelbase: 94.5 in. Overall Length: 179.0 in. Height: 76.4 in. Width: 69.3 in. Front Tread: 54.9 in. Rear Tread: 57.3 in. Standard Tires: 185R14C.

TECHNICAL

DASHER: Layout: front-engine, front-wheel-drive. Transmission: four-speed manual. Suspension (front): MacPherson struts, lower wishbones, coil springs and tubular shock absorbers. Suspension (rear): Beam axle with integral anti-sway bar, semi-trailing arms. Panhard rod, coil springs and tunular shocks. Steering: rack-and-pinion. Steering ratio: 20.2:1. Turns lock-to-lock: 3.94. Turning circle: 34 ft. Brakes: Front disc/rear drum. Body construction: Unit body and frame construction. Tires: 155SR x 13.

BEETLE: Layout: rear-engine, rear-drive. Transmission: four-speed manual. Suspension (front): transverse torsion bars with upper/lower trailing arms. Suspension (rear): independent with semi-trailing arms and torsion bars.

SUPER BEETLE: Layout: rear-engine, rear-drive. Transmission: four-speed manual. Suspension (front): (Super Beetle) MacPherson struts with coil springs. Suspension (rear): independent with semi-trailing arms and torsion bars.

KARMANN-GHIA: Layout: rear-engine, rear-drive. Transmission: four-speed manual. Suspension (front): transverse torsion bars with upper/lower trailing arms and ant-sway bar. Suspension (rear): independent with semi-trailing arms, diagonal links and torsion bars. Steering: worm-and-roller type. Brakes: Front disc/rear drum. Transmission: Four-speed manual. Final drive ratio: 3.875:1. Gas tank: 10.6 gal. Turning diameter: 36.9 ft.

412: Layout: rear-engine, rear-drive except. Transmission: four-speed manual. Suspension (front): MacPherson struts with coil springs. Suspension (rear): semi-trailing arms with coil springs.

The VW 412 series was powered by a 76.5-hp, 102.5-cid engine.

TRANSPORTER: Layout: rear-engine, rear-drive. Transmission: four-speed manual. Suspension (front): transverse torsion bars with upper/lower trailing arms. Suspension (rear): independent with semi-trailing arms and torsion bars.

OPTIONS

SUPER BEETLE: Air conditioning. AM radio.

PERFORMANCE: (Dasher 0-60 mph) 14.9 sec. (Dasher 1/4-mile): 20.09 sec. At 69.23 mph. Overall fuel economy 24.4 mpg. (Karmann-Ghia with manual transmission top speed) 88 mph. (Karmann-Ghia with automatic transmission top speed) 90 mph.

PRODUCTION/SALES: 336,257 Volkswagens were sold in the United States during 1974 (including tourist deliveries).

MANUFACTURER: Volkswagenwerk AG, Wolfsburg, West Germany.

DISTRIBUTOR: Volkswagen of America Inc., Englewood Cliffs, New Jersey.

HISTORICAL FOOTNOTES: A special Beetle that did 0-to-60 mph in 7.2 seconds and had a top speed of 130 mph was featured in the March 1974 issue of *Road Test* magazine. The VW Nordstadt was made by a German "tuner" company and required 2000 hours of labor to create. The car used a VW/Porsche 914 chassis and a 2687-cc 210-hp flat six Carrera engine. It carried a base price of $23,000.

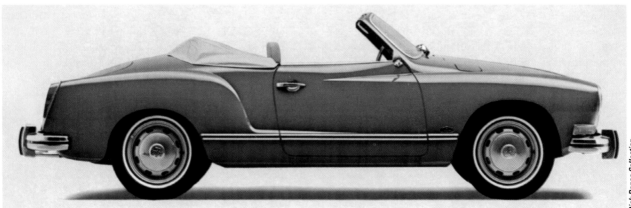

The Karmann-Ghia, introduced in the 1950s, still looked good in 1974.

1975

DASHER—FOUR Production of the front-engined, front-wheel-drive Volkswagen Dasher, introduced for 1974, continued into 1975 with little change. For 1976, a larger (1588-cc) engine replaced the original 1471-cc unit.

RABBIT—FOUR A transverse-mounted 1471-cc engine went into the new front-wheel-drive Rabbit. Early Rabbits had all-drum brakes. Deluxe and Custom models added open-up vent windows.

SCIROCCO—FOUR Following the demise of the Karmann-Ghia, Volkswagen needed another sporty model and found it in the Scirocco hatchback coupe. It was named for a North African wind. "German sports car, Italian style" was the slogan. Like the Rabbit and Dasher, the Scirocco used front-wheel drive. Styling features included quad round headlights and a short tail. *Road Test* magazine (May 1974) described the Scirocco as possibly "the most important new car launched from Wolfsburg since the original, air-cooled flat four." The Scirocco shared Volkswagen's optional 1.5-liter engine with the Dasher. Like the Dasher, it was developed by Italian designer Giorgetto Giugiaro. It had a wedge-shaped body.

Small spoilers front and rear improved air flow. The rain gutters were specially designed to hold down wind noise. The Scirocco came only as a two-door hatchback coupe. Design goals for the car included a large wheelbase for a relatively small car. The car rode high off of its 13-inch wheels and had a very flat drive shaft tunnel. Two adults fit easily in front and two kids could squeeze in back. Plain, L, LS and TS models were offered. The L included rubber bumper strips, an electrically-heated rear window, reclining seats, interval wipers, a resettable trip odometer and a trunk light. The TS included dual iodine headlights, "tombstone" seats, a sporty leatherette steering wheel, a console and a tachometer. Extras included a leatherette seat (in place of a plaid one), alloy wheels, headlight washers and tinted glass.

Above: **New from Volkswagen in 1975 was the practical Rabbit sedan.**

Phil Hall

The new 1975 Rabbit had a front-mounted engine and front-wheel drive.

Dick Dance Collection

Volkswagen needed another sporty model and found it in the Scirocco hatchback coupe.

Bottom: **The new VW for those seeking a sports car was the 1975 Scirocco.**

Dick Dance Collection

1975 VOLKSWAGEN PRODUCTION CHART

1975 VOLKSWAGEN PRODUCTION CHART

Model Code	Body Type & Seating	POE Price	Weight (lbs.)	ProductionTotal
DASHER				
3241	2d Hatchback-4/5P	4510	1995	Note 1
3441	4d Hatchback-4/5P	4650	2050	Note 1
3643	4d Station Wagon-4/5P	4875	2105	Note 1
RABBIT				
1701	2d Hatchback-4/5P	3330	1757	Note 1
RABBIT CUSTOM				
1721	2d Hatchback-4/5P	3660	1797	Note 1
1741	4d Hatchback-4/5P	3800	1827	Note 1
RABBIT DELUXE				
1761	2d Hatchback-4/5P	3890	1817	Note 1
1781	4d Hatchback-4/5P	4030	1847	Note 1
SCIROCCO				
5311	2d Coupe-4P	4949	1847	Note 1
BEETLE				
1101	2d Sedan-4P	2999	1831	Note 1
1111	2d Sedan-4P	3295	1831	Note 1
1511	2d Convertible-4P	3595	1955	Note 1
TRANSPORTER (TYPE II)				
2301	3d Kombi	4750	2825	Note 2
2211	3d Station Wagon-7P	5100	2946	Note 2
2231	3d Station Wagon-9P	5150	2946	Note 2
2391	3d Campmobile	6174	2719	Note 2

Note 1: 904,005 Volkswagen passenger cars (all models) were produced in 1975.
Note 2: 29,082 Transporters were produced in 1975.

BEETLE—FOUR Electronic fuel injection became standard in Beetles for 1975.

TRANSPORTER—FOUR Electronic fuel injection was now standard in the boxy station wagon's rear engine.

I.D. DATA: Volkswagen's 10-symbol serial number is on the upper left of the dashboard, visible through the windshield. The first two digits indicate the model, the next digit identifies the model year, and the final seven digits form the sequential production number.

ENGINE

BASE FOUR (Dasher, Rabbit, Scirocco): Inline, overhead-cam four-cylinder (water cooled). Displacement: 89.7 cid (1471 cc). Bore & Stroke: 3.01 x 3.15 in. (76.5 x 80 mm). Compression Ratio: 8.2:1. Brake Horsepower: 70 at 5800 rpm. Torque: 81 lbs.-ft. at 3500 rpm. Solid valve lifters. Two-barrel carburetor.

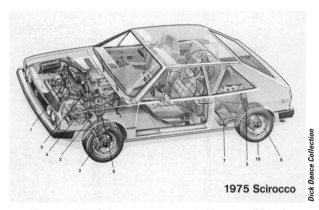

1975 Scirocco

Dick Dance Collection

The new 1975 Scirocco was promoted by a traditional Volkswagen diagram

Electronic fuel injection was a new feature in the 1975 VW Beetle.

BASE FOUR (Beetle): Horizontally opposed, overhead-valve four-cylinder (air cooled). Displacement: 96.7 cid (1585 cc). Bore & Stroke: 3.36 x 2.72 in. (85 x 69 mm). Compression Ratio: 7.3:1. Brake Horsepower: 48 at 4200 rpm. Torque: 73.1 lbs.-ft. at 2800 rpm. Four main bearings. Solid valve lifters. Electronic fuel injection.

BASE FOUR (Transporter): Horizontally opposed, overhead-valve four-cylinder (air cooled). Displacement: 109.5 cid (1795 cc). Bore & Stroke: 3.66 x 2.59 in. (93 x 66 mm). Compression Ratio: 7.3:1. Brake Horsepower: 67 at 4400 rpm. Torque: 90 lbs.-ft. at 2400 rpm. Four main bearings. Solid valve lifters. Electronic fuel injection.

CHASSIS

DASHER: Wheelbase: 97.2 in. Overall Length: 172.8 in. Height: 53.9. Width: 63 in. Front Tread: 52.7 in. Rear Tread: 52.6 in. Standard Tires: 155SR13.

RABBIT: Wheelbase: 94.5 in. Overall Length: 155.3 in. Height: 55.5 in. Width: 63.4 in. Front Tread: 54.7 in. Rear Tread: 53.1 in. Standard Tires: 145x13.

SCIROCCO: Wheelbase: 94.5 in. Overall Length: 155.7 in. Height: 51.5 in. Width: 64.0 in. Front Tread: 54.7 in. Rear Tread: 53.1 in. Standard Tires: 155SR 13 steel-belted radials.

BEETLE: Wheelbase: 94.5 in. Overall Length: 163.4 in. Height: 59.1 in. Width: 61.0 in. Front Tread: 51.5 in. Rear Tread: 53.1 in. Standard Tires: 6.00 x 15L.

TRANSPORTER: Wheelbase: 94.5 in. Overall Length: 179.0 in. Height: 76.4 in. Width: 69.3 in. Front Tread: 54.9 in. Rear Tread: 57.3 in. Standard Tires: 185R14C.

TECHNICAL

DASHER: Layout: front-engine, front-wheel-drive. Transmission: four-speed manual. Suspension (front): MacPherson struts, lower wishbones, coil springs and tubular shock absorbers. Suspension (rear): Beam axle with integral anti-sway bar, semi-trailing arms. Panhard rod, coil springs and tunular shocks. Steering: rack-and-pinion. Steering ratio: 20.2:1. Turns lock-to-lock: 3.94. Turning circle: 34 ft. Brakes: Front disc/rear drum. Body construction: Unit body and frame construction. Tires: 155SR x 13.

RABBIT: Layout: front-engine, front-wheel-drive. Transmission: four-speed manual. Suspension (front): MacPherson struts with coil springs. Suspension (rear): independent stabilizer axle with struts and coil springs. Brakes: front/rear drum, (others) front disc, rear drum.

SCIROCCO: Layout: front-engine, front-wheel-drive. Transmission: four-speed manual. Suspension (front): Independent with wishbones, spring legs and stabilizer. Suspension (rear): Rear torque tube rubber-bushed to chassis with trailing arms and spring legs. Brakes: front/rear drum, (others) front disc, rear drum.

BEETLE: Layout: rear-engine, rear-drive. Transmission: four-speed manual. Suspension (front): transverse torsion bars with upper/lower trailing arms. Suspension (rear): independent with semi-trailing arms and torsion bars.

TRANSPORTER: Layout: rear-engine, rear-drive. Transmission: four-speed manual. Suspension (front): transverse torsion bars with upper/lower trailing arms. Suspension (rear): independent with semi-trailing arms and torsion bars.

PERFORMANCE: Top Speed: (Dasher) 100 mph claimed, (Rabbit) 93 mph claimed, (Scirocco) 103 mph claimed (100 mph with automatic).

PRODUCTION/SALES: 268,751 Volkswagens were sold in the United States during 1975 (including tourist deliveries).

MANUFACTURER: Volkswagenwerk AG, Wolfsburg, West Germany.

DISTRIBUTOR: Volkswagen of America Inc., Englewood Cliffs, New Jersey.

"*The family car of the future... for the next 25 years!*" POPULAR MECHANICS

DASHER

The 1975 VW Dasher was available in two- and four-door hatchbacks and a wagon.

Right: **Electronic fuel injection was a new feature in the 1975 VW Beetle.**

Dick Dance Collection

1976

DASHER—FOUR Production of the front-engined, front-wheel-drive Volkswagen, introduced for 1974, continued into 1976 and a larger 1588-cc engine replaced the original 1471-cc unit.

RABBIT—FOUR A transverse-mounted 1588-cc four-cylinder engine went into the front-wheel-drive 1976 Volkswagen Rabbit. Custom models had opening vent windows.

Above: **The VW Beetle continued to be a presence in the 1976 Volkswagen product line.**
Phil Hall

SCIROCCO—FOUR After one year on the market, the Scirocco adopted a larger 1588-cc four. Styling features included quad round headlights and a short tail.

BEETLE—FOUR Sporty new wheels were used on the 1976 Beetle. A rear window defogger was also installed.

TRANSPORTER—FOUR The 1976 Volkswagen Transporters got a larger new 1970-cc engine. Also starting in 1976, an exposed fuel filler cap was used.

I.D. DATA: Volkswagen's 10-symbol serial number is on the upper left of the dashboard, visible through the

Model Code	Body Type & Seating	POE Price	Weight (lbs.)	ProductionTotal
	DASHER			
3241	2d Hatchback-4/5P	5195	2129	Note 1
3441	4d Hatchback-4/5P	5275	2184	Note 1
3643	4d Station Wagon-4/5P	5525	2302	Note 1
	RABBIT			
1701	2d Hatchback-4/5P	3499	1782	Note 1
	RABBIT CUSTOM			
1721	2d Hatchback-4/5P	3895	1842	Note 1
1741	4d Hatchback-4/5P	4035	1872	Note 1
	RABBIT DELUXE			
1721	2d Hatchback-4/5P	4175	1862	Note 1
1741	4d Hatchback-4/5P	4315	1892	Note 1
	SCIROCCO			
5311	2d Coupe-4P	4995	1937	Note 1
	BEETLE			
1111	2d Sedan-4P	3499	1720	Note 1
1511	2d Convertible-4P	4545	2110	Note 1
	TRANSPORTER (TYPE II)			
2301	3d Kombi	5235	2693	Note 2
2211	3d Station Wagon-7P	2946	2946	Note 2
2231	3d Station Wagon-9P	5545	2946	Note 2
2391	3d Campmobile	5194	2719	Note 2

Note 1: 1,061,940 Volkswagen passenger cars (all models) were produced in 1976.
Note 2: 31,390 Transporters were produced in 1976.

More than 200,000 Volkswagens were sold in the United States in 1976.

windshield. The first two digits indicate the model, the next digit identifies the model year, and the final seven digits form the sequential production number.

ENGINE

BASE FOUR (Rabbit, Scirocco): Inline, overhead-cam four-cylinder (water cooled). Cast-iron block and aluminum alloy head. Displacement: 97.0 cid (1588 cc). Bore & Stroke: 3.13 x 3.15 in. (79.5 x 80 mm). Compression Ratio: 8.2:1. Brake Horsepower: 71 at 5600 rpm. Torque: 82 lbs.-ft. at 3300 rpm. Five main bearings. Solid valve lifters. Zenith two-barrel carburetor.

BASE FOUR (Dasher): Inline, overhead-cam four-cylinder (water cooled). Cast-iron block and aluminum alloy head. Displacement: 97.0 cid (1588 cc). Bore & Stroke: 3.13 x 3.15 in. (79.5 x 80 mm). Compression Ratio: 8.2:1. Brake Horsepower: 78 at 5500 rpm. Torque: 82 lbs.-ft. at 3300 rpm. Five main bearings. Solid valve lifters. CIS fuel injection.

BASE FOUR (Beetle): Horizontally opposed, overhead-valve four-cylinder (air cooled). Displacement: 96.7 cid (1585 cc). Bore & Stroke: 3.36 x 2.72 in. (85 x 69 mm). Compression Ratio: 7.3:1. Brake Horsepower: 48 at 4200 rpm. Torque: 73.1 lbs.-ft. at 2800 rpm. Four main bearings. Solid valve lifters. Electronic fuel injection.

BASE FOUR (Transporter): Horizontally opposed, overhead-valve four- cylinder (air cooled). Displacement: 120.2 cid (1970 cc). Bore & Stroke: 3.70 x 2.80 in. (94 x 71 mm). Compression Ratio: 7.3:1. Brake Horsepower: 67 at 4200 rpm. Torque: 101 lbs.- ft. at 3000 rpm. Four main bearings. Solid valve lifters. Electronic fuel injection.

CHASSIS

DASHER: Wheelbase: 97.2 in. Overall Length: 172.8 in. Height: 53.9 in. Width: 63 in. Front Tread: 52.7 in. Rear Tread: 52.6 in. Standard Tires: 155SR13.

RABBIT: Wheelbase: 94.5 in. Overall Length: 155.3 in. Height: 55.5 in. Width: 63.4 in. Front Tread: 54.7 in. Rear Tread: 53.1 in. Standard Tires: 145x13.

SCIROCCO: Wheelbase: 94.5 in. Overall Length: 155.7 in. Height: 51.5 in. Width: 64.0 in. Front Tread: 54.7 in. Rear Tread: 53.1 in. Standard Tires: 175/70SR13.

BEETLE: Wheelbase: 94.5 in. Overall Length: 163.4 in. Height: 59.1 in. Width: 61.0 in. Front Tread: 51.5 in. Rear Tread: 53.1 in. Standard Tires: 6.00 x 15L.

TRANSPORTER: Wheelbase: 94.5 in. Overall Length: 179.0 in. Height: 76.4 in. Width: 69.3 in. Front Tread: 54.9 in. Rear Tread: 57.3 in. Standard Tires: 185R14C.

TECHNICAL

DASHER: Layout: front-engine, front-wheel-drive. Transmission: four-speed manual. Suspension (front): MacPherson struts, lower wishbones, coil springs and tubular shock absorbers. Suspension (rear): Beam axle with integral anti-sway bar, semi-trailing arms. Panhard

Whether they were coming or going, the VW Beetle was a special car for drivers in 1976.

Phil Hall

rod, coil springs and tunular shocks. Steering: rack-and-pinion. Steering ratio: 20.2:1. Turns lock-to-lock: 3.94. Turning circle: 34 ft. Brakes: Front disc/rear drum. Body construction: Unit body and frame construction. Tires: 155SR x 13.

RABBIT: Layout: front-engine, front-wheel-drive. Transmission: four-speed manual. Suspension (front): MacPherson struts with coil springs. Suspension (rear): independent stabilizer axle with struts and coil springs. Brakes: front/rear drum, (others) front disc, rear drum.

SCIROCCO: Layout: front-engine, front-wheel-drive. Transmission: four-speed manual. Suspension (front): Independent with wishbones, spring legs and stabilizer. Suspension (rear): Rear torque tube rubber-bushed to chassis with trailing arms and spring legs. Brakes: front/rear drum, (others) front disc, rear drum.

BEETLE: Layout: rear-engine, rear-drive. Transmission: four-speed manual. Suspension (front): transverse torsion bars with upper/lower trailing arms. Suspension (rear): independent with semi-trailing arms and torsion bars.

TRANSPORTER: Layout: rear-engine, rear-drive. Transmission: four-speed manual. Suspension (front): transverse torsion bars with upper/lower trailing arms. Suspension (rear): independent with semi-trailing arms and torsion bars.

PERFORMANCE: Top Speed: (Dasher) 100 mph claimed, (Rabbit) 93 mph claimed, (Scirocco) 103 mph claimed, but 100 mph with automatic transmission.

PRODUCTION/SALES: 203,234 Volkswagens were sold in the United States during 1976 (including tourist deliveries).

MANUFACTURER: Volkswagenwerk AG, Wolfsburg, West Germany.

DISTRIBUTOR: Volkswagen of America Inc., Englewood Cliffs, New Jersey.

John Gunnell

The VW Campmobile was listed at $5,194 and weighed 2,719 pounds in 1976.

1977

DASHER—FOUR Production of the front-engined, front-wheel-drive Volkswagen with the 1588-cc engine continued into 1977 with little change.

RABBIT—FOUR The Rabbit's 1588-cc four was now fuel injected. A diesel engine also became available in 1977. After 1977, the Rabbit would also be built in the United States

SCIROCCO—FOUR Standard equipment in the 1977 version of Volkswagen's sporty coupe included tinted glass, styled wheels, a clock, reclining bucket seats and a rear defogger.

BEETLE—FOUR This was the Beetle sedan's last year in the U.S. market.

TRANSPORTER—FOUR Any changes in the 1977 Transporter were modest ones.

I.D. DATA: Volkswagen's 10-symbol serial number is on the upper left of the dashboard, visible through the windshield. The first two digits indicate the model, the next digit identifies the model year, and the final seven digits form the sequential production number.

ENGINE

BASE FOUR (1976 Rabbit, Scirocco): Inline, overhead-cam four-cylinder (water cooled). Cast-iron block and aluminum alloy head. Displacement: 97.0 cid (1588 cc). Bore & Stroke: 3.13 x 3.15 in. (79.5 x 80 mm). Compression Ratio: 8.2:1. Brake Horsepower: 78 at 5500 rpm. Torque: 82 lbs.-ft. at 3300 rpm. Five main bearings. Solid valve lifters. CIS fuel injection.

Note: *Starting in 1977, a 1471-cc diesel engine became available in Rabbits.*

ENGINE BASE FOUR (Beetle): Horizontally opposed, overhead-valve four-cylinder (air cooled). Displacement: 96.7 cid (1585 cc). Bore & Stroke: 3.36 x 2.72 in. (85 x 69 mm). Compression Ratio: 7.3:1. Brake Horsepower: 48 at 4200 rpm. Torque: 73.1 lbs.-ft. at 2800 rpm. Four main bearings. Solid valve lifters. Electronic fuel injection.

BASE FOUR (Transporter): Horizontally opposed, overhead-valve four- cylinder (air cooled). Displacement: 120.2 cid (1970 cc). Bore & Stroke: 3.70 x 2.80 in. (94 x 71 mm). Compression Ratio: 7.3:1. Brake Horsepower: 67 at 4200 rpm. Torque: 101 lbs.- ft. at 3000 rpm. Four main bearings. Solid valve lifters. Electronic fuel injection.

Left: **While the last year for the Beetle sedan, the convertible was still popular in 1977.**

Paul Smith

The 1977 model year was the last time buyers could purchase a new Beetle sedan in the United States.

1977 VOLKSWAGEN PRODUCTION CHART

Model Code	Body Type & Seating	POE Price	Weight (lbs.)	ProductionTotal
DASHER				
3241	2d Hatchback-4/5P	5399	2085	Note 1
3441	4d Hatchback-4/5P	5499	2140	Note 1
3643	4d Station Wagon-4/5P	5749	2180	Note 1
RABBIT				
1701	2d Hatchback-4/5P	3599	1800	Note 1
RABBIT CUSTOM				
1721	2d Hatchback-4/5P	4079	1856	Note 1
1741	4d Hatchback-4/5P	4219	1911	Note 1
RABBIT DELUXE				
1721	2d Hatchback-4/5P	4379	1856	Note 1
1741	4d Hatchback-4/5P	4519	1911	Note 1
SCIROCCO				
5311	2d Coupe-4P	5295	1888	Note 1
BEETLE				
1111	2d Sedan-4P	3699	1905	Note 1
1511	2d Convertible-4P	4799	2030	Note 1
TRANSPORTER (TYPE II)				
2301	3d Kombi	5249	2701	Note 2
2211	3d Station Wagon-7P	5725	2952	Note 2
2231	3d Station Wagon-9P	5775	2952	Note 2
2391	3d Campmobile	5299	2724	Note 2

Note 1: 1,123,575 Volkswagen passenger cars (all models) were produced in 1977.
Note 2: 38,068 Transporters were produced in 1977.

The Dashers were powered by a 1588-cc engine during the 1977 model year.

CHASSIS

DASHER: Wheelbase: 97.2 in. Overall Length: 172.8 in. Height: 53.9 in. Width: 63 in. Front Tread: 52.7 in. Rear Tread: 52.6 in. Standard Tires: 155SR13.

RABBIT: Wheelbase: 94.5 in. Overall Length: 155.3 in. Height: 55.5 in. Width: 63.4 in. Front Tread: 54.7 in. Rear Tread: 53.1 in. Standard Tires: 145x13.

SCIROCCO: Wheelbase: 94.5 in. Overall Length: 155.7 in. Height: 51.5 in. Width: 64.0 in. Front Tread: 54.7 in. Rear Tread: 53.1 in. Standard Tires: 175/70SR13.

BEETLE: Wheelbase: 94.5 in. Overall Length: 163.4 in. Height: 59.1 in. Width: 61.0 in. Front Tread: 51.5 in. Rear Tread: 53.1 in. Standard Tires: 6.00 x 15L.

TRANSPORTER: Wheelbase: 94.5 in. Overall Length: 179.0 in. Height: 76.4 in. Width: 69.3 in. Front Tread: 54.9 in. Rear Tread: 57.3 in. Standard Tires: 185R14C.

TECHNICAL

DASHER: Layout: front-engine, front-wheel-drive. Transmission: four-speed manual. Suspension (front): MacPherson struts, lower wishbones, coil springs and tubular shock absorbers. Suspension (rear): Beam axle with integral anti-sway bar, semi-trailing arms. Panhard rod, coil springs and tunular shocks. Steering: rack-and-pinion. Steering ratio: 20.2:1. Turns lock-to-lock: 3.94. Turning circle: 34 ft. Brakes: Front disc/rear drum. Body construction: Unit body and frame construction. Tires: 155SR x 13.

RABBIT: Layout: front-engine, front-wheel-drive. Transmission: four-speed manual. Suspension (front): MacPherson struts with coil springs. Suspension (rear): independent stabilizer axle with struts and coil springs. Brakes: front/rear drum, (others) front disc, rear drum.

SCIROCCO: Layout: front-engine, front-wheel-drive. Transmission: four-speed manual. Suspension (front): Independent with wishbones, spring legs and stabilizer. Suspension (rear): Rear torque tube rubber-bushed to chassis with trailing arms and spring legs. Brakes: front/rear drum, (others) front disc, rear drum.

BEETLE: Layout: rear-engine, rear-drive. Transmission: four-speed manual. Suspension (front): transverse torsion bars with upper/lower trailing arms. Suspension (rear): independent with semi-trailing arms and torsion bars.

TRANSPORTER: Layout: rear-engine, rear-drive. Transmission: four-speed manual. Suspension (front): transverse torsion bars with upper/lower trailing arms. Suspension (rear): independent with semi-trailing arms and torsion bars.

PERFORMANCE: Top Speed: (Dasher) 100 mph claimed, (Rabbit) 93 mph claimed, (Scirocco) 103 mph claimed (100 mph with automatic).

PRODUCTION/SALES: 262,932 Volkswagens were sold in the United States during 1977.

MANUFACTURER: Volkswagenwerk AG, Wolfsburg, West Germany.

DISTRIBUTOR: Volkswagen of America Inc., Englewood Cliffs, New Jersey.

The popularity of the VW Campmobile continued in 1977.

Rabbits came with fuel injection or diesel engine choices in 1977.

1978

DASHER—FOUR Quad round headlights replaced the former single round units on Volkswagen's first front-wheel-drive model. The headlights, combined with a new grille and hood line, that gave the car a fresh look. It somewhat resembled the new Audi 5000. Large amber safety lights were installed at the front fender tips. The rear end had wraparound taillights and polyurethane-coated bumpers. As before, the Dasher came as a two-door hatchback, a four-door sedan or a four-door station wagon. The trim was upgraded at this time and the ride quality was softened. The seats had velour upholstery.

RABBIT—FOUR A smaller (1457-cc) engine went into the Rabbit for 1978, and the radiator was enlarged. Otherwise, production continued with little change except for additional chrome. Starting in 1978, Rabbits were also produced in America. German-built Rabbits kept their round headlights, while those from Pennsylvania switched to rectangular headlights. A "Champagne Edition" introduced in mid-1978 included Silver-Green or Rose Metallic paint with crushed velour upholstery. The diesel-engined Rabbit, rated 48 hp, earned an EPA rating of 53 mpg (highway) and 40 mpg (city). The diesel model was built only in Germany.

SCIROCCO—FOUR A smaller 1457-cc engine was installed in 1978 Sciroccos. A new polyurethane-coated front bumper extended back to the front wheel openings and new black metal moldings went around the side windows. The Scirocco grille was restyled and a woodgrained instrument panel was added. A Limited Edition Scirocco was offered in 1978 and included body striping and a spoiler.

BEETLE—FOUR Only the Beetle convertible remained in the United States market after 1977. *Car and Driver* declared that the top-down Beetle "can be one of the world's finest convertibles." Though "terribly slow . . . the flat-out driving style required to keep it moving compensates for a lot of flaws." With so "few weaknesses" remaining, they added, it should be regarded "as an institution rather than an automobile." Only a four-speed manual gearbox was available.

TRANSPORTER—FOUR The Transporter again had no changes. Power came from a 2.0-liter horizontally-opposed rear-mounted engine. EPA mileage ratings by 1978 were 18 mpg (city) and 25 mpg (highway) with manual shift, dropping to 16/22 with automatic transmission.

Above: **The square-shaped VW Rabbit was a popular, American-made car in 1978.**

Dick Dance Collection

Model Code	Body Type & Seating	POE Price	Weight (lbs.)	ProductionTotal
DASHER				
3241	2d Hatchback-4/5P	5975	2085	Note 1
3441	4d Hatchback-4/5P	6075	2140	Note 1
3641	4d Station Wagon-4/5P	6375	2181	Note 1
RABBIT				
1701	2d Hatchback-4/5P	4220	1777	Note 1
RABBIT CUSTOM				
1721	2d Hatchback-4/5P	4699	1900	Note 1
1741	4d Hatchback-4/5P	4839	1955	Note 1
RABBIT DELUXE				
1761	2d Hatchback-4/5P	5060	1900	Note 1
1781	4d Hatchback-4/5P	5200	1955	Note 1
SCIROCCO				
5311	2d Coupe-4P	6095	1888	Note 1
BEETLE (TYPE I)				
1511	2d Convertible-4P	5695	2059	Note 1
TRANSPORTER (TYPE II)				
2321	3d Kombi	6185	2831	Note 2
2211	3d Station Wagon-7P	6445	2952	Note 2
2231	3d Station Wagon-9P	6495	2952	Note 2
2391	3d Campmobile	6145	2724	Note 2

Note 1: 1,177,106 Volkswagen passenger cars (all models) were produced in 1978.
Note 2: 34,331 Transporters were produced in 1978.

The Rabbit became a popular choice for VW buyers in 1978.

Dick Dance Collection

The Dasher Wagon was a practical and stylish offering.

Dick Dance Collection

Quad headlights and velour upholstery were among changes to the 1977 Dashers.

I.D. DATA: Volkswagen's 10-symbol serial number is on the upper left of the dashboard, visible through the windshield. The first two digits indicate the model, the next digit identifies the model year, and the final seven digits form the sequential production number.

ENGINE

BASE FOUR (Rabbit, Scirocco): Inline, overhead-cam four-cylinder (water cooled). Cast-iron block and aluminum alloy head. Displacement: 88.9 cid (1457 cc). Bore & Stroke: 3.13 x 2.89 in. (79.5 x 73.4 mm). Compression Ratio: 8.0:1. Brake Horsepower: 71 at 5800 rpm. Torque: 73 lbs.-ft. at 3500 rpm. Five main bearings. Solid valve lifters. Fuel injection.

Note: A 1471-cc diesel engine, rated 48 hp at 5000 rpm, was also available in Rabbits. Gasoline-engine horsepower ratings were lower in California.

BASE FOUR (Dasher): Inline, overhead-cam four-cylinder (water cooled). Cast-iron block and aluminum alloy head. Displacement: 97.0 cid (1588 cc). Bore & Stroke: 3.13 x 3.15 in. (79.5 x 80 mm). Compression Ratio: 8.0:1. Brake Horsepower: 78 at 5500 rpm. Torque: 84 lbs.-ft. at 3200 rpm. Five main bearings. Solid valve lifters. CIS fuel injection.

BASE FOUR (Beetle): Horizontally opposed, overhead-valve four-cylinder (air cooled). Displacement: 96.7 cid (1585 cc). Bore & Stroke: 3.36 x 2.72 in. (85 x 69 mm). Compression Ratio: 7.3:1. Brake Horsepower: 48 at 4200 rpm. Torque: 73.1 lbs.-ft. at 2800 rpm. Four main bearings. Solid valve lifters. Electronic fuel injection.

BASE FOUR (TRANSPORTER): Horizontally opposed, overhead-valve four-cylinder (air cooled). Displacement: 120.2 cid (1970 cc). Bore & Stroke: 3.70 x 2.80 in. (94 x 71 mm). Compression Ratio: 7.3:1. Brake Horsepower: 67 at 4200 rpm. Torque: 101 lbs.-ft. at 3000 rpm. Four main bearings. Solid valve lifters. Electronic fuel injection.

CHASSIS

DASHER: Wheelbase: 96.7 in., (diesel) 97.2 in. Overall Length: 172.4 in. Height: 53.5 in. Width: 63.0 in. Front Tread: 52.7 in. Rear Tread: 52.5 in. Standard Tires: 155SR13.

RABBIT: Wheelbase: 94.4 in. Overall Length: 155.3 in. Height: 55.5 in. Width: 63.4 in. Front Tread: 54.7 in. Rear

David Lyon

The 1978 VW Beetle was still considered a top choice for convertible buyers.

Tread: 53.5 in., (Scirocco) 53.5 in. Standard Tires: 145 x 13, (diesel) 155SR13.

SCIROCCO: Wheelbase: 94.5 in. Overall Length: 155.7 in. Height: 51.5 in. Width: 63.9 in., (Transporter) 69.3 in. Front Tread: 54.7 in. Rear Tread: 53.5 in. Standard Tires: 175/70SR13.

BEETLE (TYPE II): Wheelbase: 94.5 in. Overall Length: 164.8 in. Height: 59.1 in. Width: 62.4 in. Front Tread: 54.9 in., Rear Tread: 54.7 in. Standard Tires: 165SR15.

TRANSPORTER: Wheelbase: 94.5 in. Overall Length: 179.0 in. Height: 77 in. Width: 69.3 in. Front Tread: 54.9 in. Rear Tread: 57.3 in. Standard Tires: 185R14C.

TECHNICAL

DASHER: Layout: front-engine, front-wheel-drive. Transmission: four-speed manual. Suspension (front): MacPherson struts, lower wishbones, coil springs and tubular shock absorbers. Suspension (rear): Beam axle with integral anti-sway bar, semi-trailing arms. Panhard

John Gunnell

VW sales success was news in 1978 as Japanese cars were dominant imports.

rod, coil springs and tunular shocks. Steering: rack-and-pinion. Steering ratio: 20.2:1. Turns lock-to-lock: 3.94. Turning circle: 34 ft. Brakes: Front disc/rear drum. Body construction: Unit body and frame construction. Tires: 155SR x 13.

RABBIT: Layout: front-engine, front-wheel-drive. Transmission: four-speed manual. Front suspension: MacPherson struts with coil springs. Rear suspension: independent with trailing arms and coil springs. Brakes: front disc, rear drum.

SCIROCCO: Layout: front-engine, front-wheel-drive. Transmission: four-speed manual. Suspension (front): Independent with wishbones, spring legs and stabilizer. Suspension (rear): Rear torque tube rubber-bushed to chassis with trailing arms and spring legs. Brakes: front/rear drum, (others) front disc, rear drum.

BEETLE (TYPE II): Layout: rear-engine, rear-drive. Transmission: four-speed manual. Front suspension: MacPherson struts with coil springs. Rear suspension: semi-trailing arms with torsion bars. Brakes: front/rear drum.

TRANSPORTER (TYPE II): Layout: rear-engine, rear-drive. Transmission: four-speed manual. Front suspension: MacPherson struts with coil springs. Rear suspension: semi-trailing arms with torsion bars. Brakes: front/rear drum.

PRODUCTION/SALES: 219,414 Volkswagens were sold in the United States during 1978.

MANUFACTURER: Volkswagenwerk AG, Wolfsburg, West Germany.

DISTRIBUTOR: Volkswagen of America Inc., Englewood Cliffs, New Jersey.

HISTORICAL FOOTNOTES: Difficulty in meeting emissions standards contributed to the demise of the Beetle, as did certain safety problems.

Left: **Volkswagen promoted specially prepared Champagne Edition models in 1978.**

Dick Dance Collection

Right: **The 1978 Rabbit was given the traditional Volkswagen diagram treatment.**

Dick Dance Collection

1979

DASHER—FOUR As before, the Dasher came as a two-door hatchback, four-door sedan, or four-door station wagon. A diesel engine became available in 1979 Dashers.

RABBIT—FOUR Rabbit production continued with little change. A five-speed manual gearbox became available by 1979. The diesel-engined Rabbit, rated 48 hp was still built only in Germany.

SCIROCCO—FOUR By model-year 1979, the 1588-cc four-cylinder engine returned. The new model also added a bright molding surrounding the grille. The choice of a four- or five-speed manual gearbox was offered, along with an optional three-speed automatic transmission.

BEETLE—FOUR Only the Beetle convertible remained once again.

TRANSPORTER—FOUR The Transporter again was little changed.

Above: **One of the final Beetle convertibles, this 1979 model still is driven and enjoyed by its owner.**
Vance Day

I.D. DATA: Volkswagen's 10-symbol serial number is on the upper left of the dashboard, visible through the windshield. The first two digits indicate the model, the next digit identifies the model year, and the final seven digits form the sequential production number.

ENGINE

BASE FOUR (Rabbit): Inline, overhead-cam four-cylinder (water cooled). Cast-iron block and aluminum alloy head. Displacement: 88.9 cid (1457 cc). Bore & Stroke: 3.13 x 2.89 in. (79.5 x 73.4 mm). Compression Ratio: 8.0:1. Brake Horsepower: 71 at 5800 rpm. Torque: 73 lbs.-ft. at 3500 rpm. Five main bearings. Solid valve lifters. Fuel injection.

Note: A 1471-cc diesel engine, rated 48 hp at 5000 rpm, was also available in Rabbits. Gasoline-engine horsepower ratings were lower in California.

BASE FOUR (Dasher, Scirocco): Inline, overhead-cam four-cylinder (water cooled). Cast-iron block and aluminum alloy head. Displacement: 97.0 cid (1588 cc). Bore & Stroke: 3.13 x 3.15 in. (79.5 x 80 mm). Compression Ratio: 8.0:1. Brake Horsepower: 78 at 5500 rpm. Torque: 84 lbs.-ft. at 3200 rpm. Five main bearings. Solid valve lifters. CIS fuel injection.

Model Code	Body Type & Seating	POE Price	Weight (lbs.)	ProductionTotal
DASHER				
3241	2d Hatchback-4/5P	7228	2085	Note 1
3441	4d Hatchback-4/5P	7418	2140	Note 1
3641	4d Station Wagon-4/5P	7673	2180	Note 1
RABBIT				
1701	2d Hatchback-4/5P	4799	1719	Note 1
RABBIT CUSTOM				
1721	2d Hatchback-4/5P	5199	1900	Note 1
1741	4d Hatchback-4/5P	5359	1900	Note 1
RABBIT DELUXE				
1761	2d Hatchback-4/5P	5649	1900	Note 1
1781	4d Hatchback-4/5P	5809	1900	Note 1
SCIROCCO				
5311	3d Coupe-4P	7090	1888	Note 1
BEETLE (TYPE I)				
1511	2d Convertible-4P	6800	2059	Note 1
TRANSPORTER (TYPE II)				
2321	3d Kombi	7285	2831	Note 2
2211	3d Station Wagon-7P	2952	2952	Note 2
2231	3d Station Wagon-9P	7987	2952	Note 2
2391	3d Campmobile	7295	2724	Note 2

Note 1: 1,156,455 Volkswagen passenger cars (all models) were produced in 1979.
Note 2: 22,384 Transporters were produced in 1979.

More than 129,000 Volkswagens were sold in the United States in 1979.

The 1979 model year marked the final run of the Beetle convertible in the U.S. market.

Tom Glatch

BASE FOUR (Beetle): Horizontally opposed, overhead-valve four-cylinder (air cooled). Displacement: 96.7 cid (1585 cc). Bore & Stroke: 3.36 x 2.72 in. (85 x 69 mm). Compression Ratio: 7.3:1. Brake Horsepower: 48 at 4200 rpm. Torque: 73.1 lbs.-ft. at 2800 rpm. Four main bearings. Solid valve lifters. Electronic fuel injection.

BASE FOUR (TRANSPORTER): Horizontally opposed, overhead-valve four-cylinder (air cooled). Displacement: 120.2 cid (1970 cc). Bore & Stroke: 3.70 x 2.80 in. (94 x 71 mm). Compression Ratio: 7.3:1. Brake Horsepower: 67 at 4200 rpm. Torque: 101 lbs.-ft. at 3000 rpm. Four main bearings. Solid valve lifters. Electronic fuel injection.

CHASSIS

DASHER: Wheelbase: 96.7 in., (diesel) 97.2 in. Overall Length: 172.4 in. Height: 53.5 in. Width: 63.0 in. Front Tread: 52.7 in. Rear Tread: 52.5 in. Standard Tires: 155SR13.

RABBIT: Wheelbase: 94.4 in. Overall Length: 155.3 in. Height: 55.5 in. Width: 63.4 in. Front Tread: 54.7 in. Rear Tread: 53.5 in., (Scirocco) 53.5 in. Standard Tires: 145 x 13, (diesel) 155SR13.

SCIROCCO: Wheelbase: 94.5 in. Overall Length: 155.7 in. Height: 51.5 in. Width: 63.9 in., (Transporter) 69.3 in. Front Tread: 54.7 in. Rear Tread: 53.5 in. Standard Tires: 175/70SR13.

BEETLE (TYPE II): Wheelbase: 94.5 in. Overall Length: 164.8 in. Height: 59.1 in. Width: 62.4 in. Front Tread: 54.9 in., Rear Tread: 54.7 in. Standard Tires: 165SR15.

TRANSPORTER: Wheelbase: 94.5 in. Overall Length: 179.0 in. Height: 77 in. Width: 69.3 in. Front Tread: 54.9 in. Rear Tread: 57.3 in. Standard Tires: 185R14C.

TECHNICAL

DASHER: Layout: front-engine, front-wheel-drive. Transmission: four-speed manual. Suspension (front): MacPherson struts, lower wishbones, coil springs and tubular shock absorbers. Suspension (rear): Beam axle with integral anti-sway bar, semi-trailing arms. Panhard rod, coil springs and tunular shocks. Steering: rack-and-pinion. Steering ratio: 20.2:1. Turns lock-to-lock: 3.94. Turning circle: 34 ft. Brakes: Front disc/rear drum. Body construction: Unit body and frame construction. Tires: 155SR x 13.

RABBIT: Layout: front-engine, front-wheel-drive. Transmission: four-speed manual. Front suspension: MacPherson struts with coil springs. Rear suspension: independent with trailing arms and coil springs. Brakes: front disc, rear drum.

SCIROCCO: Layout: front-engine, front-wheel-drive. Transmission: four-speed manual. Front suspension: MacPherson struts with coil springs. Rear suspension: independent with trailing arms and coil springs. Brakes: front disc, rear drum.

BEETLE (TYPE II): Layout: rear-engine, rear-drive. Transmission: four-speed manual. Front suspension: MacPherson struts with coil springs. Rear suspension: semi-trailing arms with torsion bars. Brakes: front/rear drum.

TRANSPORTER (TYPE II): Layout: rear-engine, rear-drive. Transmission: four-speed manual. Front suspension: MacPherson struts with coil springs. Rear suspension: semi-trailing arms with torsion bars. Brakes: front/rear drum.

PRODUCTION/SALES: 129,779 Volkswagens were sold in the United States during 1979.

MANUFACTURER: Volkswagenwerk AG, Wolfsburg, West Germany.

DISTRIBUTOR: Volkswagen of America Inc., Englewood Cliffs, New Jersey.

HISTORICAL FOOTNOTES: Difficulty in meeting emissions standards contributed to the demise of the Beetle, as did certain safety problems.

Right: **This 1979 Volkswagen Beetle convertible is the pride and joy of its owners.**
Randy and Pam Miller

1980

DASHER—FOUR Little change was evident in the 1980 Volkswagen Dasher.

RABBIT—FOUR With the Beetle-based convertible gone, Volkswagen needed a ragtop and created one with the Rabbit Cabriolet. This new convertible had a Targa-style roll bar, but was otherwise strictly an open car. A carbureted version of the Rabbit's 1457-cc engine replaced the fuel-injected edition as standard, but a larger (1588-cc) fuel-injected four was optional. So was the diesel engine.

JETTA—FOUR The Jetta was another front-wheel-drive Volkswagen that debuted in 1980. It was powered by a 1588-cc fuel-injected four-cylinder engine. The Jetta was offered as a two- or four-door sedan. Ranking as a more plush version of the Rabbit, the Jetta rode a similar-size wheelbase, but measured a foot longer overall.

SCIROCCO—FOUR Production of the sporty coupe continued with minimal change in 1980. The 1588-cc engine was under the hood. Europeans could get a turbo Scirocco, but that wasn't ready for America.

VANAGON—FOUR Though still rear-engined, the Volkswagen Microbus series was restyled for 1980. The

new version was a longer, wider and cleaner-looking vehicle than its predecessor. Rather than "Transporter," the new series adopted the "Vanagon" designation.

I.D. DATA: Volkswagen's 10-symbol serial number is on the upper left of the dashboard, visible through the windshield. The first two digits indicate the model, the next digit identifies the model year, and the final seven digits form the sequential production number.

ENGINE

BASE FOUR (Rabbit): Inline, overhead-cam four-cylinder (water cooled). Cast-iron block and aluminum alloy head. Displacement: 88.9 cid (1457 cc). Bore & Stroke: 3.13 x 2.89 in. (79.5 x 73.4 mm). Compression Ratio: 8.0:1. Brake Horsepower: 62 at 5400 rpm. Torque: 76.6 lbs.-ft. at 3000 rpm. Five main bearings. Solid valve lifters. One single-barrel carburetor.

BASE FOUR (Dasher, Rabbit Convertible, Jetta, Scirocco); OPTIONAL FOUR (Rabbit)]: Inline, overhead-valve four-cylinder (water cooled). Cast-iron block and aluminum alloy head. Displacement: 97.0 cid (1588 cc). Bore & Stroke: 3.13 x 3.15 in. (79.5 x 80 mm). Compression Ratio: 8.2:1. Brake Horsepower: 76 at 5500

Left: **The Rabbit Cabriolet offered open-air fun and sportiness for buyers in 1980.**

Phil Hall

Bottom: **A popular version in the new 1980 Vanagon series was the Camper model.**

Phil Hall

1980 VOLKSWAGEN PRODUCTION CHART

Model Code	Body Type & Seating	POE Price	Weight (lbs.)	ProductionTotal
DASHER				
3214	2d Hatchback-4/5P	7970	2085	Note 1
3234	4d Hatchback-4/5P	8190	2140	Note 1
3314	4d Station Wagon-4/5P	8470	2181	Note 1
RABBIT				
1751	2d Hatchback-4/5P	5215	1750	Note 1
RABBIT CUSTOM				
1752	2d Hatchback-4/5P	5695	1781	Note 1
1772	4d Hatchback-4/5P	5890	1845	Note 1
RABBIT DELUXE				
1753	2d Hatchback-4/5P	6095	1821	Note 1
1773	4d Hatchback-4/5P	6290	1844	Note 1
1555	2d Convertible-4P	9340	2126	Note 1
JETTA				
1614	2d Sedan-5P	7650	1946	Note 1
1634	4d Sedan-5P	7870	2001	Note 1
SCIROCCO				
5315	2d Coupe-4P	8130	1888	Note 1
5315	2d S Coupe-4P	8860	1933	Note 1
VANAGON (TRANSPORTER TYPE II)				
2535	3d Kombi	9540	2976	Note 2
2554	3d Station Wagon-7P	9900	3075	Note 2
2555	3d Station Wagon-9P	9950	3075	Note 2
2539	3d Campmobile	9540	3427	Note 2

Note 1: 1,064,534 Volkswagen passenger cars (all models) were produced in 1980.
Note 2: 28,673 Vanagons were produced in 1980.

rpm. Torque: 82.7 lbs.-ft. at 3200 rpm. Five main bearings. Solid valve lifters. Fuel injection.

Note: A 1471-cc diesel engine, rated 48 hp at 5000 rpm, was available in 1980 Rabbits and Dashers (enlarged to 1588-cc for 1981).

BASE FOUR (Vanagon): Horizontally opposed, overhead-valve four-cylinder (air cooled). Displacement: 120.2 cid (1970 cc). Bore & Stroke: 3.70 x 2.80 in. (94 x 71 mm). Compression Ratio: 7.3:1. Brake Horsepower: 67 at 4200 rpm. Torque: 101 lbs.-ft. at 3000 rpm. Four main bearings. Solid valve lifters. Electronic fuel injection.

CHASSIS

DASHER: Wheelbase: 97.2 in. Overall Length: 173.1 in. Height: 53.5 in. Width: 63.6 in. Front Tread: 52.7 in. Rear Tread: 53.1 in. Standard Tires: 155SR13.

RABBIT: Wheelbase: 94.5 in. Overall Length: 155.3 in. Height: 55.5 in. Width: 63.4 in. Front Tread: 54.7 in. Rear Tread: 53.5 in. Standard Tires: (Sedan) 155 x 13, (Convertible) 175SR13.

JETTA: Wheelbase: 94.4 in. Overall Length: 167.8 in. Height: 55.5 in. Width: 63.4 in. Front Tread: 54.7 in. Rear Tread: 53.5 in. Standard Tires: 175/70SR13.

SCIROCCO: Wheelbase: 94.5 in. Overall Length: 155.7 in. Height: 51.5 in. Width: 63.9 in. Front Tread: 54.7 in. Rear Tread: 53.5 in. Standard Tires: 175/70SR13.

Phill Hall

Restyled in 1980, the venerable Transporter series bus now was called the Vanagon.

Left and Bottom: Sporty 1980 VW Sciroccos came with a 1588-cc engine under the hood.
Phil Hall

VANAGON (TRANSPORTER TYPE II): Wheelbase: 96.8 in. Overall Length: 179.0 in. Height: 77 in. Width: 69.3 in. Front Tread: 54.9 in. Rear Tread: 57.3 in. Standard Tires: 185R14C.

TECHNICAL

DASHER: Layout: front-engine, front-wheel-drive. Transmission: four-speed manual. Suspension (front): MacPherson struts, lower wishbones, coil springs and tubular shock absorbers. Suspension (rear): Beam axle with integral anti-sway bar, semi-trailing arms. Panhard rod, coil springs and tunular shocks. Steering: rack-and-pinion. Steering ratio: 20.2:1. Turns lock-to-lock: 3.94. Turning circle: 34 ft. Brakes: Front disc/rear drum. Body construction: Unit body and frame construction. Tires: 155SR x 13.springs. Rear suspension: rigid axle with Panhard rod and coil springs. Brakes: front disc, rear drum.

RABBIT: Layout: front-engine, front-wheel-drive. Transmission: manual. Front suspension: MacPherson struts with coil springs. Rear suspension: independent with trailing arms and coil springs. Brakes: front disc, rear drum.

JETTA: Layout: front-engine, front-wheel-drive. Transmission: manual. Front suspension: MacPherson struts with coil springs. Rear suspension: independent with trailing arms and coil springs. Brakes: front disc, rear drum.

SCIROCCO: Layout: front-engine, front-wheel-drive. Transmission: manual. Front suspension: MacPherson struts with coil springs. Rear suspension: independent with trailing arms and coil springs. Brakes: front disc, rear drum.

VANAGON: Layout: rear-engine, rear-drive. Transmission: manual. Front suspension: MacPherson struts with coil springs. Rear suspension: semi-trailing arms with torsion bars. Brakes: front disc/rear drum.

PRODUCTION/SALES: 90,952 Volkswagens were sold in the United States during 1980 (not including United States-built Rabbits).

ADDITIONAL MODELS: Volkswagen also introduced a small front-wheel-drive pickup truck at this time, to take the place of the Transporter-based pickups and vans that had been offered all along.

MANUFACTURER: Volkswagenwerk AG, Wolfsburg, West Germany.

DISTRIBUTOR: Volkswagen of America Inc., Englewood Cliffs, New Jersey.

Background, Dasher four-door wagon in Diamond Silver Metallic. Foreground, Onyx Metallic. Sliding sunroof is a popular option on all models.

Phill Hall

Dashers continued to be offered in two hatchback styles and a station wagon in 1980.

1981

DASHER—FOUR Little change was evident in the looks of the 1981 Dasher. Only diesel-engined Dashers were offered this year.

RABBIT—FOUR The base 1981 Rabbit came with a four-speed manual gearbox. The Rabbit S came wirth a five-speed. The Custom became the Rabbit L and the Deluxe became the Rabbit LS. The convertible came only in S trim. Larger gasoline and diesel engines were installed this year.

JETTA—FOUR Like the Rabbit that it was based on, the Jetta got a larger (1.7-liter) gasoline engines for 1981, as well as diesel option.

SCIROCCO—FOUR Production of the sporty coupe continued with minimal change, but a larger 1.7-liter engine became standard equipment.

VANAGON—FOUR The 1981 Vanagon looked like the 1980 Vanagon with only the most minor changes.

I.D. DATA: Volkswagen's Vehicle Identification Number (VIN) now had 17 symbols. The first three symbols identified the manufacturer, make and type of vehicle. The fourth symbol was a letter designating the body type.

The fifth symbol was a letter identifying the engine. The sixth symbol designated the type of restraint system. The seventh and eighth symbols idenitified the model. The ninth symbol was a check digit. The 10th symbol was a letter designating the model year. The 11th symbol designated the assembly plant. The last six symbols were the sequential production number.

ENGINE

BASE FOUR (Rabbit, Jetta, Scirocco): Inline, overhead-cam four-cylinder (water cooled). Cast-iron block and aluminum alloy head. Displacement: 105 cid (1715 cc). Bore & Stroke: 3.13 x 3.40 in. (79.5 x 86.4 mm). Compression Ratio: 8.2:1. Brake Horsepower: 74 at 5000 rpm. Torque: 89.6 lbs.-ft. at 3000 rpm. Five main bearings. Solid valve lifters. Fuel injection.

BASE FOUR (Dasher): A 1588-cc diesel engine, rated 52 hp at 5000 rpm was used in Dashers.

BASE FOUR (Vanagon): Horizontally opposed, overhead-valve four-cylinder (air cooled). Displacement: 120.2 cid (1970 cc). Bore & Stroke: 3.70 x 2.80 in. (94 x 71 mm). Compression Ratio: 7.3:1. Brake Horsepower: 67 at 4200 rpm. Torque: 101 lbs.-ft. at 3000 rpm. Four main bearings. Solid valve lifters. Electronic fuel injection.

Left and Bottom: **1981 VW Rabbits were available in plain, S, L, LS and diesel variations.**

Phil Hall

Model Code	Body Type & Seating	POE Price	Weight (lbs.)	ProductionTotal
DASHER (DIESEL)				
3234	4d Hatchback-4/5P	8830	2140	Note 1
3314	4d Station Wagon-4/5P	9110	2181	Note 1
RABBIT (4-SPEED)				
1751	2d Hatchback-4/5P	5765	1805	Note 1
RABBIT S (5-SPEED)				
1751	2d Hatchback-4/5P	5765	1805	Note 1
RABBIT L				
1752	2d Hatchback-4/5P	6360	1856	Note 1
1772	4d Hatchback-4/5P	6570	1887	Note 1
RABBIT LS				
1753	2d Hatchback-4/5P	6760	1884	Note 1
1773	4d Hatchback-4/5P	6970	1929	Note 1
1555	2d Convertible-4P	10100	2126	Note 1
JETTA				
1614	2d Sedan-5P	7975	1946	Note 1
1634	4d Sedan-5P	8195	2001	Note 1
SCIROCCO				
5315	2d Coupe-4P	8495	1933	Note 1
5315	2d S Coupe-4P	9015	1933	Note 1
VANAGON (TRANSPORTER TYPE II)				
2535	3d Kombi	10380	2976	Note 2
2554	3d Station Wagon-7P	10690	3075	Note 2
2555	3d Station Wagon-9P	10740	3075	Note 2
2539	3d Campmobile	10330	3427	Note 2

Note 1: 981,471 Volkswagen passenger cars (all models) were produced in 1981.
Note 2: 25,083 Vanagons were produced in 1981.

Phil Hall

The 1981 Dashers were available only with a diesel engine in the U.S. market.

CHASSIS

DASHER: Wheelbase: 97.2 in. Overall Length: 173.1 in. Height: 53.5 in. Width: 63.6 in. Front Tread: 52.7 in. Rear Tread: 53.1 in. Standard Tires: 155SR13.

RABBIT: Wheelbase: 94.5 in. Overall Length: 155.3 in. Height: 55.5 in. Width: 63.4 in. Front Tread: 54.7 in. Rear Tread: 53.5 in. Standard Tires: (Sedan) 155 x 13, (Convertible) 175SR13.

JETTA: Wheelbase: 94.4 in. Overall Length: 167.8 in. Height: 55.5 in. Width: 63.4 in. Front Tread: 54.7 in. Rear Tread: 53.5 in. Standard Tires: 175/70SR13.

SCIROCCO: Wheelbase: 94.5 in. Overall Length: 155.7 in. Height: 51.5 in. Width: 63.9 in. Front Tread: 54.7 in. Rear Tread: 53.5 in. Standard Tires: 175/70SR13.

VANAGON (TRANSPORTER TYPE II): Wheelbase: 96.8 in. Overall Length: 179.0 in. Height: 77 in. Width: 69.3 in. Front Tread: 54.9 in. Rear Tread: 57.3 in. Standard Tires: 185R14C.

TECHNICAL

DASHER: Layout: front-engine, front-wheel-drive. Transmission: four-speed manual. Suspension (front): MacPherson struts, lower wishbones, coil springs and tubular shock absorbers. Suspension (rear): Beam axle with integral anti-sway bar, semi-trailing arms. Panhard rod, coil springs and tunular shocks. Steering: rack-and-pinion. Steering ratio: 20.2:1. Turns lock-to-lock: 3.94. Turning circle: 34 ft. Brakes: Front disc/rear drum. Body construction: Unit body and frame construction. Tires: 155SR x 13.

RABBIT: Layout: front-engine, front-wheel-drive. Transmission: manual. Front suspension: MacPherson struts with coil springs. Rear suspension: independent with trailing arms and coil springs. Brakes: front disc, rear drum.

JETTA: Layout: front-engine, front-wheel-drive. Transmission: manual. Front suspension: MacPherson struts with coil springs. Rear suspension: independent with trailing arms and coil springs. Brakes: front disc, rear drum.

SCIROCCO: Layout: front-engine, front-wheel-drive. Transmission: manual. Front suspension: MacPherson struts with coil springs. Rear suspension: independent with trailing arms and coil springs. Brakes: front disc, rear drum.

VANAGON: Layout: rear-engine, rear-drive. Transmission: manual. Front suspension: MacPherson struts with coil springs. Rear suspension: semi-trailing arms with torsion bars. Brakes: front disc/rear drum.

PRODUCTION/SALES: 82,173 Volkswagens were sold in the United States during 1981 (not United States-built Rabbits.

ADDITIONAL MODELS: Volkswagen also introduced a small front-wheel-drive pickup truck at this time. It took the place of the Transporter-based pickups and vans that had been built since the 1950s.

MANUFACTURER: Volkswagenwerk AG, Wolfsburg, West Germany.

DISTRIBUTOR: Volkswagen of America Inc., Englewood Cliffs, New Jersey.

The 1981 Jetta was in its second year in the U.S. market.

Right: **The 1981 Vanagon continued to be a practical source of transportation.**
Old Car Weekly Archive

1982

RABBIT—FOUR Production of the front-wheel-drive Rabbit and Rabbit-based convertible continued with little change in 1982. Standard Rabbit equipment included a four- or five-speed manual gearbox (automatic available), power brakes, bright body moldings, reclining front seats, tinted glass and a clock. The Rabbit LS added opening front vent windows, dual remote mirrors, full wheel covers, intermittent windshield wipers, a woodgrained instrument panel applique and a cigarette lighter. The Rabbit convertible included a floor console, an integral roll bar, a passenger vanity mirror, a lockable gas cap, a dual-tone horn, a digital clock, a padded steering wheel and carpeted lower door panels.

JETTA—FOUR The Jetta sedan was similar to the Rabbit, but more luxurious. This model had minimal change for 1982. Standard equipment included a five-speed manual gearbox (an automatic transmission was optional), power brakes, an electric rear window defroster, dual remote outside mirrors, an AM/FM stereo radio, intermittent windshield wipers, tinted glass, a floor console, a padded steering wheel and a woodgrained instrument panel applique.

QUANTUM—FOUR Volkswagen's replacement for the Dasher rode a 100.4-inch wheelbase and was powered by a 1715-cc engine. Three body styles were offered: a hatchback coupe with a fastback roof line, a notchback four-door sedan and a four-door station wagon. Standard equipment included a five-speed manual gearbox (three-speed automatic transmission optional), an electric rear-window defroster, a quartz clock, reclining front bucket seats, tinted glass, dual remote-control outside mirrors and light alloy wheels. A GL option added cruise control, power door locks, electric remote mirrors, a lighted visor vanity mirror and power windows.

SCIROCCO—FOUR Mechanical details changed little, but the sporty Scirocco coupe wore an all-new, more rounded body designed to reduce air drag. The wheelbase remained the same, but the car grew in overall length. This added space to the rear passenger compartment and the trunk. The more expansive window area included a deeper back window, which curved downward to reach the hatchback door. A small under-the-bumper lip spoiler was installed

Above: **Some Vanagons were powered by a diesel engine in 1982.**

Old Cars Weekly Archives

1982 VOLKSWAGEN PRODUCTION CHART

Model Code	Body Type & Seating	POE Price	Weight (lbs.)	ProductionTotal
RABBIT				
1751	2d Hatchback-4/5P	5990	1805	Note 1
RABBIT L				
1752	2d Hatchback-4/5P	6615	1858	Note 1
1772	4d Hatchback-4/5P	6825	1915	Note 1
RABBIT LS				
1753	2d Hatchback-4/5P	7065	1920	Note 1
1773	4d Hatchback-4/5P	7275	1964	Note 1
RABBIT S (5-SPEED)				
1754	2d Hatchback-4/5P	7305	1920	Note 1
1555	2d Convrtible-4P	10595	2126	Note 1
JETTA				
1614	2d Sedan-5P	8375	1946	Note 1
1634	4d Sedan-5P	8595	2001	Note 1
QUANTUM				
3213	2d Coupe-5P	10770	2389	Note 1
3273	4d Sedan-5P	11070	2140	Note 1
3313	4d Station Wagon-5P	11470	2455	Note 1
QUANTUM GL				
3219	2d Coupe-5P	11520	2389	Note 1
3279	4d Sedan-5P	11870	2140	Note 1
3319	4d Station Wagon-5P	11270	2455	Note 1
SCIROCCO				
5335	2d Coupe-4P	10150	1933	Note 1
VANAGON				
2554	3d Station Wagon-7P	10860	3075	Note 2
2555	3d Station Wagon-9P	10915	3075	Note 2
2539	3d Campmobile	14900	3475	Note 2

Note 1: 974,140 Volkswagen passenger cars (all models) were produced in 1982.
Note 2: 24,203 Vanagons were produced in 1982.

The Volkswagen Quantum was introduced to the American market in 1982.

up front. Standard equipment included power brakes, an electric rear defroster, tinted glass, a remote-control driver's mirror, an AM/FM stereo radio with cassette player, reclining front bucket seats with height adjusters, front and rear spoilers and a four-spoke sport steering wheel. The GL trim package included power windows, power remote-contol outside mirrors, and a power antenna.

VANAGON—FOUR Production of the Vanagon continued without major change.

I.D. DATA: Volkswagen's Vehicle Identification Number (VIN) now had 17 symbols. The first three symbols identified the manufacturer, make and type of vehicle. The fourth symbol was a letter designating the body type. The fifth symbol was a letter identifying the engine. The sixth symbol designated the type of restraint system. The seventh and eighth symbols idenitified the model (same as first two numbers in column 1 in table below). The ninth symbol was a check digit. The 10th symbol was a letter designating the model year. The 11th symbol designated the assembly plant. The last six symbols were the sequential production number.

ENGINE

BASE FOUR (Rabbit, Jetta, Scirocco, Quantum): Inline, overhead-cam four-cylinder (water cooled). Cast-iron block and aluminum alloy head. Displacement: 105 cid (1715 cc). Bore & Stroke: 3.13 x 3.40 in. (79.5 x 86.4 mm). Compression Ratio: 8.2:1. Brake Horsepower: 74 at 5000 rpm. Torque: 89.6 lbs.-ft. at 3000 rpm. Five main bearings. Solid valve lifters. Fuel injection.

Note: A 1.6-liter diesel engine was available in Rabbits and Jettas. It was rated for 52 hp at 4800 rpm and 72 lbs.-ft. of torque at 3000 rpm.

BASE FOUR (Vanagon): Horizontally opposed, overhead-valve four-cylinder (air cooled). Displacement: 120.2 cid (1970 cc). Bore & Stroke: 3.70 x 2.80 in. (94 x 71 mm). Compression Ratio: 7.3:1. Brake Horsepower: 67 at 4200 rpm. Torque: 101 lbs.-ft. at 3000 rpm. Four main bearings. Solid valve lifters. Electronic fuel injection.

CHASSIS

RABBIT: Wheelbase: 94.5 in. Overall Length: 155.3 in. Height: 55.5 in. Width: 63.4 in. Front Tread: 54.7 in. Rear Tread: 53.1 in.

JETTA: Wheelbase: 94.5 in. Overall Length: 167.8 in. Height: 55.5 in. Width: 63.4 in. Front Tread: 54.7 in. Rear Tread: 53.1 in.

QUANTUM: 100.4 in. Overall Length: (Coupe) 178.2 in., (Sedan) 180.2 in. Height: Quantum 55.1 in. Width: 66.9 in. Front Tread: 55.7 in. Rear Tread: 56.0 in.

SCIROCCO: Wheelbase: 94.5 in. Overall Length: 165.7 in. Height: 51.4 in. Width: 64.0 in. Front Tread: 54.7 in. Rear Tread: 53.5 in.

VANAGON: Wheelbase: 96.9 in. Overall Length: 179.9 in. Height: 77.2 in. Width: 72.6 in. Front Tread: 61.8 in. Rear Tread: 61.8 in.

TECHNICAL

RABBIT: Layout: front-engine, front-wheel-drive. Transmission: manual. Front suspension: MacPherson struts with lower control arms and coil springs. Rear suspension: Beam axle with coil springs. Brakes: front disc, rear drum. Body construction: steel unibody. Fuel tank: 10 gal.

JETTA: Layout: front-engine, front-wheel-drive. Transmission: Five-speed manual. Front suspension: MacPherson struts with lower control arms and coil springs. Rear suspension: Beam axle with coil springs and anti roll bar. Brakes: front disc, rear drum. Body construction: steel unibody. Fuel tank: 10.6 gal.

SCIROCCO: Layout: front-engine, front-wheel-drive. Transmission: Five-speed manual. Front suspension: MacPherson struts with lower control arms and coil springs. Rear suspension: Beam axle with anti-roll function, trailing arms, coil springs and anti roll bar. Brakes: front disc, rear drum. Body construction: steel unibody. Fuel tank: 10.6 gal.

VANAGON: Layout: rear-engine, rear-drive. Transmission: manual. Front suspension: MacPherson struts with coil springs. Rear suspension: semi-trailing arms with torsion bars. Brakes: front disc/rear drum.

QUANTUM: Layout: front-engine, front-wheel-drive. Transmission: Five-speed manual. Steering: rack and pinion. Front suspension: MacPherson struts with lower control arms, coil springs and anti roll bar. Rear suspension: Beam twist axle with anti-roll function and coil springs. Brakes: front disc, rear drum. Body construction: steel unibody. Fuel tank: 15.8 gal.

OPTIONS: Air conditioning. Electric rear defroster (Rabbit). Leatherette upholstery (Rabbit L/ Rabbit LS, Quantum wagon). AM/FM radio (Rabbit). AM/ FM stereo (Rabbit). AM/ FM stereo with cassette player (Rabbit/Jetta/Quantum). Metallic paint. Sunroof (Scirocco). Electric sunroof (Quantum). Alloy wheels (Quantum). Rear wiper/washer (Scirocco).

PRODUCTION/SALES: 67,350 imported Volkswagens were sold in the United States during 1982.

MANUFACTURER: Volkswagenwerk AG, Wolfsburg, West Germany, and Volkswagen of America Inc. (plant in Pennsylvania).

DISTRIBUTOR: Volkswagen of America Inc.

HISTORICAL FOOTNOTES: Rabbit sales fell by almost 50 percent in the 1982 model year.

In 1982, one version of the VW Rabbit came all dressed up as a Black Tie edition.

The 1982 Jetta continued to be available in two-door and four-door versions.

A pickup version of the Rabbit was introduced early in the 1980s.

1983

RABBIT—FOUR A new sporty GTI two-door hatchback model carried an enlarged 1.8-liter engine derived from the 1.7-liter fuel-injected four-cylinder power plant now standard in the Rabbit LS and Rabbit GL models. Standard GTI equipment included a close-ratio five-speed manual gearbox, wider wheels and tires, black body trim, flared wheel wells, a Sport steering wheel, Sport front seats, special instruments and a tuned exhaust system. A carbureted version of the 1.7-liter four powered the Rabbit L. Rabbits could also have a 1.6-liter diesel four or a new turbocharged diesel. Standard equipment was similar to that offered in 1982.

JETTA—FOUR Jetta two- and four-door notchback sedans came with the same 1.7-liter fuel-injected engine as the upper Rabbit models. Diesel and turbodiesel engines were available. Standard equipment was similar to 1982.

QUANTUM—FOUR Little change was evident in the Quantum fastback coupe, sedan and wagon. There was an additional engine choice–the turbodiesel four-cylinder. Base engine remained the 1.7-liter four with fuel injection hooked to a five-speed manual gearbox. A three-speed automatic transmission was optional. Turbodiesel models could have an "E-Mode" transmission with special economy position, which employed a form of freewheeling (disconnecting the engine whenever the gas pedal was released). An Audi five-cylinder engine became available at midyear.

Above: **Introduced to North America in 1982, the Quantum was the Dasher replacement.**

Old Cars Weekly Archives

SCIROCCO—FOUR Volkswagen's sporty coupe continued with no significant change. The Scirocco rode the Rabbit/Jetta chassis and was powered by the 1.7-liter fuel-injected four-cylinder engine. Standard equipment was similar to that of the 1982 model. Scirocco bodies were built by the famous German coachbuilder Karmann.

VANAGON—FOUR Volkswagen also continued to produce the Vanagon station wagon and Campmobile, as well as a line of pickup trucks (including the Sportruck). A water-cooled engine became standard during the 1983 model year. See engine listings for details.

I.D. DATA: Volkswagen's Vehicle Identification Number (VIN) now had 17 symbols. The first three symbols identified the manufacturer, make and type of vehicle. The fourth symbol was a letter designating the body type. The fifth symbol was a letter identifying the engine. The sixth symbol designated the type of restraint system. The seventh and eighth symbols idenitified the model (same as first two numbers in column 1 in table below). The ninth symbol was a check digit. The 10th symbol was a letter designating the model year. The 11th symbol designated the assembly plant. The last six symbols were the sequential production number.

ENGINE

BASE FOUR (Rabbit L): Inline, overhead-cam four-cylinder. Cast-iron block and light alloy head. Displacement: 105 cid (1715 cc). Bore & Stroke: 3.13 x 3.40 (79.5 x 86.4 mm). Compression Ratio: 8.0:1. Brake

1983 VOLKSWAGEN PRODUCTION CHART

Model Code	Body Type & Seating	POE Price	Weight (lbs.)	ProductionTotal
RABBIT L				
1752	2d Hatchback-4/5P	6415	1845	Note 1
1772	4d Hatchback-4/5P	6625	1880	Note 1
RABBIT LS				
1753	2d Hatchback-4/5P	6890	1850	Note 1
1773	4d Hatchback-4/5P	7100	1885	Note 1
RABBIT GL (5-SPEED)				
1753	2d Hatchback-4/5P	7490	1966	Note 1
1773	4d Hatchback-4/5P	7700	2010	Note 1
RABBIT CONVERTIBLE (5-SPEED)				
1555	2d Conv-4P	10595	2101	Note 1
RABBIT GTI (5-SPEED)				
1751	2d Hatchback-4/5P	7990	1918	Note 1
JETTA (5-SPEED)				
1614	2d Sedan-5P	7990	2072	Note 1
1634	4d Sedan-5P	8210	2127	Note 1
QUANTUM (5-SPEED)				
3213	2d Coupe-5P	10770	2389	Note 1
3273	4d Sedan-5P	11280	2140	Note 1
3313	4d Station Wagon-5P	11680	2455	Note 1
SCIROCCO				
5335	2d Coupe-4P	10150	2079	Note 1
VANAGON				
2554	3d Station Wagon-7P	10950	3075	Note 2
2555	3d Station Wagon-9P	11005	3075	Note 2
2539	3d Campmobile	14990	3427	Note 2

Note 1: 77,009 imported Volkswagens were sold in the United States during 1983.
Note 2: Vanagon production not available.

In 1983, Volkswagen Rabbits were American-made vehicles.

Horsepower: 65 at 5000 rpm. Torque: 88 lbs.-ft. at 2800 rpm. Five main bearings. Two-barrel carburetor.

BASE FOUR (Rabbit LS/GL, Jetta, Quantum, Scirocco): Inline, overhead-cam four-cylinder. Cast-iron block and light alloy head. Displacement: 105 cid (1715 cc). Bore & Stroke: 3.13 x 3.40 (79.5 x 86.4 mm). Compression Ratio: 8.0:1. Brake Horsepower: 74 at 5000 rpm. Torque: 90 lbs.-ft. at 3000 rpm. Five main bearings. Fuel injection.

BASE FOUR (Rabbit GTI, late Scirocco): Inline, overhead-cam four-cylinder. Cast-iron block and light alloy head. Displacement: 109 cid (1786 cc). Bore & Stroke: 3.19 x 3.40 (81 x 86.4 mm). Compression Ratio: 8.5:1. Brake Horsepower: 90 at 5500 rpm. Torque: 100 lbs.-ft. at 3000 rpm. Five main bearings. Fuel injection.

DIESEL FOUR (Rabbit, Jetta): Inline, overhead-cam four-cylinder. Cast-iron block and light alloy head. Displacement: 97 cid (1588 cc). Bore & Stroke: 3.01 x 3.40 (76.5 x 86.4 mm). Compression Ratio: 23.0:1. Brake Horsepower: 52 at 4800 rpm. Torque: 72 lbs.- ft. at 2000 rpm. Five main bearings. Fuel injection.

TURBODIESEL FOUR (Rabbit, Jetta, Quantum): Inline, overhead-cam four-cylinder. Cast-iron block and light alloy head. Displacement: 97 cid (1588 cc). Bore & Stroke: 3.01 x 3.40 (76.5 x 86.4 mm). Compression Ratio: 23.0:1.

Brake Horsepower: 68 at 4500 rpm. Torque: 98 lbs.-ft. at 2800 rpm. Five main bearings. Fuel injection.

BASE FOUR (Vanagon): Four-cylinder. Horizontally-opposed. Water-cooled. Displacement: 1915 cc. Bore & Stroke: 3.70 x 3.72. Compression ratio: 8.6:1. Brake Horsepower: 82. at 4800 rpm. Torque: 105 lbs.-ft. at 2600 rpm.

John Gunnell

In 1983, one way to have a lot of fun was driving the sporty VW Rabbit LE.

CHASSIS

RABBIT: Wheelbase: 94.5 in. Overall Length: 155.3 in. Height: 55.5 in. Width: 63.4 in. Front Tread: 54.7 in. Rear Tread: 53.1 in.

JETTA: Wheelbase: 94.5 in. Overall Length: 167.8 in. Height: 55.5 in. Width: 63.4 in. Front Tread: 54.7 in. Rear Tread: 53.1 in.

QUANTUM: Wheelbase: 100.4 in. Overall Length: (Coupe) 178.2 in., (Sedan) 180.2 in., (Wagon) 183.1 in. Height: Quantum 55.1 in. Width: 66.9 in. Front Tread: 55.7 in. Rear Tread: 56.0 in.

SCIROCCO: Wheelbase: 94.5 in. Overall Length: 165.7 in. Height: 51.4 in. Width: 64.0 in. Front Tread: 54.7 in. Rear Tread: 53.5 in.

VANAGON: Wheelbase: 96.9 in. Overall Length: 179.9 in. Height: 77.2 in. Width: 72.6 in. Front Tread: 61.8 in. Rear Tread: 61.8 in.

TECHNICAL

RABBIT: Layout: front-engine, front-wheel-drive. Transmission: manual. Front suspension: MacPherson struts with lower control arms and coil springs. Rear suspension: Beam axle with coil springs. Brakes: front disc, rear drum. Body construction: steel unibody. Fuel tank: 10 gal.

JETTA: Layout: front-engine, front-wheel-drive. Transmission: Five-speed manual. Front suspension: MacPherson struts with lower control arms and coil springs. Rear suspension: Beam axle with coil springs and anti roll bar. Brakes: front disc, rear drum. Body construction: steel unibody. Fuel tank: 10.6 gal.

SCIROCCO: Layout: front-engine, front-wheel-drive. Transmission: Five-speed manual. Front suspension: MacPherson struts with lower control arms and coil springs. Rear suspension: Beam axle with anti-roll function, trailing arms, coil springs and anti roll bar. Brakes: front disc, rear drum. Body construction: steel unibody. Fuel tank: 10.6 gal.

QUANTUM: Layout: front-engine, front-wheel-drive. Transmission: Five-speed manual. Steering: rack and pinion. Front suspension: MacPherson struts with lower control arms, coil springs and anti roll bar. Rear suspension: Beam twist axle with anti-roll function and coil springs. Brakes: front disc, rear drum. Body construction: steel unibody. Fuel tank: 15.8 gal.

VANAGON: Layout: rear-engine, rear-drive. Transmission: manual. Front suspension: MacPherson struts with coil springs. Rear suspension: semi-trailing arms with torsion bars. Brakes: front disc/rear drum.

OPTIONS: Air conditioning. Electric rear defroster (Rabbit). Leatherette upholstery (Rabbit L/ Rabbit LS, Quantum wagon). AM/FM radio (Rabbit). AM/ FM stereo (Rabbit). AM/ FM stereo with cassette player (Rabbit/Jetta/Quantum). Metallic paint. Sunroof (Scirocco). Electric sunroof (Quantum). Alloy wheels (Quantum). Rear wiper/washer (Scirocco).

MANUFACTURER: Volkswagenwerk AG, Wolfsburg, West Germany, and Volkswagen of America Inc. (plant in Pennsylvania).

DISTRIBUTOR: Volkswagen of America Inc., Troy, Michigan.

HISTORICAL FOOTNOTES: Volkswagen's 1983 models were introduced in the United States in October 1982. Rabbits were made in the United States, Jettas and other models in Germany.

A special edition of the Vanagon introduced at mid-year 1983 was the Waterboxer.

A special version of the 1983 Rabbit was the Wolfsburg LE model.

1984

RABBIT—FOUR Apart from a reshuffling of the model lineup, little was new in the 1984 Rabbit line. The LS series was dropped. The Rabbit GLs used the carbureted 1.7-liter engine, while the Rabbit convertible carried the same 1.8-liter engine as the high-performance GTI hatchback coupe.

JETTA—FOUR Not much was new with 1984 Jetta sedans. Base models could have a standard 1.6-liter diesel engine, while the GL came standard with a 1.7-liter gas engine. A turbodiesel was also available. The high-performance Jetta GLI used the same engine as the Rabbit GTI.

QUANTUM—FOUR/FIVE Only a four-door sedan and a station wagon were available in the Quantum series. A five-cylinder Audi engine and five-speed gearbox were base equipment. A 1.6-liter turbodiesel and a three-speed automatic transmission were optional.

SCIROCCO—FOUR A 1.8-liter engine and a close-ratio five-speed gearbox had become standard in Sciroccos during the 1983 model year.

VANAGON—FOUR Volkswagen also continued to produce the Vanagon station wagon and Camper bus. Vanagons came in three price levels: L, GL, and Camper (with pop-up top). Installation of the water-cooled engine allowed Volkswagen to add a second heater under the back seat. Either a four-speed manual gearbox or three- speed automatic transmission was available.

I.D. DATA: Volkswagen's Vehicle Identification Number (VIN) now had 17 symbols. The first three symbols identified the manufacturer, make and type of vehicle. The fourth symbol was a letter designating the body type. The fifth symbol was a letter identifying the engine. The sixth symbol designated the type of restraint system. The seventh and eighth symbols idenitified the model (same as two numbers in column 1 in table below). The ninth symbol was a check digit. The 10th symbol was a letter designating the model year. The 11th symbol designated the assembly plant. The last six symbols were the sequential production number.

ENGINE

BASE FOUR (Rabbit L): Inline, overhead-cam four-cylinder. Cast-iron block and light alloy head. Displacement: 105 cid (1715 cc). Bore & Stroke: 3.13 x 3.40 (79.5 x 86.4 mm). Compression Ratio: 8.2:1. Brake Horsepower: 65 at 5000 rpm. Torque: 88 lbs.-ft. at 2800 rpm. Five main bearings. Two-barrel carburetor.

Above: **Volkswagen promoted its upscale Wolfsburg Edition Rabbit in 1984 advertising.**
John Gunnell

1984 VOLKSWAGEN PRODUCTION CHART

Model Code	Body Type & Seating	POE Price	Weight (lbs.)	ProductionTotal
	RABBIT L			
17	2d Hatchback-4P	6530	1834	Note 1
17	4d Hatchback-4P	6740	1878	Note 1
	RABBIT GL			
17	4d Hatchback-4P	7130	1945	Note 1
	RABBIT GTI (5-SPEED)			
17	2d Hatchback-4P	8350	1950	Note 1
	RABBIT CONVERTIBLE (5-SPEED)			
15	2d Convertible-4P	10980	2145	Note 1
	JETTA (5-SPEED)			
16	2d Sedan-4P	7630	1998	Note 1
16	4d Sedan-4P	7850	2048	Note 1
	JETTA GL (5-SPEED)			
16	4d Sedan-4P	8210	2053	Note 1
	JETTA GLI (5-SPEED)			
16	4d Sedan-4P	8690	2064	Note 1
	QUANTUM GL (5-SPEED)			
32	4d Sedan-5P	12980	2516	Note 1
	QUANTUM WAGON (5-SPEED)			
33	5d Wagon-4P	13780	2604	Note 1
	SCIROCCO (5-SPEED)			
53	2d Coupe-4P	10870	2070	Note 1
	VANAGON			
25	3d Station Wagon-7P	11675	3170	Note 2
	VANAGON GL			
25	3d Station Wagon-9P	12175	3360	Note 2
	VANAGON CAMPER			
25	3d Campmobile	15800	3522	Note 2

Note 1: 103,479 imported Volkswagens were sold in the United States during 1984.
Note 2: Vanagon production not available.

The Jetta was a popular Volkswagen choice in the 1984 model year.

BASE FOUR (Rabbit GL, Jetta): Inline, overhead-cam four-cylinder. Cast-iron block and light alloy head. Displacement: 105 cid (1715 cc). Bore & Stroke: 3.13 x 3.40 (79.5 x 86.4 mm). Compression Ratio: 8.2:1. Brake Horsepower: 74 at 5000 rpm. Torque: 90 lbs.-ft. at 3000 rpm. Five main bearings. Two-barrel carburetor.

BASE FOUR (Rabbit GTI, convertible, Jetta GLI, Scirocco): Inline, overhead-cam four-cylinder. Cast-iron block and light alloy head. Displacement: 109 cid (1786 cc). Bore & Stroke: 3.19 x 3.40 (81 x 86.4 mm). Compression Ratio: 8.5:1. Brake Horsepower: 90 at 5500 rpm. Torque: 100 lbs.-ft. at 3000 rpm. Five main bearings. Multi-point fuel injection.

DIESEL FOUR (Rabbit, Jetta): Inline, overhead-cam four-cylinder. Cast-iron block and light alloy head. Displacement: 97 cid (1588 cc). Bore & Stroke: 3.01 x 3.40 (76.5 x 86.4 mm). Compression Ratio: 23.0:1. Brake Horsepower: 52 at 4800 rpm. Torque: 72 lbs.- ft. at 2000 rpm. Five main bearings. Fuel injection.

TURBODIESEL FOUR (Rabbit, Jetta, Quantum): Inline, overhead-cam four-cylinder. Cast-iron block and light alloy head. Displacement: 97 cid (1588 cc). Bore & Stroke: 3.01 x 3.40 (76.5 x 86.4 mm). Compression Ratio: 23.0:1.

Brake Horsepower: 68 at 4500 rpm. Torque: 98 lbs.-ft. at 2800 rpm. Five main bearings. Fuel injection.

BASE FIVE (Quantum): Inline, overhead-cam five-cylinder. Cast-iron block and light alloy head. Displacement: 131 cid (2144 cc). Bore & Stroke: 3.13 x 3.40 (79.5 x 86.4 mm). Compression Ratio: 8.2:1. Brake Horsepower: 100 at 5100 rpm. Torque: 112 lbs.-ft. at 3000 rpm. Six main bearings. Multi-point fuel injection.

BASE FOUR (Vanagon): Four-cylinder. Horizontally-opposed. Water-cooled. Displacement: 1915 cc. Bore & Stroke: 3.70 x 3.72. Compression ratio: 8.6:1. Brake Horsepower: 82. at 4800 rpm. Torque: 105 lbs.-ft. at 2600 rpm.

CHASSIS

RABBIT: Wheelbase: 94.5 in. Overall Length: (Hatchback) 155.3 in, (Convertible) 159.3 in. Height: (Hatchback) 55.5 in., (Convertible) 55.6 in. Width: (Hatchback) 63.4 in., (Convertible) 64.2 in. Front Tread: 54.7 in. Rear Tread: 53.1 in.

JETTA: Wheelbase: 94.5 in. Overall Length: 167.8 in. Height: 55.5 in. Width: 63.4 in. Front Tread: 54.7 in. Rear Tread: 53.1 in.

QUANTUM: Wheelbase: 100.4 in. Overall Length: (Sedan) 180.2 in., (Wagon) 183.1 in. Height: 55.1 in. Width: 66.9 in. Front Tread: 55.7 in. Rear Tread: 56.0 in.

SCIROCCO: Wheelbase: 94.5 in. Overall Length: 165.7 in. Height: 51.4 in. Width: 64.0 in. Front Tread: 54.7 in. Rear Tread: 53.5 in.

VANAGON: Wheelbase: 96.9 in. Overall Length: 179.9 in. Height: 77.2 in. Width: 72.6 in. Front Tread: 61.8 in. Rear Tread: 61.8 in.

TECHNICAL

RABBIT: Layout: front-engine, front-wheel-drive. Transmission: manual. Front suspension: MacPherson struts with lower control arms and coil springs. Rear suspension: Beam axle with coil springs. Brakes: front disc, rear drum. Body construction: steel unibody. Fuel tank: 10 gal.

JETTA: Layout: front-engine, front-wheel-drive. Transmission: Five-speed manual. Front suspension: MacPherson struts with lower control arms and coil springs. Rear suspension: Beam axle with coil springs and anti roll bar. Brakes: front disc, rear drum. Body construction: steel unibody. Fuel tank: 10.6 gal.

SCIROCCO: Layout: front-engine, front-wheel-drive. Transmission: Five-speed manual. Front suspension: MacPherson struts with lower control arms and coil springs. Rear suspension: Beam axle with anti-roll function, trailing arms, coil springs and anti roll bar. Brakes: front disc, rear drum. Body construction: steel unibody. Fuel tank: 10.6 gal.

QUANTUM: Layout: front-engine, front-wheel-drive. Transmission: Five-speed manual. Steering: rack and pinion. Front suspension: MacPherson struts with lower control arms, coil springs and anti roll bar. Rear suspension: Beam twist axle with anti-roll function and coil springs. Brakes: front disc, rear drum. Body construction: steel unibody. Fuel tank: 15.8 gal.

VANAGON: Layout: rear-engine, rear-drive. Transmission: manual. Front suspension: MacPherson struts with coil springs. Rear suspension: semi-trailing arms with torsion bars. Brakes: front disc/rear drum.

OPTIONS

RABBIT: Air conditioning ($650, except $700 in convertible). Cruise control ($180, except $200 in convertible). Power steering ($220, except $265 in convertible). Sliding sunroof ($300). Rear wiper/washer ($130). Leatherette upholstery ($80). AM/FM radio ($165). AM/FM stereo ($260). AM/FM stereo with cassette ($365). Electronic-tuning AM/FM stereo with cassette ($575). Sport seats in convertible ($220). Metallic paint ($140). Alloy wheels ($220, except $280 in convertible).

JETTA: Air conditioning ($700). Power steering ($265). AM/FM stereo with cassette ($565). Sport package for coupe ($290). Sliding sunroof ($315). Cruise control ($200). Leatherette interior ($80).

QUANTUM: Leatherette interior in station wagon ($80). Electric sunroof ($575). Alloy wheels ($340). Metallic paint ($140).

SCIROCCO: Air conditioning ($700). Power steering ($265). Slide/tilt sunroof ($445). Cruise control ($200). Leather interior trim ($695). Power windows and antenna ($490).

MANUFACTURER: Volkswagenwerk AG, Wolfsburg, West Germany, and Volkswagen of America Inc. (plant in Pennsylvania).

DISTRIBUTOR: Volkswagen of America Inc., Troy, Michigan.

HISTORICAL FOOTNOTES: Volkswagen's 1984 models were introduced in the United States in October 1983. Rabbits were made in the United States, Jettas and other models in Germany.

John Gunnell

VW's Jettas came in base, GI and GLI versions in the 1984 model year.

1985

CABRIOLET—FOUR Except for minor changes and new name badges, the "new" 1985 Cabriolet was the former Rabbit convertible. It was the only model that continued to use the original, subcompact Rabbit body. A 1.8-liter 90-hp engine provided the propulsion.

GOLF—FOUR The Rabbit was restyled and became the new Golf model. The Golf name had previously been used outside the United States. Larger dimensions caused the EPA to re-classify the Golf as a compact car, rather than a subcompact model. It was now a full five-passenger vehicle. The wheelbase was almost three inches longer than before and the front and rear tread dimensions were wider. The front suspension was revised and a new torsion beam axle was provided. It was similar to the one used in the Quantum. The Golf came in two- and four-door hatchback models. Under the hood was a modified version of the 1.8-liter engine, developing 85 hp. The GTI two-door hatchback was also part of the series.

Above: The 1985 Jetta was restyled and was powered by a 1.8-liter engine.

Old Cars Weekly Archive

JETTA—FOUR The 1985 Jetta was revised along the same lines as the Golf, but remained notchback sedans. Under the hood was a modified version of the 1.8-liter engine that developed 85 hp. Two- and four-door sedans came in base trim. Also in the model lineup were GL and GLI versions of the four-door model.

QUANTUM—FOUR/FIVE For 1985, both the Quantum sedan and station wagon were marketed. Audi's 2.1-liter five-cylinder engine was no longer available, so a 2.2-liter version became standard in the sedan. Wagons used a 1.8-liter four. Otherwise, production continued with little change.

SCIROCCO—FOUR Little was new for Volkswagen's sporty coupe except for the addition of black bumpers and a larger rear spoiler. The latter was included in the optional Wolfsburg Limited Edition package.

VANAGON—FOUR Volkswagen also continued to produce the Vanagon station wagon and Camper, with additional standard equipment for 1985. This equipment was similar to that included in the Wolfsburg Limited Edition option

A popular variation of the new VW Golf was the GTI hatchback.

Above: **The exciting GTI from Volkswagen made waves as the 1985 "Car of the Year."**

Old Cars Weekly Archive

1985 VOLKSWAGEN PRODUCTION CHART

Model Code	Body Type & Seating	POE Price	Weight (lbs.)	ProductionTotal
		CABRIOLET		
15	2d Convertible-4P	11595	2254	Note 1
		GOLF		
17	2d Hatchback-5P	6990	2150	Note 1
17	4d Hatchback-5P	7200	2150	Note 1
		GOLF		
GTI	2d Hatchback-5P	8990	2196	Note 1
		JETTA		
16	2d Sedan-5P	7975	2275	Note 1
16	4d Sedan-5P	8195	2252	Note 1
		JETTA GL		
16	4d Sedan-5P	8495	2252	Note 1
		JETTA GLI		
16	4d Sedan-5P	9995	2252	Note 1
		QUANTUM GL		
32	4d Sedan-5P	13295	2661	Note 1
		QUANTUM WAGON		
33	5d Wagon-4P	11570	2563	Note 1
		SCIROCCO		
53	2d Coupe-4P	9980	2181	Note 1
		VANAGON L		
25	3d Station Wagon	12290	3270	Note 2
		VANAGON GL		
25	3d Station Wagon-9P	13140	3370	Note 2
		VANAGON CAMPER		
25	3d Campmobile	17190	3622	Note 2

Note 1: 140,505 imported Volkswagens were sold in the United States during 1985.
Note 2: Vanagon production not available.

package, which became available during the 1984 model year. The GL could get a "Weekender" option with a rear bench seat that turned into a double bed.

I.D. DATA: Volkswagen's Vehicle Identification Number (VIN) now had 17 symbols. The first three symbols identified the manufacturer, make and type of vehicle. The fourth symbol was a letter designating the body type. The fifth symbol was a letter identifying the engine. The sixth symbol designated the type of restraint system. The seventh and eighth symbols idenitfied the model (same as number in column 1 of table below). The 10th symbol was a letter designating the model year. The 11th symbol designated the assembly plant. The last six symbols were the sequential production number starting with 000001.

ENGINE

BASE FOUR (Cabriolet, Golf, Jeta, Quantum Wagon, Scirocco): Inline, overhead-cam four-cylinder. Cast-iron block and light alloy head. Displacement: 109 cid (1786 cc). Bore & Stroke: 3.19 x 3.40 (81 x 86.4 mm). Compression Ratio: 8.5:1 (Quantum, 9.0:1). Brake Horsepower: (Golf/Jetta) 85 at 5250 rpm, (Quantum) 88 at 5500 rpm, (Cabriolet/Scirocco) 90 at 5550 rpm) Torque: (Golf/Jetta) 98 lbs.-ft. at 3000 rpm, (Quantum)

96 at 3250 rpm, (Cabrilet/Scirocc0) 100 at 3000 rpm. Five main bearings. Multi-point fuel injection.

DIESEL FOUR (Golf, Jetta): Inline, overhead-cam four-cylinder. Cast-iron block and light alloy head. Displacement: 97 cid (1588 cc). Bore & Stroke: 3.01 x 3.40 (76.5 x 86.4 mm). Compression Ratio: 23.0:1. Brake Horsepower: 52 at 4800 rpm. Torque: 71 lbs.-ft. at 2000 rpm. Five main bearings. Fuel injection.

TURBO DIESEL FOUR (Golf, Jetta GL, Quantum): Inline, overhead-cam four-cylinder. Cast-iron block and light alloy head. Displacement: 97 cid (1588 cc). Bore & Stroke: 3.01 x 3.40 (76.5 x 86.4 mm). Compression Ratio: 23.0:1. Brake Horsepower: 68 at 4500. Torque: 98 lbs.-ft. at 2500 rpm. Five main bearings. Fuel injection. Turbocharged.

BASE FIVE (Quantum sedan): Inline, overhead-cam five-cylinder. Cast-iron block and light alloy head. Displacement: 136 cid (2229 cc). Bore & Stroke: 3.19 x 3.40 (81 x 86.4 mm). Compression Ratio: 8.5:1. Brake Horsepower: 110 at 5500 rpm. Torque: 126 lbs.-ft. at 3000 rpm. Six main bearings. Multi-point fuel injection.

BASE FOUR (Vanagon): Four-cylinder. Horizontally-opposed. Water-cooled. Displacement: 1915 cc. Bore & Stroke: 3.70 x 3.72. Compression ratio: 8.6:1. Brake Horsepower: 82. at 4800 rpm. Torque: 105 lbs.-ft. at 2600 rpm.

CHASSIS

CABRIOLET: Wheelbase: 94.5 in. Overall Length: 159.3 in. Height: 55.6 in. Width: 64.2 in. Front Tread: 54.7 in. Rear Tread: 53.5 in.

GOLF/GTI: Wheelbase: 97.3 in. Overall Length: 158.0 in. Height: 55.7 in. Width: 65.5 in. Front Tread: 56.3 in. Rear Tread: 56.0 in.

JETTA: Wheelbase: 97.3 in. Overall Length: 171.7 in. Height: 55.7 in. Width: 65.5 in. Front Tread: 56.3 in. Rear Tread: 56.0 in.

QUANTUM: Wheelbase: 100.4 in. Overall Length: (Sedan) 180.2 in., (Wagon) 183.1 in. Height: 55.1 in. Width: 66.9 in. Front Tread: 55.7 in. Rear Tread: 56.0 in.

SCIROCCO: Wheelbase: 94.5 in. Overall Length: 165.7 in. Height: 51.4 in. Width: 64.0 in. Front Tread: 54.7 in. Rear Tread: 53.5 in.

VANAGON: Wheelbase: 96.9 in. Overall Length: 179.9 in. Height: 77.2 in. Width: 72.6 in. Front Tread: 61.8 in. Rear Tread: 61.8 in.

TECHNICAL

CABRIOLET: Layout: front-engine, front-wheel-drive. Transmission: five-speed manual. Steering: rack and pinion. Suspension (front): MacPherson struts with coil springs. Suspension (rear): torsion beam axle with trailing arms and coil springss. Brakes: front disc, rear drum. Body Construction: steel unibody.

GOLF/GTI: Layout: front-engine, front-wheel-drive. Transmission: five-speed manual. Steering: rack and pinion. Suspension (front): MacPherson struts with coil springs. Suspension (rear): torsion beam axle with trailing arms and coil springss. Brakes: front disc, rear drum. Body Construction: steel unibody.

JETTA: Layout: front-engine, front-wheel-drive. Transmission: five-speed manual. Steering: rack and pinion. Suspension (front): MacPherson struts with coil springs. Suspension (rear): torsion beam axle with trailing arms and coil springss. Brakes: front disc, rear drum. Body Construction: steel unibody.

QUANTUM: Layout: front-engine, front-wheel-drive. Transmission: five-speed manual. Steering: rack and pinion. Suspension (front): MacPherson struts with coil springs. Suspension (rear): torsion beam axle with trailing arms and coil springss. Brakes: front disc, rear drum. Body Construction: steel unibody.

SCIROCCO: Layout: front-engine, front-wheel-drive. Transmission: five-speed manual. Steering: rack and pinion. Suspension (front): MacPherson struts with coil springs. Suspension (rear): torsion beam axle with trailing arms and coil springss. Brakes: front disc, rear drum. Body Construction: steel unibody.Suspension (rear): torsion beam axle with coil springs. Brakes: front disc, rear drum. Body Construction: steel unibody.

VANAGON: Layout: rear-engine, rear-drive. Transmission: manual. Front suspension: MacPherson struts with coil springs. Rear suspension: semi-trailing arms with torsion bars. Brakes: front disc/rear drum.

MANUFACTURER: Volkswagenwerk AG, Wolfsburg, West Germany, and Volkswagen of America Inc. (plant in Pennsylvania).

DISTRIBUTOR: Volkswagen of America Inc., Troy, Michigan.

Old Cars Weekly Archives

In 1985, the famed VW Golf was introduced to the United States marketplace.

1986

CABRIOLET—FOUR Except for minor changes the "new" 1986 Cabriolet was the smaller Rabbit convertible using the "old" subcompact Rabbit body. A 1.8-liter 90-hp four was used.

GOLF—FOUR The Golf again came in two- and four-door hatchback models. Under the hood was a modified version of the 1.8-liter engine, developing 85 hp. The GTI two-door hatchback was again part of the series.

JETTA—FOUR The Jetta was similar to the Golf, but with notchback bodies. Two- and four-door sedans came in base trim. Also in the model lineup were GL and GLI renditions of the four-door sedan.

QUANTUM—FOUR/FIVE Audi's 2.1-liter five-cylinder engine was no longer available, but a 2.2-liter version became standard on the sedan. Wagons used a 1.8-liter four. Otherwise, production continued with little change. For 1986, a Synchro wagon with automatic four-wheel-drive was added to the series.

SCIROCCO—FOUR The Scirocco saw practically no changes in 1986.

VANAGON—FOUR For 1986, Volkswagen introduced an automatic four-wheel-drive version of the Vanagon. It was called the Syncro. Engines in all Vanagons grew to 2.1-liter displacement and 95 hp.

I.D. DATA: Volkswagen's Vehicle Identification Number (VIN) now had 17 symbols. The first three symbols identified the manufacturer, make and type of vehicle. The fourth symbol was a letter designating the body type. The fifth symbol was a letter identifying the engine. The sixth symbol designated the type of restraint system. The seventh and eighth symbols idenitfied the model (same as number in column 1 of table below). The ninth symbol was a check digit. The 10th symbol was a letter designating the model year. The 11th symbol designated the assembly plant. The last six symbols were the sequential production number starting with 000001.

ENGINE

BASE FOUR (Cabriolet, Golf, Jeta, Quantum wagon, Scirocco): Inline, overhead-cam four-cylinder. Cast-iron block and light alloy head. Displacement: 109 cid (1786 cc). Bore & Stroke: 3.19 x 3.40 (81 x 86.4 mm). Compression Ratio: 8.5:1 (Quantum, 9.0:1). Brake Horsepower: (Golf/Jetta) 85 at 5250 rpm, (Quantum) 88 at 5500 rpm, (Cabriolet/Scirocco) 90 at 5550 rpm) Torque: (Golf/Jetta) 98 lbs.-ft. at 3000 rpm, (Quantum) 96 at 3250 rpm, (Cabrilet/Scirocc0) 100 at 3000 rpm. Five main bearings. Multi-point fuel injection.

DIESEL FOUR (Golf, Jetta): Inline, overhead-cam four-cylinder. Cast-iron block and light alloy head.

Above: **Drivers enjoyed open-air fun driving the 1986 1/2 Wolfsburg Edition Cabriolet.**

Old Cars Weekly Archive

Volkswagen offered a modified 1.8 liter engine in 1986 Golf models.

Bottom: **One edition of the 1986 Vanagon was the surfer-inspired Hobie Cat.**

Old Cars Weekly Archives

Model Code	Body Type & Seating	POE Price	Weight (lbs.)	ProductionTotal
CABRIOLET				
15	2d Convertible-4P	11895	2254	Note 1
GOLF				
17	2d Hatchback-5P	7190	2150	Note 1
17	4d Hatchback-5P	7400	2222	Note 1
GOLF GTI				
GTI	2d Hatchback-5P	9190	2196	Note 1
JETTA				
16	2d Sedan-5P	150	2275	Note 1
16	4d Sedan-5P	8370	2319	Note 1
JETTA GL				
16	4d Sedan-5P	8670	2330	Note 1
JETTA GLI				
16	4d Sedan-5P	10190	2348	Note 1
QUANTUM GL				
32	4d Sedan-5P	13595	2661	Note 1
QUANTUM WAGON				
33	5d Wagon-4P	11870	2563	Note 1
33	5d Synchro Wagon-4P	15995	2800	Note 1
SCIROCCO				
53	2d Coupe-4P	9980	2181	Note 1
VANAGON				
25	3d Station Wagon	10120	3270	Note 2
VANAGON L				
25	3d Station Wagon	12290	3270	Note 2
VANAGON GL				
25	3d Station Wagon-9P	13140	3460	Note 2
25	3d Station Wag Synchro	15315	3600	Note 2
VANAGON CAMPER				
25	3d Camper	14700	3622	Note 2
25	3d Camper Synchro	18875	3952	Note 2
25	3d Camper GL	17190	3622	Note 2
25	3d Camper GL Synchro	19365	3952	Note 2

Note 1: 143,319 imported Volkswagens were sold in the United States during 1986.
Note 2: Vanagon production not available.

Displacement: 97 cid (1588 cc). Bore & Stroke: 3.01 x 3.40 (76.5 x 86.4 mm). Compression Ratio: 23.0:1. Brake Horsepower: 52 at 4800 rpm. Torque: 71 lbs.-ft. at 2000 rpm. Five main bearings. Fuel injection.

TURBO DIESEL FOUR (Golf, Jetta GL, Quantum): Inline, overhead-cam four-cylinder. Cast-iron block and light alloy head. Displacement: 97 cid (1588 cc). Bore & Stroke: 3.01 x 3.40 (76.5 x 86.4 mm). Compression Ratio: 23.0:1. Brake Horsepower: 68 at 4500. Torque: 98 lbs.-ft. at 2500 rpm. Five main bearings. Fuel injection. Turbocharged.

BASE FIVE (Quantum sedan): Inline, overhead-cam five-cylinder. Cast-iron block and light alloy head. Displacement: 136 cid (2229 cc). Bore & Stroke: 3.19 x 3.40 (81 x 86.4 mm). Compression Ratio: 8.5:1. Brake Horsepower: 110 at 5500 rpm. Torque: 126 lbs.-ft. at 3000 rpm. Six main bearings. Multi-point fuel injection.

In 1985, Volkswagen produced a 50th Anniversary Beetle, not available in the U.S.

Old Cars Weekly Archive

BASE FOUR (Vanagon): Four-cylinder. Horizontally-opposed. Water-cooled. Displacement: 2109 cc. Bore & Stroke: 3.70 x 3.99. Compression ratio: 8.6:1. Brake Horsepower: 90-95. at 4800 rpm. Torque: NA.

CHASSIS

CABRIOLET: Wheelbase: 94.5 in. Overall Length: 159.3 in. Height: 55.6 in. Width: 64.2 in. Front Tread: 54.7 in. Rear Tread: 53.5 in.

There were vehicles for many tastes and budgets in the 1986 Volkswagen lineup.

John Gunnell

GOLF/GTI: Wheelbase: 97.3 in. Overall Length: 158.0 in. Height: 55.7 in. Width: 65.5 in. Front Tread: 56.3 in. Rear Tread: 56.0 in.

JETTA: Wheelbase: 97.3 in. Overall Length: 171.7 in. Height: 55.7 in. Width: 65.5 in. Front Tread: 56.3 in. Rear Tread: 56.0 in.

QUANTUM: Wheelbase: 100.4 in. Overall Length: (Sedan) 180.2 in., (Wagon) 183.1 in. Height: 55.1 in. Width: 66.9 in. Front Tread: 55.7 in. Rear Tread: 56.0 in.

SCIROCCO: Wheelbase: 94.5 in. Overall Length: 165.7 in. Height: 51.4 in. Width: 64.0 in. Front Tread: 54.7 in. Rear Tread: 53.5 in.

VANAGON: Wheelbase: 96.9 in. Overall Length: 179.9 in. Height: 77.2 in. Width: 72.6 in. Front Tread: 61.8 in. Rear Tread: 61.8 in.

TECHNICAL

CABRIOLET: Layout: front-engine, front-wheel-drive. Transmission: five-speed manual. Steering: rack and pinion. Suspension (front): MacPherson struts with coil springs. Suspension (rear): torsion beam axle with trailing arms and coil springss. Brakes: front disc, rear drum. Body Construction: steel unibody.

GOLF/GTI: Layout: front-engine, front-wheel-drive. Transmission: five-speed manual. Steering: rack and pinion. Suspension (front): MacPherson struts with coil springs. Suspension (rear): torsion beam axle with trailing arms and coil springss. Brakes: front disc, rear drum. Body Construction: steel unibody.

JETTA: Layout: front-engine, front-wheel-drive. Transmission: five-speed manual. Steering: rack and pinion. Suspension (front): MacPherson struts with coil springs. Suspension (rear): torsion beam axle with trailing arms and coil springss. Brakes: front disc, rear drum. Body Construction: steel unibody.

QUANTUM: Layout: front-engine, front-wheel-drive. Transmission: five-speed manual. Steering: rack and pinion. Suspension (front): MacPherson struts with coil springs. Suspension (rear): torsion beam axle with trailing arms and coil springss. Brakes: front disc, rear drum. Body Construction: steel unibody.

SCIROCCO: Layout: front-engine, front-wheel-drive. Transmission: five-speed manual. Steering: rack and pinion. Suspension (front): MacPherson struts with coil springs. Suspension (rear): torsion beam axle with trailing arms and coil springs. Brakes: front disc, rear drum. Body Construction: steel unibody.Suspension (rear): torsion beam axle with coil springs. Brakes: front disc, rear drum. Body Construction: steel unibody.

VANAGON: Layout: rear-engine, rear-drive. Transmission: manual. Front suspension: MacPherson struts with coil springs. Rear suspension: semi-trailing arms with torsion bars. Brakes: front disc/rear drum.

MANUFACTURER: Volkswagenwerk AG, Wolfsburg, West Germany, and Volkswagen of America Inc. (plant in Pennsylvania).

DISTRIBUTOR: Volkswagen of America Inc., Troy, Michigan

1987

FOX—FOUR Another front-wheel-drive Volkswagen emerged for 1987. The Fox was built in Brazil. The new subcompact came as a two-door sedan, a four-door sedan or a two-door station wagon. Under the hood was Volkswagen's familiar 1.8-liter engine rated at 81 hp. Only a four-speed manual transmission was available in 1987 models.

CABRIOLET—FOUR Little change was evident in Volkswagen's convertible, which was again based on the old subcompact Rabbit platform.

GOLF—FOUR Production of the hatchback Golf continued with little change, except that the 16-valve engine from the Scirocco 16V became available in the GTI/GLI editions. This was a "hot" 123-hp engine. GT versions adopted the 102-hp engine.

JETTA—FOUR Production of the notchback Jetta also continued with little change, except that the 16-valve 123-hp engine from the Scirocco 16V became available in the GLI editions.

QUANTUM—FIVE The 1987 Quantum line offered the four-wheel-drive Syncro wagon and the two-wheel-drive sedan. Both had very little change. Both models used an Audi five-cylinder engine.

SCIROCCO—FOUR The stronger 123-hp engine was installed in the 16V edition of Volkswagen's Sport Coupe. Base Sciroccos retained the 90-hp engine.

VANAGON—FOUR Volkswagen also continued to produce the Vanagon station wagon and Camper bus, with two- or four-wheel drive. The Vanagon GL added a second sliding side door for 1987.

I.D. DATA: Volkswagen's Vehicle Identification Number (VIN) now had 17 symbols. The first three symbols identified the manufacturer, make and type of vehicle. The fourth symbol was a letter designating the body type. The fifth symbol was a letter identifying the engine. The sixth symbol designated the type of restraint system. The seventh and eighth symbols idenitified the model (same as number in column 1 of table below). The ninth symbol was a check digit. The 10th symbol was a letter designating the model year. The 11th symbol designated the assembly plant. The last six symbols were the sequential production number starting with 000001.

ENGINE

BASE FOUR (Fox, Cabriolet, Golf, Jetta, Scirocco): Inline, overhead-cam four- cylinder. Cast-iron block and light alloy head. Displacement: 109 cid (1786 cc). Bore & Stroke: 3.19 x 3.40 (81 x 86.4 mm). Compression Ratio: (Fox) 9.0:1, (Golf/Jetta) 8.5:1, Brake Horsepower: (Fox) 81 at 5500 rpm, (Golf/Jetta) 85 at 5250 rpm, (Cabriolet/Scirocco) 90 at 5550 rpm. Torque: (Fox) 93 lbs.-ft. at 3250 rpm, (Golf/Jetta) 98 lbs.-ft. at 3000 rpm, (Cabriolet/Scirocco) 100 at 3000 rpm. Five main bearings. Multi-point fuel injection.

Above**: The VW Quantum used a five-cylinder Audi engine in the 1987 models.**

Old Cars Weekly Archives

The Brazilian-built Fox model was introduced to the United States in 1987.

Bottom: **The 123-hp Scirocco engine powered the Volkswagen GTI as well in 1987.**
Old Cars Weekly Archives

Bottom: **The 1987 VW Golf was a presence on American highways, as well as, the autobahn.**
Old Cars Weekly Archives

1987 VOLKSWAGEN PRODUCTION CHART

Model Code	Body Type & Seating	POE Price	Weight (lbs.)	Production Total
FOX				
30	2d Sedan-4P	5690	2150	Note 1
FOX GL				
30	4d Sedan-4P	6490	2190	Note 1
30	2d Station Wagon-4P	6590	2190	Note 1
CABRIOLET				
15	2d Convertible-4P	13250	2254	Note 1
GOLF GL				
17	2d Hatchback-5P	8190	2137	Note 1
17	4d Hatchback-5P	8400	NA	Note 1
GOLF GT				
17	2d Hatchback-5P	9675	2137	Note 1
17	4d Hatchback-5P	9885	2310	Note 1
GOLF GTI				
17	2d Hatchback-5P	10325	2203	Note 1
GOLF GTI 16V				
17	2d Hatchback-5P	12240	NA	Note 1
JETTA				
16	2d Sedan-5P	9290	2275	Note 1
16	4d Sedan-5P	9510	2330	Note 1
JETTA GL				
16	4d Sedan-5P	9990	2330	Note 1
JETTA GLI				
16	4d Sedan-5P	11690	2348	Note 1
JETTA GLI 16V				
16	4d Sedan-5P	13725	NA	Note 1
QUANTUM				
33	5d Station Wagon-5P	13450	2745	Note 1
QUANTUM GL				
32	4d Sedan-5P	14985	2661	Note 1
QUANTUM SYNCHRO				
33	5d Station Wagon-5P	16645	2976	Note 1
SCIROCCO				
53	2d Coupe-4P	10680	2221	Note 1
SCIROCCO 16V				
53	2d Coupe-4P	12980	2287	Note 1
VANAGON				
25	3d Station Wagon	11560	3270	Note 2
VANAGON GL				
25	3d Station Wagon-9P	14730	3270	Note 2
25	3d Station Wag Synchro	16905	3600	Note 2
VANAGON CAMPER				
25	3d Camper	16660	3622	Note 2
25	3d Camper Synchro	18835	3952	Note 2
VANAGON CAMPER GL				
25	3d Camper GL	19225	3622	Note 2
25	3d Camper GL Synchro	21500	3952	Note 2

Note 1: 130,641 imported Volkswagens were sold in the United States in 1987
Note 2: Separate Vanagon production not available..

OPTIONAL FOUR (Golf GTI, Jetta GLI): Inline, overhead-cam four- cylinder. Cast-iron block and light alloy head. Displacement: 109 cid (1786 cc). Bore & Stroke: 3.19 x 3.40 (81 x 86.4 mm). Compression Ratio: 10.0:1. Brake Horsepower: 102 at 5250 rpm. Torque: 110 lbs.-ft. at 3250 rpm. Five main bearings. Multi-point fuel injection.

BASE FOUR (Golf GTI 16V, Jetta GLI 16V, Scirocco 16V): Inline, overhead-cam four-cylinder (16-valve). Cast-iron block and light alloy head. Displacement: 109

cid (1786 cc). Bore & Stroke: 3.19 x 3.40 (81 x 86.4 mm). Compression Ratio: 10.0:1. Brake Horsepower: 123 at 5800 rpm. Torque: 120 lbs.-ft. at 4250 rpm. Five main bearings. Multi-point fuel injection.

ENGINE DIESEL FOUR (Golf, Jetta): Inline, overhead-cam four-cylinder. Cast-iron block and light alloy head. Displacement: 97 cid (1588 cc). Bore & Stroke: 3.01 x 3.40 (76.5 x 86.4 mm). Compression Ratio: 23.0:1. Brake

Horsepower: 52 at 4800 rpm. Torque: 71 lbs.- ft. at 2000 rpm. Five main bearings. Fuel injection.

BASE FIVE (Quantum): Inline, overhead-cam five-cylinder. Cast-iron block and light alloy head. Displacement: 136 cid (2229 cc). Bore & Stroke: 3.19 x 3.40 (81 x 86.4 mm). Compression Ratio: 8.5:1. Brake Horsepower: 110/115 at 5500 rpm. Torque: 122/126 lbs.-ft. at 3000 rpm. Six main bearings. Multi-point fuel injection.

BASE FOUR (Vanagon): Four-cylinder. Horizontally-opposed. Water-cooled. Displacement: 2109 cc. Bore & Stroke: 3.70 x 3.99. Compression ratio: 8.6:1. Brake Horsepower: 90-95. at 4800 rpm. Torque: NA.

CHASSIS

FOX: Wheelbase: 92.8 in. Overall Length: 163.4 in. Height: 53.7-54.3 in. Width: 63.0-63.9 in. Front Tread: 53.1 in. Rear Tread: 53.9 in.

CABRIOLET: Wheelbase: 94.5 in. Overall Length: 159.3 in. Height: 55.6 in. Width: 64.2 in. Front Tread: 54.7 in. Rear Tread: 53.5 in.

GOLF/GTI: Wheelbase: 97.3 in. Overall Length: 158.0 in. Height: 55.7 in. Width: 65.5 in. Front Tread: 56.3 in. Rear Tread: 56.0 in.

JETTA: Wheelbase: 97.3 in. Overall Length: 171.7 in. Height: 55.7 in. Width: 65.5 in. Front Tread: 56.3 in. Rear Tread: 56.0 in.

QUANTUM: Wheelbase: 100.4 in. Overall Length: (Sedan) 180.2 in., (Wagon) 183.1 in. Height: 55.1 in. Width: 66.7-66.9 in. Front Tread: 55.7 in. Rear Tread: 56.0 in.

SCIROCCO: Wheelbase: 94.5 in. Overall Length: 165.7 in. Height: 51.4 in. Width: 64.0 in. Front Tread: 54.7 in. Rear Tread: 53.5 in.

VANAGON: Wheelbase: 96.9 in. Overall Length: 179.9 in. Height: 77.2 in. Width: 72.6 in. Front Tread: 61.8 in. Rear Tread: 61.8 in.

TECHNICAL

FOX: Layout: front-engine, front-wheel-drive. Transmission: four-speed manual. Steering: rack and pinion. Suspension (front): MacPherson struts with coil springs. Suspension (rear): torsion beam axle with trailing arms and coil springsBrakes: front disc, rear drum except. Body Construction: steel unibody.

CABRIOLET: Layout: front-engine, front-wheel-drive. Transmission: five-speed manual. Steering: rack and pinion. Suspension (front): MacPherson struts with coil springs. Suspension (rear): torsion beam axle with trailing arms and coil springss. Brakes: front disc, rear drum. Body Construction: steel unibody.

GOLF/GTI: Layout: front-engine, front-wheel-drive. Transmission: five-speed manual. Steering: rack and pinion. Suspension (front): MacPherson struts with coil springs. Suspension (rear): torsion beam axle with trailing arms and coil springss. Brakes: front disc, rear drum. Body Construction: steel unibody.

JETTA: Layout: front-engine, front-wheel-drive. Transmission: five-speed manual. Steering: rack and pinion. Suspension (front): MacPherson struts with coil springs. Suspension (rear): torsion beam axle with trailing arms and coil springss. Brakes: front disc, rear drum. Body Construction: steel unibody.

QUANTUM: Layout: front-engine, front-wheel-drive. Transmission: five-speed manual. Steering: rack and pinion. Suspension (front): MacPherson struts with coil springs. Suspension (rear): torsion beam axle with trailing arms and coil springss. Brakes: front disc, rear drum. Body Construction: steel unibody.

SCIROCCO: Layout: front-engine, front-wheel-drive. Transmission: five-speed manual. Steering: rack and pinion. Suspension (front): MacPherson struts with coil springs. Suspension (rear): torsion beam axle with trailing arms and coil springss. Brakes: front disc, rear drum. Body Construction: steel unibody. Suspension (rear): torsion beam axle with coil springs. Brakes: front disc, rear drum (except Scirocco 16V 4-wheel disc). Body Construction: steel unibody.

VANAGON: Layout: rear-engine, rear-drive. Transmission: manual. Front suspension: MacPherson struts with coil springs. Rear suspension: semi-trailing arms with torsion bars. Brakes: front disc/rear drum.

MANUFACTURER: Volkswagenwerk AG, Wolfsburg, West Germany or Volkswagen of America Inc., Pennsylvania (Fox built in Brazil).

DISTRIBUTOR: Volkswagen of America Inc., Troy, Michigan.

1988

FOX—FOUR No major changes were made in the 1988 Fox.

CABRIOLET—FOUR Little change was evident in Volkswagen's convertible, which continued to be based on the previous-generation subcompact Rabbit platform.

GOLF—FOUR Little changed in the 1988 Golf series, too, but horsepower ratings went up for some models.

JETTA—FOUR Jettas had the same changes as Golf models.

QUANTUM—FIVE This was the last year for the Quantum sedan, wagon and Synchro wagon.

SCIROCCO—FOUR The Scirocco was another on-its-way-out model that remained available into 1988, but then was dropped.

Above: **The 1988 model year was the final time buyers could choose the VW Quantum series.**

Phil Hall

VANAGON—FOUR Not much change for the new-generation Transporters either, but the model offerings were cut way back.

I.D. DATA: Volkswagen's Vehicle Identification Number (VIN) now had 17 symbols. The first three symbols identified the manufacturer, make and type of vehicle. The fourth symbol was a letter designating the body type. The fifth symbol was a letter identifying the engine. The sixth symbol designated the type of restraint system. The seventh and eighth symbols idenitified the model (same as number in column 1 of table below). The ninth symbol was a check digit. The 10th symbol was a letter designating the model year. The 11th symbol designated the assembly plant. The last six symbols were the sequential production number starting with 000001.

ENGINE

BASE FOUR (Fox, Cabriolet, Golf, Jetta, Scirocco): Inline, overhead-cam four- cylinder. Cast-iron block and light alloy head. Displacement: 109 cid (1786 cc). Bore & Stroke: 3.19 x 3.40 (81 x 86.4 mm). Compression Ratio: (Fox) 9.0:1, (Golf/Jetta) 8.5:1, Brake Horsepower: (Fox)

Model Code	Body Type & Seating	POE Price	Weight (lbs.)	ProductionTotal
	FOX			
30	2d Sedan-4P	5990	2150	Note 1
	FOX GL			
30	4d Sedan-4P	6890	2190	Note 1
30	2d Station Wagon-4P	6990	2190	Note 1
	CABRIOLET			
15	2d Convertible-4P	14450	2254	Note 1
	GOLF			
17	2d Hatchback-5P	7990	2150	Note 1
	GOLF GL			
17	2d Hatchback-5P	8490	2150	Note 1
17	4d Hatchback-5P	**8700**	2209	Note 1
	GOLF GT			
17	2d Hatchback-5P	9975	2154	Note 1
17	4d Hatchback-5P	10185	2213	Note 1
	GOLF GTI 16V			
17	2d Hatchback-5P	12725	2267	Note 1
	JETTA			
16	2d Sedan-5P	8990	2305	Note 1
16	4d Sedan-5P	9210	2330	Note 1
	JETTA GL			
16	4d Sedan-5P	10340	2330	Note 1
	JETTA CARAT			
16	4d Sedan-5P	14200	2433	Note 1
	JETTA GLI 16V			
16	4d Sedan-5P	13725	2460	Note 1
	QUANTUM GL			
32	4d Sedan-5P	17525	2646	Note 1
33	5d Station Wagon-5P	17925	2745	Note 1
	QUANTUM SYNCHRO			
33	5d Station Wagon-5P	20705	2976	Note 1
	SCIROCCO 16V			
53	2d Coupe-4P	14090	2287	Note 1
	VANAGON			
25	3d Station Wagon	11560	3270	Note 2
	VANAGON GL			
25	3d Station Wagon-9P	16240	3460	Note 2
	VANAGON CAMPER GL			
25	3d Camper GL	21180	3622	Note 2

Note 1: 128,503 imported Volkswagens were sold in the United States in 1987.

Note 2: Separate production total for Vanagon not available.

A five-cylinder, 136-cid engine was available for the 1988 Volkswagen Quantum.

81 at 5500 rpm, (Golf/Jetta) 100 at 5250 rpm, (Cabriolet/Scirocco) 90 at 5550 rpm. Torque: (Fox) 93 lbs.-ft. at 3250 rpm, (Golf/Jetta) 98 lbs.-ft. at 3000 rpm, (Cabriolet/Scirocco) 100 at 3000 rpm. Five main bearings. Multi-point fuel injection.

OPTIONAL FOUR (Golf GTI, Jetta GLI): Inline, overhead-cam four- cylinder. Cast-iron block and light alloy head. Displacement: 109 cid (1786 cc). Bore & Stroke: 3.19 x 3.40 (81 x 86.4 mm). Compression Ratio: 10.0:1. Brake Horsepower: 105 at 5250 rpm. Torque: 110 lbs.-ft. at 3250 rpm. Five main bearings. Multi-point fuel injection.

BASE FOUR (Golf GTI 16V, Jetta GLI 16V, Scirocco 16V): Inline, overhead-cam four-cylinder (16-valve). Cast-iron block and light alloy head. Displacement: 109 cid (1786 cc). Bore & Stroke: 3.19 x 3.40 (81 x 86.4 mm).

Compression Ratio: 10.0:1. Brake Horsepower: 123 at 5800 rpm. Torque: 120 lbs.-ft. at 4250 rpm. Five main bearings. Multi-point fuel injection.

DIESEL FOUR (Golf, Jetta): Inline, overhead-cam four-cylinder. Cast-iron block and light alloy head. Displacement: 97 cid (1588 cc). Bore & Stroke: 3.01 x 3.40 (76.5 x 86.4 mm). Compression Ratio: 23.0:1. Brake Horsepower: 52 at 4800 rpm. Torque: 71 lbs.- ft. at 2000 rpm. Five main bearings. Fuel injection.

BASE FIVE (Quantum): Inline, overhead-cam five-cylinder. Cast-iron block and light alloy head. Displacement: 136 cid (2229 cc). Bore & Stroke: 3.19 x 3.40 (81 x 86.4 mm). Compression Ratio: 8.5:1. Brake Horsepower: 110/115 at 5500 rpm. Torque: 122/126 lbs.-ft. at 3000 rpm. Six main bearings. Multi-point fuel injection.

BASE FOUR (Vanagon): Four-cylinder. Horizontally-opposed. Water-cooled. Displacement: 2109 cc. Bore & Stroke: 3.70 x 3.99. Compression ratio: 8.6:1. Brake Horsepower: 90-95. at 4800 rpm. Torque: NA.

CHASSIS

FOX: Wheelbase: 92.8 in. Overall Length: 163.4 in. Height: 53.7-54.3 in. Width: 63.0-63.9 in. Front Tread: 53.1 in. Rear Tread: 53.9 in.

CABRIOLET: Wheelbase: 94.5 in. Overall Length: 159.3 in. Height: 55.6 in. Width: 64.2 in. Front Tread: 54.7 in. Rear Tread: 53.5 in.

GOLF/GTI: Wheelbase: 97.3 in. Overall Length: 158.0 in. Height: 55.7 in. Width: 65.5 in. Front Tread: 56.3 in. Rear Tread: 56.0 in.

JETTA: Wheelbase: 97.3 in. Overall Length: 171.7 in. Height: 55.7 in. Width: 65.5 in. Front Tread: 56.3 in. Rear Tread: 56.0 in.,

QUANTUM: Wheelbase: 100.4 in. Overall Length: (Sedan) 180.2 in., (Wagon) 183.1 in. Height: 55.1 in. Width: 66.7-66.9 in. Front Tread: 55.7 in. Rear Tread: 56.0 in.

SCIROCCO: Wheelbase: 94.5 in. Overall Length: 165.7 in. Height: 51.4 in. Width: 64.0 in. Front Tread: 54.7 in. Rear Tread: 53.5 in.

VANAGON: Wheelbase: 96.9 in. Overall Length: 179.9 in. Height: 77.2 in. Width: 72.6 in. Front Tread: 61.8 in. Rear Tread: 61.8 in.

TECHNICAL

FOX: Layout: front-engine, front-wheel-drive. Transmission: four-speed manual. Steering: rack and pinion. Suspension (front): MacPherson struts with coil springs. Suspension (rear): torsion beam axle with trailing arms and coil springsBrakes: front disc, rear drum except. Body Construction: steel unibody.

CABRIOLET: Layout: front-engine, front-wheel-drive. Transmission: five-speed manual. Steering: rack and pinion. Suspension (front): MacPherson struts with coil springs. Suspension (rear): torsion beam axle with trailing arms and coil springss. Brakes: front disc, rear drum. Body Construction: steel unibody.

GOLF/GTI: Layout: front-engine, front-wheel-drive. Transmission: five-speed manual. Steering: rack and pinion. Suspension (front): MacPherson struts with coil springs. Suspension (rear): torsion beam axle with trailing arms and coil springss. Brakes: front disc, rear drum. Body Construction: steel unibody.

JETTA: Layout: front-engine, front-wheel-drive. Transmission: five-speed manual. Steering: rack and pinion. Suspension (front): MacPherson struts with coil springs. Suspension (rear): torsion beam axle with trailing arms and coil springss. Brakes: front disc, rear drum. Body Construction: steel unibody.

QUANTUM: Layout: front-engine, front-wheel-drive. Transmission: five-speed manual. Steering: rack and pinion. Suspension (front): MacPherson struts with coil springs. Suspension (rear): torsion beam axle with trailing arms and coil springss. Brakes: front disc, rear drum. Body Construction: steel unibody.

SCIROCCO: Layout: front-engine, front-wheel-drive. Transmission: five-speed manual. Steering: rack and pinion. Suspension (front): MacPherson struts with coil springs. Suspension (rear): torsion beam axle with trailing arms and coil springss. Brakes: front disc, rear drum. Body Construction: steel unibody. Suspension (rear): torsion beam axle with coil springs. Brakes: front disc, rear drum (except Scirocco 16V 4-wheel disc). Body Construction: steel unibody.

VANAGON: Layout: rear-engine, rear-drive. Transmission: manual. Front suspension: MacPherson struts with coil springs. Rear suspension: semi-trailing arms with torsion bars. Brakes: front disc/rear drum.

MANUFACTURER: Volkswagenwerk AG, Wolfsburg, West Germany or Volkswagen of America Inc., Pennsylvania (Fox built in Brazil).

DISTRIBUTOR: Volkswagen of America Inc., Troy, Michigan.

1989

FOX—FOUR The front-wheel-drive Fox subcompact got a five-speed transmission in 1989. It came in base and GL trim levels, plus a new GL Sport line. Also new was the GL two-door sedan. The base model came only as a two-door sedan. The other trim levels offered that model plus a four-door sedan and two-door station wagon. The 1.8-liter 81-hp engine was used again.

CABRIOLET—FOUR Once again, little change was evident in Volkswagen's front-wheel-drive convertible. It continued to use the older, sub-compact-sized Rabbit body.

GOLF—FOUR The front-wheel-drive Golf lineup was reduced by two models in 1989. Remaining was a base two-door hatchback, two- and four-door GL hatchbacks and the two-door hatchback GTI with the 16-valve engine. Anti-lock braking became optional for 1989 on the top-level models.

JETTA—FOUR The lineup of front-wheel-drive Jetta models was unchanged. The base offerings were two- and four-door notchback sedans. The four-door came with GL trim. The Carat was a four-door as well, as was the 16-valve GLI.

VANAGON—FOUR Volkswagen's only U.S.-market rear-wheel-drive passenger-vehicle line offered GL station wagons and campers, a Carat station wagon and four-wheel-drive "Synchro" versions of both the GL Station Wagon and GL Camper.

I.D. DATA: Volkswagen's Vehicle Identification Number (VIN) now had 17 symbols. The first three symbols identified the manufacturer, make and type of vehicle. The fourth symbol was a letter designating the body type. The fifth symbol was a letter identifying the engine. The sixth symbol designated the type of restraint system. The seventh and eighth symbols idenitified the model (same as number in column 1 of table below). The ninth symbol was a check digit. The 10th symbol was a letter designating the model year. The 11th symbol designated the assembly plant. The last six symbols were the sequential production number starting with 000001.

More than 129,000 Volkswagens were sold in the United States in 1989.

Left: **In 1981, Jetta offered the upscale Wolfsburg Limited Edition sedan.**

Old Cars Weekly Archives

Bottom: **A dressed-up Cabriolet was offered in 1989 as the Wolfsburg Limited Edition.**

Old Cars Weekly Archives

1989 VOLKSWAGEN PRODUCTION CHART

Model Code	Body Type & Seating	POE Price	Weight (lbs.)	ProductionTotal
FOX				
30	2d Sedan-4P	6890	2126	Note 1
FOX GL				
30	2d Sedan-4P	7720	2126	Note 1
30	4d Sedan-4P	7920	2203	Note 1
30	2d Station Wagon-4P	8150	2214	Note 1
FOX GL SPORT				
30	2d Sedan-4P	8195	2126	Note 1
30	4d Sedan-4P	8395	2203	Note 1
CABRIOLET				
15	2d Convertible-4P	15195	2274	Note 1
GOLF				
17	2d Hatchback-5P	8465	2194	Note 1
GOLF GL				
17	2d Hatchback-5P	9170	2246	Note 1
17	4d Hatchback-5P	9380	2246	Note 1
GOLF GTI 16V				
17	2d Hatchback-5P	13650	2267	Note 1
JETTA				
16	2d Sedan-5P	9690	2305	Note 1
16	4d Sedan-5P	9910	2330	Note 1
JETTA GL				
16	4d Sedan-5P	11120	2330	Note 1
JETTA CARAT				
16	4d Sedan-5P	15140	2433	Note 1
JETTA GLI 16V				
16	4d Sedan-5P	14770	2416	Note 1
VANAGON GL				
25	3d Station Wagon-9P	17035	3460	Note 2
25	3d Camper	22235	3622	Note 2
VANAGON CARAT				
25	3d Station Wagon-9P	19355	3460	Note 2
VANAGON GL SYNCHRO				
25	3d Station Wagon-9P	20560	3600	Note 2
25	3d Camper GL	25760	3952	Note 2

Note 1: 129,705 imported Volkswagens were sold in the United States in 1987.

Note 2: Separate production total for Vanagon not available.

ENGINE

BASE FOUR (Fox, Cabriolet, Golf, Jetta): Inline, overhead-cam four-cylinder. Cast-iron block and light alloy head. Displacement: 109 cid (1786 cc). Bore & Stroke: 3.19 x 3.40 (81 x 86.4 mm). Compression Ratio: (Fox) 9.0:1, (Golf/Jetta) 8.5:1, Brake Horsepower: (Fox) 81 at 5500 rpm, (Golf/Jetta) 100 at 5250 rpm, (Cabriolet/Scirocco) 90 at 5550 rpm. Torque: (Fox) 93 lbs.-ft. at 3250 rpm, (Golf/Jetta) 98 lbs.-ft. at 3000 rpm, (Cabriolet/Scirocco) 100 at 3000 rpm. Five main bearings. Multi-point fuel injection.

OPTIONAL FOUR (Golf GTI, Jetta GLI): Inline, overhead-cam four- cylinder. Cast-iron block and light alloy head. Displacement: 109 cid (1786 cc). Bore & Stroke: 3.19 x 3.40 (81 x 86.4 mm). Compression Ratio: 10.0:1. Brake Horsepower: 105 at 5250 rpm. Torque: 110 lbs.-ft. at 3250 rpm. Five main bearings. Multi-point fuel injection.

BASE FOUR (Golf GTI 16V, Jetta GLI 16V, Scirocco 16V): Inline, overhead-cam four-cylinder (16-valve). Cast-iron block and light alloy head. Displacement: 109 cid (1786 cc). Bore & Stroke: 3.19 x 3.40 (81 x 86.4 mm). Compression Ratio: 10.0:1. Brake Horsepower: 123 at 5800 rpm. Torque: 120 lbs.-ft. at 4250 rpm. Five main bearings. Multi-point fuel injection.

DIESEL FOUR (Golf, Jetta): Inline, overhead-cam four-cylinder. Cast-iron block and light alloy head.

John Gunnell

In 1989, Volkswagen offered excitement with its Jetta GLI 16-valve sedan.

Displacement: 97 cid (1588 cc). Bore & Stroke: 3.01 x 3.40 (76.5 x 86.4 mm). Compression Ratio: 23.0:1. Brake Horsepower: 52 at 4800 rpm. Torque: 71 lbs.- ft. at 2000 rpm. Five main bearings. Fuel injection.

BASE FOUR (Vanagon): Four-cylinder. Horizontally-opposed. Water-cooled. Displacement: 2109 cc. Bore & Stroke: 3.70 x 3.99. Compression ratio: 8.6:1. Brake Horsepower: 90-95. at 4800 rpm. Torque: NA.

CHASSIS

FOX: Wheelbase: 92.8 in. Overall Length: 163.4 in. Height: 53.7-54.3 in. Width: 63.0-63.9 in. Front Tread: 53.1 in. Rear Tread: 53.9 in.

CABRIOLET: Wheelbase: 94.5 in. Overall Length: 159.3 in. Height: 55.6 in. Width: 64.2 in. Front Tread: 54.7 in. Rear Tread: 53.5 in.

GOLF/GTI: Wheelbase: 97.3 in. Overall Length: 158.0 in. Height: 55.7 in. Width: 65.5 in. Front Tread: 56.3 in. Rear Tread: 56.0 in.

JETTA: Wheelbase: 97.3 in. Overall Length: 171.7 in. Height: 55.7 in. Width: 65.5 in. Front Tread: 56.3 in. Rear Tread: 56.0 in.,

QUANTUM: Wheelbase: 100.4 in. Overall Length: (Sedan) 180.2 in., (Wagon) 183.1 in. Height: 55.1 in. Width: 66.7-66.9 in. Front Tread: 55.7 in. Rear Tread: 56.0 in.

SCIROCCO: Wheelbase: 94.5 in. Overall Length: 165.7 in. Height: 51.4 in. Width: 64.0 in. Front Tread: 54.7 in. Rear Tread: 53.5 in.

VANAGON: Wheelbase: 96.9 in. Overall Length: 179.9 in. Height: 77.2 in. Width: 72.6 in. Front Tread: 61.8 in. Rear Tread: 61.8 in.

TECHNICAL

FOX: Layout: front-engine, front-wheel-drive. Transmission: four-speed manual. Steering: rack and pinion. Suspension (front): MacPherson struts with coil springs. Suspension (rear): torsion beam axle with trailing arms and coil springsBrakes: front disc, rear drum except. Body Construction: steel unibody.

CABRIOLET: Layout: front-engine, front-wheel-drive. Transmission: five-speed manual. Steering: rack and pinion. Suspension (front): MacPherson struts with coil springs. Suspension (rear): torsion beam axle with trailing arms and coil springss. Brakes: front disc, rear drum. Body Construction: steel unibody.

GOLF/GTI: Layout: front-engine, front-wheel-drive. Transmission: five-speed manual. Steering: rack and pinion. Suspension (front): MacPherson struts with coil springs. Suspension (rear): torsion beam axle with trailing arms and coil springss. Brakes: front disc, rear drum. Body Construction: steel unibody.

JETTA: Layout: front-engine, front-wheel-drive. Transmission: five-speed manual. Steering: rack and pinion. Suspension (front): MacPherson struts with coil springs. Suspension (rear): torsion beam axle with trailing arms and coil springss. Brakes: front disc, rear drum. Body Construction: steel unibody.

QUANTUM: Layout: front-engine, front-wheel-drive. Transmission: five-speed manual. Steering: rack and pinion. Suspension (front): MacPherson struts with coil springs. Suspension (rear): torsion beam axle with trailing arms and coil springss. Brakes: front disc, rear drum. Body Construction: steel unibody.

SCIROCCO: Layout: front-engine, front-wheel-drive. Transmission: five-speed manual. Steering: rack and pinion. Suspension (front): MacPherson struts with coil springs. Suspension (rear): torsion beam axle with trailing arms and coil springss. Brakes: front disc, rear drum. Body Construction: steel unibody. Suspension (rear): torsion beam axle with coil springs. Brakes: front disc, rear drum (except Scirocco 16V 4-wheel disc). Body Construction: steel unibody.

VANAGON: Layout: rear-engine, rear-drive. Transmission: manual. Front suspension: MacPherson struts with coil springs. Rear suspension: semi-trailing arms with torsion bars. Brakes: front disc/rear drum.

MANUFACTURER: Volkswagenwerk AG, Wolfsburg, West Germany or Volkswagen of America Inc., Pennsylvania (Fox built in Brazil).

DISTRIBUTOR: Volkswagen of America Inc., Troy, Michigan.

The Golf GL was one of four models offered in the Golf series in 1989.

Our car the movie star.

You are looking at the romantic lead of a big new Hollywood picture.

Please, no autographs.

The picture is Walt Disney Studio's "The Love Bug." And our VW appears (in all its real life splendor) as Herbie, the main character.

Why would a big film studio want to make a movie star out of the bug?

Why not?

Signing one up for a lifetime costs only $1,799.* That's less than they have to pay other movie stars in a single day.

Once signed up, the bug won't suddenly start making crazy demands. (A gallon of gas for every 27 miles or so is all.)

No studio could ask for a less temperamental star. (It'll work in any weather.)

Or one with fewer bad habits. (It doesn't even drink water.)

Or one that ages so gracefully.

And of course, there isn't a performer around that's better known to the public.

Who else makes three million personal appearances on the road every day?

1990

FOX—FOUR The Fox front-wheel-drive subcompact returned without any really basic changes, but the model lineup was reshuffled a bit. Two models were discontinued – the two-door GL sedan and the four-door GL Sport sedan.

CABRIOLET—FOUR Volkswagen's front-wheel-drive subcompact convertible continued to use the older Rabbit body and platform. A driver's airbag became standard in the Cabriolet for 1990.

GOLF—FOUR The front-wheel-drive Golf lineup was reduced by one model in 1990 as the base two-door hatchback was dropped. Remaining were two- and four-door GL hatchbacks and the two-door hatchback GTI, now with a much lower price tag, since the 16-valve engine was no longer standard. It was replaced by a larger, but more potent 2.0-liter 131-hp engine. Overall, Golf prices came down slightly to prompt sales in a tight economy.

JETTA—FOUR As in 1989, the Jetta front-wheel-drive series had five models, but they were not the same models. The base two- and four-door sedans were dropped. The GL line gained a two-door sedan and the GL four-door

Above: **The new-to-America 1990 Passat was offered in sedan and station wagon versions.**
John Gunnell

sedan was offered with gas or diesel power. The Jetta GLI continued to use the hot 16-valve engine.

PASSAT—FOUR Volkswagen's new Passat four-door GL sedan and station wagon arrived during the 1990 model year. Both were powered by a 2.0-liter 134-hp engine. Both models shared a 103.3-inch wheelbase.

CORRADO—FOUR Also introduced for 1990 was a supercharged Corrado hatchback coupe, promoted as Volkswagen's "first full-blooded sports car." The four-seat, front-wheel-drive coupe carried a "G-Charger" engine (so called because the supercharger was G-shaped) that developed 158 hp at 5600 rpm. Only a five-speed manual gearbox was available. Four-wheel disc brakes were standard, with anti-locking optional. Corrado also had an automatic "active" rear spoiler that rose at speeds above 45 mph to reduce lift, then retracted when speed fell below 12 mph. Price was $17,900, and the Corrado rode a 97.3-inch wheelbase.

VANAGON—FOUR The Vanagon line grew to six models. The base Station Wagon and base Synchro Station Wagon were both new. The GL Station Wagon and GL Camper returned, but the GL Synchro Station Wagon was gone. The Carat Station Wagon returned, as did the GL Camper and the GL Camper Synchro. The "Synchro" versions included four-wheel drive.

Above: **A driver's side airbag was the primary addition to the 1990 VW Cabriolet.**

Old Cars Weekly Archives

Above: **The subcompact VW Fox continued to be offered to American buyers in 1990.**

Old Cars Weekly Archives

1990 VOLKSWAGEN PRODUCTION CHART

Model Code	Body Type & Seating	POE Price	Weight (lbs.)	ProductionTotal
FOX				
30	2d Sedan-4P	7225	2126	Note 1
FOX GL				
30	4d Sedan-4P	8310	2203	Note 1
30	2d Station Wagon-4P	8550	2214	Note 1
FOX GL SPORT				
30	2d Sedan-4P	8595	2126	Note 1
CABRIOLET				
15	2d Convertible-4P	15485	2274	Note 1
GOLF GL				
17	2d Hatchback-5P	8695	2194	Note 1
17	4d Hatchback-5P	8995	2246	Note 1
GOLF GTI 16V				
17	2d Hatchback-5P	9995	2267	Note 1
JETTA GL				
16	2d Sedan-5P	9995	2312	Note 1
16	4d Sedan-5P	10295	2331	Note 1
JETTA GL DIESEL				
16	4d Sedan-5P	10495	2264	Note 1
JETTA CARAT				
16	4d Sedan-5P	10990	2331	Note 1
JETTA GLI 16V				
16	4d Sedan-5P	13750	2416	Note 1
PASSAT GL				
31	4d Sedan-5P	14770	2612	Note 1
31	4d Station Wagon-5P	15885	NA	Note 1
CORRADO				
50	2d Coupe-5P	17900	2660	Note 1
VANAGON				
25	3d Station Wagon-9P	14080	3460	Note 1
VANAGON SYNCHRO				
25	3d Station Wagon-9P	17605	3780	Note 1
VANAGON GL				
25	3d Station Wagon-9P	16490	3460	Note 1
25	3d Camper	20990	3622	Note 1
VANAGON CARAT				
25	3d Station Wagon-9P	18670	NA	Note 1
CAMPER GL SYNCHRO				
25	3d Camper GL	25575	3942	Note 1

Note 1: Production data not available.

I.D. DATA: Volkswagen's Vehicle Identification Number (VIN) now had 17 symbols. The first three symbols identified the manufacturer, make and type of vehicle. The fourth symbol was a letter designating the body type. The fifth symbol was a letter identifying the engine. The sixth symbol designated the type of restraint system. The seventh and eighth symbols idenitified the model (same as number in column 1 of table below). The ninth symbol was a check digit. The 10th symbol was a letter designating the model year. The 11th symbol designated the assembly plant. The last six symbols were the sequential production number starting with 000001.

ENGINE

BASE FOUR (Fox): Inline, overhead-cam four-cylinder (8-valve). Cast-iron block and light alloy head. Displacement: 109 cid (1780 cc). Bore & Stroke: 3.19 x 3.40 in. (81.0 x 86.4 mm). Compression Ratio: 9.0:1. Brake Horsepower: 81 at 5500 rpm. Torque: 93 lbs.- ft. at 3250 rpm. Five main bearings. Fuel injection.

Base Diesel (Jetta ECOdiesel): Inline, overhead-cam four-cylinder diesel (8- valve). Cast-iron block and light alloy head. Displacement: 97 cid (1590cc). Bore & Stroke: 3.01 x 3.40 in. (76.5 x 86.4 mm). Compression Ratio: 23.0:1. Brake Horsepower: 52 at 4800 rpm. Torque: 71 lbs.-ft. at 2000 rpm. Five main bearings. Fuel injection.

BASE FOUR (Cabriolet, Golf, Jetta): Inline, overhead-cam four-cylinder (8-valve). Cast-iron block and light alloy head. Displacement: 109 cid (1780cc). Bore & Stroke: 3.19 x 3.40 in. (81.0 x 86.4 mm). Compression Ratio: 10.0:1. Brake Horsepower: 94 at 5400 rpm. Tor

BASE FOUR (Corrado): Inline, overhead-cam four-cylinder with supercharger (8-valve). Cast-iron block and light alloy head. Displacement: 109 cid (1781 cc). Bore & Stroke: 3.19 x 3.40 in. (81.0 x 86.4 mm). Compression Ratio: 8.0:1. Brake Horsepower: 158 at 5600 rpm. Torque: 166 lbs.-ft. at 4000 rpm. Five main bearings. Fuel injection.

BASE FOUR (GTI 16V, Jetta 16V, Passat): Inline, dual-overhead-cam four-cylinder (16-valve). Cast-iron block and light alloy head. Displacement: 121 cid (1984 cc). Bore & Stroke: 3.25 x 3.65 in. (82.5 x 92.8 mm). Compression Ratio: 10.8:1. Brake Horsepower: 134 at 5800 rpm. Torque: 133 lbs.-ft. at 4400 rpm. Five main bearings. Fuel injection.

BASE FOUR (Vanagon): Four-cylinder. Horizontally-opposed. Water-cooled. Displacement: 2109 cc. Bore & Stroke: 3.70 x 3.99. Compression ratio: 8.6:1. Brake Horsepower: 90-95. at 4800 rpm. Torque: NA.

CHASSIS

FOX: Wheelbase: 92.8 in. Overall Length: 163.4 in. Height: 53.7-54.3 in. Width: 63.0-63.9 in. Front Tread: 53.1 in. Rear Tread: 53.9 in.

CABRIOLET: Wheelbase: 94.5 in. Overall Length: 159.3 in. Height: 55.6 in. Width: 64.2 in. Front Tread: 54.7 in. Rear Tread: 53.5 in.

GOLF/GTI: Wheelbase: 97.3 in. Overall Length: 158.0 in. Height: 55.7 in. Width: 65.5 in. Front Tread: 56.3 in. Rear Tread: 56.0 in.

JETTA: Wheelbase: 97.3 in. Overall Length: 171.7 in. Height: 55.7 in. Width: 65.5 in. Front Tread: 56.3 in. Rear Tread: 56.0 in.,

PASSAT: Wheelbase: 103.3 in. Overall Length: 180.0 in. Height: 56.2 in. Width: 67.1 in. Front Tread: 58.4 in. Rear Tread: 56.2 in.

CORRADO: Wheelbase: 97.3 in. Overall Length: 159.4 in. Height: 51.9 in. Width: 65.9 in. Front Tread: 56.5 in. Rear Tread: 56.2 in.

VANAGON: Wheelbase: 96.9 in. Overall Length: 179.9 in. Height: 77.2 in. Width: 72.6 in. Front Tread: 61.8 in. Rear Tread: 61.8 in.

TECHNICAL

FOX: Layout: front-engine, front-wheel-drive. Transmission: four-speed manual. Steering: rack and pinion. Suspension (front): MacPherson struts with coil springs. Suspension (rear): torsion beam axle with trailing arms and coil springs. Brakes: front disc, rear drum except. Body Construction: steel unibody.

CABRIOLET: Layout: front-engine, front-wheel-drive. Transmission: five-speed manual. Steering: rack and pinion. Suspension (front): MacPherson struts with coil springs. Suspension (rear): torsion beam axle with trailing arms and coil springs. Brakes: front disc, rear drum. Body Construction: steel unibody.

GOLF/GTI: Layout: front-engine, front-wheel-drive. Transmission: five-speed manual. Steering: rack and pinion. Suspension (front): MacPherson struts with coil springs. Suspension (rear): torsion beam axle with trailing arms and coil springs. Brakes: front disc, rear drum. Body Construction: steel unibody.

JETTA: Layout: front-engine, front-wheel-drive. Transmission: five-speed manual. Steering: rack and pinion. Suspension (front): MacPherson struts with coil springs. Suspension (rear): torsion beam axle with trailing arms and coil springs. Brakes: front disc, rear drum. Body Construction: steel unibody.

PASSAT: Layout: front-engine, front-wheel-drive. Transmission: five-speed manual. Steering: rack and pinion. Brakes: 4-wheel discs. Body Construction: steel unibody.

CORRADO: Layout: front-engine, front-wheel-drive. Transmission: five-speed manual. Steering: rack and pinion. Brakes: 4-wheel discs. Body Construction: steel unibody.

VANAGON: Layout: rear-engine, rear-drive. Transmission: manual. Front suspension: MacPherson struts with coil springs. Rear suspension: semi-trailing arms with torsion bars. Brakes: front disc/rear drum.

MANUFACTURER: Volkswagenwerk AG, Wolfsburg, West Germany or Volkswagen of America Inc., Pennsylvania (Fox built in Brazil).

DISTRIBUTOR: Volkswagen of America Inc., Troy, Michigan.

Old Cars Weekly Archives

The new 1990 Corrado was called Volkswagen's "...first full-blooded sports car."

1991

FOX—FOUR The GL Sport and GL Wagon were no longer available. Both front and rear end styling received a new more rounded look. The four-speed manual transmission was replaced by the five-speed manual as standard equipment.

GOLF—FOUR The GTI added a tilt steering wheel and received new interior trim. Automatic transmission became available.

CABRIOLET—FOUR Volkswagen celebrated their 35th year of open-air motoring by offering an "Etienne Aigner" designer edition and an optional power top.

JETTA—FOUR The Jetta offered the widest choice of power plants in a 1991 Volkswagen. One could choose between the 100-hp 1.8-liter, the 134-hp 2.0-liter, or select the fuel-efficient diesel engine.

PASSAT—FOUR Introduced in 1990, the Passat was Volkswagen's first entry into the mid-size market. A front end without a grille marked early models. A recessed Volkswagen logo acted as an inlet for intake air, and the radiator was cooled through an opening under the bumper.

CORRADO—FOUR The newly issued Corrado received BBS alloy wheels as standard equipment, revised instrumentation, and a four-speed automatic transmission became optional. Power was provided by a 1.8-liter four equipped with a G60 "scroll-type" supercharger called the G-Charger.

VANAGON—FOUR The Vanagon looked just about the same and no changes were made in the model lineup.

I.D. DATA: Volkswagen's Vehicle Identification Number (VIN) now had 17 symbols. The first three symbols identified the manufacturer, make and type of vehicle. The fourth symbol was a letter designating the body type. The fifth symbol was a letter identifying the engine. The sixth symbol designated the type of restraint system. The seventh and eighth symbols idenitified the model (same as number in column 1 of table below). The ninth symbol was a check digit. The 10th symbol was a letter designating the model year. The 11th symbol designated the assembly plant. The last six symbols were the sequential production number starting with 000001.

ENGINE

BASE FOUR (Fox): Inline, overhead-cam four-cylinder (8-valve). Cast-iron block and light alloy head. Displacement: 109 cid (1780 cc). Bore & Stroke: 3.19 x 3.40 in. (81.0 x 86.4 mm). Compression Ratio: 9.0:1. Brake Horsepower: 81 at 5500 rpm. Torque: 93 lbs.- ft. at 3250 rpm. Five main bearings. Fuel injection.

BASE DIESEL (Jetta ECO diesel): Inline, overhead-cam four-cylinder diesel (8- valve). Cast-iron block and light alloy head. Displacement: 97 cid (1590 cc). Bore & Stroke: 3.01 x 3.40 in. (76.5 x 86.4 mm). Compression Ratio:

Above: **The 1991 Vanagon Carat could seat nine passengers or plenty of cargo.**
Phil Hall

Model Code	Body Type & Seating	POE Price	Weight (lbs.)	ProductionTotal
FOX				
30	2d Sedan-4P	7225	2172	Note 1
FOX GL				
30	4d Sedan-4P	8395	2238	Note 1
GOLF GL				
1G	2d Hatchback-5P	9055	2320	Note 2
1G	4d Hatchback-5P	9355	2375	Note 2
GOLF GTI				
1G	2d Hatchback-5P	10440	2346	Note 3
GOLF GTI 16V				
1G	2d Hatchback-5P	13070	2445	Note 3
JETTA GL				
1G	2d Sedan-5P	10385	2275	Note 4
1G	4d Sedan-5P	10685	2330	Note 4
1G	4d Diesel Sedan-5P	10685	2375	Note 4
JETTA CARAT				
1G	4d Sedan-5P	11640	2428	Note 4
JETTA GLI 16-V				
1G	4d Sedan-5P	14550	2438	Note 4
PASSAT GL				
31	4d Sedan-5P	15650	2985	Note 5
31	5d Station Wagon-5P	15240	3029	Note 5
CABRIOLET				
15	2d Convertible-4P	16175	2307	5404
CORRADO				
50	2d Coupe-4P	18675	2558	4331
VANAGON				
25	3d Station Wagon-9P	14575	3460	Note 7
VANAGON SYNCHRO				
25	3d Station Wagon-9P	18225	3780	Note 7
VANAGON GL				
25	3d Station Wagon-9P	17070	3622	Note 7
25	3d Camper	18735	3622	Note 7
VANAGON CARAT				
25	3d Station Wagon-9P	21730	3460	Note 7
CAMPER GL SYNCHRO				
25	3d Camper GL	26475	3942	Note 7

Note 1: 13,463 Foxes were sold in the United States in 1991.
Note 2: 8,557 Golfs were sold in the United States in 1991.
Note 3: 5,783 Golfs were sold in the United States in 1991.
Note 4: 38,017 Jettas were sold in the United States in 1991.
Note 5: 16,139 Passats were sold in the United States in 1991.
Note 6: 96,736 Volkswagens were sold in the United States in 1991.
Note 7: Separate Vanagon production not available.

1: **A new addition available on the 1991 GTI was a tilting steering wheel.** *Phil Hall*

2: **Volkswagen offered an automatic transmission in the 1991 Golf models.** *Phil Hall*

3: **In 1991, Jetta buyers could choose one of three engines to power their cars.** *Phil Hall*

4: **Drivers of the 1991 Corrado enjoyed a supercharged 1.8-liter four cylinder engine.** *Phil Hall*

23.0:1. Brake Horsepower: 52 at 4800 rpm. Torque: 71 lbs.-ft. at 2000 rpm. Five main bearings. Fuel injection.

BASE FOUR (Cabriolet, Golf, Jetta): Inline, overhead-cam four-cylinder (8-valve). Cast-iron block and light alloy head. Displacement: 109 cid (1780 cc). Bore & Stroke: 3.19 x 3.40 in. (81.0 x 86.4 mm). Compression Ratio: 10.0:1. Brake Horsepower: 94 at 5400 rpm. Torque: 100 lbs.-ft. at 3400 rpm, (GTI) 105 hp and 110 lbs.-ft. Five main bearings. Fuel injection.

BASE FOUR (Corrado): Inline, overhead-cam four-cylinder with supercharger (8- valve). Cast-iron block and light alloy head. Displacement: 109 cid (1781 cc). Bore & Stroke: 3.19 x 3.40 in. (81.0 x 86.4 mm). Compression Ratio: 8.0:1. Brake Horsepower: 158 at 5600 rpm.

Torque: 166 lbs.-ft. at 4000 rpm. Five main bearings. Fuel injection.

BASE FOUR (GTI 16V, Jetta 16V, Passat): Inline, dual-overhead-cam four-cylinder (16-valve). Cast-iron block and light alloy head. Displacement: 121 cid (1984 cc). Bore & Stroke: 3.25 x 3.65 in. (82.5 x 92.8 mm). Compression Ratio: 10.8:1. Brake Horsepower: 134 at 5800 rpm. Torque: 133 lbs.-ft. at 4400 rpm. Five main bearings. Fuel injection.

BASE FOUR (Vanagon): Four-cylinder. Horizontally-opposed. Water-cooled. Displacement: 2109 cc. Bore & Stroke: 3.70 x 3.99. Compression ratio: 8.6:1. Brake Horsepower: 90-95. at 4800 rpm. Torque: NA.

CHASSIS

FOX: Wheelbase: 92.8 in. Overall Length: 163.4 in. Height: 53.7 in. Width: 63.0 in. Front Tread: 53.1 in. Rear Tread: 53.9 in.

CABRIOLET: Wheelbase: 94.5 in. Overall Length: 153.1 in. Height: 55.6 in. Width: 64.6 in. Front Tread: 55.3 in. Rear Tread: 54.0 in.

GOLF/GTI: Wheelbase: 97.3 in. Overall Length: 159.6 in. Height: 55.7 in. Width: 66.1 in. Front Tread: 56.3 in. Rear Tread: 56.0 in.

JETTA: Wheelbase: 97.3 in. Overall Length: 172.6 in. Height: 55.7 in. Width: 66.1 in. Front Tread: 56.3 in. Rear Tread: 56.0 in.,

PASSAT: Wheelbase: 103.3 in. Overall Length: 180.0 in. Height: 56.2 in. Width: 67.1 in. Front Tread: 58.4 in. Rear Tread: 56.2 in.

CORRADO: Wheelbase: 97.3 in. Overall Length: 159.4 in. Height: 51.9 in. Width: 65.9 in. Front Tread: 56.5 in. Rear Tread: 56.2 in.

VANAGON: Wheelbase: 96.9 in. Overall Length: 179.9 in. Height: 77.2 in. Width: 72.6 in. Front Tread: 61.8 in. Rear Tread: 61.8 in.

TECHNICAL

FOX: Layout: front-engine, front-wheel-drive. Transmission: four-speed manual. Steering: rack and pinion. Suspension (front): MacPherson struts with coil springs. Suspension (rear): torsion beam axle with trailing arms and coil springs. Brakes: front disc, rear drum. Body Construction: steel unibody.

CABRIOLET: Layout: front-engine, front-wheel-drive. Transmission: five-speed manual. Steering: rack and pinion. Suspension (front): MacPherson struts with coil springs. Suspension (rear): torsion beam axle with trailing arms and coil springs. Brakes: front disc, rear drum. Body Construction: steel unibody.

GOLF/GTI: Layout: front-engine, front-wheel-drive. Transmission: five-speed manual. Steering: rack and pinion. Suspension (front): MacPherson struts with coil springs. Suspension (rear): torsion beam axle with trailing arms and coil springs. Brakes: front disc, rear drum. Body Construction: steel unibody.

JETTA: Layout: front-engine, front-wheel-drive. Transmission: five-speed manual. Steering: rack and pinion. Suspension (front): MacPherson struts with coil springs. Suspension (rear): torsion beam axle with trailing arms and coil springs. Brakes: front disc, rear drum. Body Construction: steel unibody.

PASSAT: Layout: front-engine, front-wheel-drive. Transmission: five-speed manual. Steering: rack and pinion. Brakes: 4-wheel discs. Body Construction: steel unibody.

CORRADO: Layout: front-engine, front-wheel-drive. Transmission: five-speed manual. Steering: rack and pinion. Brakes: 4-wheel discs. Body Construction: steel unibody.

VANAGON: Layout: rear-engine, rear-drive. Transmission: manual. Front suspension: MacPherson struts with coil springs. Rear suspension: semi-trailing arms with torsion bars. Brakes: front disc/rear drum.

PERFORMANCE: Acceleration (0-60 mph): (Fox) 11.1 sec., (Golf GL) 9.4 sec., (Golf GTI) 8.9 sec., (Golf GTI 16V) 7.8 sec., (Jetta) 7.8 sec., (Cabriolet) 9.9 sec., (Passat) 8.8 sec., (Corrado) 7.5 sec. Top Speed in mph: (Fox) 100, (Golf GL) 111, (Golf GTI) 114, (Golf GTI 16V) 125, (Jetta) 125, (Cabriolet) 102, (Passat) 127, (Corrado) 140. EPA Fuel Economy in mpg: City/Highway: (Fox) 25/32, (Golf) 25/32, (Golf GTI) 25/32, (Golf GTI 16V) 21/28, (Jetta) 21/ 28, (Cabriolet) 25/32, (Passat GL) 21/30, (Corrado) 21/28.

Performance figures by *Motor Trend*.

MANUFACTURER: Volkswagenwerk AG, Wolfsburg, Germany.

DISTRIBUTOR: Volkswagen of America Inc., Troy, Michigan.

Phil Hall

The 1991 VW Passats were intended to reach mid-size car buyers in North America.

1992

FOX—FOUR The radio no longer remained on when ignition switch was shut off.

GOLF—FOUR Tilt steering wheel was dropped and both the exterior and interior trim combinations were simplified.

CABRIOLET—FOUR Three-point seat belts replaced lap-only belts for the rear seat passengers.

JETTA—FOUR The two-door Jetta was dropped and a new style full wheel cover was offered on the Jetta GL. This was the last year for the Jetta ECOdiesel.

PASSAT—FOUR/V-6 New GLS models were introduced with Volkswagen's new 2.8-liter narrow angle VR6 engine very late in 1992. This unique engine used a very narrow (15- degrees) V-6 cylinder block topped by a single cylinder head.

CORRADO—V-6 Following a short 1992 model run, the Corrado G60 was replaced by the Corrado SLC, which was powered by the narrow-angle VR6 engine. The hood, grille, turn signals, front spoiler and BBS road wheels were changed.

I.D. DATA: Volkswagen's Vehicle Identification Number (VIN) now had 17 symbols. The first three symbols identified the manufacturer, make and type of vehicle. The fourth symbol was a letter designating the body type. The fifth symbol was a letter identifying the engine. The sixth symbol designated the type of restraint system. The seventh and eighth symbols idenitified the model (same as number in column 1 of table below). The ninth symbol was a check digit. The 10th symbol was a letter designating the model year. The 11th symbol designated the assembly plant. The last six symbols were the sequential production number starting with 000001.

ENGINE

BASE FOUR (Fox): Inline, overhead-cam four-cylinder (8-valve). Cast-iron block and light alloy head. Displacement: 109 cid (1780 cc). Bore & Stroke: 3.19 x 3.40 in. (81.0 x 86.4 mm). Compression Ratio: 9.0:1. Brake Horsepower: 81 at 5500 rpm. Torque: 93 lbs.- ft. at 3250 rpm. Five main bearings. Fuel injection.

Base Diesel (Jetta ECO diesel): Inline, overhead-cam four-cylinder diesel (8- valve). Cast-iron block and light alloy head. Displacement: 97 cid (1590 cc). Bore & Stroke: 3.01 x 3.40 in. (76.5 x 86.4 mm). Compression Ratio: 23.0:1. Brake Horsepower: 59 at 4800 rpm. Torque: 81 lbs.-ft. at 2000 rpm. Five main bearings. Fuel injection.

BASE FOUR (Cabriolet, Golf, Jetta): Inline, overhead-cam four-cylinder (8-valve). Cast-iron block and light alloy head. Displacement: 109 cid (1780 cc). Bore &

Above: **A new V-6 engine was offered to buyers of the 1992 VW Passat series.**
Phil Hall

Model Code	Body Type & Seating	POE Price	Weight (lbs.)	ProductionTotal
FOX				
30	2d Sedan-4P	7670	2172	Note 1
FOX GL				
30	4d Sedan-4P	8890	2238	Note 1
GOLF GL				
1G	2d Hatchback-5P	9640	2320	Note 2
1G	4d Hatchback-5P	9950	2375	Note 2
GOLF GTI				
1G	2d Hatchback-5P	11110	2346	Note 3
GOLF GTI 16V				
1G	2d Hatchback-5P	13910	2346	Note 3
JETTA GL				
1G	4d Sedan-5P	11370	2330	Note 4
JETTA GL ECO DIESEL				
1G	4d Sedan-5P	11670	2330	Note 4
JETTA CARAT				
1G	4d Sedan-5P	12390	2428	Note 4
1G	4d Sedan-5P	15480	2438	Note 4
PASSAT CL				
31	4d Sedan-5P	14950	2985	Note 1
PASSAT GL				
31	4d Sedan-5P	17550	2985	Note 1
31	5d Station Wagon-5P	17970	3029	Note 1
CABRIOLET				
15	2d Convertible-4P	17320	2307	7031
CORRADO				
50	2d Coupe-4P	19860	2675	Note 6
CORRADO SLC				
50	2d Coupe-4P	22170	NA	Note 6

Note 1: 10,880 Foxes were sold in the United States in 1992.
Note 2: 5,300 Golfs were sold in the United States in 1992.
Note 3: 4,059 GTIs were sold in the United States in 1992.
Note 4: 29,907 Jettas were sold in the United States in 1992.
Note 5: 12,578 Passats were sold in the United States in 1992.
Note 6: 3,439 Corrados were sold in the United States.
Note 7: 75,873 Volkswagens were sold in the United States in 1992.

1: **In 1992, the only way to enjoy a Jetta in the United States was in sedan form.** *Phil Hall*

2: **Some minor exterior modifications were made to the 1992 VW Golf series.** *Phil Hall*

3: **Just over 400 GTIs were sold by Volkswagen to the U.S. market in 1992.** *Phil Hall*

4: **New for 1992 were three-point safety belts for rear seat Cabriolet passengers.** *Phil Hall*

Stroke: 3.19 x 3.40 in. (81.0 x 86.4 mm). Compression Ratio: 10.0:1. Brake Horsepower: 94 at 5400 rpm. Torque: 100 lbs.-ft. at 3400 rpm, (GTI) 105 hp and 110 lbs.-ft. Five main bearings. Fuel injection.

BASE FOUR (GTI 16V, Jetta 16V, Passat CL, GL): Inline, dual-overhead-cam four- cylinder (16-valve). Cast-iron block and light alloy head. Displacement: 121 cid (1984 cc). Bore & Stroke: 3.25 x 3.65 in. (82.5 x 92.8 mm). Compression Ratio: 10.8:1. Brake Horsepower: 134 at 5800 rpm. Torque: 133 lbs.-ft. at 4400 rpm. Five main bearings. Fuel injection.

BASE V-6 (Corrado, Passat): Narrow (15 degrees) "vee" type dual-overhead- cam six-cylinder. Cast-iron block and light alloy head. Displacement: 170 cid (2792 cc). Bore & Stroke: 3.19 x 3.56 in. (81 x 90.3 mm). Compression Ratio: 10.0:1. Brake Horsepower: 172 at 5800 rpm,

(Corrado) 178 hp. Torque: 177 lbs.-ft. at 4200 rpm. Seven main bearings. Fuel injection.

CHASSIS

FOX: Wheelbase: 92.8 in. Overall Length: 163.4 in. Height: 53.7 in. Width: 63.0 in. Front Tread: 53.1 in. Rear Tread: 53.9 in.

CABRIOLET: Wheelbase: 94.5 in. Overall Length: 153.1 in. Height: 55.6 in. Width: 64.6 in. Front Tread: 55.3 in. Rear Tread: 54.0 in.

GOLF/GTI: Wheelbase: 97.3 in. Overall Length: 159.6 in. Height: 55.7 in. Width: 66.1 in. Front Tread: 56.3 in. Rear Tread: 56.0 in.

JETTA: Wheelbase: 97.3 in. Overall Length: 172.6 in. Height: 55.7 in. Width: 66.1 in. Front Tread: 56.3 in. Rear Tread: 56.0 in.,

PASSAT: Wheelbase: 103.3 in. Overall Length: 180.0 in. Height: 56.2 in. Width: 67.1 in. Front Tread: 58.4 in. Rear Tread: 56.2 in.

CORRADO: Wheelbase: 97.3 in. Overall Length: 159.4 in. Height: 51.9 in. Width: 65.9 in. Front Tread: 56.5 in. Rear Tread: 56.2 in.

TECHNICAL

FOX: Layout: front-engine, front-wheel-drive. Transmission: four-speed manual. Steering: rack and pinion. Suspension (front): MacPherson struts with coil springs. Suspension (rear): torsion beam axle with trailing arms and coil springs. Brakes: front disc, rear drum. Body Construction: steel unibody.

CABRIOLET: Layout: front-engine, front-wheel-drive. Transmission: five-speed manual. Steering: rack and pinion. Suspension (front): MacPherson struts with coil springs. Suspension (rear): torsion beam axle with trailing arms and coil springs. Brakes: front disc, rear drum. Body Construction: steel unibody.

GOLF/GTI: Layout: front-engine, front-wheel-drive. Transmission: five-speed manual. Steering: rack and pinion. Suspension (front): MacPherson struts with coil springs. Suspension (rear): torsion beam axle with trailing arms and coil springs. Brakes: front disc, rear drum. Body Construction: steel unibody.

JETTA: Layout: front-engine, front-wheel-drive. Transmission: five-speed manual. Steering: rack and pinion. Suspension (front): MacPherson struts with coil

springs. Suspension (rear): torsion beam axle with trailing arms and coil springs. Brakes: front disc, rear drum. Body Construction: steel unibody.

PASSAT: Layout: front-engine, front-wheel-drive. Transmission: five-speed manual. Steering: rack and pinion. Brakes: 4-wheel discs. Body Construction: steel unibody.

CORRADO: Layout: front-engine, front-wheel-drive. Transmission: five-speed manual. Steering: rack and pinion. Brakes: 4-wheel discs. Body Construction: steel unibody.

PERFORMANCE: Acceleration (0-60 mph): (Fox) 11.1 sec., (Golf GTI) 8.9 sec., (Golf GTI 16V) 7.8 sec., (Jetta) 7.8 sec., (Cabriolet) 9.9 sec., (Passat GL) 8.8 sec., (Passat GLX sedan) 7.9 sec., (Passat GLX Station Wagon) 8.0 sec., (Corrado) 6.8 sec. Top Speed in mph: (Fox) 100, (Golf GTI) 114, (Golf GTI 16V) 125, (Jetta) 125, (Cabriolet) 102, (Passat GL) 127, (Passat GLX) 130, (Corrado) 140. EPA Fuel Economy in mpg: City/Highway: (Fox) 25/32, (Golf) 25/ 32, (Golf GTI) 25/32, (Golf GTI 16V) 21/28, (Jetta) 21/28, (Cabriolet) 25/32, (Passat GL) 21/ 30, (Passat GLX) 19/27, (Corrado) 18/25.

Performance Figures by *Motor Trend*.

MANUFACTURER: Volkswagenwerk AG, Wolfsburg, Germany.

DISTRIBUTOR: Volkswagen of America Inc., Troy, Michigan.

Left: **The Vanagon series was called the EuroVan beginning in the 1992 model year.**
Phil Hall

1993

FOX—FOUR The four-speed manual was no longer available. This was the final year of the Fox.

GOLF III—FOUR A new GTI was launched with more horsepower (115) and a revised exterior. The more rounded, aerodynamic shape was complemented by a body-colored grille and mirror housings. Newly designed alloy wheels, bumper integrated fog lights, and tear-drop-shaped, dual lens halogen headlights completed the makeover. The Golf III would arrive in early 1993.

CABRIOLET—FOUR Commemorating 37 years of offering a convertible, Volkswagen offered a Collector's Edition of their classic cabriolet.

JETTA III—FOUR A new 115-hp, 2.0-liter engine powered the 1993 Jetta. The Jetta was also available with a 172-hp version of the VR6 engine.

PASSAT—FOUR/V-6 With the addition of the 2.8-liter VR6, the Passat GLX became Volkswagen's fastest and quickest sedan to date. Topping out at 130 mph, and spiriting to 60 mph in 7.9 seconds, the Passat GLX offered zoom and practicality. The GL and GLS still offered four-cylinder economy.

CORRADO—V-6 Badged as a Corrado SLC (Sports Luxury Coupe) the Corrado received an interior upgrade for 1993. Besides new instrumentation, the Corrado also received an improved premium stereo, an alarm system, and new five-spoke alloy wheels.

EUROVAN—FIVE The all-new Volkswagen EuroVan was introduced at the Boston Auto Show late in 1991 and reached Volkswagen dealerships late in 1992. This van was less boxy than early Transporters and had a tapering front end with a horizontally-split grille and large rectangular headlights. For this fourth-generation Transporter, Volkswagen finally abandoned the rear-engine layout. The water-cooled up-front engine was a 109-hp 2459-cc overhead cam five-cylinder with Digifant fuel injection. Buyers had the choice of a five-speed manual geabox or an optional four-speed automatic. Up front a double wishbone front suspension with torsion bars was used. The rear had coil springs positioned by semi-trailing arms. Rack-and-pinion steering was standard and antilock brakes were optional. There were CL, GL and MV trim levels and an optional Weekender camping package. Due to production delays, supplies were limited.

Above: **The Corrado SLC received a new stereo system and interior upgrade in 1993.**

Old Cars Weekly Archives

Above: **The 1993 VW Passats could go from 0 to 60 mph in just 7.9 seconds.**

Old Cars Weekly Archives

Above: **The 1993 model year was the final time around for the Fox series in the United States.**

Old Cars Weekly Archives

Model Code	Body Type & Seating	POE Price	Weight (lbs.)	ProductionTotal
	FOX WOLFSBURG			
30	2d Sedan-4P	9410	2172	Note 1
	FOX WOLFSBURG GL			
30	4d Sedan-4P	10260	2238	Note 1
	GOLF III			
1H	2d Hatchback-5P	10560	2511	Note 2
	GOLF III GL			
1H	4d Hatchback-5P	11600	2615	Note 2
	GOLF III GTI			
1H	2d Hatchback-5P	NA	NA	Note 3
	JETTA GL			
1H	4d Sedan-5P	12800	2647	Note 4
	JETTA GLS			
1H	4d Sedan-5P	NA	2647	Note 4
	JETTA GLX			
1H	4d Sedan-5P	17000	2915	Note 4
	PASSAT GL			
31	4d Sedan-5P	17860	2985	Note 5
31	5d Station Wagon-5P	NA	2647	Note 5
	PASSAT GLS			
31	4d Sedan-5P	NA	2999	Note 5
	PASSAT GLX			
31	4d Sedan-5P	21390	3152	Note 5
31	5-dr Station Wagon-5P	21820	3197	Note 5
	CABRIOLET			
15	2d Convertible-4P	18660	2307	3846
	CORRADO SLC			
50	2d Coupe-4P	23470	2808	2111
	EUROVAN CL			
15	Passenger Van	16640	3086	Note 6
	EUROVAN GL			
15	Passenger Van	20420	3839	Note 6
	EUROVAN MV			
15	Passenger Van	21850	4246	Note 6

Note 1: 6,697 Foxes were sold in the United States in 1993.
Note 2: 4,554 Golfs were sold in the United States in 1993.
Note 3: 139 GTIs were sold in the United States in 1993.
Note 4: 14,582 Jettas were sold in the United States in 1993.
Note 5: 11,970 Passats were sold in the United States in 1993.
Note 6: EuroVan production not available.
Note 7: 49,533 imported Volkswagens were sold in the United States in 1993, the lowest amount since 1956!

I.D. DATA: Volkswagen's Vehicle Identification Number (VIN) now had 17 symbols. The first three symbols identified the manufacturer, make and type of vehicle. The fourth symbol was a letter designating the body type. The fifth symbol was a letter identifying the engine. The sixth symbol designated the type of restraint system. The seventh and eighth symbols idenitified the model (same as number in column 1 of table below). The ninth symbol was a check digit. The 10th symbol was a letter designating the model year. The 11th symbol designated the assembly plant. The last six symbols were the sequential production number starting with 000001.

ENGINE

BASE FOUR (Fox, Cabriolet, Golf, Jetta): Inline, overhead-cam four-cylinder (8-valve). Cast-iron block and light alloy head. Displacement: 109 cid (1780 cc). Bore & Stroke: 3.19 x 3.40 in. (81.0 x 86.4 mm). Compression Ratio: 10.0:1. Brake Horsepower: 94 at 5400 rpm. Torque: 100 lbs.-ft. at 3000 rpm. Five main bearings. Multi-point fuel injection.

BASE FOUR (Golf, Jetta): Inline, overhead-cam four-cylinder (8-valve). Cast-iron block and light alloy head. Displacement: 121 cid (1984 cc). Bore & Stroke: 3.25 x 3.65 in. (82.5 x 92.8 mm). Compression Ratio: 10.0:1. Brake Horsepower: 115 at 5400 rpm. Torque: 122 lbs.-ft. at 3200 rpm. Five main bearings. Multi-point fuel injection.

BASE V-6 (Corrado, Passat): Narrow (15 degrees) "vee" type dual-overhead-cam six-cylinder. Cast-iron block and light alloy head. Displacement: 170 cid (2792 cc). Bore & Stroke: 3.19 x 3.56 in. (81 x 90.3 mm). Compression

Ratio: 10.0:1. Brake Horsepower: 172 at 5800 rpm, (Corrado) 178 hp. Torque: 177 lbs.-ft. at 4200 rpm. Seven main bearings. Multi-point fuel injection.

BASE FIVE (EuroVan): Overhead cam. Displacement: 2459 cc. Bore & Stroke: 3.19 x 2.99 in. Brake Horsepower: 109. Digifant fuel injection.

CHASSIS

FOX: Wheelbase: 92.8 in. Overall Length: 163.4 in. Height: 53.7 in. Width: 63.0 in. Front Tread: 53.1 in. Rear Tread: 53.9 in.

CABRIOLET: Wheelbase: 94.5 in. Overall Length: 153.1 in. Height: 55.6 in. Width: 64.6 in. Front Tread: 55.3 in. Rear Tread: 54.0 in.

GOLF/GTI: Wheelbase: 97.3 in. Overall Length: 159.6 in. Height: 55.7 in. Width: 66.1 in. Front Tread: 56.3 in. Rear Tread: 56.0 in.

JETTA: Wheelbase: 97.3 in. Overall Length: 172.6 in. Height: 55.7 in. Width: 66.1 in. Front Tread: 56.3 in. Rear Tread: 56.0 in.,

PASSAT: Wheelbase: 103.3 in. Overall Length: 180.0 in. Height: 56.2 in. Width: 67.1 in. Front Tread: 58.4 in. Rear Tread: 56.2 in.

CORRADO: Wheelbase: 97.3 in. Overall Length: 159.4 in. Height: 51.9 in. Width: 65.9 in. Front Tread: 56.5 in. Rear Tread: 56.2 in.

EUROVAN: Wheelbase: 115 in. Overall length: 186.6 in. Height: NA. Width: 73 in. Front tread: NA. Rear tread: NA. Tires: 205/65R15.

TECHNICAL

FOX: Layout: front-engine, front-wheel-drive. Transmission: four-speed manual. Steering: rack and

The practical EuroVan continued to be a staple of the VW lineup in 1993.

The 1993 Jettas were available in 115 hp and 172 hp versions.

pinion. Suspension (front): MacPherson struts with coil springs. Suspension (rear): torsion beam axle with trailing arms and coil springsBrakes: front disc, rear drum except. Body Construction: steel unibody.

CABRIOLET: Layout: front-engine, front-wheel-drive. Transmission: five-speed manual. Steering: rack and pinion. Suspension (front): MacPherson struts with coil springs. Suspension (rear): torsion beam axle with trailing arms and coil springs. Brakes: front disc, rear drum. Body Construction: steel unibody.

GOLF/GTI: Layout: front-engine, front-wheel-drive. Transmission: five-speed manual. Steering: rack and pinion. Suspension (front): MacPherson struts with coil springs. Suspension (rear): torsion beam axle with trailing arms and coil springs. Brakes: front disc, rear drum. Body Construction: steel unibody.

JETTA: Layout: front-engine, front-wheel-drive. Transmission: five-speed manual. Steering: rack and pinion. Suspension (front): MacPherson struts with coil springs. Suspension (rear): torsion beam axle with trailing arms and coil springs. Brakes: front disc, rear drum. Body Construction: steel unibody.

PASSAT: Layout: front-engine, front-wheel-drive. Transmission: five-speed manual. Steering: rack and pinion. Brakes: 4-wheel discs. Body Construction: steel unibody.

CORRADO: Layout: front-engine, front-wheel-drive. Transmission: five-speed manual. Steering: rack and pinion. Brakes: 4-wheel discs. Body Construction: steel unibody.

EUROVAN: Layout: front-engine, front-wheel-drive. Transmission: five-speed manual. Steering: rack and pinion. Front suspension: Double wishbone. Rear suspension: Semi-trailing arms and coil springs. Brakes: Anti-lock optional. Body Construction: Unitized space-cage frame.

PERFORMANCE: Acceleration (0-60 mph): (Fox) 11.3 sec., (Cabriolet) 11.1 sec., (Passat GL) 8.8 sec., (Passat GLX sedan) 7.9 sec., (Passat GLX station wagon) 8.0 sec., (Corrado) 6.8 sec. Top Speed in mph: (Fox) 101, (Cabriolet) 101, (Passat GL) 127, (Passat GLX) 130, (Corrado) 140. EPA Fuel Economy City/Highway in mpg: (Fox) 25/33, (Cabriolet) 24/30, (Passat GL) 21/30, (Passat GLX) 19/27, (Corrado) 18/25.

Performance figures by *Motor Trend*.

MANUFACTURER: Volkswagenwerk AG, Wolfsburg, Germany.

DISTRIBUTOR: Volkswagen of America Inc., Troy, Michigan.

Old Cars Weekly Archives

In the 1993 model year, Volkswagen attached the Classic label to its Cabriolet.

1994

GOLF III—FOUR 1994 marked the official United States launch of the third generation Golf. Significantly more aerodynamic and rounded than its predecessor, the Golf offered a body-colored grille mirror housings and bumpers. Increased chassis stiffness and larger wheels and tires gave the third-generation Golf improved ride and handling.

JETTA III—FOUR FOUR/V-6 The Jetta was totally redesigned for 1994. It was available as a luxury GLS model, or as a six-cylinder performance GLX model. The exterior received sheet metal that was considerably more rounded. An increase in length meant more interior room, and an increase in track provided a smoother ride and better handling. Standard driver and passenger airbags were included.

PASSAT—V-6 Powered by Volkswagen's unique VR6 engine the Passat was the fastest mid-size sedan ever. The VR6 was an Inline V engine. The six cylinders were staggered in the block by only 15 degrees. This was close enough together that only one cylinder head was needed.

The wagon version was one of the quickest cars in its segment.

CORRADO—V-6 Powered by Volkswagen's innovative VR6, the Corrado was capable of sprinting to 60 in just 6.8 seconds. Introduced in 1992, it was Volkswagen's first six-cylinder engine sporty car. This was its final year of production.

EUROVAN—FIVE No 1994 EuroVans entered the U.S. Market due to problems with satisfying federal safety regulations. Volkswagen was working on a revised version with dual air bags. Its introduction was delayed. Apparently only camper versions were available 1995-1998. The EuroVan was reintroduced here in 1999.

I.D. DATA: Volkswagen's Vehicle Identification Number (VIN) now had 17 symbols. The first three symbols

Above: **The 1994 Concept I would play a prominent part in Volkswagen's future.**
Old Cars Weekly Archives

Above: **In 1994, Passats were available with an ultra-fast V-6 engine.**

Old Cars Weekly Archives

Above: **The Golf III was the third generation of the popular VW car.**

Old Cars Weekly Archives

Model Code	Body Type & Seating	POE Price	Weight (lbs.)	ProductionTotal
	GOLF III GL			
1H	2d Hatchback-5P	12325	2511	Note 2
1H	4d Hatchback-5P	12525	2615	Note 2
	GOLF III GTI			
1H	2d Hatchback-5P	NA	NA	Note 3
	CABRIOLET			
15	2d Convertible-4P	17320	2307	3838
	JETTA III GL			
1H	4d Sedan-5P	13750	2647	Note 4
	JETTA III GLS			
1H	4d Sedan-5P	15700	2647	Note 4
	JETTA III GLX			
1H	4d Sedan-5P	19975	2915	Note 4
	PASSAT GLX			
31	4d Sedan-5P	23075	3152	Note 5
31	5d Station Wagon-5P	23500	3217	Note 5
	CORRADO SLC			
50	2d Coupe-4P	25150	2808	1514

Note 1: 3,922 Foxes were sold in the United States in 1994.
Note 2: 16,0709 Golfs were sold in the United States in 1994.
Note 3: 315 GTIs were sold in the United States in 1994.
Note 4: 55,688 Jettas were sold in the United States in 1994.
Note 5: 11,021 Passats were sold in the United States in 1994.
Note 6: 97,043 Volkswagens were sold in the United States in 1994.

identified the manufacturer, make and type of vehicle. The fourth symbol was a letter designating the body type. The fifth symbol was a letter identifying the engine. The sixth symbol designated the type of restraint system. The seventh and eighth symbols idenitified the model (same as number in column 1 of table below). The ninth symbol was a check digit. The 10th symbol was a letter designating the model year: R=1994. The 11th symbol designated the assembly plant. The last six symbols were the sequential production number starting with 000001.

ENGINE

BASE FOUR (Golf, Jetta): Inline, overhead-cam four-cylinder (8-valve). Cast-iron block and light alloy head. Displacement: 121 cid (1984 cc). Bore & Stroke: 3.25 x 3.65 in. (82.5 x 92.8 mm). Compression Ratio: 10.0:1. Brake Horsepower: 115 at 5400 rpm. Torque: 122 lbs.-ft. at 3200 rpm. Five main bearings. Multi-point fuel injection.

BASE V-6 (Jetta GLX, Corrado, Passat): Narrow (15 degrees) "vee" type dual- overhead-cam six-cylinder. Cast-iron block and light alloy head. Displacement: 170 cid (2792 cc). Bore & Stroke: 3.19 x 3.56 in. (81 x 90.3 mm). Compression Ratio: 10.0:1. Brake Horsepower: 172 at 5800 rpm, (Corrado) 178 hp. Torque: 177 lbs.-ft. at 4200 rpm. Seven main bearings. Multi-point fuel injection.

CHASSIS

FOX: Wheelbase: 92.8 in. Overall Length: 163.4 in. Height: 53.7 in. Width: 63.0 in. Front Tread: 53.1 in. Rear Tread: 53.9 in.

CABRIOLET: Wheelbase: 94.5 in. Overall Length: 153.1 in. Height: 55.6 in. Width: 64.6 in. Front Tread: 55.3 in. Rear Tread: 54.0 in.

GOLF/GTI: Wheelbase: 97.3 in. Overall Length: 159.6 in. Height: 55.7 in. Width: 66.1 in. Front Tread: 56.3 in. Rear Tread: 56.0 in.

JETTA: Wheelbase: 97.3 in. Overall Length: 172.6 in. Height: 55.7 in. Width: 66.1 in. Front Tread: 56.3 in. Rear Tread: 56.0 in.,

PASSAT: Wheelbase: 103.3 in. Overall Length: 180.0 in. Height: 56.2 in. Width: 67.1 in. Front Tread: 58.4 in. Rear Tread: 56.2 in.

CORRADO: Wheelbase: 97.3 in. Overall Length: 159.4 in. Height: 51.9 in. Width: 65.9 in. Front Tread: 56.5 in. Rear Tread: 56.2 in.

TECHNICAL

CABRIOLET: Layout: front-engine, front-wheel-drive. Transmission: five-speed manual. Steering: rack and pinion. Suspension (front): MacPherson struts with coil springs. Suspension (rear): torsion beam axle with trailing arms and coil springs. Brakes: front disc, rear drum. Body Construction: steel unibody.

GOLF/GTI: Layout: front-engine, front-wheel-drive. Transmission: five-speed manual. Steering: rack and pinion. Suspension (front): MacPherson struts with coil springs. Suspension (rear): torsion beam axle with trailing arms and coil springs. Brakes: front disc, rear drum. Body Construction: steel unibody.

JETTA: Layout: front-engine, front-wheel-drive. Transmission: five-speed manual. Steering: rack and pinion. Suspension (front): MacPherson struts with coil springs. Suspension (rear): torsion beam axle with trailing arms and coil springs. Brakes: front disc, rear drum. Body Construction: steel unibody.

PASSAT: Layout: front-engine, front-wheel-drive. Transmission: five-speed manual. Steering: rack and pinion. Brakes: 4-wheel discs. Body Construction: steel unibody.

CORRADO: Layout: front-engine, front-wheel-drive. Transmission: five-speed manual. Steering: rack and pinion. Brakes: 4-wheel discs. Body Construction: steel unibody.

PERFORMANCE: Acceleration (0-60 mph): (Cabriolet) 11.1 sec., (Passat GL) 8.8 sec., (Passat GLX sedan) 7.9 sec., (Passat GLX sta wagon) 8.0 sec., (Corrado) 6.8 sec. Top Speed in mph: (Cabriolet) 101, (Passat GL) 127, (Passat GLX) 130, (Corrado) 140. EPA Fuel Economy in mpg: City/Highway: (Cabriolet) 24/30, (Passat GL) 21/30, (Passat GLX) 19/27, (Corrado) 18/25.

Performance figures by *Motor Trend*.

MANUFACTURER: Volkswagenwerk AG, Wolfsburg, Germany.

DISTRIBUTOR: Volkswagen of America Inc., Troy, Michigan.

HISTORICAL FOOTNOTES: No 1994 EuroVans entered the United States market, since Volkswagen was waiting to launch a revised version with dual air bags.

1995

GOLF III—FOUR The company that invented the "hot hatchback" class with the original GTI in 1982 shook up the market by dropping the potent VR6 engine into the practical Golf hatchback. The Golf Sport became the top four-cylinder Golf model.

CABRIOLET—FOUR In typical Volkswagen fashion, the Cabriolet, based on the latest Golf, reached the American market a year after the hatchback's debut. Despite its cute exterior, the Cabriolet actually offered 11 percent more room than a 1995 325i convertible. The six-layer top contained a glass rear window, complete with an electric defroster. The Cabriolet was the only convertible to offer a standard fixed roll bar, this also provided a convenient location for the seatbelt's upper anchor.

JETTA III—FOUR/V-6 The Jetta received Volkswagen's emergency seat belt tensioning system, which used a pyrotechnic device to instantly tighten belts around the front occupants in the event of a frontal impact. Color-keyed side moldings were also added.

PASSAT—V-6 Gone was the grill-less wonder. For 1995 the Passat was re-styled with a more conventional front end, including a waterfall-shaped grille and headlights that wrapped back into the fenders. The interior also got a freshening.

I.D. DATA: Volkswagen's 17-symbol VIN appears on the top left-hand surface of the instrument panel and is visible through the windshield. The first three symbols identified the country of origin, make and type of vehicle. Volkswagens made in Europe have the first three symbols WVW. Volkswagens made in Mexico have the first three synbols 3VW. The fourth symbol was a letter designating the series (see first column of table below). The fifth symbol was a letter identifying the engine. The sixth symbol designated the type of restraint system. The seventh and eighth symbols idenitified the model (1H=Golf, Jetta and GTI, 1E=Cabriolet, 3A=Passat). The ninth symbol was a check digit. The 10th symbol was a letter designating the model year: S=1995. The 11th symbol designated the assembly plant: E=Emden, Germany, K=Osnabruck, Germany, M=Mexico, W=Wolfsburg, Germany. The last six symbols were the sequential production number starting with 000001.

Above: **The GTI and the powerful VR6 were mated in 1995 making a powerful Volkswagen.**

Old Cars Weekly Archives

Above: **The 1995 Cabrio was new in America and was based on the Golf III styling.**

Old Cars Weekly Archives

1995 VOLKSWAGEN PRODUCTION CHART

Model Code	Body Type & Seating	POE Price	Weight (lbs.)	ProductionTotal
	GOLF			
O	4d Hatchback-5P	14075	2665	Note 1
	GOLF III GL			
B	2d Hatchback-5P	12500	2577	Note 1
F	4d Hatchback-5P	14075	2665	Note 1
	GOLF III SPORT			
B	2d Hatchback-5P	15250	2599	Note 1
	GOLF III GTI VR6			
H	2d Hatchback-5P	18875	2818	Note 2
	CABRIOLET			
B	2d Convertible-4P	19975	2762	5538
	JETTA III			
O	4d Sedan-5P	13475	2647	Note 3
	JETTA III GL			
R	4d Sedan-5P	16450	2735	Note 3
	JETTA III GLS			
S	4d Sedan-5P	17025	2735	Note 3
	JETTA III GLX			
T	4d Sedan-5P	19975	2980	Note 3
	PASSAT GLS			
C	4d Sedan-5P	17990	2919	Note 4
	PASSAT GLX VR6			
E	4d Sedan-5P	20890	3197	Note 4
F	5d Wagon-5P	21320	3267	Note 4

Note1: 15,853 Golfs were sold in the United States in 1995.
Note 2: 2,576 GTIs were sold in the United States in 1995.
Note 3: 75,393 Jettas were sold in the United States in 1995.
Note 4: 14,010 Passats were sold in the United States in 1995.
Note 5: 115,114 Volkswagens were sold in the United States in 1995.

ENGINE

BASE FOUR (Golf, Jetta): Inline, overhead-cam four-cylinder (8-valve). Cast-iron block and light alloy head. Displacement: 121 cid (1984 cc). Bore & Stroke: 3.25 x 3.65 in. (82.5 x 92.8 mm). Compression Ratio: 10.0:1. Brake Horsepower: 115 at 5400 rpm. Torque: 122 lbs.-ft. at 3200 rpm. Five main bearings. Multi-point fuel injection.

BASE V-6 (Golf GTI, Jetta GLX, Passat): Narrow (15 degrees) "vee" type dual- overhead-cam six-cylinder. Cast-iron block and light alloy head. Displacement: 170 cid (2792 cc). Bore & Stroke: 3.19 x 3.56 in. (81 x 90.3 mm). Compression Ratio: 10.0:1. Brake Horsepower: 172 at 5800 rpm. Torque: 177 lbs.-ft. at 4200 rpm. Seven main bearings. Multi-point fuel injection.

CHASSIS

CABRIOLET: Wheelbase: 97.2 in. Overall Length: 160.4 in. Height: 56 in. Width: 66.7 in. Front Tread: 56.7 in. Rear Tread: 57.6 in.

GOLF/GTI: Wheelbase: 97.3 in. Overall Length: 160.4 in. Height: 56.2 in. Width: 66.7 in. Front Tread: 56.7 in. Rear Tread: 56.9 in.

JETTA: Wheelbase: 97.4 in. Overall Length: 173.4 in. Height: 56.1 in. Width: 66.7 in. Front Tread: 56.7 in. Rear Tread: 56.9 in.,

PASSAT: Wheelbase: 103.3 in. Overall Length: 181.5 in. Height: 56.4 in. Width: 67.5 in. Front Tread: 58.4 in. Rear Tread: 56.2 in.

TECHNICAL

CABRIOLET: Layout: front-engine, front-wheel-drive. Transmission: five-speed manual. Steering: rack and pinion. Suspension (front): MacPherson struts with coil springs. Suspension (rear): torsion beam axle with trailing arms and coil springs. Brakes: front disc, rear drum. Body Construction: steel unibody.

GOLF/GTI: Layout: front-engine, front-wheel-drive. Transmission: five-speed manual. Steering: rack and pinion. Suspension (front): MacPherson struts with coil springs. Suspension (rear): torsion beam axle with trailing arms and coil springs. Brakes: front disc, rear drum. Body Construction: steel unibody.

JETTA: Layout: front-engine, front-wheel-drive. Transmission: five-speed manual. Steering: rack and pinion. Suspension (front): MacPherson struts with coil springs. Suspension (rear): torsion beam axle with trailing arms and coil springs. Brakes: front disc, rear drum. Body Construction: steel unibody.

PASSAT: Layout: front-engine, front-wheel-drive. Transmission: five-speed manual. Steering: rack and pinion. Brakes: 4-wheel discs. Body Construction: steel unibody.

PERFORMANCE: Acceleration (0-60 mph): (Cabriolet) 11.1 sec., (Passat GL) 8.8 sec., (Passat GLX sedan) 7.9 sec., (Passat GLX sta wagon) 8.0 sec. Top Speed in mph: (Cabriolet) 101., (Passat GL) 127., (Passat GLX) 130. EPA Fuel Economy in mpg: City/Highway: (Cabriolet) 24/30, (Passat GL) 21/30, (Passat GLX) 19/27.

Performance figures by *Motor Trend*.

MANUFACTURER: Volkswagenwerk AG, Wolfsburg, Germany.

DISTRIBUTOR: Volkswagen of America Inc., Troy, Michigan.

HISTORICAL FOOTNOTES: The arrival of the EuroVan with dual air bags was delayed, so the only version offered in 1995 was a Camper created as a joint venture with Winnebago Industries, the American recreational vehicle maker. Only a handful of these campers were marketed in 1995-1996. Selling of the EuroVan through the United States marketplace would have to wait until 1999.

The restyled Golf III marked its second year in the U.S. market in 1995.

The Jetta was available in four sedan versions in Volkswagen's 1995 lineup.

Among the changes to the 1995 Passat was a new-look grille and headlight treatment.

In 1995, Volkswagen's new Concept car appeared at the Tokyo Motor Show.

The Weekender was one model in the 1995 Volkswagen EuroVan offerings.

1996

GOLF—FOUR Volkswagen found the VR6 GTI to be so popular that the company added a 115-hp four-cylinder version of the hot hatchback. The GTI VR6's suspension was lowered by 10 mm. The handling was improved and newly rated gas shock absorbers were added. Central locking was added as standard equipment.

CABRIOLET—FOUR The Cabriolet was unchanged from its 1995 launch save for a new metallic color, Cinnabar.

JETTA—FOUR/V-6 New front-end styling for the 1996 Jetta included a body-colored three bar grille. The GLX front suspension was lowered by 10 mm for better handling.

PASSAT—FOUR/V-6 Starting in mid-1995, Volkswagen offered a Passat GLS model. It was powered by the 2.0-liter four, instead of the VR6 engine. This allowed the company to advertise "the lowest price European mid-size model sold in the United States." Central locking was added as standard equipment.

I.D. DATA: Volkswagen's 17-symbol VIN appears on the top left-hand surface of the instrument panel and is visible through the windshield. The first three symbols identified the country of origin, make and type of vehicle. Volkswagens made in Europe have the first three symbols WVW. Volkswagens made in Mexico have the first three synbols 3VW. The fourth symbol was a letter designating the series (see first column of table below). The fifth symbol was a letter identifying the engine: A=2.0-liter four-cylinder 115 hp; B=2.0-liter four cylinder 115 hp; C=2.0-liter four cylinder 115 hp; D=2.8-liter V-6 172 hp; E=2.8-liter V-6 172 hp; F=1.9-liter four-cylinder diesel 90 hp; J=1.8-liter four-cylinder diesel 148 hp; K=1.8-liter four-cylinder 90 hp; L=2.0-liter four-cylinder 115 hp; The sixth symbol designated the type of restraint system: 8=Active belts. The seventh and eighth symbols idenitified the model (1H=Golf, Jetta and GTI, 1E=Cabriolet, 3A=Passat). The ninth symbol was a check digit. The 10th symbol was a letter designating the model year: T=1996. The 11th symbol designated the assembly plant: E=Emden, Germany, K=Osnabruck, Germany, M=Mexico, W=Wolfsburg, Germany. The last six symbols were the sequential production number starting with 000001.

ENGINE

BASE FOUR (Golf, Jetta, Passat GLS): Inline, overhead-cam four-cylinder (8-valve). Cast-iron block and light alloy head. Displacement: 121 cid (1984 cc). Bore & Stroke: 3.25 x 3.65 in. (82.5 x 92.8 mm). Compression Ratio:

Above: **The 1996 Cabrio had the shortest wheel base of the American VWs, 97.2 inches.**

Old Cars Weekly Archives

Above: **The small and powerful 1996 GTI continued to be fun to drive.**

Old Cars Weekly Archives

Above: **Slightly more then 16,000 Golfs were sold by Volkswagen in 1996.**

Old Cars Weekly Archives

1996 VOLKSWAGEN PRODUCTION CHART

Model Code	Body Type & Seating	POE Price	Weight (lbs.)	ProductionTotal
GOLF III GL				
F	4d Hatchback-5P	13150	2529	Note 1
GTI				
D	2d Hatchback-5P	16000	2557	Note 2
GTI VR6				
H	2d Hatchback-5P	19685	2811	Note 2
CABRIOLET				
B	2d Convertible-4P	19975	2701	5828
JETTA GL				
R	4d Sedan-5P	14250	2667	Note 3
JETTA GLS				
S	4d Sedan-5P	15425	2723	Note 3
JETTA GLX VR6				
T	4d Sedan-5P	20610	2954	Note 3
PASSAT GLS				
G	4d Sedan-5P	18490	2890	Note 4
H	5d Wagon-5P	NA	NA	Note 4
PASSAT GLS TDI (FOUR)				
G	4d Sedan-5P	21890	3097	Note 4
H	5d Wagon-5P	NA	3175	Note 4
PASSAT GLX VR6 (V-6)				
E	4d Sedan-5P	21890	3097	Note 4
F	5d Station Wag-5P	NA	3175	Note 4

Note 1: 16,802 Golfs were sold in the United States in 1996.
Note 2: 7,406 GTIs were sold in the United States in 1996.
Note 3: 85,022 Jettas were sold in the United States in 1996.
Note 4: 19,850 Passats were sold in the United States in 1996.
Note 5: 135,807 Volkswagens were sold in the United States in 1996.

10.0:1. Brake Horsepower: 115 at 5400 rpm. Torque: 122 lbs.-ft. at 3200 rpm. Five main bearings. Multi-point fuel injection.

DIESEL FOUR (Golf, Jetta, Passat GTI): Four-cylinder. Displacement: 116 cid (1.9 liter). Bore & Stroke: 3.13 x 3.76 in. Brake Horsepower: 90. Diesel.

DIESEL FOUR (Golf): 1.8-liter four-cylinder. Specifications not available.

BASE V-6 (Golf GTI, Jetta GLX, Passat): Narrow (15 degrees) "vee" type dual-overhead-cam six-cylinder. Cast-iron block and light alloy head. Displacement: 170 cid (2792 cc). Bore & Stroke: 3.19 x 3.56 in. (81 x 90.3 mm). Compression Ratio: 10.0:1. Brake Horsepower: 172 at 5800 rpm. Torque: 177 lbs.-ft. at 4200 rpm. Seven main bearings. Multi-point fuel injection.

CHASSIS

CABRIOLET: Wheelbase: 97.2 in. Overall Length: 160.4 in. Height: 56.0 in. Width: 66.7 in. Front Tread: 57.6 in. Rear Tread: 57.6 in.

GOLF/GTI: Wheelbase: 97.3 in. Overall Length: 160.4 in. Height: 56.2 in. Width: 66.7 in. Front Tread: 57.6 in. Rear Tread: 56.9 in.

JETTA: Wheelbase: 97.4 in. Overall Length: 173.4 in. Height: 56.1 in. Width: 66.7 in. Front Tread: 57.6 in. Rear Tread: 56.9 in.

PASSAT: Wheelbase: 103.3 in. Overall Length: (Sedan) 181.0 in., (Wagon) 181.5 in. Height: (Sedan) 56.4 in., (Wagon) 58.7 in. Width: 67.5 in. Front Tread: 58.4 in. Rear Tread: 56.2 in.

TECHNICAL

CABRIOLET: Layout: front-engine, front-wheel-drive. Transmission: five-speed manual. Steering: rack and pinion. Suspension (front): MacPherson struts with coil springs. Suspension (rear): torsion beam axle with trailing arms and coil springs. Brakes: front disc, rear drum. Body Construction: steel unibody.

GOLF/GTI: Layout: front-engine, front-wheel-drive. Transmission: five-speed manual. Steering: rack and pinion. Suspension (front): MacPherson struts with coil springs. Suspension (rear): torsion beam axle with trailing arms and coil springs. Brakes: front disc, rear drum (except GTI VR6 4-wheel discs). Body Construction: steel unibody.

JETTA: Layout: front-engine, front-wheel-drive. Transmission: five-speed manual. Steering: rack and pinion. Suspension (front): MacPherson struts with coil springs. Suspension (rear): torsion beam axle with trailing arms and coil springs. Brakes: front disc, rear drum. Body Construction: steel unibody.

PASSAT: Layout: front-engine, front-wheel-drive. Transmission: five-speed manual. Steering: rack and pinion. Brakes: 4-wheel discs. Body Construction: steel unibody.

PERFORMANCE: Acceleration: (0-60 mph): (Cabriolet) 11.1 sec., (Passat GL) 8.8 sec., (Passat GLX sedan) 7.9 sec., (Passat GLX sta wagon) 8.0 sec. Top Speed in mph:

(Cabriolet) 101, (Passat GL) 127, (Passat GLX) 130. EPA Fuel Economy in mpg: City/Highway: (Cabriolet) 24/30, (Passat GL) 21/30, (Passat GLX) 19/27.

Performance figures by *Motor Trend*.

MANUFACTURER: Volkswagenwerk AG, Wolfsburg, Germany.

DISTRIBUTOR: Volkswagen of America Inc., Troy, Michigan.

The Jetta featured new front-end styling for the 1996 models.

In 1996, Passat buyers could opt for the economical four or potent V-6 engines.

1997

GOLF—FOUR Cartoon figure Speed Racer let us know that his choice, after his Mach 5, would be a 1997 Volkswagen GTI. In the standard Golf, a modified intake swirl duct and cross-flow cylinder head provided smoother power delivery.

CABRIOLET—FOUR The Cabriolet lineup got a second decontented model in order to have the price start at under $18,000. The up-level model became known as the Highline and included standard leather seating surfaces.

JETTA—FOUR/V-6 Flushed with the success of the V-6 Jetta GLX, Volkswagen added a Jetta GT model for 1997. It came standard with unique alloy wheels, a rear spoiler, fog lights, darkened taillights and a "specially designed, attention-grabbing" cloth interior.

PASSAT—FOUR/V-6/DIESEL How often do you find a mid-size car capable of returning 47 mpg? Well, in this case it was per gallon of diesel fuel, not gasoline. Thanks to the remarkable 1.9 TDI (Turbo Diesel Injection) engine, the roomy Passat was rated for 47 highway and 38-mpg city. Besides being able to go 870 miles on a tank of fuel, the TDI engine offered a non-diesel feel to it. Thanks to a turbocharger and an intercooler, the engine reached its peak torque of 149 lbs.-ft. at just 1900 rpm. This provided plenty of get up and go around town. TDI also meant

that fuel was injected directly into the cylinder head, rather than into a separate combustion prechamber which resulted in significant heat loss. This engine was made available in both the sedan and the wagon.

I.D. DATA: Volkswagen's 17-symbol VIN appears on the top left-hand surface of the instrument panel and is visible through the windshield. The first three symbols identified the country of origin, make and type of vehicle. Volkswagens made in Europe have the first three symbols WVW. Volkswagens made in Mexico have the first three symbols 3VW. The fourth symbol was a letter designating the series (see first column of table below). The fifth symbol was a letter identifying the engine: A=2.0-liter four-cylinder 115 hp; B=2.0-liter four cylinder 115 hp; C=2.0-liter four cylinder 115 hp; D=2.8-liter V-6 172 hp; E=2.8-liter V-6 172 hp; F=1.9-liter four-cylinder diesel 90 hp; J=1.8-liter four-cylinder diesel 148 hp; K=1.8-liter four-cylinder 90 hp; L=2.0-liter four-cylinder 115 hp; The sixth symbol designated the type of restraint system: 8=Active belts. The seventh and eighth symbols identified the model (1H=Golf, Jetta and GTI, 1E=Cabriolet, 3A=Passat). The ninth symbol was a check digit. The 10th symbol was a letter designating the model year:

Above: **In 1997, the Golf GL was the entry level choice in the Volkswagen lineup.**

Old Cars Weekly Archives

Above: **Passats were offered with gasoline or advanced diesel engines in 1997.**

Old Cars Weekly Archives

Above: **The 1997 Volkswagen GTI VR6 still produced 172 hp.**

Old Cars Weekly Archives

1997 VOLKSWAGEN PRODUCTION CHART

Model Code	Body Type & Seating	POE Price	Weight (lbs.)	ProductionTotal
	GOLF GL			
F	4d Hatchback-5P	13470	2525	Note 1
	GOLF GTI			
D	2d Hatchback-5P	16320	2564	Note 2
	GOLF GTI VR6			
H	2d Hatchback-5P	19710	2800	Note 2
	CABRIOLET GL			
A	2d Convertible-4P	17925	2701	Note 3
	CABRIOLET GLS			
B	2d Convertible-4P	21675	2767	Note 3
	JETTA GL			
R	4d Sedan-5P	14570	2591	Note 4
	JETTA GT			
V	4d Sedan-5P	14965	2591	Note 4
	JETTA GLS			
S	4d Sedan-5P	16920	2675	Note 4
	JETTA GLX			
T	4d Sedan-5P	20930	2928	Note 4
	PASSAT TDI			
G	4d Sedan-5P	19430	3009	Note 5
H	4d Wagon-5P	19860	3075	Note 5
	PASSAT GLX			
T	4d Sedan-5P	21890	3097	Note 5
F	5d Wagon-5P	22320	3175	Note 5

Note 1: 14,673 Golfs were sold in the United States in 1997.
Note 2: 6,029 GTIs were sold in the United States in 1997.
Note 3: 9,583 Cabriolets were sold in the United States in 1997.
Note 4: 90,964 Jettas were sold in the United States in 1997.
Note 5: 14,868 Passats were sold in the United States in 1997.
Note 6: 137,855 Volkswagens were sold in the United States in 1997.

V=1997. The 11th symbol designated the assembly plant: B=Brussels, Belgium, E=Emden, Germany, H=Hanover, Germany, K=Osnabruck, Germany, M=Mexico, W=Wolfsburg, Germany. The last six symbols were the sequential production number starting with 000001.

ENGINE

BASE FOUR (Golf, Jetta): Inline, overhead-cam four-cylinder (8-valve). Cast-iron block and light alloy head. Displacement: 121 cid (1984 cc). Bore & Stroke: 3.25 x 3.65 in. (82.5 x 92.8 mm). Compression Ratio: 10.0:1. Brake Horsepower: 115 at 5400 rpm. Torque: 122 lbs.-ft. at 3200 rpm. Five main bearings. Multi-point fuel injection.

DIESEL FOUR(Passat TDI): Inline, overhead-cam four-cylinder with turbocharger and intercooler (8-valve). Cast-iron block and light alloy head. Displacement: 116 cid (1896 cc). Bore & Stroke: 3.13 x 3.76 in. Compression Ratio: 19.5:1. Brake Horsepower: 90 at 3750 rpm. Torque: 149 lbs.-ft. at 1900 rpm. Five main bearings. Multi-point fuel injection.

DIESEL FOUR (Golf): 1.8-liter four-cylinder. Specifications not available.

BASE V-6 (Golf GTI, Jetta GLX, Passat): Narrow (15 degrees) "vee" type dual- overhead-cam six-cylinder. Cast-iron block and light alloy head. Displacement: 170 cid (2792 cc). Bore & Stroke: 3.19 x 3.56 in. (81 x 90.3 mm). Compression Ratio: 10.0:1. Brake Horsepower: 172 at 5800 rpm. Torque: 177 lbs.-ft. at 4200 rpm. Seven main bearings. Multi-point fuel injection.

CHASSIS

CABRIOLET: Wheelbase: 97.2 in. Overall Length: 160.4 in. Height: 56.0 in. Width: 66.7 in. Front Tread: 57.5 in. Rear Tread: 57.6 in.

GOLF/GTI: Wheelbase: 97.4 in. Overall Length: 160.4 in. Height: 56.2 in. Width: 66.7 in. Front Tread: 57.5 in. Rear Tread: 57.0 in.

JETTA: Wheelbase: 97.4 in. Overall Length: 173.4 in. Height: 56.1 in. Width: 66.7 in. Front Tread: 57.5 in. Rear Tread: 57.0 in.

PASSAT: Wheelbase: 103.3 in. Overall Length: (Sedan) 181.0 in., (Wagon) 181.5 in. Height: (Sedan) 56.4 in., (Wagon) 58.7 in. Width: 67.5 in. Front Tread: 58.4 in. Rear Tread: 56.2 in.

TECHNICAL

CABRIOLET: Layout: front-engine, front-wheel-drive. Transmission: five-speed manual. Steering: rack and pinion. Suspension (front): MacPherson struts with coil springs. Suspension (rear): torsion beam axle with trailing arms and coil springs. Brakes: front disc, rear drum. Body Construction: steel unibody.

GOLF/GTI: Layout: front-engine, front-wheel-drive. Transmission: five-speed manual. Steering: rack and pinion. Suspension (front): MacPherson struts with coil springs. Suspension (rear): torsion beam axle with trailing arms and coil springs. Brakes: front disc, rear drum (except GTI VR6 4-wheel discs). Body Construction: steel unibody.

JETTA: Layout: front-engine, front-wheel-drive. Transmission: five-speed manual. Steering: rack and pinion. Suspension (front): MacPherson struts with coil springs. Suspension (rear): torsion beam axle with trailing arms and coil springs. Brakes: front disc, rear drum. Body Construction: steel unibody.

PASSAT: Layout: front-engine, front-wheel-drive. Transmission: five-speed manual. Steering: rack and pinion. Brakes: 4-wheel discs. Body Construction: steel unibody.

PERFORMANCE: Acceleration (0-60 mph): (Cabriolet) 11.1 sec., (Passat GL) 8.8 sec., (Passat GLX sedan) 7.9 sec., (Passat GLX sta wagon) 8.0 sec. Top Speed in mph: (Cabriolet) 101, (Passat GL) 127, (Passat GLX) 130. EPA Fuel Economy City/Highway in mpg: (Cabriolet) 24/ 30, (Passat GL) 21/30, (Passat GLX) 19/27.

Performance figures by *Motor Trend*.

MANUFACTURER: Volkswagenwerk AG, Wolfsburg, Germany.

DISTRIBUTOR: Volkswagen of America Inc., Troy, Michigan.

The 1997 Jettas were offered in four trim levels by Volkswagen.

1998

1998

NEW BEETLE—FOUR The retro-styled New Beetle was a modern rendition of the classic "People's Car" and it really turned people on. With zooming sales, the cute little "Bug" was a major hit. Released in the spring of 1998, this car surpassed success in the automobile arena to become a major new pop culture phenomenon. There was so much interest generated by the clever ad campaign that cars were soon selling for a premium far over their sticker price. Based directly on the Golf chassis, the New Beetle offered considerably less utility, thanks to its sloped roof. But, oh the excitement! Initial owners of this vehicle were unable to park their car without someone coming up to them and regaling them with tales of Beetles of their youth. Not long after the car debuted with the 2.0-liter gas engine, the 1.9 TDI engine was made available.

GOLF—FOUR Seat mounted side air bags became an available option for the GTI, which also received new seven-spoke alloy wheels and twin chrome tailpipes.

CABRIOLET—FOUR The former Highline was renamed the GLS. It received the Cabriolet's first ever power convertible top. Seat mounted side airbags became an available option. Rear disc brakes replaced rear drums.

Above: **The 1998 Jettas continud to be the leading sellers in America for Volkswagen.**

Old Cars Weekly Archives

JETTA—FOUR/V-6/DIESEL Seat mounted side air bags also became an available option for the Jetta. Though the TDI diesel was dropped from the new Passat lineup, it reappeared in the Jetta TDI.

PASSAT—FOUR A brand-new Passat offered sleek styling that helped set it off from the crowd. The roof line sloped gently into the back window and created a shape that pleased many. A potent 5-vavle-per-cylinder, turbocharged, intercooled four-cylinder engine became the base engine. This remarkable 1.8-liter engine pumped out 150 hp and made 155 lbs.-ft. of torque from 1750 to 4600 rpms. The rear seat legroom in the 1998 Passat rivaled that of many full-size cars. A new multi-link front suspension created a virtual center steering axis in which the wheels were steered directly from their center points, rather than at the end of lever arms. The result was a virtual elimination of torque steer. The V-6, diesel and station wagon models were dropped.

I.D. DATA: Volkswagen's 17-symbol VIN appears on the top left-hand surface of the instrument panel and is visible through the windshield. The first three symbols identified the country of origin, make and type of vehicle. Volkswagens made in Europe have the first three symbols WVW. Volkswagens made in Mexico have the first three synbols 3VW. The fourth symbol was a letter designating the series (see first column of table below). The fifth

Above: **Among the additions to the 1998 Cabrio was an available power top.**

Old Cars Weekly Archives

Above: **In 1998, the Golf GL continued to be the entry-level VW in America.**

McLellan's Automotive History

1998 VOLKSWAGEN PRODUCTION CHART

Model Code	Body Type & Seating	POE Price	Weight (lbs.)	ProductionTotal
	NEW BEETLE			
B	2d Hatchback-5P	15200	2712	Note 1
	NEW BEETLE TDI			
B	2d Hatchback-5P	16475	2810	Note 1
	GOLF GL			
F	2d Hatchback-5P	13495	2544	Note 2
	GOLF GTI			
D	2d Hatchback-5P	16670	2565	Note 3
R6H	V2d Hatchback-5P	20235	2800	Note 3
	CABRIOLET			
A	2d Convertible-4P	17975	2771	Note 4
	CABRIOLET GLS			
B	2d Convertible-4P	22290	2867	Note 4
	JETTA GL			
R	4d Sedan-5P	14595	2590	Note 5
	JETTA GT			
V	4d Sedan-5P	14990	2590	Note 5
	JETTA TDI			
R	4d Sedan-5P	15770	2525	Note 5
	JETTA WOLFSBURG			
P	4d Sedan-5P	16500	2678	Note 5
	JETTA GLS			
S	4d Sedan-5P	16945	2729	Note 5
	JETTA GLX VR6			
T	4d Sedan-5P	20955	2927	Note 5
	PASSAT GLS FOUR TDI			
M	4d Sedan-5P	21200	3133	Note 6
	PASSAT GLS FOUR TURBO			
M	4d Sedan-5P	20750	3120	Note 6
N	4d Wagon -5P	21900	3194	Note 6
	PASSAT GLS V-6			
M	4d –Sedan-5P	23190	3243	Note 6
	PASSAT GLX V-6			
P	4d Sedan-5P	26250	3250	Note 6

Note 1: 55,842 New Beetles were sold in the United States in 1998.
Note 2: 11,866 Golfs were sold in the United States in 1998.
Note 3: 6,416 GTIs were sold in the United States in 1998.
Note 4: 15,230 Cabriolets were sold in the United States in 1998.
Note 5: 89,311 Jettas were sold in the United States in 1998.
Note 6: 39,272 Passats were sold in the United States in 1998.
Note 7: 219,679 Volkswagens were sold in the United States in 1998.

symbol was a letter identifying the engine: A=2.0-liter four-cylinder 115 hp; B=2.0-liter four cylinder 115 hp; D=2.8-liter V-6 172 hp; F=1.9-liter four-cylinder diesel 90 hp. The sixth symbol designated the type of restraint system: 8=Active belts with driver and passenger air bags, 6= Active belts with driver and passenger air bags, plus side airbags. The seventh and eighth symbols idenitified the model (1C=New Beetle, 1H=Golf, Jetta and GTI, 1E=Cabriolet, 3A=Passat). The ninth symbol was a check digit. The 10th symbol was a letter designating the model year: W=1998. The 11th symbol designated the assembly plant: B=Brussels, Belgium, E=Emden, Germany, H=Hanover, Germany, M=Mexico, W=Wolfsburg, Germany. The last six symbols were the sequential production number starting with 000001.

ENGINE

BASE FOUR (New Beetle, Golf, Jetta): Inline, overhead-cam four-cylinder (8- valve). Cast-iron block and light alloy head. Displacement: 121 cid (1984 cc). Bore & Stroke: 3.25 x 3.65 in. (82.5 x 92.8 mm). Compression Ratio: 10.0:1. Brake Horsepower: 115 at 5400 rpm. Torque: 122 lbs.-ft. at 3200 rpm. Five main bearings. Multi-point fuel injection.

BASE FOUR (Passat): Inline, dual-overhead-cam four-cylinder with turbocharger and intercooler (20-valve). Cast-iron block and light alloy head. Displacement: 108.7 cid (1781 cc). Bore & Stroke: 3.19 x 3.40 in. Compression Ratio: 9.5:1. Brake Horsepower: 150 at 5700 rpm. Torque: 155 lbs.-ft. at 1750-4600 rpm. Five main bearings. Multi-point fuel injection.

DIESEL FOUR (Jetta TDI): Inline, overhead-cam four-cylinder with turbocharger and intercooler (8-valve). Cast-iron block and light alloy head. Displacement: 116 cid (1896 cc). Bore & Stroke: 3.13 x 3.76 in. Compression Ratio: 19.5:1. Brake Horsepower: 90 at 3750 rpm. Torque: 149 lbs.-ft. at 1900 rpm. Five main bearings. Multi-point fuel injection.

BASE V-6 (Golf GTI, Jetta GLX, Passat): Narrow (15 degrees) "vee" type dual- overhead-cam six-cylinder. Cast-iron block and light alloy head. Displacement: 170 cid (2792 cc). Bore & Stroke: 3.19 x 3.56 in. (81 x 90.3 mm). Compression Ratio: 10.0:1. Brake Horsepower: 172 at 5800 rpm. Torque: 177 lbs.-ft. at 4200 rpm. Seven main bearings. Multi-point fuel injection.

CHASSIS

NEW BEETLE: Wheelbase: 98.9 in. Overall Length: 161.1 in. Height: 59.5 in. Width: 67.9 in. Front Tread: 59.6 in. Rear Tread: 58.7 in.

CABRIOLET: Wheelbase: 97.2 in. Overall Length: 160.4 in. Height: 56.0 in. Width: 66.7 in. Front Tread: 57.5 in. Rear Tread: 57.6 in.

GOLF/GTI: Wheelbase: 97.4 in. Overall Length: 160.4 in. Height: 56.2 in. Width: 66.7 in. Front Tread: 57.5 in. Rear Tread: 57.0 in.

JETTA: Wheelbase: 97.4 in. Overall Length: 173.4 in. Height: 56.1 in. Width: 66.7 in. Front Tread: 57.5 in. Rear Tread: 57.0 in.

PASSAT: Wheelbase: 106.4 in. Overall Length: 184.1 in. Height: 57.4 in. Width: 68.5 in. Front Tread: 59.0 in. Rear Tread: 59.1 in.

TECHNICAL

NEW BEETLE: Layout: front-engine, front-wheel-drive. Transmission: five-speed manual. Steering: rack and pinion. Brakes: 4-wheel discs. Body Construction: steel unibody.

CABRIOLET: Layout: front-engine, front-wheel-drive. Transmission: five-speed manual. Steering: rack and pinion. Suspension (front): MacPherson struts with coil springs. Suspension (rear): torsion beam axle with trailing arms and coil springs. Brakes: 4-wheel disc. Body Construction: steel unibody.

GOLF/GTI: Layout: front-engine, front-wheel-drive. Transmission: five-speed manual. Steering: rack and pinion. Suspension (front): MacPherson struts with coil springs. Suspension (rear): torsion beam axle with trailing arms and coil springs. Brakes: front disc, rear drum (except GTI VR6 4-wheel discs). Body Construction: steel unibody.

JETTA: Layout: front-engine, front-wheel-drive. Transmission: five-speed manual. Steering: rack and pinion. Suspension (front): MacPherson struts with coil springs. Suspension (rear): torsion beam axle with trailing arms and coil springs. Brakes: front disc, rear drum. Body Construction: steel unibody.

PASSAT: Layout: front-engine, front-wheel-drive. Transmission: five-speed manual. Steering: rack and pinion. Brakes: 4-wheel discs. Body Construction: steel unibody.

PERFORMANCE: Acceleration (0-60 mph): (Cabriolet) 11.1 sec., (Passat GL) 8.8 sec., (Passat GLX sedan) 7.9 sec., (Passat GLX sta wagon) 8.0 sec. Top Speed in mph: (Cabriolet) 101, (Passat GL) 127, (Passat GLX) 130. EPA Fuel Economy City/Highway in mpg: (Cabriolet) 24/ 30, (Passat GL) 21/30, (Passat GLX) 19/27.

Performance Figures by *Motor Trend*.

MANUFACTURER: Volkswagenwerk AG, Wolfsburg, Germany.

The GTI continued its presence as the Volkswagen that roared in 1998.

Passats received trimming styling in the 1998 model year.

1999

NEW BEETLE—FOUR "The world's most talked about car" is what Volkswagen called this marketing phenomenon. Rather than being typical company hyperbole, this was actually an understatement. For 1999, an antilock braking system was standard. In the second half of the model year, the 1.8 T engine was added. In addition to getting this 150-hp power plant, the GLS or GLX trim Turbo Beetles received six-spoke alloy wheels, a speed-activated rear spoiler and leather seating.

GOLF—FOUR/V-6/DIESEL While Volkswagen called this new Golf the "fourth-generation," it was so far removed from the original Rabbit that leapt to our shores, that it seemed to be a completely different car. Interior and exterior dimensions grew slightly, as did torsional rigidity and aerodynamic sleekness. Standard features included side air bags and ABS brakes. Trim levels jumped from 3 to 6, as the TDI engine became available. In the GTI, a new intake manifold bumped up power and torque slightly in the already potent VR6 engine.

Above: **In its second model year, the 1999 New Beetle received much attention.**

Old Cars Weekly Archives

CABRIOLET—FOUR Unlike previous years, the Cabriolet debuted along with its Golf and Jetta siblings. This time GL and GLS versions were offered. Inside, a striking indigo blue light contrasted with glowing red instrument dials.

JETTA—FOUR/V-6/DIESEL The fourth-generation Jetta hit our shores in the fall of 1998. Offering a more aerodynamic body that cloaked a stiffer chassis, this new Jetta moved up a notch on the sophistication scale. The VR6 engine became available in the GLS trim level. While the horsepower ratings were identical, a newly-refined 2.0-liter engine was standard equipment. The TDI engine was made available at mid-model year.

PASSAT—FOUR/V-6 A station wagon joined the model lineup and the 1.8 T four-cylinder engine was supplemented by the addition of the 2.8-liter V-6 previously available in Audi's A4. This five-valve-per-cylinder engine made 190 hp and produced a very healthy 105 lbs.-ft. of torque.

EUROVAN—V-6 The EuroVan returned to U.S. shores in two models. The GLS van was the less expensive version and the MV van cost a bit more. Options included a power-

Above: **In 1999, the Jetta received a styling update and a choice of engines.**

Old Cars Weekly

Above: **A new intake brought the 1999 GTI VR6 even more power than ever before.**

Old Cars Weekly Archives

Above: **The station wagon was new to the Passat lineup in the 1999 model year.**

Old Cars Weekly Archives

The Passat station wagon was a new Volkswagen model in 1999.

Model Code	Body Type & Seating	POE Price	Weight (lbs.)	ProductionTotal
	NEW BEETLE GL			
B	2d Hatchback-5P	15900	2769	Note 1
	NEW BEETLE GLS			
C	2d Hatchback-5P	16850	2785	Note 1
	NEW BEETLE GLS 1.8T			
C	2d Hatchback 5-P	19000	2785	Note 1
	NEW BEETLE TDI			
C	2d Hatchback-5P	17900	2867	Note 1
	NEW BEETLE GLS TURBO			
D	2d Hatchback 5-P	19000	2921	Note 1
	NEW BEETLE GLX TURBO			
D	2d Hatchback 5-P	20900	2959	Note 1
	GOLF GL			
F	4d Hatchback-5P	13495	2544	Note 2
	GOLF WOLFSBURG			
J	4d Hatchback-5P	15275	NA	Note 2
	GOLF GTI VR6			
F	2d Hatchback-5P	20235	2800	Note 2
	NEW GOLF GL			
B	2d Hatchback-5P	14900	2723	Note 2
	NEW GOLF GL TDI			
B	2d Hatchback-5P	16195	2791	Note 2
	NEW GOLF GTI GLS			
D	2d Hatchback-5P	17500	2762	Note 2
	NEW GOLF GTI GLX VR6			
D	2d Hatchback-5P	22150	2890	Note 3
	NEW GOLF GLS			
G	2d Hatchback-5P	16350	2820	Note 2
	NEW GOLF GTI TDI			
G	2d Hatchback-5P	17400	2875	Note 3
	NEW CABRIO GL			
GL	2d Convertible-4P	19900	3079	Note 4
	NEW CABRIO GLS			
GLS	2d Convertible-4P	23300	3167	Note 4
	JETTA GL			
GL	4d Sedan-5P	16700	2853	Note 5
	JETTA GL TDI			
GL	TDI 4d Sedan-5P	17995	2873	Note 5
	JETTA GLS FOUR			
GLS	4d Sedan-5P	17650	2862	Note 5
	JETTA GLS TDI			
GLS	TDI 4d Sedan-5P	18700	2891	Note 5
	JETTA GLS V-6			
GLS	4d Sedan-5P	19950	2994	Note 5
	JETTA GLX V-6			
GLX	4d Sedan-5P	23500	3019	Note 5
	PASSAT GLS			
GLS	4d Sedan-5P	21200	3122	Note 6
GLS	4d Wagon-5P	21750	3201	Note 6
	PASSAT GLS V-6			
GLS V6	4d Sedan-5P	23800	3245	Note 6
	PASSAT GLX V-6			
GLX	4d Sedan-5P	28150	3380	Note 6
	EUROVAN GLS V-6			
K	Van-8P	29900	4220	Note 7
	EUROVAN MV V-6			
M	Van-8P	31400	4348	Note 7

Note 1: 83,434 New Beetles were sold in the United States in 1999.
Note 2: 13,816 Golfs were sold in the United States in 1999.
Note 3: 5,174 GTIs were sold in the United States in 1999.
Note 4: 11,539 Cabriolets were sold in the United States in 1999.
Note 5: 130,054 Jettas were sold in the United States in 1999.
Note 6: 68,151 Passats were sold in the United States in 1999.
Note 7: EuroVan production not available.
Note 8: 315,563 Volkswagens were sold in the United States in 1999.

operated sun roof, a compact disc player, aluminum alloy wheels and an anti-theft and vehicle recovery system.

I.D. DATA: Volkswagen's 17-symbol VIN appears on the top left-hand surface of the instrument panel and is visible through the windshield. The first three symbols identified the country of origin, make and type of vehicle. Volkswagens made in Europe have the first three symbols WVW. Volkswagens made in Mexico have the first three synbols 3VW. The fourth symbol was a letter designating the series (see first column of table below). The fifth symbol was a letter identifying the engine: A=2.0-liter four-cylinder 115 hp; B=2.0-liter four-cylinder 115 hp; C=2.0-liter four-cylinder 115 hp; D=1.8-liter four-cylinder 148 hp; E=2.8-liter V-6 174-hp; F=1.9-liter four-cylinder diesel 90 hp. The sixth symbol designated the type of restraint system. The seventh and eighth symbols idenitified the model (1C=New Beetle, 1H=Golf, Jetta and GTI, 1E=Cabriolet, 1J Golf/GTI, 3B=Passat, 9M=Jetta). The ninth symbol was a check digit. The 10th symbol was a letter designating the model year: X=1999. The 11th symbol designated the assembly plant: E=Emden, Germany, H=Hanover, Germany, M=Mexico, W=Wolfsburg, Germany. The last six symbols were the sequential production number starting with 000001.

ENGINE

BASE FOUR (Golf, Jetta): Inline, overhead-cam four-cylinder (8-valve). Cast-iron block and light alloy head. Displacement: 121 cid (1984 cc). Bore & Stroke: 3.25 x 3.65 in. (82.5 x 92.8 mm). Compression Ratio: 10.0:1. Brake Horsepower: 115 at 5200 rpm. Torque: 122 lbs.-ft. at 2600 rpm. Five main bearings. Multi-point fuel injection.

BASE FOUR (Passat, New Beetle 1.8T): Inline, dual-overhead-cam four-cylinder (20-valve). Cast-iron block and light alloy head. Displacement: 108.7 cid (1781 cc). Bore & Stroke: 3.19 x 3.40 in. Compression Ratio: 9.5:1. Brake Horsepower: 150 at 5700 rpm. Torque: 155 lbs.-ft. at 1750-4600 rpm. Five main bearings. Multi-point fuel injection.

DIESEL FOUR (Golf TDI, Jetta TDI): Inline, overhead-cam four-cylinder with turbocharger and intercooler (8-valve). Cast-iron block and light alloy head. Displacement: 116 cid (1896 cc). Bore & Stroke: 3.13 x 3.76 in. Compression Ratio: 19.5:1. Brake Horsepower: 90 at 3750 rpm. Torque: 149 lbs.-ft. at 1900 rpm. Five main bearings. Multi-point fuel injection.

BASE V-6 (Golf GTI GLX, Jetta GLX): Narrow (15 degrees) "vee" type dual- overhead-cam six-cylinder. Cast-iron block and light alloy head. Displacement: 170 cid (2792 cc). Bore & Stroke: 3.19 x 3.56 in. (81 x 90.3 mm). Compression Ratio: 10.0:1. Brake Horsepower: 174 at 5800 rpm. Torque: 181 lbs.-ft. at 3200 rpm. Seven main bearings. Multi-point fuel injection.

BASE V-6 (Passat GLS): "Vee" type dual-overhead-cam six-cylinder. Cast-iron block and light alloy head. Displacement: 169.1 cid (2771 cc). Bore & Stroke: 3.25 x 3.40 in. (82.5 x 86.4 mm). Compression Ratio: 10.6:1. Brake Horsepower: 160 at 6000 rpm. Torque: 206 lbs.-ft. at 3200 rpm. Four main bearings. Sequential multi-point fuel injection.

BASE V-6 (EuroVan): "Vee" type six-cylinder. Displacement: 170 cid. Bore & Stroke: 3.19 x 3.54 in. Brake Horsepower: 140-201 at 6000 rpm. Fuel injection.

CHASSIS

NEW BEETLE: Wheelbase: 98.9 in. Overall Length: 161.1 in. Height: 59.5 in. Width: 67.9 in. Front Tread: 59.6 in. Rear Tread: 58.7 in.

CABRIOLET: Wheelbase: 97.4 in. Overall Length: 160.4 in. Height: 56.0 in. Width: 66.7 in. Front Tread: 57.6 in. Rear Tread: 57.6 in.

GOLF/GTI: Wheelbase: 98.9 in. Overall Length: 163.3 in. Height: 56.7 in. Width: 66.7 in. Front Tread: 59.6 in. Rear Tread: 58.8 in.

JETTA: Wheelbase: 98.9 in. Overall Length: 172.3 in. Height: 56.9 in. Width: 66.7 in. Front Tread: 59.6 in. Rear Tread: 58.8 in.

PASSAT: Wheelbase: 106.4 in. Overall Length: 184.1 in. Height: 57.4 in. Width: 68.5 in. Front Tread: 59.0 in. Rear Tread: 59.1 in.

EUROVAN: Wheelbase: 115 in. Overall Length: NA in. Height: NA in. Width: NA in. Front Tread: NA in. Rear Tread: NA in.

TECHNICAL

NEW BEETLE: Layout: front-engine, front-wheel-drive. Transmission: five-speed manual. Steering: rack and pinion. Brakes: 4-wheel discs. Body Construction: steel unibody.

CABRIOLET: Layout: front-engine, front-wheel-drive. Transmission: five-speed manual. Steering: rack and pinion. Suspension (front): MacPherson struts with coil springs. Suspension (rear): torsion beam axle with trailing arms and coil springs. Brakes: 4-wheel disc. Body Construction: steel unibody.

GOLF/GTI: Layout: front-engine, front-wheel-drive. Transmission: five-speed manual. Steering: rack and pinion. Suspension (front): MacPherson struts with coil springs. Suspension (rear): torsion beam axle with trailing arms and coil springs. Brakes: front disc, rear drum (except GTI VR6 4-wheel discs). Body Construction: steel unibody.

JETTA: Layout: front-engine, front-wheel-drive. Transmission: five-speed manual. Steering: rack and pinion. Suspension (front): MacPherson struts with coil springs. Suspension (rear): torsion beam axle with trailing arms and coil springs. Brakes: front disc, rear drum. Body Construction: steel unibody.

PASSAT: Layout: front-engine, front-wheel-drive. Transmission: five-speed manual. Steering: rack and pinion. Brakes: 4-wheel discs. Body Construction: steel unibody.

PERFORMANCE: Acceleration (0-60 mph): (Cabriolet) 11.1 sec., (Passat GL) 8.8 sec., (Passat GLX sedan) 7.9 sec., (Passat GLX Station Wagon) 8.0 sec. Top Speed in mph: (Cabriolet) 101, (Passat GL) 127, (Passat GLX) 130. EPA Fuel Economy City/Highway in mpg: (Cabriolet) 24/ 30, (Passat GL) 21/30, (Passat GLX) 19/27.

Performance figures by *Motor Trend*.

MANUFACTURER: Volkswagenwerk AG, Wolfsburg, Germany.

DISTRIBUTOR: Volkswagen of America Inc., Auburn Hills, Michigan.

Old Cars Weekly Archives

In 1999, the EuroVan continued to be a dependable choice for VW buyers.

2000

NEW BEETLE—FOUR The Immobilizer anti-theft system became standard equipment on the New Beetle. The 1.8T versions had ASR (Anti-Slip Regulation) added to the existing traction control EDL (Electronic Differential Lock).

GOLF—FOUR/V-6/DIESEL Security featured prominently in the 2000 Golf. The Immobilizer system was added, a coded key had to be used in order for the vehicle to start. Child seat tether anchorage points were added, and the 100-watt, eight-channel Monsoon Audio system became available as an option. It was standard on the GTI GLX. The GTI GLX also received standard all-speed traction control equipped with ASR (Anti-Slip Regulation).

CABRIOLET—FOUR Side turn signals were mounted in the front fenders, a non-smokers package with power outlet and storage cubbies replaced the ashtray. A driver's-door-mounted central locking switch was added. The Immobilizer was also standard.

JETTA—FOUR/V-6/DIESEL Security featured prominently in the 2000 Jetta. The Immobilizer system was added, a coded key had to be used in order for the vehicle to start. Child seat tether anchorage points were added, and the 100-watt, eight-channel Monsoon Audio system became available as an option.

Above: **The potent 2000 GTI VR6 produced 174 hp from its 170-cid engine.**

McLellan's Automotive History

PASSAT—FOUR/V-6 A five-speed automatic transmission with Porsche's patented Tiptronic sequential shifting mechanism was added to the Passat lineup. The five-speed manual was also made available in all levels of the Passat. A Monsoon audio system and enhanced traction control were also available.

EUROVAN—V-6 The EuroVan continued to be offered in two models. The GLS van was the less expensive version and the MV van cost a bit more. Options included a power-operated sun roof, a compact disc player, alumiunm alloy wheels and an anti-theft and vehicle recovery system. EuroVans were in the 5600-5838-pound GVW range.

I.D. DATA: Volkswagen's 17-symbol VIN appears on the top left-hand surface of the instrument panel and is visible through the windshield. The first three symbols identified the country of origin, make and type of vehicle. Volkswagens made in Europe have the first three symbols WVW. Volkswagens made in Mexico have the first three synbols 3VW. Volkswagens made in Brazil have the first three synbols 9BW. The fourth symbol was a letter designating the series (see first column of table below). The fifth symbol was a letter identifying the engine: A=2.0-liter four-cylinder 115 hp; B=2.0-liter four cylinder 115 hp; D=2.8-liter V-6 172 hp; F=1.9-liter four-cylinder diesel 90 hp. The sixth symbol designated the type of restraint system. The seventh and eighth symbols idenitified the model (1C=New Beetle, 1J=Golf, Jetta and Jetta Wagon, 1V=Cabrio, 3B=Passat, New Passat

Above: **The 2000 Golf GLS was available with improved safety and audio systems.**

McLellan's Automotive History

Above: **The unique New Beetle was one of the top selling Volkswagens in 2000.**

McLellan's Automotive History

2000 VOLKSWAGEN PRODUCTION CHART

Model Code	Body Type & Seating	POE Price	Weight (lbs.)	ProductionTotal
	NEW BEETLE GL			
B	2d Hatchback-5P	15900	2769	Note 1
	NEW BEETLE GLS			
C	2d Hatchback-5P	16850	2825	Note 1
	NEW BEETLE TDI			
C	2d Hatchback-5P	17900	2867	Note 1
	NEW BEETLE GLS 1.8 T			
C	2d Hatchback-5P	19000	2785	Note 1
	NEW BEETLE GLX 1.8 T			
D	2d Hatchback-5P	21075	2964	Note 1
	GOLF GL			
B	2d Hatchback-5P	14900	2767	Note 2
	GOLF GL TDI			
B	2d Hatchback-5P	16195	2847	Note 2
	GOLF GTI GLS			
D	2d Hatchback-5P	17675	2762	Note 3
	GOLF GTI GLS 1.8T			
D	2d Hatchback-5P	19225	2811	Note 3
	GOLF GLS			
G	4d Hatchback-5P	16350	2864	Note 2
	GOLF GLS TDI			
G	2d Hatchback-5P	17400	2944	Note 2
	GOLF GTI GLX VR6			
D	2d Hatchback-5P	22620	2890	Note 3
	GOLF GLS 1.8T			
G	4d Hatchback-5P	17400	2906	Note 2
	CABRIO GL			
C	2d Convertible-4P	19900	2831	Note 4
	CABRIO GLS			
D	2d Convertible-4P	23300	2853	Note 4
	JETTA GL			
R	4d Sedan-5P	16700	2884	Note 5
	JETTA GL TDI			
R	4d Sedan-5P	17995	2974	Note 5
	JETTA GLS			
S	4d Sedan-5P	17650	2934	Note 5
	JETTA GLS TDI			
S	4d Sedan-5P	18700	3036	Note 5

and 9M=Jetta). The ninth symbol was a check digit. The 10th symbol was a letter designating the model year: Y=2000. The 11th symbol designated the assembly plant: E=Emden, Germany, H=Hanover, Germany, M=Mexico, P=Mosel, Germany, W=Wolfsburg, Germany, 4=Curitiba, Brazil. The last six symbols were the sequential production number starting with 000001.

ENGINE

BASE FOUR (Golf, Jetta): Inline, overhead-cam four-cylinder (8-valve). Cast-iron block and light alloy head. Displacement: 121 cid (1984 cc). Bore & Stroke: 3.25 x 3.65 (82.5 x 92.8 mm). Compression Ratio: 10.0:1. Brake Horsepower: 115 at 5200 rpm. Torque: 122 lbs.-ft. at 2600 rpm. Five main bearings. Multi-point fuel injection.

BASE FOUR (Passat): Inline, dual-overhead-cam four-cylinder (20-valve). Cast-iron block and light alloy head.

Displacement: 108.7 cid (1781 cc). Bore & Stroke: 3.19 x 3.40 in. Compression Ratio: 9.5:1. Brake Horsepower: 150 at 5700 rpm. Torque: 155 lbs.-ft. at 1750-4600 rpm. Five main bearings. Multi-point fuel injection.

DIESEL FOUR (Golf TDI, Jetta TDI): Inline, overhead-cam four-cylinder with turbocharger and intercooler (8-valve). Cast-iron block and light alloy head. Displacement: 116 cid (1896 cc). Bore & Stroke: 3.13 x 3.76 in. Compression Ratio: 19.5:1. Brake Horsepower: 90 at 3750 rpm. Torque: 149 lbs.-ft. at 1900 rpm. Five main bearings. Multi-point fuel injection.

BASE V-6 (Golf GTI GLX, Jetta GLX): Narrow (15 degrees) "vee" type dual overhead-cam six-cylinder. Cast-iron block and light alloy head. Displacement: 170 cid (2792 cc). Bore & Stroke: 3.19 x 3.56 in. (81 x 90.3 mm). Compression Ratio: 10.0:1. Brake Horsepower: 174 at

Model Code	Body Type & Seating	POE Price	Weight (lbs.)	Production Total
JETTA GLS 1.8T				
S	4d Sedan-5P	19200	2922	Note 5
JETTA GLS 1.8T				
S	4d Sedan-5P	19200	2922	Note 5
JETTA GLS VR6				
S	4d Sedan-5P	19950	3086	Note 5
JETTA GLX VR6				
T	4d Sedan-5P	24170	3106	Note 5
PASSAT GLS TURBO FOUR				
M	4d Sedan-5P	21200	3043	Note 6
N	4d Wagon-5P	22000	3136	Note 6
PASSAT GLS V-6				
M	4d Sedan-5P	23800	3151	Note 6
N	4d Wagon-5P	24600	3244	Note 6
PASSAT GLS MOTION V-6				
T	4d Sedan-5P	25450	3532	Note 6
R	4d Wagon-5P	26250	3655	Note 6
PASSAT GLX V-6				
P	4d Sedan-5P	27655	3181	Note 6
W	4d Wagon-5P	28455	3269	Note 6
PASSAT GLX MOTION V-6				
U	4d Sedan-5P	29305	3532	Note 6
W	4d Wagon-5P	30105	3655	Note 6
EUROVAN GLS V-6				
K	Van-8P	31300	4220	Note 7
EUROVAN MV V-6				
M	Van-8P	4438	4438	Note 7

Note 1: 81,134 New Beetles were sold in the United States in 2000.
Note 2: 20,747 Golfs were sold in the United States in 2000.
Note 3:: 7,377 GTIs were sold in the United States in 2000.
Note 4: 14,133 Cabriolets were sold in the United States in 2000.
Note 5: 144,853 Jettas were sold in the United States in 2000.
Note 6: 84,521 Passats were sold in the United States in 2000.
Note 7: EuroVan production not available.
Note 8: 355,479 Volkswagens were sold in the United States in 2000.

Above: **There were seven variations of the popular Jetta available in 2000.**
McLellan's Automotive History

Above: **There five trim levels available among the 2000 Passat choices.**
McLellan's Automotive History

5800 rpm. Torque: 181 lbs.-ft. at 3200 rpm. Seven main bearings. Multi-point fuel injection.

BASE V-6 (Passat GLS): "Vee" type dual overhead-cam six-cylinder. Cast-iron block and light alloy head. Displacement: 169.1 cid (2771 cc). Bore & Stroke: 3.25 x 3.40 in. (82.5 x 86.4 mm). Compression Ratio: 10.6:1. Brake Horsepower: 160, at 6000 rpm. Torque: 206 lbs.-ft. at 3200 rpm. Four main bearings. Sequential multi-point fuel injection.

BASE V-6 (EuroVan): "Vee" type six-cylinder. Displacement: 170 cid. Bore & Stroke: 3.19 x 3.54 in. Brake Horsepower: 140-201 at 6000 rpm. Fuel injection.

CHASSIS

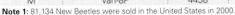

NEW BEETLE: Wheelbase: 98.9 in. Overall Length: 161.1 in. Height: 59.5 in. Width: 67.9 in. Front Tread: 59.6 in. Rear Tread: 58.7 in.

CABRIOLET: Wheelbase: 97.4 in. Overall Length: 160.4 in. Height: 56.0 in. Width: 66.7 in. Front Tread: 57.6 in. Rear Tread: 57.6 in.

GOLF/GTI: Wheelbase: 98.9 in. Overall Length: 163.3 in. Height: 56.7 in. Width: 68.3 in. Front Tread: 59.6 in. Rear Tread: 58.8 in.

JETTA: Wheelbase: 98.9 in. Overall Length: 172.3 in. Height: 56.9 in. Width: 68.3 in. Front Tread: 59.6 in. Rear Tread: 58.8 in.

PASSAT: Wheelbase: 106.4 in. Overall Length: 184.1 in. Height: 57.4 in. Width: 68.5 in. Front Tread: 59.0 in. Rear Tread: 59.1 in.

EUROVAN: Wheelbase: 115 in. Overall Length: NA in. Height: NA in. Width: NA in. Front Tread: NA in. Rear Tread: NA in.

TECHNICAL

NEW BEETLE: Layout: front-engine, front-wheel-drive. Transmission: five-speed manual. Steering: rack and pinion. Brakes: 4-wheel discs. Body Construction: steel unibody.

CABRIOLET: Layout: front-engine, front-wheel-drive. Transmission: five-speed manual. Steering: rack and pinion. Suspension (front): MacPherson struts with coil springs. Suspension (rear): torsion beam axle with trailing arms and coil springss. Brakes: 4-wheel disc. Body Construction: steel unibody.

GOLF/GTI: Layout: front-engine, front-wheel-drive. Transmission: five-speed manual. Steering: rack and pinion. Suspension (front): MacPherson struts with coil springs. Suspension (rear): torsion beam axle with trailing arms and coil springss. Brakes: front disc, rear drum (except GTI VR6 4-wheel discs). Body Construction: steel unibody.

JETTA: Layout: front-engine, front-wheel-drive. Transmission: five-speed manual. Steering: rack and pinion. Suspension (front): MacPherson struts with coil springs. Suspension (rear): torsion beam axle with trailing arms and coil springss. Brakes: front disc, rear drum. Body Construction: steel unibody.

PASSAT: Layout: front-engine, front-wheel-drive. Transmission: five-speed manual. Steering: rack and pinion. Brakes: 4-wheel discs. Body Construction: steel unibody.

PERFORMANCE: Acceleration (0-60 mph): (Cabriolet) 11.1 sec. (Passat GL) 8.8 sec., (Passat GLX sedan) 7.9 sec., (Passat GLX Station Wagon) 8.0 sec. Top Speed in mph: (Cabriolet) 101, (Passat GL) 127, (Passat GLX) 130. EPA Fuel Economy in mpg: City/Highway: (Cabriolet) 24/30, (Passat GL) 21/30, (Passat GLX) 19/27. Performance Figures by *Motor Trend*.

MANUFACTURER: Volkswagenwerk AG, Wolfsburg, Germany.

DISTRIBUTOR: Volkswagen of America Inc., Auburn Hills, Michigan.

McLellan's Automotive History

The EuroVan continued to be a staple of the VW lineup in America for 2000.

2001

NEW BEETLE--FOUR The arch-shaped New Beetle resembled the old bug. It had a real "don't-know-if-it's-coming-or-going" look. The large round headlamps resembled cartoon-character eyes. A limited edition GLS 1.8T model with a sporty flavor was added to the 2001 New Beetle model range. It included leather seats, 17-in. alloy wheels, a Monsoon audio system with eight speakers, a sun roof and a cold weather package. All New Beetles received larger side mirrors, redesigned cup holders and an emergency release button to press if you got trapped in the trunk. Added to the GLX model's standard equipment list was a Monsoon sound system, rain-sensing windshield wipers and a self-dimming rearview mirror. You could get Monsoon sound and 17-in. alloy wheels for the GLS at extra cost. The GL powered by the 2.0-liter SOHC four was the base model, but didn't skimp on equipment. The GLS added a console, one-touch power windows and cruise control. The GLS TDI added the 1.9-liter turbo-diesel four that could deliver 48 mpg. The GLS 1.8T had the smallest engine, but it was a high-tech power plant that produced 150 hp and went fast. The GLX had the 1.8T engine, alloy rims, leather seats, a glass sun roof and other goodies. The New Beetle was built in Puebla, Mexico.

GOLF/GTI—FOUR/V-6/DIESEL Golf models for 2001 were fourth-generation hatchback models with a long sloping windshield. The horizontal-bars grille held a VW

Above: **The 2001 Passat's 4Motion option brought power to all four wheels.**

McLellan's Automotive History

center emblem and horizontal clear halogen headlights at either end. The more letters in the name, the higher the trim level. The 2.0-liter four was base engine and the 1.9-liter TDI four were offered and the 1.8T was optional (but standard in the high-performance GTI). All 2001 Golf models got clear side marker lights, a trunk entrapment release button, new cup holders and "curtain" type head-protection air bags. This type of air bag protected both front and rear passengers in a side collision. A new optional sport suspension was available on the 1.8T model. The GTI GLX received a multi-function (stereo and cruise control) control steering wheel. The Golf and GTI were built in Wolfsburg, Germany and Sao Bernardo, Brazil. Base model was the well-equipped GL. The GL TDI added the turbo diesel. The GLS hatchback added velour upholstery, a console, air conditioning and more. The GLS TDI added the turbo diesel. The GLS 1.8T added the hot turbo four. The GTI GLS had that engine, a glass sun roof, cloth upholstery, fatter tires, cruise, tilt steering, a tach and much more. The GTI GLX had the 2.8-liter V-6, leather upholstery, auto-dimming mirrors, a wood-trimmed shifter and many other ammenities.

CABRIOLET—FOUR The Cabrio looked like a shoe on wheels with a handle. The handle was the rollover bar. A 6-layer convertible top latched tightly to the windshield header. A long list of equipment was standard on the base GL model. The GLS added heated seats, power windows, power mirrors and cruise. The GLX added new-design 14-in. alloy rims, a power top, Sport front seats and leather

Above: **In 2001, the Mexican-built Cabrio came with a long list of standard features.**

McLellan's Automotive History

Above: **For 2001, the EuroVan was powered by a new V-6 engine.**

McLellan's Automotive History

Above: **The award for the most fun in the VW lineup once again went to the 2001 GTI series.**

McLellan's Automotive History

2001 VOLKWAGEN PRODUCTION CHART

Model Code	Body Type & Seating	POE Price	Weight (lbs.)	ProductionTotal
	NEW BEETLE GL			
B	2d Hatchback-5P	15900	2769	Notes 1 / 2
	NEW BEETLE GLS			
C	2d Hatchback-5P	16850	2785	Notes 1 & 2
	NEW BEETLE GLS TDI			
C	2d Hatchback-5P	17900	2867	Notes 1 & 2
	NEW BEETLE GLS 1.8TURBO			
C	2d Hatchback-5P	19000	2921	Notes 1 & 2
	NEW BEETLE GLX 1.8TURBO			
D	2d Hatchback-5P	21175	2959	Notes 1 & 2
	GOLF GL			
B	2d Hatchback-5P	14900	2767	Notes 1 & 2
	GOLF GL TDI			
B	2d Hatchback-5P	16195	2847	Notes 1 & 2
	GOLF GTI GLS 1.8 TURBO			
D	2d Hatchback-5P	19275	2860	Notes 1 & 2
	GOLF GTI GLX VR6			
P	2d Hatchback-5P	22900	2999	Notes 1 & 2
	GOLF GLS			
G	4d Hatchback-5P	16350	2864	Notes 1 & 2
	GOLF GLS TDI			
G	4d Hatchback-5P	17400	2944	Notes 1 & 2
	GOLF GLS 1.8TURBO			
G	4d Hatchback-5P	17,900	2906	Notes 1 & 2
	CABRIOLET GL			
B	2d Convertible-4P	19600	2825	Notes 1 & 2
	CABRIOLET GLS			
C	2d Convertible-4P	20600	2834	Notes 1 & 2
	CABRIOLET GLX			
D	2d Convertible-4P	22300	2857	Notes 1 & 2
	JETTA GL			
R	4d Sedan-5P	16700	2893	Notes 1 & 2
	JETTA GL TDI			
R	4d Sedan-5P	17995	2975	Notes 1 & 2
	JETTA GLS FOUR			
S	4d Sedan-5P	17650	2908	Notes 1 & 2

upholstery. All models were powered by the 2.0-liter four. The Cabrio was built in Puebla, Mexico.

JETTA—FOUR/V-6/DIESEL The Jetta came as a notchback sedan with a "ducktail" rear or a wagon. The grille up front looked like a slanted, upside-down trapezoid with horizontal bars and a big VW emblem in the center. The streamlined headlights sat outboard of the grille. The base GL and the GLS got improved velour upholstery. In addition to standard Side Curtain air bags, the Jetta received optional 17-in. alloy wheels for 1.8T and VR6 models equipped with the sport package. The same steering wheel controls on the GTI wheel were standard on the GLX and optional on the GLS. The GL was the basic model, with a very non-basic equipment list. The 2.0-liter four was base engine. The GLS added power windows, power mirrors and cruise control. The GL TDI added the 90-hp turbo-diesel engine. The GLS was also available with this motor, making it a GLD TDI. The GLS Wolfsburg Edition added 16-in. alloys, P205/55HR16 tires, Sport front seats and a leather-wrapped steering wheel. The GLS 1.8T included the 150-hp turbo DOHC four. There was a GLS VR6 with P195/65HR15 tires, full wheel covers, height-adjustable front bucket seats and more. The GLX sedan added P205/55HR16 tires, alloys, fog lights, glass sunroof, heated seats, Monsoon sound and much more. Wagon trims aped those available for the sedans. The Jetta was built in Puebla, Mexico.

PASSAT—FOUR/V-6 The 2001 Passat had updated styling, minor interior revisions and a hotter four-cylinder power plant. New features included side curtain air bags, optional redundant controls on the steering wheel, and a trunk entrapment feature. At long last the 4MOTION option was available on the Passat. This traction-enhancing system distributed power to all four wheels using an automatic- locking Torsen center differential to allocate engine torque front to back. The base GLS model included many features. The GLS V6 added a V-6 engine, shiftable five-speed automatic transmission, full-time four-wheel-drive, a pass-through center armrest and more. The GLX had alloys, fatter P205/55HR15 tires,

Model Code	Body Type & Seating	POE Price	Weight (lbs.)	Production Total
JETTA GLS TDI				
S	4d Sedan-5P	18700	2983	Notes 1 & 2
JETTA GLS 1.8T				
S	2d Sedan-5P	19200	2952	Notes 1 & 2
JETTA WOLFSBURG				
P	4d Sedan-5P	19600	3054	Notes 1 & 2
JETTA GLS VR6				
S	4d Sedan-5P	19950	3045	Notes 1 & 2
JETTA GLX VR6				
T	4d Sedan-5P	24300	3144	Notes 1 & 2
PASSAT GLS TURBO FOUR				
A	4d Sedan-5P	21450	3043	Notes 1 & 2
H	4d Wagon-5P	22250	3136	Notes 1 & 2
PASSAT GLS V-6				
A	4d Sedan-5P	24050	3151	Notes 1 & 2
H	4d Wagon-5P	24850	3244	Notes 1 & 2
PASSAT GLX V-6				
B	4d Sedan-5P	28210	3180	Notes 1 & 2
J	4d Wagon-5P	29010	3269	Notes 1 & 2
PASSAT GLS 4MOTION V-6				
D	4d Sedan-5P	26875	3472	Notes 1 & 2
K	4d Wagon-5P	27675	3574	Notes 1 & 2
PASSAT GLX 4MOTIONV-6				
B	4d Sedan-5P	26875	3502	Notes 1 & 2
L	4d Wagon-5P	27675	3603	Notes 1 & 2
EUROVAN GLS V-6				
K	Van-8P	26200	4285	Notes 1 & 2
EUROVAN MV V-6				
M	Van-8P	27700	4474	Notes 1 & 2

Note 1: Volkswagen built a total of 1,282, 552 cars in Germany in 2001. This included 113,822 Polos, 565,602 Golfs, 41,716 Lupos, 486,023 Passats, 371 Phaetons, 37,534 Caravelles and 37,484 vans and ambulances.

Note 2: Volkswagen built a total of 241,639 cars in Mexico for the U.S. market. These units included 72,375 Beetles, 15,481 Cabrios and 153,783 Jettas.

Above: **The new Beetle reflected owner tastes in customizing.**

McLellan's Automotive History

leather trim, Monsoon sound, wood dash trim and other niceties. The GLX 4Motion was the top trim level with the full-time four-wheel-drive system. Also offered were GLS, GLS 4Motion and GLX wagons. The Passat was built in Emden, Germany.

EUROVAN—V-6 Equipped with a more powerful V-6 and electronic stability control system, the 2001 EuroVan had updates including a new premium sound system, individual seats for second row seating and standard integrated fog lights. Standard equipment also included a Climatronic system, a six-speaker stereo system, power OSRV mirrors, lighted visor-vanity mirrors and a four-speed automatic transmission. The EuroVan continued to be offered in two models. The GLS van was the less expensive version and the MV van cost a bit more. The EuroVan was built in Hanover, Germany.

I.D. DATA: Volkswagen's 17-symbol VIN appears on the top left-hand surface of the instrument panel and is visible through the windshield. The first three symbols identified the country of origin, make and type of vehicle. Volkswagens made in Europe have the first three symbols WVW. Volkswagens made in Mexico have the first three symbols 3VW. Volkswagens made in Brazil have the first three synbols 9BW. The fourth symbol was a letter designating the series (see first column of table below). The fifth symbol was a letter identifying the engine: A=2.0-liter four-cylinder 115 hp; C=1.8-liter 150-hp four cylinder 115 hp; D=1.8-liter four-cylinder 150 hp; G=2.8-liter V-6 174 hp; H=1.8-liter four-cylinder 150 hp; K=2.0-liter four-cylinder 115 hp; P=1.9-liter 90-hp four-cylinder diesel; S=2.0-liter four-cylinder 115 hp; T=2.0-liter four-cylinder 115 hp. The sixth symbol designated the type of restraint system. The seventh and eighth symbols idenitified the model (1C=New Beetle, 1J=Golf, Jetta and Jetta Wagon, 1V=Cabrio, 3B=Passat, New Passat and 9M=Jetta). The ninth symbol was a check digit. The 10th symbol was a letter designating the model year: 1=2001. The 11th symbol designated the assembly plant: E=Emden, Germany; H=Hanover, Germany, M=Mexico, P=Mosel, Germany, W=Wolfsburg, Germany, 4=Curitba, Brazil. The last six symbols were the sequential production number starting with 000001.

ENGINE

2.0-LITER FOUR (Golf, Cabrio, Jetta, New Beetle): Inline, overhead-cam four-cylinder (8-valve). Cast-iron block and light alloy head. Displacement: 121 cid (1984 cc). Bore & Stroke: 3.25 x 3.65 in. (82.5 x 92.8 mm).

Compression Ratio: 10.0:1. Brake Horsepower: 115 at 5200 rpm. Torque: 122 lbs.-ft. at 2600 rpm. Five main bearings. Sequential multi-point fuel injection.

1.8-LITER TURBO "1.8T" FOUR (New Beetle, Golf GLS, GTI, Jetta, Passat): Inline, dual-overhead-cam 20-valve four-cylinder. Cast- iron block and light alloy head. Displacement: 108.7 cid (1781 cc). Bore & Stroke: 3.19 x 3.40 in. Compression Ratio: 9.5:1. Brake Horsepower: 150 at 5700 rpm. Torque: 155 lbs.-ft. at 1750-4600 rpm. Five main bearings. Sequential multi-point fuel injection.

1.9-LITER DIESEL TDI FOUR (New Beetle TDI, Golf TDI, Jetta TDI): Inline, overhead-cam four-cylinder with turbocharger and intercooler (8-valve). Cast-iron block and light alloy head. Displacement: 116 cid (1896 cc). Bore & Stroke: 3.13 x 3.76 in. Compression Ratio: 19.5:1. Brake Horsepower: 90 at 3750 rpm. Torque: 149 lbs.-ft. at 1900 rpm. Five main bearings. Sequential multi-point fuel injection.

2.8-LITER V-6 "30-VALVE" (Golf GTI GLX, Jetta GLS VR6, Jetta GLX VR6): Narrow (15 degrees) "vee" type dual-overhead-cam 12-valve six-cylinder. Cast-iron block and light alloy head. Displacement: 170 cid (2792 cc). Bore & Stroke: 3.19 x 3.56 in. (81 x 90.3 mm). Compression Ratio: 10.0:1. Brake Horsepower: 174 at 5800 rpm. Torque: 181 lbs.-ft. at 3200 rpm. Seven main bearings. Sequential multi-point fuel injection.

2.8-LITER V-6 "12-VALVE" (Passat GLS): "Vee" type dual overhead-cam 30-valve six-cylinder. Cast-iron block and light alloy head. Displacement: 169.1 cid (2771 cc). Bore & Stroke: 3.25 x 3.40 in. (82.5 x 86.4 mm). Compression Ratio: 10.6:1. Brake Horsepower: 190 at 6000 rpm. Torque: 206 lbs.-ft. at 3200 rpm. Four main bearings. Sequential multi-point fuel injection.

2.8-LITER V-6 (EuroVan): "Vee" type six-cylinder. Displacement: 170 cid. Bore & Stroke: 3.19 x 3.54 in. Brake Horsepower: 140-201 at 6000 rpm. Sequential multi-point fuel injection.

CHASSIS

NEW BEETLE: Wheelbase: 98.7 in. Overall length: 161.1 in. Height: 59.0 in. Width: 67.9 in. Front tread: 59.6 in. Rear tread: 58.7 in. Standard tires: (Except Turbo S): P205/55HR16.

GOLF: Wheelbase: 98.9 in. Overall length: 164.9 in. Height: 56.9 in. Width: 68.3 in. Front tread: 59.6 in. Rear tread: 58.8 in. Standard tires: P195/65HR15.

GTI: Wheelbase: 98.9 in. Overall length: 164.9 in. Height: 56.9 in. Width: 68.3 in. Front tread: 59.6 in. Rear tread: 58.8 in. Standard tires: P205/55HR16.

CABRIO: Wheelbase: 97.4 in. Overall length: 160.4 in. Height: 56.0 in. Width: 66.7 in. Front tread: 57.6 in. Rear tread: 57.6 in. Standard tires: P195/60HR14.

JETTA: Wheelbase: 98.9 in. Overall length: (Sedan) 172.3 in., (Wagon) 173.6 in. Height: (Sedan) 56.9 in., (Wagon) 58.5. Width: (All) 68.3 in. Front tread: 59.6 in. Rear tread: 58.8 in. Standard tires: (Except GLX) P195/65HR15. Standard tires: (GLX) P205/55HR16.

PASSAT: Wheelbase: 106.4 in. Overall length: (Sedan) 185.2 in., (Wagon) 184.3 in. Height: (Sedan) 57.6 in., (Wagon) 59.0. Width: (All) 68.7 in. Front tread: 59.0 in. Rear tread: 59.1 in. Standard tires: (Except GLX) P195/65HR15. Standard tires: (GLX) P205/55HR16.

EUROVAN (NORMAL LENGTH): Wheelbase: 115.0 in. Overall length: 188.5 in. Height: 76.4. Width: 72.4 in. Standard tires: P225/60HR16.

TECHNICAL

NEW BEETLE: Layout: front-engine, front-wheel-drive. Transmission: five-speed manual or four speed automatic. Steering: power rack and pinion. Brakes: Antilock brakes with ventilated front disc and solid rear disc.

GOLF: Layout: front-engine, front-wheel-drive. Transmission: five-speed manual or four speed automatic. Steering: power rack and pinion. Brakes: Antilock brakes with ventilated front disc and solid rear disc.

GTI: Layout: front-engine, front-wheel-drive. Transmission: five-speed manual or four speed automatic (automatic standard in GLX). Steering: power rack and pinion. Brakes: Antilock brakes with ventilated front disc and solid rear disc. Traction control.

The 2001 Golf GL received some updated styling and halogen headlamps.

CABRIO: Layout: front-engine, front-wheel-drive. Transmission: five-speed manual or four speed automatic. Steering: power rack and pinion. Brakes: Antilock brakes with ventilated front disc and solid rear disc.

JETTA: Layout: front-engine, front-wheel-drive. Transmission: five-speed manual or four speed automatic. Steering: power rack and pinion. Brakes: Antilock brakes with ventilated front disc and solid rear disc.

PASSAT: Layout: front-engine, front-wheel-drive. Transmission: five-speed manual or four speed automatic (automatic standard in 4Motion models). Steering: power rack and pinion. Brakes: Antilock brakes with ventilated front disc and rear disc. Traction control.

EUROVAN: Layout: front-engine, front-wheel-drive. Transmission: four speed automatic. Steering: power rack and pinion. Brakes: Antilock brakes with ventilated front disc and solid rear disc. Traction control.

OPTIONS

NEW BEETLE: PDA Luxury package for GLS ($1,225). PLA Leather package for GLS ($900). PLS Limited-Edition Lifestyle package for GLS 2.0L ($2,125). PMC California and Northeast emissions requirements ($100). PSA 17-in. alloy wheels for GLX ($400). PZA Sports Luxury package for GLS Turbo ($1,625). PCA cold weather package for GLS ($150).

GOLF: PJA 17-in. alloy wheels for GTI GLS ($600). PJA 17-in. alloy wheels for GTI GLX ($400). PLB Leather package for GTI GLS ($1,050). PLX Luxury package for GLS ($1,225). PMC California and Northeast emissions ($100). PSF Sport suspension for GLS 1.8 ($200). RMA Monsoon sound system for GLS ($325). WW1 Cold weather package for GLS ($150).

CABRIO: PMC California and Northeast emissions ($100).

JETTA: 3FE power sunroof ($915). PCA cold weather package for GLS ($150). PDA Luxury package for GLS VR6 ($1,425). PEA Luxury package for GLS ($1,225). PLA Leather package for GLS Sedan ($1,050). PLA Leather package for GLS Wagon ($1,050). PMC emissions ($100). PMF Multi-function steering wheel for GLX ($150). PVA sport suspension ($200). PZA Sport luxury package ($2,025). RMA Monsoon sound system in GLS ($325).

PASSAT: PJ6 Luxury package for GLS Sedan ($1,550). PJ6 Luxury package for GLS Wagon ($1,435). PLD

leather package for GLS ($1,500). PMC emissions (no charge). RMA Monsoon sound system in GLS ($325). VC1 HomeLink in GLS ($130). WW1 Cold weather package for GLS ($325).

EUROVAN: Clearcoat pearl paint ($345). 4A3 heatable front seats ($400). PMC emissions (no charge). W33 Weekender package ($3,335). ZD1 power sunroof ($1,000).

PERFORMANCE: Acceleration (0-60 mph): (Cabriolet) 11.1 sec., (Passat GL) 8.8 sec., (Passat GLX sedan) 7.9 sec., (Passat GLX Station Wagon) 8.0 sec. Top Speed in mph: (Cabriolet) 101, (Passat GL) 127, (Passat GLX) 130. EPA Fuel Economy in mpg: City/Highway: (Cabriolet) 24/30, (Passat GL) 21/30, (Passat GLX) 19/27. Performance Figures by *Motor Trend*.

MANUFACTURER: Volkswagenwerk AG, Wolfsburg, Germany.

DISTRIBUTOR: Volkswagen of America Inc., Auburn Hills, Michigan.

There were five levels in the 2001 New Beetle hatchback lineup.

The Jetta GLX sedan included such amenities as a top sound system in 2001.

2002

NEW BEETLE—FOUR The cuddly pseudo-classic from Volkswagen returned in 2002 to offer buyers a safe, enjoyable, practical car that gave good value for the money. A new Turbo S model with a turbocharged 180-hp engine and six-speed manual transmission topped the changes for the year. It has special "Turbo S" badges, 1an electronic stabilization profram (EPS), a stiffer suspension, revised turn signals, foglights, a front spoiler, a redesigned rear bumper, brushed alloy accents and 17-in. Delta X alloy wheels to set it off. The Turbo S came only in Reflex Silver, Black, Red ot Platinum Gray and had a special rear spoiler that deployed when the car reached 45 mph. Other updates included a cruise control indicator light, several limited-edition exterior colors (Snap Orange and Riviera Blue), upgraded seat upholstery and optional 16-in. alloy wheels for the GL and GLS models. The GL two-door hatchback was the well-equipped base model. The GLS included fog lights, power windows and cruise control. The GLS TDI included the turbo diesel engine. The GLS 1.8T included the smaller, but more powerful, DOHC turbo four, traction control and a rear spoiler. The GLX 1.8T added leather seats, a power sunroof, a Monsoon premium sound system and more upgrades. The Turbo S added 30 hp, stability control, fancier wheels, larger tires and more.

GOLF—FOUR/V-6/DIESEL For 2002, the GL trim level was offered for the Golf four-door hatchback, as well as the three-door hatchback. A premium casette/CD sound system became standard on the GLS. All model with cruise control got an indicator light that showed when the "cruise" was turned on. The speedy 1.8-lter turbo four-door hatchback was dropped. A new Mojave Beige color was added. Volkswagen improved its warranty protection. The GL was the base model. The TDI added the turbo diesel engine. GLS trim included velour seats, a console and equipment and audio upgrades. A GLS TDI four-door was offered.

GTI—FOUR/V-6 For 2002, the GTI was viewed as a separate, single-trim-level series. Power offerings included the 1.8-liter turbocharged four-cylinder or the 2.8-liter 12-valve V-6 at first, but the V-6 was replaced at midyear by a 24-valve six that cranked up 201 hp. The price of the V-6 model was reduced. The four gained 30 hp. It was available with and optional five-speed automatic transmission with Tiptronic manual shift control. New features included the cruise control indicator light, a premium casette/CD audio system and an on/off switch for the auto dimming rearview mirror. The base 1.8T hatchback was as well equipped as any modern automobile. The VR6 version included he V-6, 17 x 7 rims, fat tires, a trip computer and an external temperature display.

CABRIOLET—FOUR A trunk entrapment release and an on/off switch for the auto-dimming rearview mirror were standard equipment in 2002 Cabrios. Reflex Silver body finish with a Gray top and Flannel Gray interior was a

Above: **The potent 2000 GTI VR6 produced 174 hp from its 170-cid engine.**

McLellan's Automotive History

Above: **The Volkswagen GTI became a separate series in the 2002 model year.**
McLellan's Automotive History

Above: **The 2002 Golf was available with a four cylinder, V-6 or diesel engine.**
McLellan's Automotive History

Model Code	Body Type & Seating	POE Price	Weight (lbs.)	Production Total
	NEW BEETLE GL			
B	2d Hatchback-5P	15900	2817	NA
	NEW BEETLE GLS			
C	2d Hatchback-5P	16850	2855	NA
	NEW BEETLE GLS TDI			
C	2d Hatchback-5P	17900	2899	NA
	NEW BEETLE GLS 1.8 TURBO			
C	2d Hatchback-5P	19200	2954	NA
	NEW BEETLE SPORT			
E	2d Hatchback-5P	20250	NA	NA
	NEW BEETLE GLX 1.8 TURBO			
D	2d Hatchback-5P	21500	2958	NA
	NEW BEETLE TURBO S			
F	2d Hatchback-5P	23400	3005	NA
	GOLF GL			
B	2d Hatchback-5P	15050	2771	NA
	GOLF GL TDI			
B	2d Hatchback-5P	16345	2853	NA
	GOLF GL			
F	4d Hatchback-5P	15250	2857	NA
	GOLF GL TDI			
F	4d Hatchback-5P	16545	2936	NA
	GOLF GLS			
G	4d Hatchback-5P	16600	2897	NA
	GOLF GLS TDI			
S	4d Hatchback-5P	18700	2983	NA
	GTI 1.8T			
D	2d Hatchback-5P	18910	2932	NA
	GTI 337 (6-speed)			
D	2d Hatchback-5P	22225	NA	NA
	GTI VR6			
P	2d Hatchback-5P	20295	3011	NA
	GTI VR6 24V (6-speed)			
P	2d Hatchback-5P	21775	3036	NA
	CABRIOLET GL			
B	2d Convertible-4P	19600	2824	NA
	CABRIOLET GLS			
C	2d Convertible-4P	20600	2833	NA
	CABRIOLET GLX			
D	2d Convertible-4P	22300	2857	NA
	JETTA GL			
R	4d Sedan-5P	16850	2893	NA
	JETTA GL TDI			
R	4d Sedan-5P	18145	2975	NA
	JETTA GLS FOUR			
S	4d Sedan-5P	17900	2908	NA

new color combination. As on all 2002 Volkswagens, the warranty was enhanced. Standard features of the base GL version made a long list of equipment including side airbags, ABS and a glass rear window. The GLS added heated seats, 1-touch power windows, power mirrors and cruise control. Alloy rims, a power top and leather seats were part of the GLX model.

JETTA—FOUR/V-6/DIESEL For speed freaks a new 24-valve 2.8-liter V-6 with over 200 hp was a mid year change for the Jetta. The five-speed Tiptronic automatic transmission was added at the same time. The V-6 was

also available with a stick-shifted six-speed. The 1.8T gained 30 hp and was available with the five-speed Tiptronic automatic transmission. The GLS and GLX were enhanced with a premium casette/CD audio system, cruise contol indicator light and auto-dimming mirror on/off switch. The Jetta sedan got a trunk entrapment release. Wagon buyers were offered the 1.9-liter Turbo four in both GL and GLS models. Reflex Silver paint replaced Silver Arrow paint. The GL base model had lots of goodies to start with. The GLS added velour seats, a console, one-touch power windows and stereo upgrades. The GL TDI added the turbo diesel (also available with traction control

Model Code	Body Type & Seating	POE Price	Weight (lbs.)	ProductionTotal
	JETTA GLS TDI			
S	4d Sedan-5P	18950	2983	NA
	JETTA GLS 1.8T			
S	2d Sedan-5P	19550	2952	NA
	JETTA GLS VR6			
S	4d Sedan-5P	20200	3054	NA
	JETTA GLI VR6 (6-speed)			
V	4d Sedan-5P	22950	3179	NA
	JETTA GLX VR6 (6-speed)			
T	4d Sedan-5P	24700	3144	NA
	JETTA GLX VR6 24V (5-speed Tiptronic)			
T	4d Sedan-5P	26825	3263	NA
	JETTA GL			
R	4d Wagon-5P	17650	3034	NA
	JETTA GL TDI			
R	4d Wagon-5P	18945	3121	NA
	JETTA GLS			
S	4d Wagon-5P	18700	3078	NA
	JETTA GLS TDI			
S	4d Wagon-5P	19750	3161	NA
	JETTA GLS 1.8T			
S	4d Wagon-5P	20350	3175	NA
	JETTA GLS VR6			
S	4d Wagon-5P	21000	3127	NA
	JETTA GLX VR6			
S	4d Wagon-5P	25500	3280	NA
	PASSAT GLS 1.8T			
P	4d Sedan-5P	24,250	3291	NA
V	4d Wagon-5P	25,050	3388	NA
	PASSAT GLS 4MOTION V-6			
S	4d Sedan-5P	27075	3602	NA
X	4d Wagon-5P	27875	3717	NA
	PASSAT GLX V-6			
R	4d Sedan-5P	28750	3336	NA
W	4d Wagon-5P	29550	3428	NA
	PASSAT GLX 4MOTIONV-6			
T	4d Sedan-5P	31575	3644	NA
Y	4d Wagon-5P	32375	3757	NA
	PASSAT W8 4MOTIONV-8			
U	4d Sedan-5P	37900	3907	NA
Z	4d Wagon-5P	38700	4035	NA
	EUROVAN GLS V-6			
K	Van-8P	26200	4285	NA
	EUROVAN MV V-6			
M	Van-8P	27700	4474	NA
	EUROVAN MV WEEKENDER V-6			
N	Van-8P	30935	NA	NA

Note 1: Production for 2002 models not available at time of publication.

Above: **The Volkswagen New Beetle convertible premiered in 2003.**

Paul Smith

added in the GLS. The GLS 1.8T had the hot little DOHC turbo gas engine. The GLS VR6 added the V-6. Top of the line was the GLX VR6 sedan, which added extras like 16 x 6.5 alloys, fat tires, leather trim, power seats, Monsoon sound and more. The base GL wagon had a roof rack and rear wiper. The GLS wagon added velour seat trim and could be had with TDI power. The GLS TDI wagon added velour seats, power windows, cruise and a front storage console. The GLS 1.8T wagon came with traction control and cargo tie-downs. The GLS Vr6 wagon added the V-6 and the GLX version had a long list

of add-ons including leather upholstery, Monsoon sound and a power sun roof.

PASSAT—FOUR/V-6 Changes in Volkswagen's midsize family car were similar to those made in the other lines—cruise indicator light, auto dimming mirror switch, premium casette/CD audio and a trunk entrapment release (in sedans). One big change, however, was the mid year release of a 275-hp V-8 engine. The base GLS came with practically everything needed or wanted in a car. The one-step-up GLS V-6 sedan added wood trim on the doors. The all-wheel-drive 4Motion version included the shiftable five-speed automatic. Alloy rims, fat tires a sunroof and leather upholstery helped to set the GLX sedan apart. It also came as a 4Motion model. Base wagon was the 1.8T version with a roof rack, cargo light and rear wiper. The GLS V-6 wagon added a V-6 and wood door trim. It came as a 4Motion model. Also offered were a fancy wagon with GLX features and — if you needed a $25,000 VW—a 4Motion version of the same.

EUROVAN — V-6 The EuroVan had no major changes. New colors included Emerald Green, Reflex Silver and Black Magic Pearl on the MV with the Weekender camper package. The GLS came well-equipped. The MV also included a height-adjustable driver seat and fold-flat third row seats. The Weekender package included a pop-up roof, a two-person bed, front manual air conditioning, window screens, a fixed driver side rear-facing seat with refrigerator in seat base, a second battery, a 120-amp alternator, sliding window curtains and a screen for the rear hatch.

I.D. DATA: Volkswagen's 17-symbol VIN appears on the top left-hand surface of the instrument panel and is visible through the windshield. The first three symbols identified the country of origin, make and type of vehicle. Volkswagens made in Europe have the first three symbols WVW. Volkswagens made in Mexico have the first three synbols 3VW. Volkswagens made in Brazil have the first three synbols 9BW. The fourth symbol was a letter designating the series (see first column of table below). The fifth symbol was a letter identifying the engine: B=2.0-liter four-cylinder 115 hp; C=12.0-liter four-cylinder 115 hp; D=1.8-liter four-cylinder 150 hp; E=1.8-liter DOHC Turbo 180 hp; G=2.8-liter V-6 174 hp; H=2.8-liter V-6 200 hp; K=2.0-liter four-cylinder 115 hp; P=1.9-liter 90-hp four-cylinder diesel; NA=4.0-liter V-8 275 hp. The sixth symbol designated the type of restraint system: 2=Front and front side airbags, 6=Front air bags and front side curtain air bags. The seventh and eighth symbols idenitified the model (1C=New Beetle, 1J=Golf, Jetta and Jetta Wagon, 1V=Cabrio, 3B=Passat, 9M=Jetta, 7=EuroVan). The ninth symbol was a check digit. The 10th symbol was a letter designating the model year: 2=2002. The 11th symbol designated the assembly plant: E=Emden, Germany, H=Hanover, Germany, M=Mexico, P=Mosel, Germany, W=Wolfsburg, Germany, 4=Curitiba, Brazil. The last six symbols were the sequential production number starting with 000001.

ENGINE

2.0-LITER FOUR (Beetle, Cabrio, Golf, Jetta): Inline, overhead-cam four-cylinder (8-valve). Cast-iron block and light alloy head. Displacement: 2.0-liter (1984 cc). Bore & Stroke: 3.25 x 3.65 in. (82.5 x 92.8 mm). Compression Ratio: 10.0:1. Brake Horsepower: 115 at 5200 rpm. Torque: 122 lbs.-ft. at 2600 rpm. Five main bearings. Sequential multi-point fuel injection.

1.8L TURBO FOUR (Beetle): Inline, dual-overhead-cam four-cylinder (20-valve). Cast-iron block and light alloy head. Displacement: 1.8-liter (1781 cc). Bore & Stroke: 3.19 x 3.40 in. Compression Ratio: 9.3:1. Brake Horsepower: 150 at 5700 rpm. Torque: 155 lbs.-ft. at 1750-4600 rpm. Five main bearings. Sequential multi-point fuel injection.

1.8L TURBO DOHC FOUR (Passat): Inline, dual-overhead-cam four-cylinder (20-valve). Cast-iron block and light alloy head. Displacement: 1.8-liter (1781 cc). Bore & Stroke: 3.19 x 3.40 in. Compression Ratio: 9.3:1. Brake Horsepower: 170 at 5900 rpm. Torque: 166 lbs.-ft. at 1950 rpm. Five main bearings. Sequential multi-point fuel injection.

1.8L TURBO DOHC FOUR (GTI, Jetta): Inline, dual-overhead-cam four-cylinder (20-valve). Cast-iron block and light alloy head. Displacement: 1.8-liter (1781 cc). Bore & Stroke: 3.19 x 3.40 in. Compression Ratio: 9.5:1. Brake Horsepower: 180 at 5500 rpm. Torque: 174 lbs.-ft. at 1950 rpm. Five main bearings. Sequential multi-point fuel injection.

1.9-LITER TURBO DIESEL (TDI) FOUR (Beetle, Golf, Jetta): Inline, overhead-cam four-cylinder with turbocharger and intercooler (8-valve). Cast-iron block and light alloy head. Displacement: 1.9-liter (1896 cc). Bore & Stroke: 3.13 x 3.76 in. Compression Ratio: 19.5:1. Brake Horsepower: 90 at 3750 rpm. Torque: 155 lbs.-ft. at 1900 rpm. Five main bearings. Sequential multi-point fuel injection.

2.8-LITER V-6 (GTI, Jetta): Narrow (15 degrees) "vee" type dual-overhead-cam 12-valve six-cylinder. Cast-iron block and light alloy head. Displacement: 2.8-liter (2792 cc). Bore & Stroke: 3.19 x 3.56 in. (81 x 90.3 mm). Compression Ratio: 10.0:1. Brake Horsepower: 174 at 5800 rpm. Torque: 181 lbs.-ft. at 3200 rpm. Seven main bearings. Sequential multi-point fuel injection.

2.8-LITER V-6 (Passat): "Vee" type dual overhead-cam 30-valve six-cylinder. Cast-iron block and light alloy head. Displacement: 169.1 cid (2771 cc). Bore & Stroke: 3.25 x 3.40 in. (82.5 x 86.4 mm). Compression Ratio: 10.6:1. Brake Horsepower: 190 at 6000 rpm. Torque: 206 lbs.-ft. at 3200 rpm. Four main bearings. Sequential multi-point fuel injection.

2.8-LITER V-6 (EuroVan): Narrow (15 degrees) "vee" type dual-overhead-cam six-cylinder. Cast-iron block and light alloy head. Displacement: 2.8-liter (2792 cc). Bore & Stroke: 3.19 x 3.56 in. (81 x 90.3 mm). Compression Ratio: 10.0:1. Brake Horsepower: 201 at 6200 rpm. Torque: 245 lbs.-ft. at 2500 rpm. Seven main bearings. Sequential multi-point fuel injection.

4.0-LITER V-8 (Passat/Fall 2002): "Vee" type eight. Cast-iron block and light alloy heads. Displacement: 4.0-liter (245 cid). Bore & Stroke: 3.31 x 3.55 in. Brake Horsepower: 275. Sequential multi-point fuel injection.

CHASSIS

NEW BEETLE: Wheelbase: 98.7 in. Overall length: 161.1 in. Height: 59.0 in. Width: 67.9 in. Front tread: 59.6 in. Rear tread: 58.7 in. Standard tires (Except Turbo S): P205/55HR16.

GOLF: Wheelbase: 98.9 in. Overall length: 164.9 in. Height: 56.7 in. Width: 68.3 in. Front tread: 59.6 in. Rear tread: 58.8 in. Standard tires: P195/65HR15.

GTI: Wheelbase: 98.9 in. Overall length: 164.9 in. Height: 56.9 in. Width: 68.3 in. Front tread: 59.6 in. Rear tread: 58.8 in. Standard tires: P205/55HR16.

CABRIO: Wheelbase: 97.4 in. Overall length: 160.4 in. Height: 56.0 in. Width: 66.7 in. Front tread: 57.6 in. Rear tread: 57.6 in. Standard tires: P195/60HR14.

JETTA: Wheelbase: 98.9 in. Overall length: (Sedan) 172.3 in., (Wagon) 173.6 in. Height: (Sedan) 56.9 in., (Wagon) 58.5. Width: (All) 68.3 in. Front tread: 59.6 in. Rear tread: 58.8 in. Standard tires: (Except GLX) P195/65HR15. Standard tires: (GLX) P205/55HR16.

PASSAT: Wheelbase: 106.4 in. Overall length: (Sedan) 185.2 in., (Wagon) 184.3 in. Height: (Sedan) 57.6 in., (Wagon) 59.0. Width: (All) 68.7 in. Front tread: 59.0 in. Rear tread: 59.1 in. Standard tires: (Except GLX) P195/65HR15. Standard tires: (GLX) P205/55HR16.

EUROVAN (NORMAL LENGTH): Wheelbase: 115.0 in. Overall length: 188.5 in. Height: 76.1 in. Width: 72.4 in. Standard tires: P225/60HR16.

TECHNICAL

NEW BEETLE: Layout: front-engine, front-wheel-drive. Transmission: five-speed manual or four speed automatic. Steering: power rack and pinion. Brakes: Antilock brakes with ventilated front disc and solid rear disc.

GOLF: Layout: front-engine, front-wheel-drive. Transmission: five-speed manual or four speed automatic. Steering: power rack and pinion. Brakes: Antilock brakes with ventilated front disc and solid rear disc.

GTI: Layout: front-engine, front-wheel-drive. Transmission: five-speed manual or four speed automatic (automatic standard in GLX). Steering: power rack and pinion. Brakes: Antilock brakes with ventilated front disc and solid rear disc. Traction control.

CABRIO: Layout: front-engine, front-wheel-drive. Transmission: five-speed manual or four speed automatic. Steering: power rack and pinion. Brakes: Antilock brakes with ventilated front disc and solid rear disc.

JETTA: Layout: front-engine, front-wheel-drive. Transmission: five-speed manual or four speed automatic. Steering: power rack and pinion. Brakes: Antilock brakes with ventilated front disc and solid rear disc.

PASSAT: Layout: front-engine, front-wheel-drive. Transmission: five-speed manual or four speed automatic (automatic standard in 4Motion models). Steering: power rack and pinion. Brakes: Antilock brakes with ventilated front disc and rear disc. Traction control.

EUROVAN: Layout: front-engine, front-wheel-drive. Transmission: four speed automatic. Steering: power rack and pinion. Brakes: Antilock brakes with ventilated front disc and solid rear disc. Traction control.

OPTIONS

NEW BEETLE: PJ1 Luxury package for non-Turbo GLS ($1,225). PJ2 17 x 7 "Daytona" alloy wheels for GLX ($400). PJ3 luxury package for GLS 1.8 Turbo ($1,625). PL1 Leather package for GLS 1.8 Turbo ($900). PL1 Leather package for other models ($900). PLS Lifestyle package for GLS 1.8 Turbo ($1,550). PMC California and Northeast emissions requirements ($100). PRB Riviera Blue package for GLS 2.0 (NA). PRT Riviera Blue package for GLS 1.8 Turbo (NA). PS1 power sunroof package for GLS 1.8 Turbo ($915). PWA cold weather package for GLS ($150). RSM monsoon sound system for GLS ($325).

GOLF: PLX Luxury package for GLS ($1,225). PMC California and Northeast emissions ($100). RMA Monsoon sound system for GLS ($325). WW1 Cold weather package for GLS ($150).

GTI: PJA 17-in. alloy wheels for 1.8T ($400). PLB lather package ($900). PLY Luxury package ($1,240). PMC California and Northeast emissions ($100). PTA technology package for VR6 ($755). WW1 Cold weather package for GLS ($150).

CABRIO: PMC California and Northeast emissions ($100).

JETTA: 3FE power sunroof ($915). 9AK Climatronic climate control in GLX sedan ($350). PDA Luxury package for GLS VR6 ($1,425). PJ1 Luxury package for GLS Sedan VR6 ($1425). PJ2 17 x 7 alloy rims and Sport suspension ($600). PJ3 Sport Luxury package for GLS VR6 or 1.8T ($2,025). PJ4 Luxury package ($1,225). PJ8 17 x 7 alloy rims and tireds for GLX sedan ($400). PJA 17 x 7 alloy wheels, all-season tires and sports suspension for GLX wagon ($600). PL1 leather package for GLS sedan ($1,050). PLD leather package for GLS wagon ($1,050). PLX Luxury package ($1,225). PMC emissions ($100). PSF sport suspension ($200). PVA sport suspension ($200). PW1 cold weather package ($150). PZA Sport luxury package ($2,025). RMA Monsoon sound system in GLS wagon ($325). RSM Monsoon sound system in GLS sedan ($325). WW1 Cold weather package for GLS wagon ($150).

PASSAT: PJ6 Luxury package for GLS Sedan ($1550). PJ6 Luxury package for GLS Wagon ($1435). PLD leather package for GLS ($1,500). PMC emissions (no charge). RMA Monsoon sound system in GLS ($325). VC1 HomeLink in GLS ($130). WW1 Cold weather package for GLS ($325).

EUROVAN: Clearcoat pearl paint ($345). 4A3 heatable front seats ($400). PMC emissions (no charge). W33 Weekender package ($3,335). ZD1 power sunroof ($1,000).

PERFORMANCE: Acceleration (0-60 mph): (Cabriolet) 11.1 sec., (Passat GL) 8.8 sec., (Passat GLX sedan) 7.9 sec., (Passat GLX Station Wagon) 8.0 sec. Top Speed in mph: (Cabriolet) 101, (Passat GL) 127, (Passat GLX) 130. EPA Fuel Economy in mpg: City/Highway: (Cabriolet) 24/30, (Passat GL) 21/30, (Passat GLX) 19/27. Performance Figures by *Motor Trend*.

MANUFACTURER: Volkswagenwerk AG, Wolfsburg, Germany.

DISTRIBUTOR: Volkswagen of America Inc., Auburn Hills, Michigan.

2003

NEW BEETLE—FOUR A New Beetle convertible announced for introduction in the winter of 2003 was the year's big Volkswagen news. Other changes included putting the hot TDI and 1.8T engines on the GL option list. All GLs also came with power windows and cruise. The GL 1.8T and all GLS versions rode on alloy rims. The EPS stability control system, heated seats and Monsoon stereos were now available in all "Bugs." All Beetles, except GLs, had sun roofs and a larger center console. New cloth trim was used in GL and GLS versions. All models had a rearview mirror with a clock-temperature readout, blinkers built into the OSRV mirrors and a more comfy rear seat. The GL included air, casette, 4-wheel ABS discs, side air bags, 16-in. wheels, power locks, power-adjustable mirrors, seat height adjusters, a telescopic steering wheel and a dashboard-mounted bud vase. The GLS added a sun roof, storage armrest, alloys and fog lights. The GLX included leather seats, Monsoon sound and more. The

Above & Left: **Like the hatchback, the 2003 New Beetle convertible came in several trim levels.**

Old Cars Weekly Archive

Model Code	Body Type & Seating	POE Price	Weight (lbs.)	ProductionTotal
NEW BEETLE GL				
B	2d Hatchback-5P	15950	2817	NA
B	2d Convertible-5P	20450	3075	NA
NEW BEETLE GL TDI				
B	2d Hatchback-5P	17195	2899	NA
NEW BEETLE GL 1.8 TURBO				
B	2d Hatchback-5P	18450	2820	NA
NEW BEETLE GLS				
C	2d Hatchback-5P	17815	2855	NA
C	2d Convertible-5P	21850	3082	NA
NEW BEETLE GLS TDI				
C	2d Hatchback-5P	18995	3018	NA
NEW BEETLE GLS 1.8 TURBO				
C	2d Hatchback-5P	19855	2954	NA
C	2d Convertible-5P	24100	3166	NA
NEW BEETLE GLX 1.8 TURBO				
D	2d Hatchback-5P	21640	2958	NA
D	2d Convertible-5P	25550	170	NA
NEW BEETLE TURBO S				
F	2d Hatchback-5P	23540	3005	NA
GOLF GL				
B	2d Hatchback-5P	15295	2771	NA
F	4d Hatchback-5P	15495	2857	NA
GOLF GL TDI				
B	2d Hatchback-5P	16720	2853	NA
F	4d Hatchback-5P	16920	2937	NA
GOLF GLS				
G	4d Hatchback-5P	17520	2897	NA
GOLF GLS TDI				
G	4d Hatchback-5P	18710	2976	NA
GTI 1.8T				
D	2d Hatchback-5P	19065	2932	NA
GTI VR6 24V (6-speed)				
D	2d Hatchback-5P	21995	3036	NA
GTI 20TH ANNIVERSARY (6-speed)				
D	2d Hatchback-5P	23225	2916	NA
JETTA GL				
R	4d Sedan-5P	17100	2892	NA
R	4d Wagon-5P	17900	3034	NA
JETTA GL TDI				
R	4d Sedan-5P	18490	2974	NA
R	4d Wagon-5P	19290	3122	NA

Sport model was dropped but the Turbo S returned. Its highlights included sport-tuned underpinnings, 17-in. alloys and tires, metallic trim and the 45-mile spoiler. The ragtop bowed in GLS 2.0 format, but GL and GLX versions came later, as well as the 1.8T engine as an option. Another extra was a power folding top. With the New Beetle convertible out, the Cabrio was gone.

GOLF—FOUR/DIESEL For 2003, Volkswagen marketed the Golf coupe in GL trim and the sedan in GL and GLS trim. The GL came with air, 4-wheel ABS discs, side and curtain air bags, five headrests, a telescopic steering wheel, driver seat height adjusters, a CD player, cruise, remote keyless entry, an alarm, electric windows, power locks and power mirrors. The GLS versions had a sun roof, alloy wheels, velour seats and a storage armrest. EPS was

available for all Golfs. Monsoon sound was optional in all. The 2.0-liter four was now ultra-low-emissions-vehicle (ULEV) compliant and the base stereo had new back-lit buttons.

GTI—FOUR/V-6 For 2003, the GTI power offerings included the 1.8-liter turbocharged four-cylinder or the 2.8-liter 24-valve six that cranked up 200 hp. EPS stability control was optional on the four and standard with the V-6. Both models now included a leather-wrapped steering wheel, shifter and hand brake. The curtain air bags were improved with more padding, the stereo buttons were back-lit and the sun roof and windshield wipers were refined. A new Silverstone Gray paint color was brought out. A 20th Anniversary package was added at midyear. It included a Rabbit logo and red GTI badge on the grille and

Model Code	Body Type & Seating	POE Price	Weight (lbs.)	Production Total
JETTA GL 1.8T				
R	2d Sedan-5P	18750	2974	NA
R	4d Wagon-5P	19550	3130	NA
JETTA GLS FOUR				
S	4d Sedan-5P	18790	2934	NA
S	4d Wagon-5P	19590	3078	NA
JETTA GLS TDI				
S	4d Sedan-5P	19970	3009	NA
S	4d Wagon-5P	20770	3161	NA
JETTA GLS 1.8T				
S	4d Sedan-5P	20440	3037	NA
S	4d Wagon-5P	21240	3175	NA
JETTA GLS 1.8T PREMIUM				
T	4d Wagon-5P	24635	NA	NA
JETTA WOLFSBURG				
P	4d Sedan-5P	19500	2974	NA
JETTA GLI VR6 (6-speed)				
V	4d Sedan-5P	22950	3179	NA
JETTA GLX VR6 (6-speed)				
T	4d Sedan-5P	26940	3274	NA
PASSAT GL 1.8T				
M	4d Sedan-5P	21750	3212	NA
N	4d Wagon-5P	22550	3307	NA
PASSAT GLS 1.8T				
P	4d Sedan-5P	22885	3240	NA
V	4d Wagon-5P	23685	3388	NA
PASSAT GLS V-6				
M	4d Sedan-5P	25385	3373	NA
N	4d Wagon-5P	26185	3461	NA
PASSAT GLX V-6				
P	4d Sedan-5P	28750	3413	NA
V	4d Wagon-5P	29550	3499	NA
PASSAT GLX 4MOTION V-6				
T	4d Sedan-5P	31575	3721	NA
Y	4d Wagon-5P	32375	3840	NA
PASSAT W8 4MOTION V-8				
U	4d Sedan-5P	37900	3953	NA
Z	4d Wagon-5P	38700	4067	NA
EUROVAN GLS V-6				
K	Van-8P	26200	4285	NA
EUROVAN MV V-6				
M	Van-8P	27700	4474	NA
EUROVAN MV WEEKENDER V-6				
N	Van-8P	31035	NA	NA

Note 1: Production for 2003 models not available at time of publication.

rear hatchback, a lowered rear bumper, a polished exhaust pipe, a dashboard serial number plate, a drilled-aluminum dead pedal, metal door sill trim, red-trimmed Recaro front seats, red-trimmed seat belts, a large gearshift knob, 18-in. 15-spoke alloy wheels, red-finished brake calipers and the 1.8-liter turbocharged engine (180 hp at 5,000 rpm and 173 lb.-ft. of torque at 1,950-5,000 rpm.

JETTA—FOUR/V-6/DIESEL In Jetta-land, Volkswagen erased the GLX wagon. The 1.8T engine now came in the GL sedan and wagon. GLs gained electric windows, power-adjustable mirrors, cruise and a CD player. New standard equipment for the GLS included a sun roof and alloys. EPS was available for all models, along with heated

seats and a Monsoon stereo. Jettas with the 2.0-liter four were ULEV rated. They also got the new back-lit stereo buttons and redesigned cup holders. The Jetta sedan came in GL, GLS, GLX and GLI models. The GL was a fairly loaded vehicle. The GLS added a center armrest, alloys and a sun roof. The GLX added 16-in. wheels. The GLI was a sports version which included 17-in. rims, a sport suspension, EPS and sport seats.

PASSAT—FOUR/V-6/W8 New 2003 Passat models included a GL sedan and wagon. The 1.8T engine was standard, along with much more including a CD player, electric windows and keyless entry. A sun roof and alloy wheels were additions on the GLS. The V-6-powered

GLS was no longer offered with the 4Motion all-wheel-drive system, but you could get any Passat with the ESP option and W8s could have a six-speed manual gearbox and a firm-ride suspension with 17-in. wheels. The GL was the kick-off model and was fairly loaded. The GLS added a sun roof, alloy wheels and more. The GLX had power seats, rain-sensing windshield wipers, an auto dimming mirror and 16-in. wheels. The V-8-powered W8 had vented 4-wheel discs, xeon headlights and a one-step-up trip computer. The "W8" designation indicated that the engine had staggered cylinders.

EUROVAN—V-6 The EuroVan had no major changes. New colors included Emerald Green. The GLS came well-equipped. The MV also included a height-adjustable driver seat and fold-flat third row seats. The Weekender package included a pop-up roof, a two-person bed, front manual air conditioning, window screens, a fixed driver side rear-facing seat with refrigerator in seat base, a second battery, a 120-amp alternator, sliding window curtains and a screen for the rear hatch.

I.D. DATA: Volkswagen's 17-symbol VIN appears on the top left-hand surface of the instrument panel and is visible through the windshield. The first three symbols identified the country of origin, make and type of vehicle. Volkswagens made in Europe have the first three symbols WVW. Volkswagens made in Mexico have the first three synbols 3VW. Volkswagens made in Brazil have the first three synbols 9BW. The fourth symbol was a letter designating the series (see first column of table below). The fifth symbol was a letter identifying the engine: B=2.0-liter four-cylinder 115 hp; C=12.0-liter four-cylinder 115 hp; D=1.8-liter four-cylinder 150 hp; E=1.8-liter DOHC Turbo 180 hp; G=2.8-liter V-6 174 hp; H=2.8-liter V-6 200 hp; K=2.0-liter four-cylinder 115 hp; P=1.9-liter 90-hp four-cylinder diesel; NA=4.0-liter V-8 275 hp. The sixth symbol designated the type of restraint system: 2=Front and front side airbags, 6=Front air bags and front side curtain air bags. The seventh and eighth symbols idenitified the model (1C=New Beetle, 1J=Golf, Jetta and Jetta Wagon, 1V=Cabrio, 3B=Passat, 9M=Jetta, 7=EuroVan). The ninth symbol was a check digit. The 10th symbol was a letter designating the model year: 3=2003. The 11th symbol designated the assembly plant: E=Emden, Germany, H=Hanover, Germany, M=Mexico, P=Mosel, Germany, W=Wolfsburg, Germany, 4=Curitiba, Brazil. The last six symbols were the sequential production number starting with 000001.

ENGINE

2.0-LITER FOUR (Beetle, Cabrio, Golf, Jetta): Inline, overhead-cam four-cylinder (8-valve). Cast-iron block and light alloy head. Displacement: 2.0-liter (1984 cc). Bore & Stroke: 3.25 x 3.65 in. (82.5 x 92.8 mm). Compression Ratio: 10.0:1. Brake Horsepower: 115 at 5200 rpm. Torque: 122 lbs.-ft. at 2600 rpm. Five main bearings. Sequential multi-point fuel injection.

1.8L TURBO FOUR (Beetle): Inline, dual-overhead-cam four-cylinder (20-valve). Cast- iron block and light alloy head. Displacement: 1.8-liter (1781 cc). Bore & Stroke: 3.19 x 3.40 in. Compression Ratio: 9.3:1. Brake Horsepower: 150 at 5700 rpm. Torque: 162 lbs.-ft. at 1750-4600 rpm. Five main bearings. Sequential multi-point fuel injection.

1.8L TURBO DOHC FOUR (Passat): Inline, dual-overhead-cam four-cylinder (20-valve). Cast-iron block and light alloy head. Displacement: 1.8-liter (1781 cc). Bore & Stroke: 3.19 x 3.40 in. Compression Ratio: 9.3:1. Brake Horsepower: 170 at 5900 rpm. Torque: 166 lbs.-ft. at 1950 rpm. Five main bearings. Sequential multi-point fuel injection.

1.8L TURBO DOHC FOUR (GTI, Jetta, Beetle): Inline, dual-overhead-cam four-cylinder (20-valve). Cast-iron block and light alloy head. Displacement: 1.8-liter (1781 cc). Bore & Stroke: 3.19 x 3.40 in. Compression Ratio: 9.5:1. Brake Horsepower: 180 at 5500 rpm. Torque: 174 lbs.-ft. at 1950 rpm. Five main bearings. Sequential multi-point fuel injection.

1.9-LITER TURBO DIESEL (TDI) FOUR (Beetle, Golf, Jetta): Inline, overhead-cam four-cylinder with turbo-charger and intercooler (8-valve). Cast-iron block and light alloy head. Displacement: 1.9-liter (1896 cc). Bore & Stroke: 3.13 x 3.76 in. Compression Ratio: 19.5:1. Brake Horsepower: 90 at 3750 rpm. Torque: 155 lbs.-ft. at 1900 rpm. Five main bearings. Sequential multi-point fuel injection.

2.8-LITER V-6 (GTI, Jetta): Narrow (15 degrees) "vee" type dual-overhead-cam 12-valve six-cylinder. Cast-iron block and light alloy head. Displacement: 2.8-liter (2792 cc). Bore & Stroke: 3.19 x 3.56 in. (81 x 90.3 mm). Compression Ratio: 10.0:1. Brake Horsepower: 200 at 5800 rpm. Torque: 195 lbs.-ft. at 3200 rpm. Seven main bearings. Sequential multi-point fuel injection.

2.8-LITER V-6 (Passat): "Vee" type dual overhead-cam 30-valve six-cylinder. Cast-iron block and light alloy head. Displacement: 169.1 cid (2771 cc). Bore & Stroke: 3.25 x 3.40 in. (82.5 x 86.4 mm). Compression Ratio: 10.6:1. Brake Horsepower: 190 at 6000 rpm. Torque: 206 lbs.-ft. at 3200 rpm. Four main bearings. Sequential multi-point fuel injection.

2.8-LITER V-6 (EuroVan): Narrow (15 degrees) "vee" type dual-overhead-cam six-cylinder. Cast-iron block and light alloy head. Displacement: 2.8-liter (2792 cc). Bore & Stroke: 3.19 x 3.56 in. (81 x 90.3 mm). Compression Ratio: 10.0:1. Brake Horsepower: 201 at 6200 rpm. Torque: 245 lbs.-ft. at 2500 rpm. Seven main bearings. Sequential multi-point fuel injection.

4.0-LITER V-8 (Passat/Fall 2002): "Vee" type eight. Cast-iron block and light alloy heads. Displacement: 4.0-liter (245 cid). Bore & Stroke: 3.31 x 3.55 in. Brake Horsepower: 270. Torque: 273 lbs.-ft. Sequential multi-point fuel injection.

CHASSIS

NEW BEETLE: Wheelbase: 98.7 in. Overall length: 161.1 in. Height: 59.0 in. Width: 67.9 in. Front tread: 59.6 in. Rear tread: 58.7 in. Standard tires (Except Turbo S): P205/55HR16.

GOLF: Wheelbase: 98.9 in. Overall length: 164.9 in. Height: 56.7 in. Width: 68.3 in. Front tread: 59.6 in. Rear tread: 58.8 in. Standard tires: P195/65HR15.

GTI: Wheelbase: 98.9 in. Overall length: 164.9 in. Height: 56.9 in. Width: 68.3 in. Front tread: 59.6 in. Rear tread: 58.8 in. Standard tires: P205/55HR16.

CABRIO: Wheelbase: 97.4 in. Overall length: 160.4 in. Height: 56.0 in. Width: 66.7 in. Front tread: 57.6 in. Rear tread: 57.6 in. Standard tires: P195/60HR14.

JETTA: Wheelbase: 98.9 in. Overall length: (Sedan) 172.3 in., (Wagon) 173.6 in. Height: (Sedan) 56.9 in., (Wagon) 58.5. Width: (All) 68.3 in. Front tread: 59.6 in. Rear tread: 58.8 in. Standard tires: (Except GLX) P195/65HR15. Standard tires: (GLX) P205/55HR16.

PASSAT: Wheelbase: 106.4 in. Overall length: (Sedan) 185.2 in., (Wagon) 184.3 in. Height: (Sedan) 57.6 in., (Wagon) 59.0. Width: (All) 68.7 in. Front tread: 59.0 in. Rear tread: 59.1 in. Standard tires: (Except GLX) P195/65HR15. Standard tires: (GLX) P205/55HR16.

EUROVAN (NORMAL LENGTH): Wheelbase: 115.0 in. Overall length: 188.5 in. Height: 76.1. Width: 72.4 in. Standard tires: P225/60HR16.

TECHNICAL

NEW BEETLE: Layout: front-engine, front-wheel-drive. Transmission: five-speed manual or four speed automatic. Steering: power rack and pinion. Brakes: Antilock brakes with ventilated front disc and solid rear disc.

GOLF: Layout: front-engine, front-wheel-drive. Transmission: five-speed manual or four speed automatic. Steering: power rack and pinion. Brakes: Antilock brakes with ventilated front disc and solid rear disc.

GTI: Layout: front-engine, front-wheel-drive. Transmission: five-speed manual or four speed automatic (automatic standard in GLX). Steering: power rack and pinion. Brakes: Antilock brakes with ventilated front disc and solid rear disc. Traction control.

CABRIO: Layout: front-engine, front-wheel-drive. Transmission: five-speed manual or four speed automatic. Steering: power rack and pinion. Brakes: Antilock brakes with ventilated front disc and solid rear disc.

JETTA: Layout: front-engine, front-wheel-drive. Transmission: five-speed manual or four speed automatic. Steering: power rack and pinion. Brakes: Antilock brakes with ventilated front disc and solid rear disc.

PASSAT: Layout: front-engine, front-wheel-drive. Transmission: five-speed manual or four speed automatic (automatic standard in 4Motion models). Steering: power rack and pinion. Brakes: Antilock brakes with ventilated front disc and rear disc. Traction control.

EUROVAN: Layout: front-engine, front-wheel-drive. Transmission: four speed automatic. Steering: power rack

Left: **The 2003 Volkswagen New Beetle was offered in eight trim levels.**
Old Cars Weekly Archive

and pinion. Brakes: Antilock brakes with ventilated front disc and solid rear disc. Traction control.

OPTIONS

NEW BEETLE: PJ1 Luxury package for non-Turbo GLS ($1,225). PJ2 17 x 7 "Daytona" alloy wheels for GLX ($400). PJ3 luxury package for GLS 1.8 Turbo ($1,625). PL1 Leather package for GLS 1.8 Turbo ($900). PL1 Leather package for other models ($900). PLS Lifestyle package for GLS 1.8 Turbo ($1,550). PMC California and Northeast emissions requirements ($100). PRB Riviera Blue package for GLS 2.0 (NA). PRT Riviera Blue package for GLS 1.8 Turbo (NA). PS1 power sunroof package for GLS 1.8 Turbo ($915). PWA cold weather package for GLS ($150). RSM monsoon sound system for GLS ($325).

GOLF: PLX Luxury package for GLS ($1,225). PMC California and Northeast emissions ($100). RMA Monsoon sound system for GLS ($325). WW1 Cold weather package for GLS ($150).

GTI: PJA 17-in. alloy wheels for 1.8T ($400). PLB lather package ($900). PLY Luxury package ($1,240). PMC California and Northeast emissions ($100). PTA technology package for VR6 ($755). WW1 Cold weather package for GLS ($150).

CABRIO: PMC California and Northeast emissions ($100).

JETTA: 3FE power sunroof ($915). 9AK Climatronic climate control in GLX sedan ($350). PDA Luxury package for GLS VR6 ($1,425). PJ1 Luxury package for GLS Sedan VR6 ($1425). PJ2 17 x 7 alloy rims and Sport suspension ($600). PJ3 Sport Luxury package for GLS Vr6 or 1.8T ($2,025). PJ4 Lusury package ($1,225). PJ8

17 x 7 alloy rims and tireds for GLX sedan ($400). PJA 17 x 7 alloy wheels, all-season tires and sports suspension for GLX wagon ($600). PL1 leather package for GLS sedan ($1,050). PLD leather package for GLS wagon ($1,050). PLX Luxury package ($1,225). PMC emissions ($100). PSF sport suspension ($200). PVA sport suspension ($200). PW1 cold weather package ($150). PZA Sport luxury package ($2,025). RMA Monsoon sound system in GLS wagon ($325). RSM Monsoon sound system in GLS sedan ($325). WW1 Cold weather package for GLS wagon ($150).

PASSAT: PJ6 Luxury package for GLS Sedan ($1550). PJ6 Luxury package for GLS Wagon ($1435). PLD leather package for GLS ($1,500). PMC emissions (no charge). RMA Monsoon sound system in GLS ($325). VC1 HomeLink in GLS ($130). WW1 Cold weather package for GLS ($325).

EUROVAN: Clearcoat pearl pain ($345). 4A3 heatable front seats ($400). PMC emissions (no charge). W33 Weekender package ($3,335). ZD1 power sunroof ($1,000).

PERFORMANCE: Acceleration (0-60 mph): (Cabriolet) 11.1 sec., (Passat GL) 8.8 sec., (Passat GLX sedan) 7.9 sec., (Passat GLX Station Wagon) 8.0 sec. Top Speed in mph: (Cabriolet) 101, (Passat GL) 127, (Passat GLX) 130. EPA Fuel Economy in mpg: City/Highway: (Cabriolet) 24/30, (Passat GL) 21/30, (Passat GLX) 19/27. Performance Figures by *Motor Trend*.

MANUFACTURER: Volkswagenwerk AG, Wolfsburg, Germany.

DISTRIBUTOR: Volkswagen of America Inc., Auburn Hills, Michigan.

Left: **The Volkswagen Golf continued to offer buyers a practical car with many options.**
Old Cars Weekly Archive

2004

NEW BEETLE—FOUR/TDI FOUR By 2004 the New Beetle was getting to be "the Beetle" in most people's minds, as it was no longer all-new. Buy many people across the country were still seeing the convertible version for the first time. The coupe (which was technically a hatchback) came as a GL, GLS or Turbo S model. The ragtop came in GL and GLS formats only. The GL included 16-in. wheels, air conditioning, a cassette stereo, electric windows, power locks, power OSRV mirrors, cruise, seat height adjusters, a telescoping steering wheel and a manual convertible top. The GL level added a sun roof, a storage armrest, alloys, fog lights and a power top. The Turbo S coupe added 17-in. wheels, a sport-tuned suspension and the 45-mph rear spoiler (although the power-activated spoiler was replaced with a fixed-position version later in the model year). The TDI four was improved this year and both 16- and 17-in. wheels were redesigned. In fact, the later-2004 Turbo S wheels were unique to that model. Volkswagen added safer curtain airrbags and headrests. Monsoon sound became regular equipment in the GLS. New colors and seat trims were offered for the ragtop and all "Bugs" had a new fuel cap with a warning light. A choice of four different four-cylinder engines was available.

GOLF—FOUR/TDI FOUR For 2004, Volkswagen again marketed the Golf coupe in GL trim and the sedan in GL and GLS trim. The GL came with air, 4-wheel ABS discs, side and curtain air bags, five headrests, a telescopic steering wheel, driver seat height adjusters, a CD player, cruise, remote keyless entry, an alarm, electric windows, power locks and power mirrors. The GLS versions had a sun roof, alloy wheels, velour seats, a storage armrest and Monsoon sound. EPS was available for all Golfs. The Golf also got the new, more powerful 1.9-liter TDI four, a warning-light fuel cap ans a seat belt monitor.

GTI—1.8T FOUR/V-6 For 2004, the GTI power offerings included a new 237-cid V-6 in the R32 model. The 1.8-liter turbocharged four-cylinder or the 2.8-liter 24-valve six remained, too. The base 1.8T model included 16-in. alloys, a full-size spare tire, sport seats with height adjusters, an 8-speaker CD sound system, a telescoping steering wheel, remote keyless entry, alarm, cruise, electric windows and power locks and mirrors. The VR6 version added a larger power plant, 17-in. wheels and a trip computer. The R32 added 18-in. wheels, special sport seats, a sun roof, a rear spoiler, specific front-rear-side body skirting and higher performance.

JETTA—FOUR/TDI FOUR/1.8T FOUR/V-6 Jetta styling was updated for 2004. The Jetta sedan came in GL, GLS and GLI models. Deletion of the GLX brought top-of-the-rtange pricing lower. The GL was a fairly loaded vehicle. The GLS added a center armrest, alloys and a sun roof. The GLI was a sports version which included 17-in. rims, a sport suspension, EPS and sport seats (but lost the standard sun roof). The Jetta got the up-rated 1.9-liter TDI engine. Late-2004 wagons had a revised instrument board design.

PASSAT—FOUR/TDI FOUR/V-6/V-8 (W8) A 2.0-liter four-cylinder diesel was added to the Passat lineup. The GLS got premium Monsoon sound and Homelink system. The optional leather seat package now included wood-grained interior trimmings. ESP became standard on the Passat GLX. Restyled 15- and 16-in. wheels and new side mirrors with built-in turn signals were other

Below: **Among the choices for 2004 Golf buyers was a 1.9 liter engine.**
Old Cars Weekly Archive

Above: **The new long-wheelbase 2004 Phaeton was the VW answer for luxury buyers.**

Old Cars Weekly Archive

Above: **One more engine option gave Passat buyers four power choices in 2004.**

Old Cars Weekly Archive

Model Code	Body Type & Seating	POE Price	Weight (lbs.)	ProductionTotal
	NEW BEETLE GL 2.0L			
B	2d Hatchback-5P	16330	2817	NA
B	2d Convertible-5P	20900	3075	NA
	NEW BEETLE GL 1.9 TDI			
B	2d Hatchback-5P	17630	2899	NA
	NEW BEETLE GLS 2.0L			
C	2d Hatchback-5P	18520	2855	NA
C	2d Convertible-5P	22640	3082	NA
	NEW BEETLE GLS 1.9 TDI			
C	2d Hatchback-5P	19760	3018	NA
	NEW BEETLE GLS 1.8T			
C	2d Hatchback-5P	19855	2954	NA
C	2d Convertible-5P	24100	3166	NA
	NEW BEETLE GLS 1.8T			
D	2d Hatchback-5P	20480	2958	NA
D	2d Convertible-5P	24820	3170	NA
	NEW BEETLE TURBO S (1.8T)			
F	2d Hatchback-5P	23850	3005	NA
	GOLF GL 2.0			
B	2d Hatchback-5P	15580	2771	NA
F	4d Hatchback-5P	15780	2857	NA
	GOLF GL 1.9 TDI			
F	4d Hatchback-5P	17200	2937	NA
	GOLF GLS 2.0			
G	4d Hatchback-5P	18140	2897	NA
	GOLF GLS 1.9 TDI			
G	4d Hatchback-5P	18049	2976	NA
	GTI 1.8T			
D	2d Hatchback-5P	19250	2932	NA
	GTI VR6			
D	2d Hatchback-5P	22070	3036	NA
	GTI R32			
D	2d Hatchback-5P	29100	3330	NA
	JETTA GL 2.0			
R	4d Sedan-5P	17430	2892	NA
R	4d Wagon-5P	18430	3034	NA
	JETTA GL 1.9 TDI			
R	4d Sedan-5P	18670	2974	NA
R	4d Wagon-5P	19670	3122	NA
	JETTA GL 1.8T			
R	2d Sedan-5P	18910	2974	NA

changes. Except for these updates, model differences were the same as in 2003.

R32—V-6 The 2004 R32 was a brand new two-door sports coupe and a mid year addition to the Volkswagen model lineup. This five-passenger car was available only with the VR6 engine and only in a single trim level. It was designed to compete with the Audi TT, the Infiniti G35 Sport Coupe and the all-new Pontiac GTO.

PHAETON—V-8/V-12 Volkswagen's new top-line car came only as a long-wheelbase sedan designed to compete with fancier Mercedes. The well-equipped V-8 (W8) was the "base" model. The upscale V-12 (W12) added even more standard equipment. Both of these models went luxury all the way. Prices started at $64,600. The 4.2-liter 335-hp V-8 could move the car from 0 to 60 in 6.7 seconds. The 420-hp 6.0-liter V-12 was good for 0-to-60 in a scant 5.9 seconds. Quietly elegant, the V-8 came standard with 4MOTION, a Torsen (TORque SENsing) center differential, air suspension, Electronic Damping Control, a four-zone Climatronic climate control system, 18-way power leather seats, 18-inch alloy wheels, all-season tires and aerodynamic Xenon headlights. The V-12's standard features included 18-inch alloy wheels and all-season tires, quad-visible exhaust pipes (the VC-8 had dual pipes), a sporty leather-wrapped, a hand-stitched heated steering wheel with multi-function controls, a world-class, four-zone Climatronic system with rear-seat climate controls and an upgraded 12-speaker, 270-watt sound system with digital sound processing. A coating of metalized infrared foil on the windows was heat-reflective and shatter-resistant. The V-12's 18-way memory power front seats were heatable, ventilated and had a 10-minute

Model Code	Body Type & Seating	POE Price	Weight (lbs.)	Production Total
JETTA GLS 2.0				
S	4d Sedan-5P	19460	2934	NA
S	4d Wagon-5P	20460	3078	NA
JETTA GLS TDI-PD				
S	4d Sedan-5P	20480	3009	NA
S	4d Wagon-5P	21480	3161	NA
JETTA GLS 1.8T				
S	4d Sedan-5P	20940	3037	NA
S	4d Wagon-5P	21940	3175	NA
JETTA GLI VR6				
V	4d Sedan-5P	23210	3179	NA
JETTA GLI 1.8T				
T	4d Sedan-5P	23800	3274	NA
PASSAT GL 1.8T				
M	4d Sedan-5P	21780	3212	NA
N	4d Wagon-5P	22780	3307	NA
PASSAT GLS 1.8T				
P	4d Sedan-5P	23380	3240	NA
V	4d Wagon-5P	24380	3388	NA
PASSAT GLX 2.8L V-6				
P	4d Sedan-5P	29780	3413	NA
N	4d Wagon-5P	30780	3461	NA
PASSAT W8 4.0L V-8				
P	4d Sedan-5P	38600	3413	NA
N	4d Wagon-5P	39660	3461	NA
PASSAT GL 2.0L TDI FOUR				
M	4d Sedan-5P	23060	3373	NA
N	4d Wagon-5P	24060	3461	NA
PASSAT GLS 2.0L TDI FOUR				
M	4d Sedan-5P	24660	3373	NA
N	4d Wagon-5P	25660	3461	NA
PHAETON 4.2L V-8 (W8)				
NA	4d Sedan-8P	64600	5194	NA
PHAETON 6.0L V-12 (W12)				
NA	4d Sedan-8P	73253	5399	NA

Note 1: Production for 2004 models not available at time of publication.

Above: **The 2004 Volkswagen Jetta sedans and wagons received a styling update.**
Old Cars Weekly Archive

Above: **In 2004, buyers could choose from three versions of Volkswagens sporty cars.**
Old Cars Weekly Archive

massage function and four-way power lumbar support. The rear seats were also heated. Interior trim on the seats, steering wheel and doors included premium wood, leather upgrades and brushed metal accents. Standard safety equipment included side curtain air bags, four-wheel anti-lock brakes (with emergency brake assist), electronic park assist, ESP and a tire pressure monitoring system. Additional equipment included a glovebox-mounted six-CD changer, a push-button automatic-closing deck lid, a HomeLink universal transmitter to program garage doors and home lights and a remote-key anti-theft alarm system. The Phaeton also came with OnStar telematics and an integrated infotainment center with numerous personal profile settings and a seven-inch color screen that functions with the CD changer, navigation system, onboard trip computer and air conditioning. Volkswagen built 330 special "Premier Edition" models of the V-12 to celebrate its arrival. These special models were available in Piano Black exterior paint finish and were ordered with identical specifications. Premier Edition Phaetons listed for $79,900 plus a special equipment package priced at

$4,990. Volkswagen estimated 2,500-3,000 Phaetons would be sold the first year.

I.D. DATA: Volkswagen's 17-symbol VIN appears on the top left-hand surface of the instrument panel and is visible through the windshield. The first three symbols identified the country of origin, make and type of vehicle. Volkswagens made in Europe have the first three symbols WVW. Volkswagens made in Mexico have the first three synbols 3VW. Volkswagens made in Brazil have the first three synbols 9BW. The fourth symbol was a letter designating the series (see first column of table below). The fifth symbol was a letter identifying the engine. The sixth symbol designated the type of restraint system. The seventh and eighth symbols idenitified the model. The 10th symbol was a letter designating the model year: 4=2004. The 11th symbol designated the assembly plant. The last six symbols were the sequential production number starting with 000001. Codes for individual models not available at date of publication. See 2003 codes for most carryover models.

ENGINE

2.0-LITER FOUR (Beetle, Golf, Jetta): Inline, overhead-cam four-cylinder (8-valve). Cast-iron block and light alloy head. Displacement: 2.0-liter (1984 cc). Bore & Stroke: 3.25 x 3.65 in. (82.5 x 92.8 mm). Compression Ratio: 10.0:1. Brake Horsepower: 115 at 5200 rpm. Torque: 122 lbs.-ft. at 2600 rpm. Five main bearings. Sequential multi-point fuel injection.

2.0-LITER TURBO DIESEL (TDI) FOUR (Passat): Inline, overhead-cam four-cylinder (8-valve). Cast-iron block and light alloy head. Displacement: 2.0-liter (1984 cc). Bore & Stroke: 3.25 x 3.65 in. (82.5 x 92.8 mm). Compression Ratio: 10.0:1. Brake Horsepower: 134. Torque: 247 lbs.-ft. Five main bearings. Sequential multi-point fuel injection.

1.8L TURBO FOUR (Beetle): Inline, dual-overhead-cam four-cylinder (20-valve). Cast-iron block and light alloy head. Displacement: 1.8-liter (1781 cc). Bore & Stroke: 3.19 x 3.40 in. Compression Ratio: 9.3:1. Brake Horsepower: 150 at 5700 rpm. Torque: 162 lbs.-ft. at 1750-4600 rpm. Five main bearings. Sequential multi-point fuel injection.

1.8L TURBO DOHC FOUR (Passat): Inline, dual-overhead-cam four-cylinder (20-valve). Cast-iron block and light alloy head. Displacement: 1.8-liter (1781 cc). Bore & Stroke: 3.19 x 3.40 in. Compression Ratio: 9.3:1. Brake Horsepower: 170 at 5900 rpm. Torque: 166 lbs.-ft. at 1950 rpm. Five main bearings. Sequential multi-point fuel injection.

1.8L TURBO DOHC FOUR (GTI, Jetta, Beetle): Inline, dual-overhead-cam four-cylinder (20-valve). Cast-iron block and light alloy head. Displacement: 1.8-liter (1781 cc). Bore & Stroke: 3.19 x 3.40 in. Compression Ratio: 9.5:1. Brake Horsepower: 180 at 5500 rpm. Torque: 174 lbs.-ft. at 1950 rpm. Five main bearings. Sequential multi-point fuel injection.

1.9-LITER TURBO DIESEL (TDI) FOUR (Beetle, Golf, Jetta): Inline, overhead-cam four-cylinder with turbocharger and intercooler (8-valve). Cast-iron block and light alloy head. Displacement: 1.9-liter (1896 cc). Bore & Stroke: 3.13 x 3.76 in. Compression Ratio: 19.5:1. Brake Horsepower: 100. Torque: 177 lbs.-ft. Five main bearings. Sequential multi-point fuel injection.

2.8-LITER V-6 (GTI, Jetta): Narrow (15 degrees) "vee" type dual-overhead-cam 12-valve six-cylinder. Cast-iron block and light alloy head. Displacement: 2.8-liter (2792 cc). Bore & Stroke: 3.19 x 3.56 in. (81 x 90.3 mm). Compression Ratio: 10.0:1. Brake Horsepower: 200 at 5800 rpm. Torque: 195 lbs.-ft. at 3200 rpm. Seven main bearings. Sequential multi-point fuel injection.

2.8-LITER V-6 (Passat): "Vee" type dual overhead-cam 30-valve six-cylinder. Cast-iron block and light alloy head. Displacement: 169.1 cid (2771 cc). Bore & Stroke: 3.25 x 3.40 in. (82.5 x 86.4 mm). Compression Ratio: 10.6:1. Brake Horsepower: 190 at 6000 rpm. Torque: 206 lbs.-ft. at 3200 rpm. Four main bearings. Sequential multi-point fuel injection.

3.2-LITER V-6 (GTI R32): Narrow angle "vee" type dual-overhead-cam 24-valve six-cylinder. Cast-iron block and light alloy head. Displacement: 3.2-liter (3189 cc). Brake Horsepower: 240 at 6250 rpm. Torque: 236 lbs.-ft. at 2800-3200 rpm. Sequential multi-point fuel injection.

4.0-LITER V-8 (Passat): "Vee" type eight. Cast-iron block and light alloy heads. Displacement: 4.0-liter (245 cid). Bore & Stroke: 3.31 x 3.55 in. Brake Horsepower: 270. Torque: 273 lbs.-ft. Sequential multi-point fuel injection.

Below: **The 2004 New Beetle convertible came in two trim levels and several color choices.**
Old Cars Weekly Archive

4.2-LITER V-8 (Phaeton): "Vee" type eight. DOHC. Cast-iron block and light alloy heads. Displacement: 4.2-liter. Bore & Stroke: 3.33 x 3.66 in. Brake Horsepower: 335 at 6500 rpm. Torque: 317 lbs.-ft. at 3500 rpm. Sequential multi-point fuel injection.

4.2-LITER V-8 (Phaeton): "Vee" type eight. DOHC. Cast-iron block and light alloy heads. Displacement: 6.0-liter (366 cid). Bore & Stroke: 3.31 x 3.55 in. Brake Horsepower: 414 at 6000 rpm. Torque: 406 lbs.-ft. at 4700 rpm. Sequential multi-point fuel injection.

CHASSIS

NEW BEETLE: Wheelbase: 98.7 in. Overall length: 161.1 in. Height: 59.0 in. Width: 67.9 in. Front tread: 59.6 in. Rear tread: 58.7 in. Standard tires (Except Turbo S): P205/55HR16.

GOLF: Wheelbase: 98.9 in. Overall length: 164.9 in. Height: 56.7 in. Width: 68.3 in. Front tread: 59.6 in. Rear tread: 58.8 in. Standard tires: P195/65HR15.

GTI: Wheelbase: 98.9 in. Overall length: 164.9 in. Height: 56.9 in. Width: 68.3 in. Front tread: 59.6 in. Rear tread: 58.8 in. Standard tires: P205/55HR16.

GTI R32: Wheelbase: 99.1 in. Overall length: 164.4 in. Height: 56.1 in. Width: 68.3 in. Front tread: 59.5 in. Rear tread: 58.7 in. Standard tires: 18 inch.

JETTA: Wheelbase: 98.9 in. Overall length: (Sedan) 172.3 in., (Wagon) 173.6 in. Height: (Sedan) 56.9 in., (Wagon) 58.5. Width: (All) 68.3 in. Front tread: 59.6 in. Rear tread: 58.8 in. Standard tires: (Except GLX) P195/65HR15. Standard tires: (GLX) P205/55HR16.

PASSAT: Wheelbase: 106.4 in. Overall length: (Sedan) 185.2 in., (Wagon) 184.3 in. Height: (Sedan) 57.6 in., (Wagon) 59.0. Width: (All) 68.7 in. Front tread: 59.0 in. Rear tread: 59.1 in. Standard tires: (Except GLX) P195/65HR15. Standard tires: (GLX) P205/55HR16.

PHAETON: Wheelbase: 118.1 in. Overall length: 203.7 in. Height: 57.1. Width: 74.9 in. Front tread: 64.1 in. Rear tread: 63.5 in. Standard tires: 235/50R18.

TECHNICAL

NEW BEETLE: Layout: front-engine, front-wheel-drive. Transmission: five-speed manual or four speed automatic. Steering: power rack and pinion. Brakes: Antilock brakes with ventilated front disc and solid rear disc.

GOLF: Layout: front-engine, front-wheel-drive. Transmission: five-speed manual or four speed automatic. Steering: power rack and pinion. Brakes: Antilock brakes with ventilated front disc and solid rear disc.

GTI: Layout: front-engine, front-wheel-drive. Transmission: five-speed manual or four speed automatic (automatic standard in GLX). Steering: power rack and pinion. Brakes: Antilock brakes with ventilated front disc and solid rear disc. Traction control.

JETTA: Layout: front-engine, front-wheel-drive. Transmission: five-speed manual or four speed automatic. Steering: power rack and pinion. Brakes: Antilock brakes with ventilated front disc and solid rear disc.

PASSAT: Layout: front-engine, front-wheel-drive. Transmission: five-speed manual or four speed automatic (automatic standard in 4Motion models). Steering: power rack and pinion. Brakes: Antilock brakes with ventilated front disc and rear disc. Traction control.

PHAETON: Layout: front-engine. All-wheel drive. Transmission: five-speed manual or four speed automatic (automatic standard in 4Motion models). Steering: power rack and pinion. Brakes: Antilock brakes with ventilated disc front and rear disc. Traction control.

OPTIONS

PERFORMANCE: Acceleration (0-60 mph): (Cabriolet) 11.1 sec., (Passat GL) 8.8 sec., (Passat GLX sedan) 7.9 sec., (Passat GLX Station Wagon) 8.0 sec., (GTI R32) 5.8 seconds, (Phaeton V-8) 6.7 sec., (Phaeton W-12) 5.9 seconds. Top Speed in mph: (Cabriolet) 101, (Passat GL) 127, (Passat GLX) 130, (GTI R32) 153 mph, (Phaeton V-8) 130 electronically governed, (Phaeton W12) 130 mph electronically governed, but given as 167 mph in some sources. EPA Fuel Economy in mpg: City/Highway: (Cabriolet) 24/ 30, (Passat GL) 21/30, (Passat GLX) 19/27.

MANUFACTURER: Volkswagenwerk AG, Wolfsburg, Germany.

DISTRIBUTOR: Volkswagen of America Inc., Auburn Hills, Michigan.

VOLKSWAGEN

PRICE GUIDE

Vehicle Condition Scale

1: **Excellent:** Restored to current maximum professional standards of quality in every area, or perfect original with components operating and apearing as new. A 95-plus point show car that is not driven.

2: **Fine:** Well-restored or a combination of superior restoration and excellent original parts. Also, extremely well-maintained original vehicle showing minimal wear.

3. **Very Good:** Complete operable original or older restoration. Also, a very good amateur restoration, all presentable and serviceable inside and out. Plus, a combination of well-done restoration and good operable components or a partially restored car with all parts necessary to compete and/or valuable NOS parts.

4: **Good:** A driveable vehicle needing no or only minor work to be functional. Also, a deteriorated restoration or a very poor amateur restoration. All components may need restoration to be "excellent," but the car is mostly useable "as is."

5. **Restorable:** Needs complete restoration of body, chassis and interior. May or may not be running, but isn't weathered, wrecked or stripped to the point of being useful only for parts.

6. **Parts car:** May or may not be running, but is weathered, wrecked and/or stripped to the point of being useful primarily for parts.

	6	5	4	3	2	1
1945 Standard, 4-cyl., 25 hp, 94.5" wb						
2d Sed	880	2,640	4,400	8,800	15,400	22,000
1946 Standard, 4-cyl., 25 hp, 94.5" wb						
2d Sed	840	2,520	4,200	8,400	14,700	21,000
1947-48 4-cyl., 25 hp, 94.5" wb						
Std	700	2,100	3,500	7,000	12,250	17,500
Export	800	2,400	4,000	8,000	14,000	20,000
1949 Standard, 4-cyl., 25 hp, 94.5" wb						
2d Sed	700	2,100	3,500	7,000	12,250	17,500
1949 DeLuxe, 4-cyl., 10 hp, 94.5" wb						
2d Sed	760	2,280	3,800	7,600	13,300	19,000
Conv	916	2,748	4,580	9,160	16,030	22,900
Heb Conv	956	2,868	4,780	9,560	16,730	23,900

NOTE: Add 10 percent for sunroof.

	6	5	4	3	2	1
1950 DeLuxe, 4-cyl., 25 hp, 94.5" wb						
2d Sed	740	2,220	3,700	7,400	12,950	18,500
Conv	820	2,460	4,100	8,200	14,350	20,500
Heb Conv	960	2,880	4,800	9,600	16,800	24,000

NOTE: Only 700 Hebmuller Cabr convertibles were built during 1949-1950.

	6	5	4	3	2	1
1950 Transporter, 4-cyl., 25 hp, 94.5" wb						
DeL Van	840	2,520	4,200	8,400	14,700	21,000
Kombi	740	2,220	3,700	7,400	12,950	18,500
1951-52 (Serial Nos. 170000-Up) DeLuxe, 4-cyl., 25 hp, 94.5" wb						
2d Sed	700	2,100	3,500	7,000	12,250	17,500
Conv	760	2,280	3,800	7,600	13,300	19,000

NOTE: Add 10 percent for sunroof.

	6	5	4	3	2	1
1951-52 Transporter, 4-cyl., 25 hp, 94.5" wb						
DeL Van	840	2,520	4,200	8,400	14,700	21,000
Kombi	740	2,220	3,700	7,400	12,950	18,500
1952-53 (Serial Nos. 1-0264198-Up) DeLuxe 4-cyl., 25 hp, 94.5" wb						
2d Sed	700	2,100	3,500	7,000	12,250	17,500
Conv	820	2,460	4,100	8,200	14,350	20,500

NOTE: Add 10 percent for sunroof.

	6	5	4	3	2	1
1952-53 Transporter, 4-cyl., 25 hp, 94.5" wb						
DeL Van	840	2,520	4,200	8,400	14,700	21,000
Kombi	740	2,220	3,700	7,400	12,950	18,500

	6	5	4	3	2	1
1953 (Serial Nos. later than March 1953) DeLuxe, 4-cyl., 94.5" wb, 25 hp						
2d Sed	700	2,100	3,500	7,000	12,250	17,500
Conv	820	2,460	4,100	8,200	14,350	20,500

NOTE: Add 10 percent for sunroof.

	6	5	4	3	2	1
1953 Transporter, 4-cyl., 25 hp, 94.5" wb						
DeL Van	740	2,220	3,700	7,400	12,950	18,500
Kombi	840	2,520	4,200	8,400	14,700	21,000
1954 DeLuxe, 4-cyl., 36 hp, 94.5" wb						
2d Sed	700	2,100	3,500	7,000	12,250	17,500
Conv	820	2,460	4,100	8,200	14,350	20,500

NOTE: Add 10 percent for sunroof.

	6	5	4	3	2	1
1954 Station Wagons, 4-cyl., 30 hp, 94.5" wb						
Microbus	820	2,460	4,100	8,200	14,350	20,500
DeL Microbus	840	2,520	4,200	8,400	14,700	21,000

NOTE: Microbus 165" overall; DeLuxe Microbus 166.1" overall; Beetle 160.3" overall.

	6	5	4	3	2	1
1955 DeLuxe, 4-cyl., 36 hp, 94.5" wb						
2d Sed	700	2,100	3,500	7,000	12,250	17,500
Conv	820	2,460	4,100	8,200	14,350	20,500

NOTE: Add 10 percent for sunroof.

	6	5	4	3	2	1
1955 Station Wagons, 4-cyl., 36 hp, 94.5" wb						
Kombi	740	2,220	3,700	7,400	12,950	18,500
Microbus	820	2,460	4,100	8,200	14,350	20,500
Microbus DeL	840	2,520	4,200	8,400	14,700	21,000
1956 DeLuxe, 4-cyl., 36 hp, 94.5" wb						
2d Sed	700	2,100	3,500	7,000	12,250	17,500
Conv	820	2,460	4,100	8,200	14,350	20,500

NOTE: Add 10 percent for sunroof.

	6	5	4	3	2	1
1956 Karmann-Ghia, 4-cyl., 36 hp, 94.5" wb						
Cpe	740	2,220	3,700	7,400	12,950	18,500
1956 Station Wagons, 4-cyl., 36 hp, 94.5" wb						
Kombi	740	2,220	3,700	7,400	12,950	18,500
Microbus	860	2,580	4,300	8,600	15,050	21,500
Microbus DeL	880	2,640	4,400	8,800	15,400	22,000
1957 Beetle, 4-cyl., 36 hp, 94.5" wb						
2d Sed	700	2,100	3,500	7,000	12,250	17,500
Conv	820	2,460	4,100	8,200	14,350	20,500

NOTE: Add 10 percent for sunroof.

	6	5	4	3	2	1

1957 Karmann-Ghia, 4-cyl., 36 hp, 94.5" wb

	6	5	4	3	2	1
Cpe	700	2,100	3,500	7,000	12,250	17,500

1957 Station Wagons, 4-cyl., 36 hp, 94.5" wb

	6	5	4	3	2	1
Kombi	780	2,340	3,900	7,800	13,650	19,500
Microbus	920	2,760	4,600	9,200	16,100	23,000
Microbus SR	940	2,820	4,700	9,400	16,450	23,500
Camper	980	2,940	4,900	9,800	17,150	24,500

NOTE: Add 10 percent for sunroof.

1958 Beetle, 4-cyl., 36 hp, 94.5" wb

	6	5	4	3	2	1
2d DeL Sed	700	2,100	3,500	7,000	12,250	17,500
Conv	820	2,460	4,100	8,200	14,350	20,500

1958 Karmann-Ghia, 4-cyl., 36 hp, 94.5" wb

	6	5	4	3	2	1
Cpe	780	2,340	3,900	7,800	13,650	19,500
Conv	820	2,460	4,100	8,200	14,350	20,500

1958 Station Wagons, 4-cyl., 36 hp, 94.5" wb

	6	5	4	3	2	1
Kombi	780	2,340	3,900	7,800	13,650	19,500
Microbus	960	2,880	4,800	9,600	16,800	24,000
Microbus DeL SR	980	2,940	4,900	9,800	17,150	24,500
Camper	1,020	3,060	5,100	10,200	17,850	25,500

1959 Beetle, 4-cyl., 36 hp, 94.5" wb

	6	5	4	3	2	1
2d Sed	680	2,040	3,400	6,800	11,900	17,000
Conv	800	2,400	4,000	8,000	14,000	20,000

NOTE: Add 10 percent for sunroof.

1959 Karmann-Ghia, 4-cyl., 36 hp, 94.5" wb

	6	5	4	3	2	1
Cpe	740	2,220	3,700	7,400	12,950	18,500
Conv	780	2,340	3,900	7,800	13,650	19,500

1959 Station Wagons, 4-cyl., 36 hp, 94.5" wb

	6	5	4	3	2	1
Kombi	780	2,340	3,900	7,800	13,650	19,500
Microbus	980	2,940	4,900	9,800	17,150	24,500
Microbus DeL SR	1,100	3,300	5,500	11,000	19,250	27,500
Camper	1,040	3,120	5,200	10,400	18,200	26,000

1960 Beetle, 4-cyl., 36 hp, 94.5" wb

	6	5	4	3	2	1
2d DeL Sed	680	2,040	3,400	6,800	11,900	17,000
Conv	800	2,400	4,000	8,000	14,000	20,000

1960 Karmann-Ghia, 4-cyl., 36 hp, 94.5" wb

	6	5	4	3	2	1
Cpe	740	2,220	3,700	7,400	12,950	18,500
Conv	780	2,340	3,900	7,800	13,650	19,500

1960 Station Wagons, 4-cyl., 36 hp, 94.5" wb

	6	5	4	3	2	1
Kombi	780	2,340	3,900	7,800	13,650	19,500
Microbus	980	2,940	4,900	9,800	17,150	24,500
Microbus DeL SR	1,100	3,300	5,500	11,000	19,250	27,500
Camper	1,040	3,120	5,200	10,400	18,200	26,000

NOTE: Add 10 percent for sunroof.

1961 Beetle, 4-cyl., 40 hp, 94.5" wb

	6	5	4	3	2	1
2d DeL Sed	680	2,040	3,400	6,800	11,900	17,000
Conv	760	2,280	3,800	7,600	13,300	19,000

1961 Karmann-Ghia, 4-cyl., 40 hp, 94.5" wb

	6	5	4	3	2	1
Cpe	780	2,340	3,900	7,800	13,650	19,500
Conv	820	2,460	4,100	8,200	14,350	20,500

1962 Beetle, 4-cyl., 40 hp, 94.5" wb

	6	5	4	3	2	1
2d DeL Sed	680	2,040	3,400	6,800	11,900	17,000
Conv	760	2,280	3,800	7,600	13,300	19,000

NOTE: Add 10 percent for sunroof.

1962 Karmann-Ghia, 4-cyl., 40 hp, 94.5" wb

	6	5	4	3	2	1
Cpe	780	2,340	3,900	7,800	13,650	19,500
Conv	820	2,460	4,100	8,200	14,350	20,500

1963 Beetle, 4-cyl., 40 hp, 94.5" wb

	6	5	4	3	2	1
2d DeL Sed	660	1,980	3,300	6,600	11,550	16,500
Conv	740	2,220	3,700	7,400	12,950	18,500

NOTE: Add 10 percent for sunroof.

1963 Karmann-Ghia, 4-cyl., 40 hp, 94.5" wb

	6	5	4	3	2	1
Cpe	740	2,220	3,700	7,400	12,950	18,500
Conv	780	2,340	3,900	7,800	13,650	19,500

1963 Station Wagons, 4-cyl., 40 hp, 94.5" wb

	6	5	4	3	2	1
Kombi	780	2,340	3,900	7,800	13,650	19,500
Sta Wag	1,040	3,120	5,200	10,400	18,200	26,000
DeL Sta Wag	1,140	3,420	5,700	11,400	19,950	28,500
Camper	1,100	3,300	5,500	11,000	19,250	27,500

1964 Beetle, 4-cyl., 40 hp, 94.5" wb

	6	5	4	3	2	1
2d DeL Sed	660	1,980	3,300	6,600	11,550	16,500
Conv	740	2,220	3,700	7,400	12,950	18,500

NOTE: Add 10 percent for sunroof.

1964 Karmann-Ghia, 4-cyl., 40 hp, 94.5" wb

	6	5	4	3	2	1
Cpe	740	2,220	3,700	7,400	12,950	18,500
Conv	780	2,340	3,900	7,800	13,650	19,500

1965 Beetle, 4-cyl., 40 hp, 94.5" wb

	6	5	4	3	2	1
2d DeL Sed	660	1,980	3,300	6,600	11,550	16,500
Conv	740	2,220	3,700	7,400	12,950	18,500

NOTE: Add 10 percent for sunroof.

1965 Karmann-Ghia, 4-cyl., 40 hp, 94.5" wb

	6	5	4	3	2	1
Cpe	740	2,220	3,700	7,400	12,950	18,500
Conv	780	2,340	3,900	7,800	13,650	19,500

1965 Station Wagons (1500 Series), 4-cyl., 40 hp, 94.5" wb

	6	5	4	3	2	1
Kombi	780	2,340	3,900	7,800	13,650	19,500
Sta Wag	1,040	3,120	5,200	10,400	18,200	26,000
DeL Sta Wag	1,140	3,420	5,700	11,400	19,950	28,500
Camper	1,100	3,300	5,500	11,000	19,250	27,500

1966 Beetle, 50 hp

	6	5	4	3	2	1
2d DeL Sed	660	1,980	3,300	6,600	11,550	16,500
Conv	740	2,220	3,700	7,400	12,950	18,500

NOTE: Add 10 percent for sunroof.

1966 Karmann-Ghia, 53 hp

	6	5	4	3	2	1
Cpe	740	2,220	3,700	7,400	12,950	18,500
Conv	780	2,340	3,900	7,800	13,650	19,500

1966 Station Wagons, 57 hp

	6	5	4	3	2	1
Kombi	780	2,340	3,900	7,800	13,650	19,500
Sta Wag	1,040	3,120	5,200	10,400	18,200	26,000
DeL Sta Wag	1,140	3,420	5,700	11,400	19,950	28,500
Camper	1,100	3,300	5,500	11,000	19,250	27,500

1966 1600 Series, 65 hp

	6	5	4	3	2	1
2d FBk Sed	304	912	1,520	3,040	5,320	7,600
2d SqBk Sed	308	924	1,540	3,080	5,390	7,700

NOTE: Add 10 percent for sunroof.

1967 Beetle, 53 hp

	6	5	4	3	2	1
2d DeL Sed	680	2,040	3,400	6,800	11,900	17,000
Conv	760	2,280	3,800	7,600	13,300	19,000

NOTE: Add 10 percent for sunroof.

1967 Karmann-Ghia, 53 hp

	6	5	4	3	2	1
Cpe	740	2,220	3,700	7,400	12,950	18,500
Conv	780	2,340	3,900	7,800	13,650	19,500

1967 Station Wagon, 57 hp

	6	5	4	3	2	1
Kombi	780	2,340	3,900	7,800	13,650	19,500
Sta Wag	1,040	3,120	5,200	10,400	18,200	26,000
DeL Sta Wag	1,140	3,420	5,700	11,400	19,950	28,500
Camper	1,100	3,300	5,500	11,000	19,250	27,500

1967 1600 Series, 65 hp

	6	5	4	3	2	1
2d FBk Sed	316	948	1,580	3,160	5,530	7,900
2d SqBk Sed	324	972	1,620	3,240	5,670	8,100

NOTE: Add 10 percent for sunroof.

1968 Beetle, 53 hp

	6	5	4	3	2	1
2d Sed	660	1,980	3,300	6,600	11,550	16,500
Conv	740	2,220	3,700	7,400	12,950	18,500

NOTE: Add 10 percent for sunroof.

1968 Karmann-Ghia, 53 hp

	6	5	4	3	2	1
Cpe	740	2,220	3,700	7,400	12,950	18,500
Conv	780	2,340	3,900	7,800	13,650	19,500

1968 1600 Series, 65 hp

	6	5	4	3	2	1
2d FBk Sed	316	948	1,580	3,160	5,530	7,900
2d SqBk Sed	324	972	1,620	3,240	5,670	8,100

NOTE: Add 10 percent for sunroof.

1968 Station Wagons, 57 hp

	6	5	4	3	2	1
Kombi	780	2,340	3,900	7,800	13,650	19,500
Sta Wag	980	2,940	4,900	9,800	17,150	24,500

	6	5	4	3	2	1
Camper	1,020	3,060	5,100	10,200	17,850	25,500

1969 Beetle, 53 hp

	6	5	4	3	2	1
2d Sed	660	1,980	3,300	6,600	11,550	16,500
Conv	740	2,220	3,700	7,400	12,950	18,500

NOTE: Add 10 percent for sunroof.

1969 Karmann-Ghia, 53 hp

	6	5	4	3	2	1
Cpe	740	2,220	3,700	7,400	12,950	18,500
Conv	780	2,340	3,900	7,800	13,650	19,500

1969 1600 Series, 65 hp

	6	5	4	3	2	1
2d FBk Sed	324	972	1,620	3,240	5,670	8,100
2d SqBk Sed	328	984	1,640	3,280	5,740	8,200

NOTE: Add 10 percent for sunroof.

1969 Station Wagons, 57 hp

	6	5	4	3	2	1
Kombi	740	2,220	3,700	7,400	12,950	18,500
Sta Wag	980	2,940	4,900	9,800	17,150	24,500
Camper	1,000	3,000	5,000	10,000	17,500	25,000

1970 Beetle, 60 hp

	6	5	4	3	2	1
2d Sed	660	1,980	3,300	6,600	11,550	16,500
Conv	740	2,220	3,700	7,400	12,950	18,500

NOTE: Add 10 percent for sunroof.

1970 Karmann-Ghia, 60 hp

	6	5	4	3	2	1
Cpe	740	2,220	3,700	7,400	12,950	18,500
Conv	780	2,340	3,900	7,800	13,650	19,500

1970 1600 Series, 65 hp

	6	5	4	3	2	1
2d FBk Sed	320	960	1,600	3,200	5,600	8,000
2d SqBk Sed	324	972	1,620	3,240	5,670	8,100

NOTE: Add 10 percent for sunroof.

1970 Station Wagons, 60 hp

	6	5	4	3	2	1
Kombi	740	2,220	3,700	7,400	12,950	18,500
Sta Wag	980	2,940	4,900	9,800	17,150	24,500
Camper	1,000	3,000	5,000	10,000	17,500	25,000

1971 Beetle, 60 hp

	6	5	4	3	2	1
2d Sed	650	1,900	3,200	6,400	11,200	16,000
2d Sup Sed	650	2,000	3,300	6,600	11,600	16,500
Conv	700	2,150	3,600	7,200	12,600	18,000

NOTE: Add 10 percent for sunroof.

1971 Karmann-Ghia

	6	5	4	3	2	1
Cpe	700	2,050	3,400	6,800	11,900	17,000
Conv	750	2,200	3,700	7,400	13,000	18,500

1971 Type 3, Sq. Back 411

	6	5	4	3	2	1
2d SqBk Sed	300	900	1,500	3,000	5,250	7,500
3d 411 Sed	304	912	1,520	3,040	5,320	7,600
4d 411 Sed	304	912	1,520	3,040	5,320	7,600
2d Type 3 Sed	300	900	1,500	3,000	5,250	7,500

1971 Transporter

	6	5	4	3	2	1
Kombi	700	2,050	3,400	6,800	11,900	17,000
Sta Wag	800	2,400	4,000	8,000	14,000	20,000
Sta Wag SR	800	2,400	4,050	8,100	14,100	20,200
Campmobile	800	2,450	4,100	8,200	14,300	20,500

1972 Beetle, 60 hp

	6	5	4	3	2	1
2d Sed	650	1,900	3,200	6,400	11,200	16,000
2d Sup Sed	650	2,000	3,300	6,600	11,600	16,500
Conv	700	2,150	3,600	7,200	12,600	18,000

NOTE: Add 10 percent for sunroof.

1972 Karmann-Ghia

	6	5	4	3	2	1
Cpe	700	2,050	3,400	6,800	11,900	17,000
Conv	750	2,200	3,700	7,400	13,000	18,500

1972 Type 3, Sq. Back 411

	6	5	4	3	2	1
2d Sed	300	900	1,500	3,000	5,250	7,500
2d Sed Type 3	300	900	1,500	3,000	5,250	7,500
2d Sed 411	304	912	1,520	3,040	5,320	7,600
4d Sed AT 411	304	912	1,520	3,040	5,320	7,600
3d Wagon 411	308	924	1,540	3,080	5,390	7,700

NOTE: Add 10 percent for sunroof.

1972 Transporter

	6	5	4	3	2	1
Kombi	700	2,050	3,400	6,800	11,900	17,000
Sta Wag	800	2,400	4,000	8,000	14,000	20,000
Campmobile	800	2,450	4,100	8,200	14,300	20,500

1973 Beetle, 46 hp

	6	5	4	3	2	1
2d Sed	650	1,900	3,200	6,400	11,200	16,000
2d Sup Sed	650	2,000	3,300	6,600	11,600	16,500
Conv	700	2,150	3,600	7,200	12,600	18,000

1973 Karmann-Ghia

	6	5	4	3	2	1
Cpe	650	1,900	3,200	6,400	11,200	16,000
Conv	700	2,150	3,600	7,200	12,600	18,000

1974 Beetle

	6	5	4	3	2	1
2d Sed	650	1,900	3,200	6,400	11,200	16,000
2d Sup Sed	650	2,000	3,300	6,600	11,600	16,500
2d Sun Bug Sed	650	2,000	3,300	6,650	11,600	16,600
Conv	700	2,100	3,500	7,000	12,300	17,500

1974 Karmann-Ghia

	6	5	4	3	2	1
Cpe	600	1,850	3,100	6,200	10,900	15,500
Conv	700	2,100	3,500	7,000	12,300	17,500

1974 Thing

	6	5	4	3	2	1
4d Conv	400	1,200	2,000	4,000	7,000	10,000

1974 Dasher

	6	5	4	3	2	1
2d Sed	300	950	1,550	3,100	5,450	7,800
4d Sed	300	950	1,600	3,150	5,550	7,900
4d Wag	300	950	1,600	3,200	5,600	8,000

1974 412

	6	5	4	3	2	1
2d Sed	300	950	1,550	3,100	5,450	7,800
4d Sed	300	950	1,600	3,150	5,550	7,900
3d Sed	300	950	1,600	3,150	5,550	7,900

1974 Transporter

	6	5	4	3	2	1
Kombi	650	1,900	3,200	6,400	11,200	16,000
Sta Wag	700	2,150	3,600	7,200	12,600	18,000
Campmobile	750	2,200	3,700	7,400	13,000	18,500

1975 Beetle

	6	5	4	3	2	1
2d Sed	600	1,800	3,000	6,000	10,500	15,000
2d Sup Sed	600	1,850	3,100	6,200	10,900	15,500
Conv	700	2,050	3,400	6,800	11,900	17,000

1975 Rabbit

	6	5	4	3	2	1
2d Cus Sed	300	900	1,500	3,050	5,300	7,600
4d Cus Sed	300	900	1,550	3,100	5,400	7,700

1975 Dasher

	6	5	4	3	2	1
2d Sed	300	900	1,500	3,050	5,300	7,600
4d Sed	300	950	1,550	3,100	5,450	7,800
HBk	300	950	1,600	3,150	5,550	7,900
4d Wag	300	950	1,600	3,200	5,600	8,000

1975 Scirocco

	6	5	4	3	2	1
Cpe	350	1,000	1,700	3,350	5,900	8,400

1975 Transporter

	6	5	4	3	2	1
Kombi	600	1,850	3,100	6,200	10,900	15,500
Sta Wag	700	2,050	3,400	6,800	11,900	17,000
Campmobile	700	2,100	3,500	7,000	12,300	17,500

1976 Beetle

	6	5	4	3	2	1
2d Sed	600	1,800	3,000	6,000	10,500	15,000
Conv	600	1,850	3,100	6,200	10,900	15,500

1976 Rabbit

	6	5	4	3	2	1
2d Sed	250	800	1,300	2,650	4,600	6,600
2d Cus Sed	250	800	1,350	2,700	4,700	6,700
4d Cus Sed	250	800	1,350	2,700	4,700	6,700

NOTE: Add 10 percent for DeLuxe.

1976 Dasher

	6	5	4	3	2	1
2d Sed	250	800	1,350	2,700	4,700	6,700
4d Sed	300	850	1,400	2,750	4,850	6,900
4d Wag	300	850	1,450	2,900	5,050	7,200

1976 Scirocco

	6	5	4	3	2	1
Cpe	300	950	1,550	3,100	5,450	7,800

1976 Transporter

	6	5	4	3	2	1
Kombi	600	1,850	3,100	6,200	10,900	15,500
Sta Wag	700	2,050	3,400	6,800	11,900	17,000
Campmobile	700	2,100	3,500	7,000	12,300	17,500

1977 Beetle

	6	5	4	3	2	1
2d Sed	600	1,800	3,000	6,000	10,500	15,000

	6	5	4	3	2	1
Conv	700	2,050	3,400	6,800	11,900	17,000
1978 Beetle						
2d Conv	650	1,900	3,200	6,400	11,200	16,000
1978 Rabbit						
2d	250	800	1,300	2,600	4,550	6,500
2d Cus	250	800	1,300	2,650	4,600	6,600
4d Cus	250	800	1,300	2,650	4,600	6,600
2d DeL	250	800	1,350	2,700	4,700	6,700
4d DeL	250	800	1,350	2,700	4,700	6,700
1978 Dasher						
2d	300	850	1,400	2,800	4,900	7,000
4d	300	850	1,400	2,800	4,900	7,000
4d Sta Wag	300	850	1,400	2,850	4,950	7,100
1978 Scirocco						
2d Cpe	300	900	1,500	3,000	5,250	7,500
1978 Transporter						
Kombi	600	1,800	3,000	6,000	10,500	15,000
Sta Wag	700	2,050	3,400	6,800	11,900	17,000
Campmobile	700	2,100	3,500	7,000	12,300	17,500
1979 Beetle						
2d Conv	650	2,000	3,300	6,600	11,600	16,500
1979 Dasher						
2d HBk	300	850	1,400	2,800	4,900	7,000
4d HBk	300	850	1,400	2,800	4,900	7,000
4d Sta Wag	300	850	1,400	2,850	4,950	7,100
1979 Scirocco						
2d Cpe	300	900	1,500	3,000	5,250	7,500
1979 Transporter						
Kombi	600	1,800	3,000	6,000	10,500	15,000
Sta Wag	700	2,050	3,400	6,800	11,900	17,000
Campmobile	700	2,100	3,500	7,000	12,300	17,500
1980 Rabbit						
2d Conv	350	1,000	1,700	3,350	5,900	8,400
2d Cus	250	700	1,200	2,400	4,200	6,000
4d Cus	250	700	1,200	2,400	4,200	6,000
2d DeL	250	750	1,200	2,450	4,250	6,100
4d DeL	250	750	1,200	2,450	4,250	6,100
1980 Jetta						
2d	250	750	1,300	2,550	4,500	6,400
4d	250	750	1,300	2,550	4,500	6,400
1980 Dasher						
2d	250	750	1,250	2,500	4,400	6,300
4d	250	750	1,250	2,500	4,400	6,300
4d Sta Wag	250	750	1,300	2,550	4,500	6,400
1980 Scirocco						
2d Cpe	250	800	1,300	2,650	4,600	6,600
2d Cpe S	250	800	1,350	2,700	4,750	6,800
1980 Pickup						
Cus	250	800	1,300	2,650	4,600	6,600
LX	250	800	1,350	2,700	4,700	6,700
Spt	250	800	1,350	2,700	4,750	6,800
1980 Vanagon Transporter						
Kombi	400	1,150	1,900	3,800	6,650	9,500
Sta Wag	400	1,250	2,100	4,200	7,350	10,500
Campmobile	600	1,800	3,000	6,000	10,500	15,000
1981 Jetta						
2d	200	650	1,100	2,150	3,800	5,400
4d	200	650	1,100	2,150	3,800	5,400
1981 Dasher						
4d	200	600	1,050	2,100	3,650	5,200
1981 Scirocco						
2d Cpe	200	650	1,100	2,250	3,900	5,600
2d Cpe S	250	700	1,150	2,300	4,000	5,700
1981 Pickup						
PU	200	650	1,100	2,250	3,900	5,600
LX	250	700	1,150	2,300	4,000	5,700
Spt	250	700	1,150	2,300	4,050	5,800

	6	5	4	3	2	1
1981 Vanagon Transporter						
Kombi	350	1,000	1,700	3,400	5,950	8,500
Sta Wag	400	1,150	1,900	3,800	6,650	9,500
Campmobile	450	1,300	2,200	4,400	7,700	11,000
1982 Rabbit						
2d Conv	300	850	1,400	2,850	4,950	7,100
2d	200	600	1,000	2,000	3,500	5,000
2d L	200	600	1,000	2,050	3,550	5,100
4d L	200	600	1,000	2,000	3,500	5,000
2d LS	200	600	1,000	2,050	3,550	5,100
4d LS	200	600	1,000	2,050	3,550	5,100
2d S	200	600	1,050	2,100	3,650	5,200
1982 Jetta						
2d	200	650	1,050	2,100	3,700	5,300
4d	200	650	1,050	2,100	3,700	5,300
1982 Quantum						
2d Cpe	250	700	1,200	2,400	4,200	6,000
4d	250	700	1,200	2,400	4,200	6,000
4d Sta Wag	250	750	1,200	2,450	4,250	6,100
1982 Vanagon						
Sta Wag	350	1,000	1,700	3,400	5,950	8,500
Campmobile	450	1,300	2,200	4,400	7,700	11,000
1983 Rabbit						
2d Conv	300	850	1,450	2,900	5,050	7,200
2d L	200	600	1,000	2,000	3,500	5,000
4d L	200	600	1,000	2,000	3,500	5,000
2d LS	200	600	1,000	2,000	3,500	5,000
4d LS	200	600	1,000	2,000	3,500	5,000
GL 2d	200	600	1,000	2,050	3,550	5,100
GL 4d	200	600	1,000	2,050	3,550	5,100
GTI 2d	200	650	1,100	2,200	3,850	5,500
1983 Jetta						
2d	200	650	1,100	2,150	3,800	5,400
4d	200	650	1,100	2,150	3,800	5,400
1983 Scirocco						
2d Cpe	250	750	1,200	2,450	4,250	6,100
1983 Quantum						
2d Cpe	250	750	1,200	2,450	4,250	6,100
4d	250	750	1,200	2,450	4,250	6,100
4d Sta Wag	250	750	1,250	2,500	4,350	6,200
1983 Vanagon						
Sta Wag	350	1,000	1,700	3,400	5,950	8,500
Campmobile	450	1,300	2,200	4,400	7,700	11,000
1984 Rabbit						
2d Conv	300	950	1,550	3,100	5,450	7,800
2d L HBk	200	600	1,000	2,000	3,500	5,000
4d L HBk	200	600	1,000	2,050	3,550	5,100
GL 4d HBk	200	650	1,100	2,200	3,850	5,500
GTI 2d HBk	250	700	1,200	2,400	4,200	6,000
1984 Jetta						
2d Sed	250	700	1,150	2,300	4,050	5,800
4d Sed	250	700	1,200	2,350	4,150	5,900
GL 4d Sed	250	700	1,200	2,400	4,200	6,000
GLi 4d Sed	250	750	1,250	2,500	4,350	6,200
1984 Scirocco						
2d Cpe	250	700	1,200	2,400	4,200	6,000
1984 Quantum						
GL 4d Sed	250	700	1,150	2,300	4,050	5,800
GL 4d Sta Wag	250	700	1,150	2,300	4,000	5,700
1984 Vanagon						
Sta Wag	300	950	1,600	3,200	5,600	8,000
Campmobile	450	1,300	2,200	4,400	7,700	11,000
1985 Golf						
2d HBk	200	600	1,000	2,050	3,550	5,100
GTI 2d HBk	200	650	1,100	2,200	3,850	5,500
4d HBk	200	600	1,050	2,100	3,650	5,200
1985 Jetta						

	6	5	4	3	2	1
2d Sed	200	600	1,050	2,100	3,650	5,200
4d Sed	200	650	1,050	2,100	3,700	5,300

NOTE: Add 5 percent for GL and GLi option.

1985 Cabriolet
	6	5	4	3	2	1
2d Conv	350	1,000	1,700	3,400	5,950	8,500

1985 Scirocco
	6	5	4	3	2	1
2d Cpe	200	650	1,100	2,200	3,850	5,500

1985 Quantum
	6	5	4	3	2	1
4d Sed	200	650	1,050	2,100	3,700	5,300
4d Sta Wag	200	650	1,100	2,150	3,800	5,400

1985 Vanagon
	6	5	4	3	2	1
Sta Wag	300	950	1,600	3,200	5,600	8,000
Camper	450	1,300	2,200	4,400	7,700	11,000

1986 Golf
	6	5	4	3	2	1
2d HBk	250	800	1,300	2,650	4,600	6,600
GTI 2d HBk	300	850	1,400	2,800	4,900	7,000
4d HBk	250	800	1,350	2,700	4,700	6,700

1986 Jetta
	6	5	4	3	2	1
2d Sed	250	800	1,350	2,700	4,700	6,700
4d Sed	250	800	1,350	2,700	4,750	6,800

NOTE: Add 5 percent for GL and GLi option.

1986 Cabriolet
	6	5	4	3	2	1
2d Conv	400	1,250	2,100	4,200	7,350	10,500

1986 Scirocco
	6	5	4	3	2	1
2d Cpe	300	850	1,400	2,800	4,900	7,000

1986 Quantum
	6	5	4	3	2	1
GL 4d Sed	250	800	1,350	2,700	4,750	6,800

1986 Vanagon
	6	5	4	3	2	1
Sta Wag	350	1,100	1,800	3,600	6,300	9,000
Camper	600	1,800	3,000	6,000	10,500	15,000

1987 Fox
	6	5	4	3	2	1
2d Sed	250	800	1,350	2,700	4,700	6,700
GL 4d Sed	250	800	1,350	2,700	4,750	6,800
GL 2d Sta Wag	300	850	1,400	2,750	4,850	6,900

1987 Golf
	6	5	4	3	2	1
2d HBk GL	250	800	1,350	2,700	4,750	6,800
GL 4d HBk	300	850	1,400	2,750	4,850	6,900
GT 2d HBk	300	850	1,400	2,750	4,850	6,900
GT 4d HBk	300	850	1,400	2,800	4,900	7,000
GTI 2d HBk	300	950	1,550	3,100	5,450	7,800
GTI 2d HBk 16V	350	1,050	1,750	3,500	6,150	8,800

1987 Jetta
	6	5	4	3	2	1
2d Sed	300	850	1,400	2,750	4,850	6,900
4d Sed	300	850	1,400	2,800	4,900	7,000
GL 4d Sed	300	850	1,450	2,900	5,050	7,200
GLi 4d Sed	300	950	1,600	3,150	5,550	7,900
GLi 4d Sed 16V	350	1,050	1,800	3,550	6,250	8,900

1988 Fox
	6	5	4	3	2	1
2d Sed	250	700	1,200	2,400	4,200	6,000
GL 4d Sed	250	750	1,250	2,500	4,350	6,200
GL 2d Sta Wag	250	800	1,300	2,600	4,550	6,500

1988 Cabriolet
	6	5	4	3	2	1
2d Conv	500	1,450	2,400	4,800	8,400	12,000

1988 Golf
	6	5	4	3	2	1
2d HBk	250	800	1,300	2,600	4,550	6,500
GL 2d HBk	300	850	1,400	2,800	4,900	7,000
GL 4d HBk	300	850	1,450	2,900	5,050	7,200
GT 2d HBk	300	900	1,500	3,050	5,300	7,600
GT 4d HBk	300	950	1,550	3,100	5,450	7,800
GTI 2d HBk	300	950	1,600	3,150	5,550	7,900

1988 Jetta
	6	5	4	3	2	1
2d Sed	300	950	1,550	3,100	5,450	7,800
4d Sed	300	950	1,600	3,250	5,650	8,100
GL 4d Sed	350	1,000	1,700	3,350	5,900	8,400

	6	5	4	3	2	1
4d Sed Carat	350	1,000	1,700	3,400	5,950	8,500
GLi 4d Sed	400	1,150	1,900	3,800	6,650	9,500

1988 Scirocco
	6	5	4	3	2	1
2d Cpe	300	950	1,550	3,100	5,450	7,800

1988 Quantum
	6	5	4	3	2	1
GL 4d Sed	300	850	1,450	2,900	5,050	7,200
GL 4d Sta Wag	300	850	1,450	2,900	5,050	7,200

1988 Vanagon
	6	5	4	3	2	1
GL Sta Wag	400	1,250	2,100	4,200	7,350	10,500
GL Camper	500	1,550	2,600	5,200	9,100	13,000

1989 Fox
	6	5	4	3	2	1
2d Sed	250	750	1,250	2,500	4,350	6,200
GL 2d Sed	250	800	1,300	2,600	4,550	6,500
GL 4d Sed	250	800	1,350	2,700	4,700	6,700
GL 4d Sta Wag	300	850	1,400	2,750	4,850	6,900

1989 Cabriolet
	6	5	4	3	2	1
2d Conv	500	1,500	2,500	5,000	8,750	12,500

1989 Golf
	6	5	4	3	2	1
2d HBk	250	800	1,350	2,700	4,700	6,700
GL 2d HBk	300	850	1,400	2,850	4,950	7,100
GL 4d HBk	300	850	1,450	2,900	5,050	7,200
GTI 2d HBk	300	950	1,600	3,200	5,600	8,000

1989 Jetta
	6	5	4	3	2	1
2d Sed	300	950	1,600	3,200	5,600	8,000
4d Sed	350	1,000	1,650	3,300	5,750	8,200
GL 4d Sed	350	1,000	1,700	3,400	5,950	8,500
4d Sed Carat	350	1,050	1,700	3,450	6,000	8,600
GLi 4d Sed	400	1,150	1,950	3,900	6,800	9,700

1989 Vanagon
	6	5	4	3	2	1
GL Sta Wag	500	1,450	2,400	4,800	8,400	12,000
GL Camper	550	1,600	2,700	5,400	9,450	13,500
Carat Sta Wag	550	1,600	2,700	5,400	9,450	13,500

1990 Fox, 4-cyl.
	6	5	4	3	2	1
2d Sed	250	700	1,200	2,400	4,200	6,000
4d Sed	250	800	1,300	2,600	4,550	6,500
2d Sta Wag	250	800	1,350	2,700	4,750	6,800
4d Spt Wag	250	800	1,300	2,650	4,600	6,600

1990 Cabriolet, 4-cyl.
	6	5	4	3	2	1
2d Conv	500	1,450	2,400	4,800	8,400	12,000

1990 Golf, 4-cyl.
	6	5	4	3	2	1
GL 2d HBk	300	850	1,400	2,800	4,900	7,000
GL 4d HBk	300	850	1,400	2,850	4,950	7,100
GTI 2d HBk	300	950	1,600	3,150	5,550	7,900

1990 Jetta, 4-cyl.
	6	5	4	3	2	1
GL 2d Sed	350	1,000	1,650	3,300	5,800	8,300
GL 4d Sed	350	1,000	1,700	3,350	5,900	8,400
GL 4d Sed Diesel	300	950	1,550	3,100	5,450	7,800
4d Carat Sed	350	1,000	1,700	3,400	5,950	8,500
GLi 4d Sed	400	1,150	1,900	3,800	6,650	9,500

1990 Passat, 4-cyl.
	6	5	4	3	2	1
4d Sed	400	1,150	1,900	3,800	6,650	9,500
4d Sta Wag	400	1,200	2,000	4,000	7,000	10,000

1990 Corrado, 4-cyl.
	6	5	4	3	2	1
2d Cpe	400	1,250	2,100	4,200	7,350	10,500

1991 Fox
	6	5	4	3	2	1
2d Sed	150	500	850	1,700	2,950	4,200
GL 4d Sed	200	550	900	1,800	3,150	4,500

1991 Cabriolet
	6	5	4	3	2	1
2d Conv	400	1,150	1,900	3,800	6,650	9,500

1991 Golf
	6	5	4	3	2	1
GL 2d HBk	250	700	1,200	2,400	4,200	6,000
GTI 2d HBk	300	900	1,500	3,000	5,250	7,500
GTI 2d HBk 16V	300	950	1,600	3,200	5,600	8,000
GL 4d HBk	250	800	1,350	2,700	4,700	6,700

1991 Jetta

	6	5	4	3	2	1
GL 2d Sed	250	800	1,300	2,600	4,550	6,500
GL 4d Sed	250	800	1,350	2,700	4,700	6,700
GL 4d Sed Diesel	200	650	1,100	2,200	3,850	5,500
4d Carat Sed	300	850	1,450	2,900	5,050	7,200
GLi 4d Sed 16V	300	950	1,600	3,200	5,600	8,000

1991 Passat

	6	5	4	3	2	1
GL 4d Sed	300	900	1,500	3,000	5,250	7,500
GL 4d Sta Wag	300	950	1,600	3,200	5,600	8,000

1991 Corrado

	6	5	4	3	2	1
2d Cpe	400	1,150	1,900	3,800	6,650	9,500

1992 Fox, 4-cyl.

	6	5	4	3	2	1
2d Sed	200	600	1,000	2,000	3,500	5,000
GL 4d Sed	200	650	1,100	2,200	3,850	5,500

1992 Golf, 4-cyl.

	6	5	4	3	2	1
GL 2d HBk	300	850	1,400	2,800	4,900	7,000
GL 4d HBk	300	900	1,500	3,000	5,250	7,500
GTI 2d HBk	300	950	1,600	3,200	5,600	8,000
GTI 2d HBk 16V	350	1,000	1,700	3,400	5,950	8,500

1992 Cabriolet, 4-cyl.

	6	5	4	3	2	1
2d Conv	400	1,150	1,900	3,800	6,650	9,500

1992 Jetta, 4-cyl.

	6	5	4	3	2	1
GL 4d Sed	300	900	1,500	3,000	5,250	7,500
GL 4d Sed Diesel	300	850	1,400	2,800	4,900	7,000
4d Carat Sed	350	1,000	1,700	3,400	5,950	8,500
GLi 4d Sed 16V	400	1,150	1,900	3,800	6,650	9,500

1992 Passat, 4-cyl.

	6	5	4	3	2	1
CL 4d Sed	300	900	1,500	3,000	5,250	7,500
GL 4d Sed	350	1,000	1,700	3,400	5,950	8,500
GL 4d Sta Wag	400	1,150	1,900	3,800	6,650	9,500

1992 Corrado, 4-cyl.

	6	5	4	3	2	1
2d G60 Cpe	450	1,300	2,200	4,400	7,700	11,000
SLC 2d Cpe	500	1,550	2,600	5,200	9,100	13,000

1993 Fox, 4-cyl.

	6	5	4	3	2	1
2d Sed	200	550	900	1,850	3,200	4,600
GL 4d Sed	200	600	950	1,900	3,350	4,800

1993 Golf

	6	5	4	3	2	1
GL 4d HBk	300	950	1,600	3,200	5,600	8,000

1993 Cabriolet, 4-cyl.

	6	5	4	3	2	1
2d Conv	400	1,150	1,950	3,900	6,800	9,700

1993 Jetta, 4-cyl.

	6	5	4	3	2	1
GL 4d Sed	300	950	1,550	3,100	5,450	7,800

1993 Passat, 4-cyl.

	6	5	4	3	2	1
GL 4d Sed	350	1,100	1,800	3,600	6,300	9,000
GLX 4d Sed	400	1,150	1,900	3,800	6,650	9,500
GLX 4d Sta Wag	400	1,200	2,000	4,000	7,000	10,000

1993 Corrado, V-6

	6	5	4	3	2	1
SLC 2d Cpe	500	1,450	2,400	4,800	8,400	12,000

1994 Golf, 4-cyl.

	6	5	4	3	2	1
GL 2d HBk	300	900	1,500	3,000	5,250	7,500
GL 4d HBk	300	950	1,550	3,100	5,450	7,800

1994 Jetta, 4-cyl.

	6	5	4	3	2	1
GL 4d Sed	350	1,000	1,700	3,400	5,950	8,500
GLS 4d Sed	350	1,100	1,800	3,600	6,300	9,000
GLX 4d Sed, V-6	400	1,250	2,100	4,200	7,350	10,500

1994 Passat, V-6

	6	5	4	3	2	1
GLX 4d Sed	450	1,300	2,200	4,400	7,700	11,000
GLX 4d Sta Wag	500	1,450	2,400	4,800	8,400	12,000

1994 Corrado, V-6

	6	5	4	3	2	1
SLC 2d Cpe	550	1,700	2,800	5,600	9,800	14,000

1995 Golf III, 4-cyl. & V-6

	6	5	4	3	2	1
4d HBk	300	900	1,450	2,900	5,100	7,300
GL 2d HBk	300	900	1,500	3,000	5,250	7,500
GL 4d HBk	300	950	1,550	3,100	5,450	7,800
2d Spt HBk	300	950	1,600	3,200	5,600	8,000
GTI 2d HBk, V-6	400	1,250	2,100	4,200	7,350	10,500

1995 Jetta III, 4-cyl. & V-6

	6	5	4	3	2	1
4d Sed	300	950	1,600	3,200	5,600	8,000
GL 4d Sed	350	1,000	1,700	3,400	5,950	8,500
GLS 4d Sed	350	1,100	1,800	3,600	6,300	9,000
GLX 4d Sed, V-6	400	1,250	2,100	4,200	7,350	10,500

1995 Cabrio, 4-cyl.

	6	5	4	3	2	1
2d Conv	450	1,300	2,200	4,400	7,700	11,000

1995 Passat, 4-cyl.

	6	5	4	3	2	1
GLS 4d Sed	350	1,000	1,700	3,400	5,950	8,500
GLX 4d Sed, V-6	450	1,300	2,200	4,400	7,700	11,000
GLX 4d Sta Wag, V-6	500	1,450	2,400	4,800	8,400	12,000

1996 Golf, 4-cyl.

	6	5	4	3	2	1
GL 4d HBk	250	800	1,350	2,700	4,750	6,800
GTI 2d HBk	300	950	1,550	3,100	5,450	7,800
GTI VR6 2d HBk (V-6 only)	400	1,150	1,900	3,800	6,650	9,500

1996 Jetta, 4-cyl.

	6	5	4	3	2	1
GL 4d Sed	300	900	1,500	3,000	5,250	7,500
GLS 4d Sed	300	950	1,600	3,200	5,600	8,000
GLX VR6 4d Sed (V-6 only)	400	1,150	1,900	3,800	6,650	9,500

1996 Cabrio, 4-cyl.

	6	5	4	3	2	1
2d Conv	400	1,200	2,000	4,000	7,000	10,000

1996 Passat, 4-cyl.

	6	5	4	3	2	1
GLS 4d Sed	300	900	1,500	3,000	5,250	7,500
TDI 4d Sed	350	1,100	1,800	3,600	6,300	9,000
TDI 4d Sta Wag	400	1,150	1,900	3,800	6,650	9,500

1996 Passat, V-6.

	6	5	4	3	2	1
GLX VR6 4d Sed	400	1,200	2,000	4,000	7,000	10,000
GLX VR6 4d Sta Wag	450	1,300	2,200	4,400	7,700	11,000

1997 Golf, 4-cyl.

	6	5	4	3	2	1
GL 4d HBk	272	816	1,360	2,720	4,760	6,800
GTI 2d HBk	312	936	1,560	3,120	5,460	7,800
GTI VR6 2d HBk (V-6 only)	380	1,140	1,900	3,800	6,650	9,500

1997 Jetta, 4-cyl.

	6	5	4	3	2	1
GL 4d Sed	300	900	1,500	3,000	5,250	7,500
GT 4d Sed	320	960	1,600	3,200	5,600	8,000
GLS 4d Sed	340	1,020	1,700	3,400	5,950	8,500
GLX VR6 4d Sed (V-6 only)	380	1,140	1,900	3,800	6,650	9,500

NOTE: Add 5 percent for TDI (diesel) engine.

1997 Cabrio, 4-cyl.

	6	5	4	3	2	1
2d Conv	400	1,200	2,000	4,000	7,000	10,000
2d Highline Conv	420	1,260	2,100	4,200	7,350	10,500

1997 Passat, TDI 4-cyl.

	6	5	4	3	2	1
4d Sed	360	1,080	1,800	3,600	6,300	9,000
4d Sta Wag	380	1,140	1,900	3,800	6,650	9,500

1997 Passat, V-6

	6	5	4	3	2	1
GLX VR6 4d Sed	400	1,200	2,000	4,000	7,000	10,000
GLX VR6 4d Sta Wag	440	1,320	2,200	4,400	7,700	11,000

VOLKSWAGENS
Around the World

Volkswagen uses many car names around the world. Here are some VWs you may not have heard of in North America:

Bjalla . . . . If you speak Icelandic, you'll recognize it as the word for "Beetle."

Bora . . . . A VW Fox-based sport station wagon made in Brazil.

Caddy . . . . Also called the Saviero. A Brazilian Fox-based pickup and high-back van.

Derby . . . . A two door VW sedan that looks like an updated two-door Fox.

Corsar . . . . A Jetta-based VW sold in some countries.

Ecomatic . . . . An economical Golf version with an engine that shuts off at stop lights.

Escarabajo . . . . The reference to the New Beetle in many Spanish-speaking nations.

Fridolin . . . . A 1960s hybrid—part VW 1500 and part Transporter—for postal delivery.

Fusca . . . . The traditional VW Beetle in the Spanish-speaking countries.

Gol . . . . Looks like a smaller version of the Golf series.

Kafer . . . . The German-language word for the Beetle.

Logus . . . . Another name for a Golf sedan in some countries.

Lupo . . . . Think of a small, two-door car made for tight spaces and maximum utility.

Match . . . . A variation of the VW Golf.

Nutzfahrzeuges . . . Think of a 1950s courier wagon and the VW Golf or Lupo.

Parati . . . . A handsome two-door VW wagon.

Pointer . . . . A hatchback sedan similar to the VW Golf.

Polo . . . . A sedan based on the Brazilian VW Fox.

Riesemobile . . . . . . The Austrian name for the VW Sharan mini van.

Rivage . . . . A deluxe version of what North Americans know as the VW Cabrio.

Senda . . . . A Jetta-like sedan, also called the VW 1.8.

Santana . . . . A slightly larger version of the VW Fox

Scala and Storm . . Special versions of the VW Scirocco.

Sharan . . . . A compact VW mini van.

Touran . . . . A slightly larger, more traditional van.

Umwelt . . . . A Golf-based diesel courier van.

VW also makes localized vehicles in several nations. One very good example is the LT flatbed mini-lorry in Australia. North Americans may have seen LT series cube vans and campers.

Volkswagens are sold in 54 nations around the world. Here is a list of the VW "homes."

Argentina	Finland	Luxembourg	Slovakia
Australia	France	Mexico	Slovenia
Austria	Greece	Netherlands	South Africa
Belgium	Guatemala	New Zealand	Spain
Bosnia-Herzogovina	Honduras	Nicaragua	Sweden
Brazil	Hong Kong	Norway	Switzerland
Canada	Hungary	Panama	Turkey
Chile	Iceland	Peru	United Kingdom
China	Indonesia	Poland	United States
Colombia	Ireland	Portugal	Uruguay
Croatia	Israel	Puerto Rico	Venezuela
Czech Republic	Italy	Romania	Yugoslavia
Denmark	Japan	Russia	
Ecuador	Latvia	Singapore	